TOURISM
OPERATIONS AND
MANAGEMENT

SUNETRA RODAY • ARCHANA BIWAL • VANDANA JOSHI

Department of Tourism
Maharashtra State Institute of Hotel Management &
Catering Technology (MSIHMCT), Pune

OXFORD
UNIVERSITY PRESS

OXFORD
UNIVERSITY PRESS

Oxford University Press is a department of the University of Oxford.
It furthers the University's objective of excellence in research, scholarship,
and education by publishing worldwide. Oxford is a registered trademark of
Oxford University Press in the UK and in certain other countries

Published in India by
Oxford University Press
Ground Floor, 2/11, Ansari Road, Daryaganj, New Delhi, 110 002, India

First published in 2009
13th impression 2018

ISBN-13: 978-0-19-806001-7
ISBN-10: 0-19-806001-7

Typeset in Baskerville
by Innovative Processor, New Delhi 110002
Printed in India by Rakmo Press, New Delhi 110 020

Dedicated to our parents
who have helped and supported us whenever we needed them

Smt. Sudha A. Shrouti and Late Col. A.W. Shrouti

Sunetra Roday

Smt. Mewadevi and Shri Ramkumar Sodi

Archana Biwal

Smt. Asha and Dr. Shripad Mahurkar

Vandana Joshi

Preface

The tourism industry is a vast industry made up of various sectors related to virtually all areas of the economy. It has steadily acquired an increasingly significant position in the global economy. The operation and magnitude of such a vast industry cannot be viewed in isolation as it is the outcome of the combined efforts of different business houses and organizations which provide tourism-related services. The Government of India has realized the tremendous potential of this industry in expanding the economy and in the Seventh Five Year Plan, tourism was accorded the status of an industry. Tourist numbers—both international and domestic—are increasing each year and an industry growing at such a phenomenal rate is bound to bring about changes and challenges. Commensurate with this has been an increase in the number of schools, colleges, and tourism organizations offering travel and tourism-related courses. Travel and tourism companies too are seeking to recruit graduates who possess essential knowledge and business skills which are relevant to this industry. Management skills of planning, organizing, development, marketing, and customer service are essential for managing any business successfully and tourism is no exception.

About the Book

This book explores the issues pertaining to tourism operations and management from a global perspective. While it has been especially designed to meet the needs of students of hotel management, travel and tourism, and hospitality courses, professionals within the industry will also find it a useful reference.

Written in an easy-to-read, student-friendly manner, this comprehensive book examines the operation and management of all the sectors of the industry. Aimed at providing a practical view of tourism operations and management, the book fills a void of a single textbook specific to the tourism profession, which covers the needs of the industry and the syllabus of the subject for hotel management and hospitality-related courses. This book discusses the principles and practices of tourism exploring relevant theoretical concepts and incorporates current industry practices.

This book has been conceptualized keeping in mind the fact that there is no comprehensive Indian text on tourism available as of now. It has been developed in consultation with tourism professionals and includes areas which need special emphasis to give the students an insight into the various aspects of this vast industry.

Pedagogical Features

Each chapter of the book includes learning objectives, definitions of important terms, figures, tables, and pictures to add interest and clarify concepts. End chapter exercises include concept review questions to test the reader's understanding of the concepts discussed in the chapter, critical thinking questions to stimulate the thought process, and projects/ assignments to help the reader develop further interest and knowledge. A chapter-wise summary and key terms are included at the end of every chapter, along with references. Every effort has been made to provide latest statistics and examples from this rapidly changing industry.

Coverage and Structure

The first five chapters of the book serve as an introduction to the tourism industry and its various sectors and sub-sectors. The book begins with the definition of tourism and the tourism industry, its significance, a historical overview of the stages in the evolution of tourism, different types of tourism, infrastructural requirements, and a descriptive section on tourist transportation.

Chapter six discusses the different tourism organizations, their roles and functions.

Chapter seven highlights the crucial role of the two intermediaries in the industry—the travel agent and the tour operator and their functions. The reader is introduced to the concept of package tours and the significance of guides and escorts. Guidelines for setting up a travel agency are also discussed in this chapter.

Chapter eight deals with travel documentation and the importance of completing various travel formalities before undertaking travel.

Chapter nine introduces the reader to geography pertaining to the airlines and the various codes and abbreviations which a tourism professional needs to know.

Chapter ten provides details of the technical aspects of planning itineraries with adequate examples, including the procedure for calculating the costing of tours.

Chapter eleven explains the unique characteristics of the tourism product and how the service product differs from goods or commodities.

Chapters twelve and thirteen consider the marketing and sales techniques and the dominant role of the tourism professional in customer satisfaction.

Chapters fourteen and fifteen provide an insight into the impact created by the tourism industry on environment, economy, culture, and society. Environmentally sensitive issues and eco-friendly practices are dealt with, along with tourism legislations. Measures for sustainable tourism development and the need for planned development are emphasized.

Chapter sixteen discusses the changing scenario of the tourism industry and stresses on the role of information technology and emerging trends in this industry. The tourism policy and initiatives taken by the government are also dealt with in this chapter.

Several forms and formats, codes and currencies for practical sessions are given as appendices.

Acknowledgements

The authors would like to acknowledge the contribution of all the people and organizations who have directly or indirectly helped in the conceptualization and compilation of this book.

We gratefully acknowledge the encouragement and inspiration from Dr S K Mahajan, Director Technical Education, Maharashtra State. We would like to thank Ms R Kayerkar, Principal, Maharashtra State Institute of Hotel Management and Catering Technology, Pune; our colleagues, especially the library staff and other support staff; and students of our institute for their contribution and assistance in completing this book.

We wish to extend our gratitude to Mr Aniket Shrouti, Addl. Check Flight Purser, Air India Ltd for his invaluable guidance and suggestions, and Mr Vikrant Roday, Senior Consultant, Capgemini, Pune for his constant assistance and technical support.

We would like to thank all the tourism professionals—travel agents, tour operators, and academicians—from Pune and Mumbai for the valuable inputs from the industry perspective.

We extend our sincere thanks to the editorial team at Oxford University Press (OUP) India, as well as the reviewers for their guidance, persistence, and continuous support.

Last, but not the least, we would like to acknowledge the patience and understanding of our families throughout this project.

Sunetra Roday
Archana Biwal
Vandana Joshi

Contents

CHAPTER 1

Introduction to Travel and Tourism

Learning Objectives

After reading this chapter you should be able to:
- understand the meaning of the word tourism
- define the basic concepts related to tourism
- describe the various constituents of the tourism industry
- know the significance of tourism
- identify and describe the five 'A's of tourism

INTRODUCTION

Every day all over the world, innumerable people make their travel plans for a pleasure or business-related trip. The trip may be of a short or long duration, for the forthcoming weekend, or for a longer holiday sometime during the coming year. Visas are applied for, flights are reserved, accommodation is booked, cars are rented, train tickets are purchased, itineraries are planned, and the World Wide Web is surfed for travel-related information and availability of seats. Thousands of people are working round-the-clock to provide these services and interact with the traveller, while another couple of thousands work behind the scenes to help the traveller have a safe and memorable holiday.

All these people form a part of one of the largest industry in the world—the tourism industry. When people make travel plans and visit different places, they contribute directly or indirectly towards the livelihood of millions who work for this industry.

Let us take a closer look at the professionals who contribute towards making our trips possible. Consider a family of four from Pune planning a week's holiday in Singapore. Their friends have just returned from a

Table 1.1 Persons/agents responsible for various travel-related tasks

Tasks	Person/Agency Responsible
• Passport document	• Ministry of External Affairs
• Visa endorsement	• Consulate
• Airline ticket to destination	• Travel agent
• Accommodation at destination	• Travel agent
• Foreign exchange	• Travel agent/bank
• Transport to airport	• Local transport services
• Collect trolley	• Airport staff
• Go to airline counter at terminal	• Airline staff
• Screen baggage	• Airports authority of India and Central Industrial Security Force (CISF)
• Weigh baggage, check visa	• Airline staff
• Get passport checked	• Immigration officer
• Customs declaration	• Customs officer (Indian Revenue Services)
• Hand baggage screening and frisking	• CISF
• Duty-free shopping	• Salespersons
• Airline gate representation	• Airline staff
• Baggage handling	• Airport staff
• Food service on board	• Flight caterers
• On board the aircraft –Other airline staff for safe flight	• Flight purser and airhostess, flight engineer, pilot, co-pilot, aircraft mechanic
• Arrival at the destination	• Changi airport staff
• Immigration	• Immigration officer (Singapore)
• Baggage claim	• Baggage handling agency of airline
• Customs clearance	• Customs officer (Singapore)
• Pick-up guests from airport	• Hotel courtesy coach driver
• Arrival at hotel	• Hotel doorman
• Registration and room allotment	• Receptionist/front desk
• Escorting to room and carrying bags	• Porter

fabulous holiday in Singapore, so they call their friends to get details about the travel agent and other travel formalities required for the trip. Little do they realize that for each step in their plan, there are hundreds of people working to ensure that things go smoothly. Take an example of the meals served aboard a flight, which are provided by special flight caterers who cater to in-flight services and employ hundreds of people to prepare the meals as per set standard specifications. Table 1.1 takes a look at some of the people/agencies involved and tasks which need to be completed to make the trip happen.

The family has just arrived at their hotel in Singapore and is yet to explore the destination, but as we can see, they have already interacted with so many people. All these individuals are from different sectors of the vast tourism industry and all will benefit from the arrival of the tourists and so will many others, whom the family will interact with during their stay in Singapore.

From the above example, it is quite clear why tourism has been declared as one of the world's largest industries today. The number of tourists and the industry itself has shown a phenomenal growth, making both the government and the private sector wake up to realize the need to study tourism and its consequences. The sheer number of travellers and even larger volume of the host population (locals at the destinations) who bear the brunt of tourists or the consequences of tourism is another aspect which needs to be considered and will be discussed at length in Chapter 14.

THE MEANING OF TOURISM

The word 'tourism' does not only mean international travel for leisure or travel by air, but has a much wider scope. Many thoughts may come to one's mind when one thinks about tourism. Tourism may bring forth pictures of cool hill stations, snow clad mountains, warm sunny beaches or long scenic drives. Enjoyment, pleasure, excitement, packing of bags, carrying documents and credit cards, shopping, and spending money are some of the things which may come to your mind when you think of tourism. How you perceive tourism will also depend on your past individual experience as a tourist. Then what exactly does the term tourism mean and what all does it encompass or include? It is necessary to understand the term tourism in its totality and identify what its main characteristics are. Tourism is the temporary short-term movement of people to destinations outside the place where they normally live and work and includes the activities they indulge in at the destination as well as all facilities and services specially created to meet their needs. Tourism does not only mean travelling to a particular destination but also includes all activities undertaken during the stay. It includes day visits and excursions.

Tourism is closely related to leisure and recreation. Leisure time is the time we have with us after carrying out our basic needs such as work and sleep. It is our free or spare time. Recreation is the activities we enjoy doing which are carried out during our leisure time.

Both leisure and recreation are necessary for all of us to overcome the mounting stress and strain of modern life. Playing a game of scrabble, swimming, or watching a movie, are all recreational activities carried out in one's leisure time at home or in a community centre. Tourism is one such recreational activity. It involves travel away from one's place of stay to participate in other recreational activities. For example, snorkelling at Andaman and Nicobar Islands is tourism whereas swimming in the neighbourhood pool is only recreation.

Most tourism activities are leisure activities except when people travel during their working hours or over the weekend for business-related work. That tourism is only a leisure activity is a misconception. When people travel to participate in meetings, seminars, conferences, trade fairs or to launch new products, it is also a tourism activity.

The tourist market may thus be divided into the following two categories:

1. The leisure tourist
2. The business tourist

Leisure tourists do not travel for monetary benefit, unlike the business tourists whose main motive for travel is making profits or expanding their businesses.

Both these tourists travel away from their normal places of residence and spend at least one night away from home. Both need transport, accommodation, food and beverage, recreation, etc. although their main motives for travel are different.

Then how do we define the term tourism? There is no single universally accepted, clear cut definition of tourism. Tourism professionals have defined tourism in many different ways over the years. It has been defined as a change from one's usual routine and what one looks forward to most. It is a travel usually undertaken out of choice and convenience, which is the reason why it is more exciting and memorable.

One of the earliest definitions of tourism was in the year 1937 by the League of Nations, 'The term tourist shall in principle be interpreted to mean any person travelling for a period of 24 hours or more in a country other than in which he usually resides.' The definition which focused on the tourist has been modified several times over to include tourism activities, impacts, day visits, and not only the geographical movement of people.

In 1977, Jafari described tourism as 'The study of man away from his usual habitat, of the industry which responds to his needs, and of the impacts that both he and the industry have on the host's socio-cultural, economic, and physical environments'.

While defining the term tourism, it must be kept in mind that tourists are short-term, temporary visitors and should not be confused with people who migrate to a country to settle permanently and become residents.

Related Concepts

Some more concepts related to tourism are discussed in the following section.

Visitors   A visitor is any person visiting a country other than that in which he/she has his/her usual place of residence, for any other reason than following an occupation from within the country visited.

Visitors may be further categorized as excursionists and tourists.

Excursionist   An excursionist is a day visitor who stays for less than 24 hours at a place. Excursionists do not stay overnight. For example, if a group of students from Pune go to the nearby hill station Lonavala early in the morning and return late in the evening, they are called excursionists.

Tourist   A tourist is a temporary visitor to a place. When people leave their usual place of residence and work to have a change from their usual routine for a short time, they are called tourists. They stay at the place overnight, i.e. for at least 24 hours.

Domestic tourism   It involves residents of a country travelling within the borders of that country. A person from Pune going for a holiday to Kerala is a domestic tourist.

International tourism   It involves people travelling from one country to another country, crossing national borders or through immigration check points.

International tourists may be *inbound* or *outbound.*

Inbound tourism   This refers to incoming tourists or tourists entering a country. For example, Malaysian citizens travelling to India would be considered as inbound tourists for India and outbound tourists for Malaysia (see Fig. 1.1).

Outbound tourism   This refers to outgoing tourists or tourists leaving their country of origin to travel to another country (see Fig. 1.1).

Traveller   A traveller is a person who travels from one place to another. It is a general term used for a person who travels, irrespective of the purpose of travel, distance travelled, or duration of stay. All tourists are travellers/visitors but all travellers/visitors are not tourists.

Transit visitor   A traveller/visitor who passes through a country without breaking journey other than for taking connecting transport is called a transit visitor. His/her destination is another country.

Hospitality   It is concerned with providing necessary meals, a place to live and sleep, and a welcoming attitude within defined levels of service for which the customer has to pay. It provides physiological and psychological comfort and security to the guest.

Destination   A destination is the place where tourists travel for leisure or business-related activities. It is the place where the tourist product is located and consumed. Destinations can be spread over a wide geographical area and it is the reason for tourism to exist. Without a

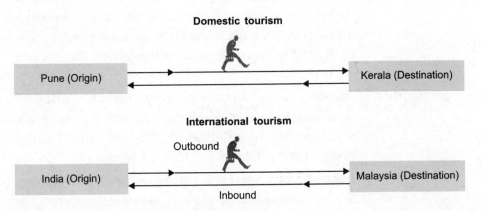

Fig. 1.1   Domestic and international tourism

destination there would be no tourism. The images and positive perceptions that people have of a destination, draw tourists to the place.

Tourism Regions of the World

The United Nations World Tourism Organization (UNWTO) has divided the world into six tourism regions on the basis of volume of tourists and the concentration of popular products and destinations (see Fig. 1.2).

These regions include both rich and poor countries as well as advanced and underdeveloped tourism destinations. Tourism activity is unevenly distributed in these regions and is developing at its own pace.

THE TOURISM INDUSTRY

The tourism industry is a vast industry made up of businesses and organizations that provide goods and services to meet the distinctive needs of tourists. These businesses and organizations are related to virtually all areas of the economy making tourism a very huge industry.

The tourism industry comprises many sectors or sub-industries such as the hospitality industry, transport industry, attractions, and entertainment. All these sectors are interconnected and integrated. They

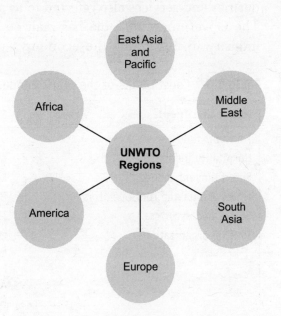

Fig. 1.2   The six tourism regions of the world

work with one another to some extent in providing goods and services as their survival depends on each other.

There is some dispute as to whether a separate tourism industry exists. Some perceive the tourism industry as a highly fragmented industry made up of many industries. However, in the Seventh Five Year Plan (1985–90) tourism was accorded the status of an industry by the Government of India.

Constituents of the Tourism Industry

The tourism industry is the outcome of the combined efforts of various sub-industries or sectors which provide tourism-related services. Large multinational companies (MNCs), small business houses, and individuals working as guides at tourist spots, all constitute the tourism industry. Some of the constituents are located at the destination itself, such as hotels, attractions, guides, shops, local transport, etc; some are encountered en route like customs, transport, foreign exchange money changers; while others are available at the place of origin of the journey, such as consulate for visa and travel agents. The tourism industry can be classified into two broad categories or sectors namely the main constituents and the secondary constituents as shown in Table 1.2.

The tourism industry, as we can see, covers a very wide range of industries and services also referred to as sectors of the tourism industry. The Government of India has realized the tremendous scope of this industry in expanding the economy, and is offering incentives and

Table 1.2 Constituents of the tourism industry

Main constituents	Secondary constituents
Transport industry	Shops and state emporiums
Hospitality industry	Arts and crafts
Entertainment industry	Local transport
Travel agents and tour operators	Banks
Guides and escorts	Insurance companies
Tourism organizations	Communication services—Media
	Performing artists
	Publishers
	Advertisers
	Hawkers and coolies
	Agents and brokers

conducting formal training programmes for service providers to give a boost to tourism in our country.

SIGNIFICANCE OF TOURISM

Tourism is a global phenomenon. It is the world's largest and fastest growing industry. According to the World Travel and Tourism Council (WTTC), tourism generates more than 230 million jobs directly and indirectly, and contributes to more than 10 per cent of the world gross domestic product (GDP). According to WTTC, the global tourism industry is a USD 5000 trillion industry giving tourism global significance. International tourist arrivals in 2006 were 842 million people and UNWTO has forecast the number to exceed 1.6 billion by the year 2020.

Not all increases in tourism arrivals or receipts are proportionately distributed throughout the receiving regions of the world. It is important to know which countries are major tourism generators and major tourism recipients. Figure 1.3 shows us the 10 most visited countries in the world in 2006 and 2007, while Fig. 1.4 depicts international tourism receipts in 2006 and 2007. It is essential for tourism managers to understand tourism flows, i.e. where do tourists travel to, from which country do they originate, and the volume of tourist flows. These statistics are collected, compiled, and disseminated by the UNWTO and WTTC.

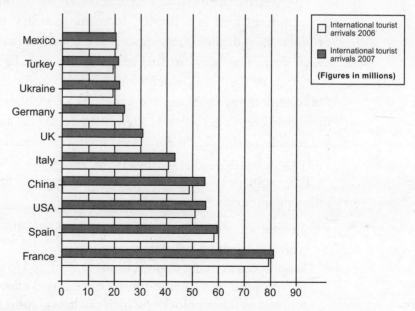

Fig. 1.3 Most visited countries in the world in 2006 and 2007

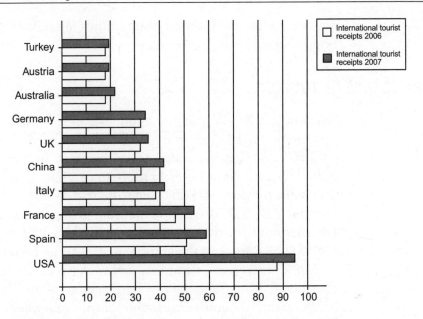

Fig. 1.4 International tourism receipts in billions (USD)

Table 1.3 shows some of the most visited tourist attractions in the world with their world rank, while Table 1.4 shows the top 15 tourism destinations in the world in 2007.

The tourism industry is characterized by constant change and development and is a highly dynamic industry offering innovative products, new destinations, and technologically advanced transportation every year. The latest in this range is the world's largest cruise liner 'Freedom of the Seas' which can accommodate over 5500 passengers. Stiff competition exists amongst the service providers, with each trying their level best to attract and retain customers. This industry is also highly vulnerable to significant events occurring around the globe such as the Hurricane Katrina, bird flu outbreaks, and even soaring oil prices.

The rapid pace of growth of this industry is directly linked to the following factors:

- Greater disposable incomes with women entering the workforce, which is spent on recreation and leisure.
- Employees in many organizations are entitled to a minimum number of days paid leave per annum. Leave travel allowance (LTA) facility is given to the employees which covers self and family.

Table 1.3   Some of the most visited tourist attractions by domestic and international tourists in 2007 with world ranking

World's ranking	Tourist attraction	City, Country
1.	Times Square	New York City, USA
2.	National Mall and Memorial Parks	Washington DC, USA
3.	Walt Disney World's Magic Kingdom	Orlando, USA
4.	Trafalgar Square	London, UK
5.	Disneyland	Anaheim, CA, USA
6.	Niagara Falls	Ontario, Canada and New York, USA
7.	Fisherman's Wharf and Golden Gate	San Francisco, CA
8.	Tokyo Disneyland and Tokyo DisneySea	Tokyo, Japan
9.	Notre-Dame de Paris	Paris, France
10.	Disneyland Paris	Paris, France
11.	The Great Wall of China	Badaling, China
18.	Eiffel Tower	Paris, France
31.	Grand Canyon	Arizona, USA
36.	Statue of Liberty	New York, USA
50.	Taj Mahal	Agra, India

Table 1.4   The world's top 15 cities in 2007 with world ranking

Ranking	City	Country	No. of visitors (in million)
1.	London	UK	15.64
2.	Bangkok	Thailand	10.35
3.	Paris	France	9.70
4.	Singapore	Singapore	9.50
5.	Hong Kong	China	8.14
6.	New York City	USA	6.22
7.	Dubai	UAE	6.12
8.	Rome	Italy	6.03
9.	Seoul	South Korea	4.92
10.	Barcelona	Spain	4.69
11.	Dublin	Ireland	4.47
12.	Bahrain	Bahrain	4.42
13.	Shangai	China	4.31
14.	Toronto	Canada	4.16
15.	Kuala Lumpur	Malaysia	4.12

Source: UNWTO (www.world-tourism.org) and Wikipedia Tourism

- Global travel is becoming more accessible for all classes of people in developed countries with advances in transport and technology and availability of low cost carriers.
- Greater awareness about travel and tourism, through the Internet, as well as through articles and advertisements published in leading magazines and dailies and on television.
- Discretionary time and money available. Double income no kids (DINK) policy being adopted by couples.
- An unquenchable thirst or desire to travel which has always existed in humankind.
- Stress and strain of routine work makes one look for a welcome break.

Today, tourism is no longer the privilege of the rich and famous exclusively, but it is an activity to be enjoyed by people from all strata of society. It is ingrained into the daily lives of many people across the globe. It involves not only the life of the tourists, but leaves its impact on the host or local population at the destination as well.

THE TOURISM SYSTEM

Tourism, as we have just read, is made up of various industries or sectors which need to work in harmony to serve the needs of tourists. Tourism has evolved from a number of academic disciplines such as geography, history, sociology, psychology, anthropology, agriculture, business management, marketing, law, political science, economics, education, architecture, and public health.

Figure 1.5 shows us the different dimensions of tourism. It can be studied from the perspective of any of these disciplines. However, the different perspectives can be confusing. Tourism as a field of study is complex and requires an interdisciplinary approach. A specific frame of reference would be useful while studying the subject of tourism.

Systems theory is one such frame of reference that can be used to study and analyse tourism. It is a useful way of investigating a phenomenon. Systems theory tries to form a complete picture of all parts of the tourism phenomenon and tries to explain how these separate parts or components work together as a whole.

A system is a collection of interrelated elements that interact to produce a desired result. Each system has a particular function to fulfil or a result to achieve. According to the systems theory, a system's external or macro-environment influences its performance. The external environment

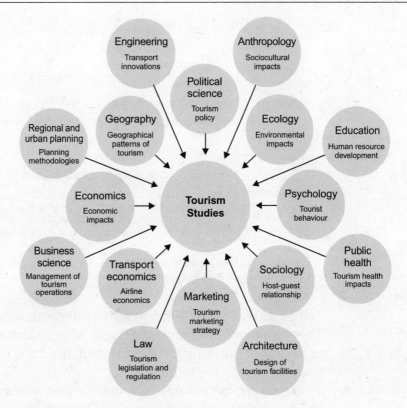

Fig. 1.5   An inter-disciplinary perspective of tourism
Source: Keyser (2002)

includes all factors outside the system that may create obstacles or help the system in achieving its objectives. These environmental factors may be sociocultural, physical, political, economic, environmental, legal, and technological.

Figure 1.6 provides a methodological framework for studying tourism and will help us in understanding the systems approach in a better manner. According to Leiper (1979), tourism is made up of the following five elements:

1. Traveller generating region
2. Transit region
3. Tourist destination region
4. Tourists and
5. Tourism industry

All of these are influenced by the external environment by which they are surrounded.

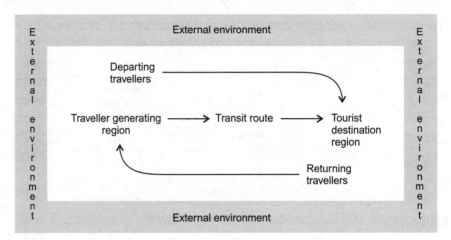

Fig. 1.6 Leiper's basic tourism system
Source: Adapted from Leiper (1979)

The success of any tourism activity depends on all the five elements. These elements are interrelated and have to function properly. Let us understand these five elements and the influence of the external environment on the tourism system.

Tourists are the people from the traveller generating region and the human participants in the system. The *transit route* is the link between the *generating region* and the destination and comprises all the places that tourists pass through en route. The *tourism industry* consists of all the sectors and sub-sectors which meet the specific needs and wants of the tourists and is located in all the three regions. For example, travel organizers are located in the generating region, transport sector is in the transit region, and hospitality sector is located in the destination region. The *destination region* is the place where the tourist is travelling to and is the focus of tourist activity and attractions.

The macro-environment or *external environment* can have a positive or negative impact on the tourism system. For example, with the advances in information technology (IT), tourists have access to hotels and destinations worldwide via the Internet, which gives the service providers more opportunities for marketing their products. However, incidents like the 9/11 terrorist attack on World Trade Center (WTC) towers in the USA in 2001 and the tsunami in December 2004 in South East Asia leave temporary negative impacts on the tourism system. The success of a destination, howsoever attractive it may be, depends on the effectiveness of the tourism system.

Some important facts related to tourism are as follows:

- tremendous growth potential;
- generates direct and indirect employment to millions across the globe;
- travel undertaken for leisure or business;
- includes short visits to other places;
- goods and services are consumed which differ from our routine;
- is an integral part of our lifestyle;
- technology such as the Internet has simplified travel bookings; and
- is multi-disciplinary and encompasses a number of disciplines.

FIVE 'A'S OF TOURISM

As we have already discussed, there can be no tourism without a destination. When people travel, they go to some particular place. For a destination to develop and sustain itself, the following five 'A's are important.

The classic five 'A's of tourism are

1. Accessibility
2. Accommodation
3. Amenities
4. Attractions
5. Activities

Accessibility   This refers to the transport and transport infrastructure to reach the destination and at the destination. Tourists look for comfort and hassle-free travel. Apart from comfort, cost, convenience, time for travelling, and safety, there are other important factors which need to be considered before undertaking a journey. For example, Port Blair in the Andaman and Nicobar Islands may not be considered easily accessible by tourists who cannot afford air travel and have to travel by sea. Rough waters, sea sickness, and cancellation of flights due to bad weather conditions can hamper accessibility.

Tourists look forward to smooth travel in terms of regular schedules, well-developed network of roads, railway lines, airports, harbours, and adequate means of safe transport. The hill station Matheran in Maharashtra is another example of poor accessibility, as private vehicles are not allowed till the top.

Accommodation   It plays a central role in tourism. Every tourist needs a place to stay and relax. Tourists look for clean, hygienic, and well maintained accommodation with a comfortable bed, clean linen, and sanitary facilities with adequate hot and cold water supply. A wide range of accommodation options exist at most destinations ranging from tourist lodges to five star deluxe hotels. Without suitable accommodation there would be no tourism as accommodation is the temporary home of the tourist at the destination and the base from which they pursue their activities.

Amenities   It refers to the facilities available at the destination which help in meeting the needs and wants of tourists. Tourist amenities include food and beverage facilities, drinking water, good communication network, local transport, automatic teller machines (ATMs), proper garbage and sewage disposal systems, medical facilities, etc. Electricity supply with minimum power cuts and adequate water supply are crucial facilities which must be available at the destination.

Attractions   This is the principal reason for undertaking travel to a particular destination. Attractions are classified basically into four categories which are as follows:

1. Natural attractions such as pristine beaches, waterfalls, scenic views, climate, heavy rainfall, snow clad mountains etc.
2. Human-made attractions such as theme parks, Ocean Park at Hong Kong, Disney World at Orlando, USA, Snow City at Singapore, etc.
3. Cultural attractions in the form of fairs, festivals, celebrations, theatre and museums, which depict the history and culture of a country.
4. Social attractions where one can meet and interact with the locals at a destination as well as meet friends and relatives.

Activities   People take a break because they want to see and do different things. Some like an active holiday and would like to go for water sports, fishing, nature trails, etc. while some would rather just sit back and relax. A number of activities may be available at the destination to suit various age groups and social backgrounds. Tourists may be attracted to a destination for any one or more of the above activities or attractions located there.

Apart from the classic five 'A's of tourism, we suggest a sixth 'A' which is extremely vital to the success of any destination.

Affordability   This is the sixth 'A' but nonetheless very important to attract tourists to the destination. Tourists should be able to afford the trip in terms of transport costs, accommodation charges, entrance fees at attractions and the number of days, which need to be spent for travel and stay; i.e. they should be able to afford the holiday in terms of time and money. Tour operators prepare package tours keeping affordability in mind. These group tours work out cheaper than individuals booking their own tickets and making itineraries for themselves.

A successful destination would have a good balance between these six 'A's and ensure that there is something to see and do for people of different ages and backgrounds so that a large number of tourists visit the place.

The tourism industry, one of the world's largest industries, is ingrained into the lives of people around the globe. The industry providing services to the tourists is growing at a rapid pace and has become a global phenomenon. This industry is dynamic and constantly changing, with various factors contributing to its growth, which we will read about in the chapters which follow. The next chapter discusses the evolution of tourism and events in history which have left their mark on this enormous industry.

SUMMARY

The tourism industry, which is one of the largest industries in the world, is directly or indirectly providing employment to millions of people around the globe. It is made up of many sub-industries such as the transport, hospitality, and entertainment. This vast industry is growing at a rapid pace.

Today tourism has reached the common man and destinations are being developed, to provide accommodation, amenities, attractions, and transport which are affordable, making tourism no longer the domain of the rich and famous, but forming a way of life for people all over the world. Tourism has been given the status of an industry. The main constituents of this industry work together for the mutual benefit of both the tourist and the industry. The secondary constituents such as banks, shops, handicrafts, and local transport, also provide essential goods and services to tourists and benefit from tourism activities at the destination.

Tourism can be best studied and understood from the systems approach as it encompasses many disciplines and is influenced by the external environment in which it operates. The successful development of a destination requires easy accessibility, clean accommodation, basic amenities, special attractions and ample activities for visitors from different age groups and socioeconomic backgrounds, besides being affordable in terms of time and money. This industry has tremendous growth potential and is growing by leaps and bounds day by day.

KEY TERMS

Domestic tourism Travel undertaken within one's own country.

Inbound tourism Incoming tourists or tourists entering a country.

Itinerary A travel plan or schedule which includes all travel details such as date, time, mode of transport, accommodation, etc. for travellers.

Leisure It is defined as using one's free or unoccupied time in a relaxed manner for entertainment or rest.

Mass tourism Transportation of a large number of people in a short time to places of leisure interest made possible by advances in technology (mass travel).

Outbound tourism It refers to outgoing tourists or tourists leaving their country of origin to travel to another country.

Recreation It means spending time to refresh and revitalize the body and mind by indulging in activities which have no monetary benefits.

Tourism industry A vast industry made up of many industries and organizations that work with one another to provide goods and services to meet the special needs of tourists.

Tourist product The tourist product is the reason of travel to the destination and may be defined as the total experience of travel and other attractions at the destination.

CONCEPT REVIEW QUESTIONS

1. Briefly define the following:
   (a) Hospitality industry
   (b) Tourism
   (c) Destination
2. Discuss the main constituents of the tourism industry.
3. List the five 'A's which are needed at a destination if tourism is to be promoted.
4. Why are tourism studies called multi-disciplinary?

CRITICAL THINKING QUESTION

Think of any holiday you have enjoyed in the past. Keeping Leiper's tourism system model in mind, identify the five elements of the tourism system in relation to your holiday.

PROJECT/ASSIGNMENT

Prepare a collage on the present tourism-related activities and events in your city.

REFERENCES

Andrews, S. 2007, *Introduction to Tourism and Hospitality Industry*, Tata McGraw-Hill Co Ltd, New Delhi.

Foster, D.L. 1994, *First class: An Introduction to Travel and Tourism*, Glencoe Macmillan/McGraw Hill, Singapore.

Gartner, W.C. 1996, *Tourism Development: Principles, Processes and Policies*, Van Nostrand Reinhold, USA.

George, R. 2007, *Managing tourism in South Africa*, Oxford University Press Southern Africa, Cape Town.

IGNOU 1994, School of Social Sciences, *Foundation Course in Tourism*.

Jafari, J. 1977, 'Editor's page', *Annals of Tourism Research*, vol. 4.

Keyser, H. 2002, *Tourism Development*, Oxford University Press Southern Africa, Cape Town.

Leiper, N. 1979, 'The Framework of Tourism', *Annals of Tourism Research*, vol. 6, no. 4.

The World Book Encyclopedia, vol. 19, World Book Inc, A Scott Fetzer Company, USA.

http://en.wikipedia.org/wiki/Industrial_revolution, accessed on 31 May 2008.

http://en.wikipedia.org/wiki/Tourism, accessed on 14 November 2008.

www.UNWTO.org, accessed on 31 August 2008.

www.wttc.org, accessed on 31 August 2008.

www.world-tourism.org, accessed on 31 August 2008.

CHAPTER 2

History of Travel and Tourism

Learning Objectives

After reading this chapter you should be able to:
- understand the evolution of tourism
- trace the history of mankind
- appreciate the events in history which contributed to the development of tourism
- describe the evolution of international tourism
- identify important milestones in the development of tourism

INTRODUCTION

In the previous chapter we were introduced to the subject 'tourism management' and read about what all it encompasses. Having understood the enormity of the tourism industry and its diversified sectors, this chapter focuses on evolution of tourism down the ages and how tourism in the past differs from modern-day tourism. The history of tourism begins with the history of travel, of man travelling on foot, in search of food, or for shelter from the forces of nature or from wild beasts.

The history of travel and tourism helps us in understanding how developments in the past have had an influence on the present-day tourism. Furthermore, knowledge of how tourism is developing in the present time will help us plan in a better manner for the future.

For the early man, the term 'travel' was not associated with the words pleasure or leisure as it is today. The word travel has originated from the word 'travail' meaning painful or laborious. The word 'holidays' can be said to have its origin from 'holy days', or a time to relax and rejoice, to be spent in celebrating festivals in the honour of our guardian saints. People have always moved from one place to another for a variety of reasons. Early travel was undertaken mainly for the purpose of trade, waging wars and conquering new lands, or for religious reasons. The pilgrimage or religious travel to perform rituals to appeal God, deities, or other sacred powers for wish fulfillment or to purify the body, had been seen in Europe after Jesus Christ was crucified. Churches maintained hospices, monasteries, and hostels for pilgrims. Pilgrims visited distant shrines for wish fulfillment or for material or spiritual betterment.

Pilgrimages and travel for treatment at natural springs or Spas was gaining popularity in the mid-seventeenth century when doctors advocated the healing powers of mineral water. They soon became important meeting places for the gentry or elite.

Travel for leisure dawned from the nineteenth century and tourism as a profession was born in the beginning of that century. The business of tourism can be traced back to the transport revolution that occurred around the same time as World War II. In its early stage, travel was a luxury available to the privileged class as transport costs were very high. Today, tourism is a full-fledged industry, very much within the reach of the common man.

The evolution of tourism in this chapter is a brief outline of the transition from travel for survival to modern-day tourism. It includes a brief account of the history of the human race, highlighting events which have created an impact on tourism.

DEVELOPMENTS IN THE HISTORY OF TOURISM

Throughout history, people have exhibited an unquenchable need to travel. There has always been a reason to change one's place and pace; be it for survival, trade, conquests, or curiosity. Inscriptions on monuments and coins and paintings on rocks show that early man undertook travel that was difficult and hazardous. People travelled on foot in search of food and shelter and moved on once the food supplies were exhausted. They carried their belongings on the head and back. Heavier items were strapped to a pole and carried by two people or dragged on primitive sledges. But people moved on braving the forces of nature and natural calamities which came their way.

Very little is known about the prehistoric period between 40,000 BC to 10,000 BC as no written records exist. The earliest archaeological records depict the westward movements of the Cro-Magnon man into Europe. Cave paintings around 20,000 BC in Lascaux are evidence of the existence of the Cro-Magnon man in modern-day France. Apart from travelling in search of food or to save one's skin, wanderlust could also have been one of the reasons for undertaking travel by the prehistoric man.

Early Civilizations

Civilizations developed around 10,000 BC to 8000 BC in the Neolithic period when people began living together and developed settlements. Instead of constantly moving about in search of food, man started using his intelligence and took control over nature. He developed farming techniques such as growing his own food and undertook the domestication of animals. Dogs were domesticated as early as 8400 BC and were used by native Indians in the USA to hunt for food and pull sledges.

Agriculture developed in 8000 BC in the Middle East leading to the formation of settlements. Agricultural implements and tools for hunting were designed. Civilizations were also developing simultaneously in India, China, and Egypt. Since man did not have to wander in search of food, he could use his time to develop other skills. Trade began amongst various settlements and the need for better transportation was felt. Travel on horseback began and was popular with the military movement to acquire land and conquer tribes.

By 5000 BC, water transportation in the form of rafts and canoes propelled by poles or paddles were developed for use in rivers, lakes, and streams (see Fig. 2.1). The development of the wheel around 3500–3000 BC by the Sumerians, ancient inhabitants of southern Mesopotamia, was a major landmark in the travel industry. Carts driven by oxen were used to carry goods and people. Later around 1000–500 BC, roads were constructed for chariots, wagons, and carriages. The roads and carriages helped both in trade and war. In 3200 BC, Egyptians developed sailboats,

Fig. 2.1 A canoe

which were used for trade, conquests, and exploration. The first merchant fleets were developed by the Phoenicians in 1000 BC, which sailed along the coastline for trade with Spain. Sails and oars were used for navigation.

The advent of civilization created a basis for tourism in the following ways:

- The concept of the word 'home' emerged in the communities in a particular area where people lived together.
- It was in these communities that culture was evolved. Different communities across the globe exhibited cultural diversity.
- Craftsmen produced goods which were traded.
- Invention of the wheel around 3500–3000 BC paved the way for future transportation of goods and people.
- Bricks were used for construction work. The Sphinx and all major pyramids were built between 2800 BC and 2175 BC by the Egyptian Pharaohs (see Fig. 2.2).

Fig. 2.2 The Sphinx

In Asia, India was the most developed region and the Indus Valley Civilization was the earliest civilization recorded in 3000 BC, during the Iron Age, followed by the Vedic period in 2000 BC (see Fig. 2.3). The excavations of Mohenjo-Daro in Sind and Harappa in Punjab are ample evidence of that era. Remains of modern cities with well-developed houses, streets, drainage systems, common baths and large courtyards have been unearthed. Seals of trade in terracotta have been found in Mohenjo-Daro which is evidence that people indulged in trade. Merchants

Fig. 2.3 The Indus Valley Civilization

travelled in groups in caravans consisting of carriages drawn by horses and oxen to protect themselves from wild beasts and bandits.

The creation and adoption of Vedic scriptures such as the great epic Mahabharata, and establishment of temples teaching Vedic scriptures attracted many students showing evidence of religious travel during the early Vedic period. The first crude grand trunk routes were created, and travel for military purpose and administration in addition to trade and commerce was undertaken.

The advent of civilization created one of the most important reasons for travel and it was during this period that the first signs of a tourism industry were visible. Inns appeared at prominent centres of trade to offer hospitality to the weary trader. After gaining control over nature and forming settlements, the desire to acquire assets and exert control over others developed. The worth of a civilization was measured in terms of its power to control others.

The Imperial Era

Tourism was established during the early empires of Egypt, Persia, Rome, China, and India. Road networks were laid for travellers, transport was made available, accommodation was provided for the traveller and the beast of burden, wells were dug for water, and security pickets were set up. Apart from travelling for trade purpose, the aristocrats travelled in style carrying provisions, water, animals, luggage, and servants along with them to enjoy the comforts of their home away from home. Folk-tales tell us about the stranger who was known to bring prosperity and the Asian tradition of courtesy was offered to the traveller who was considered a guest.

It may be said that the Western society has its roots in the civilizations of Greece and Rome. Although other civilizations were developing simultaneously, the written records of the Greeks have been used as the foundation for the scientific theories used today. The Roman empire took over Sicily in 241 BC and thereafter witnessed the greatest period of growth while Julius Caesar was in power in the last 100 years BC (see Fig. 2.4). Road systems with bridges and aqueducts, built for military purposes, became an excellent tourism infrastructure for the Romans and were used for trade and

Fig. 2.4   Julius Caesar

pleasure tourism. The Romans were the first to pave roads made of stone and gravel of 80,000-kilometre length from 100 BC to 400 AD, while paved roads appeared in Europe only after 1700 AD.

In 400 BC, the Greeks expanded the merchant fleets and developed two-mast vessels with four sails (see Fig. 2.5). Three hundred ports were formed for trade along the Mediterranean, the Black, and the Caspian Seas. Barges were developed to transport goods. Speed of travel over the land and sea was slow and expensive as food and shelter was not available en route. With the advent of road networks, resting places and food was provided along these routes.

Fig. 2.5   Merchant fleets

Wealthy Greeks and Romans travelled to Athens, Rome, and other cities to participate in or observe sporting competitions and performing arts events. Some travelled to the Oracles to pay homage to the numerous gods.

Travellers were attracted all over the world to participate in festivals held in honour of the Gods. The Olympic Games were held in Olympia, Greece, once in four years in honour of God Zeus. Athletes from all over the vast Greek empire participated in this mega event. The concept of guide services has its origin in Greece. Native guides were hired to escort tourists for sightseeing. Food, gambling, and dancing to entertain travellers have been part of the Greek hospitality.

The Roman empire was prosperous and pleasure loving. Inns were built and the business of renting various modes of transport, such as horses and carts, began to pick up. Tourism developed further during the period. Spectator sports such as gladiatorial contests were organized to overcome boredom (see Fig. 2.6). Pilgrimage, sightseeing, and health tourism in the form of bathing in mineral springs were popular activities. During this period, travel had a new dimension and was recognized as a meaningful social activity. The importance of leisure was recognized and a mention has been made in the writings of Plato and Aristotle.

Apart from the Greek and Roman civilizations, other sophisticated civilizations were being established which have contributed significantly towards modern tourism. The Pacific Islands were being explored and Mayan civilizations were spreading throughout Central America and Mexico. Extensive road networks were being built by the Mayans to

Fig. 2.6 Gladiators battle to death in an arena in Ancient Rome to entertain spectators

Fig. 2.7   The Great Wall of China

connect their centres of civilizations. The famous ruins of Chichen Itza and Tikal have observatories, temples, and sports fields, and attract millions of tourists. Even today, tourists throng to the temple of Chichen Itza during the vernal and autumnal equinox to observe a snake deity descend from the top of the temple and connect with its head at the base. These centres indicate that science, religion, and leisure were important aspects of Mayan life. Unlike the Western civilizations who believed in extending their territories by conquering land, the Chinese civilization preferred to live within a set space and constructed the Great Wall of China as a defensive structure to keep away foreign invaders. The construction work for the Great Wall began in 214 BC (see Fig. 2.7).

India's wealth and rich treasures were exposed to the Western world only after the Persian and Macedonian invasions in India. Apart from travel for military purposes and acquiring new territories, travel for trade and commerce expanded and new geographic routes were developed. The Mauryan Emperor Ashoka was responsible for the spurt in development of formal travel facilities. Emperor Ashoka's kingdom extended from Nepal in the north, to Tamil Nadu in the south and from Kabul in the west to Bangladesh in the east. After his great conquests and the sight of bloodshed, he left the administration of his vast kingdom to his officers and adopted the Buddhist teachings. He established schools, hospitals, and monasteries which also served the travellers. The grand trunk routes were improved further, trees were planted along roadways, and Ashoka pillars, with his doctrine etched on them, were erected. Rest houses were constructed along the grand trunk routes for the comfort of the travellers.

Fig. 2.8   Mughal Emperor Akbar

In India, the royalty travelled for pleasure and developed summer retreats away from the heat and dust. Milestones or *kos minar*s speak about the travel culture during Mughal rule. Caravanserais or walled rest houses were developed as trade tours became popular. Akbar established schools and colleges with boarding facilities, known as madrasas, to provide education to children (see Fig. 2.8). Education was another major reason for travel during this period. There was an increase in international trade and additional ports were developed. Before the Industrial Revolution, travel for leisûre was the privilege of the upper class of society only. Leisure travel, which is undertaken by the masses today, was unknown to the working class.

The Silk Route

The Silk Road or the Silk Route was a major trade route for caravans carrying silk and other luxury items from China to India and the Middle East which began as early as 2000 BC, and flourished during the Kushan Empire from 50 AD to 200 AD (see Fig. 2.9). The Kushan emperors opened and protected the silk road. It is the most important link in the movement of people from east to west to exchange silk, muslin, porcelain, tea, rice, and spices, or for the purpose of trade. Silk, spices, and ointments left Indian ports in ships bound for the Roman empire. Navigation was done by looking at the stars or the course of a stream or river. Rome sent back gold coins, Greek wine, and harem girls. Ideas and customs were exchanged along these routes between the people of central Asia, China, India, and Persia. This trading gave the travellers an experience of present tourism, i.e. seeing new places, cultures, interacting with people, exchanging ideas, and learning new processes. In spite of the hazardous route, travel was undertaken and profits were high.

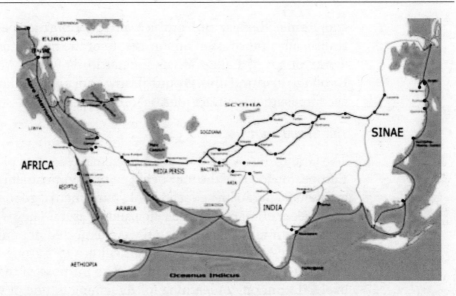

Fig. 2.9   The old Silk Route ran over 9700 kilometres, connecting China with Rome and pre-Christian Europe

It was only in 1400–1500 AD that navigation improved and longer voyages were undertaken, with the development of ships with rudder, triangular sails, and mariners' compass. Canals were built in the late eighteenth century to link the major manufacturing centres so that bulk material could be easily transported. A single canal horse could pull a load a dozen times larger than a cart at a faster pace and by 1820 a national network of canals was in existence. Water transportation was eventually taken over by the railways from 1840 onwards.

European Renaissance

The Renaissance was a great cultural movement that began in Italy in early 1300 AD and spread to England, France, Germany, Spain, and other countries in the late 1400s and ended about 1600 AD. During the Middle Ages, the Church was a patron of arts and learning and believed that people's chief responsibility was to pray to God and save their souls. Any activity considered unconventional or unorthodox was suppressed. Painters and sculptors during this period tried to give their works a spiritual quality and painted stiff and unrealistic human figures which represented religious ideas. The Renaissance or rebirth was a period of change and revival of Greek and Roman cultures. Many European scholars and artists, especially those in Italy, studied the learning and art of ancient Greece and Rome. Renaissance artists wanted to portray people and nature realistically and stressed on the beauty of the human body. The famous works of art of Italian artists Leonardo da Vinci, Michelangelo and Raphael inspired the Grand Tour, and even today, these artistic accomplishments attract tourists to Europe.

The Grand Tour

The Grand Tour was a tour of the principal cities and places of interest in Europe, the focus of the tour being cultural enrichment. It was said to be an essential part of the education of young men of good birth and fortune undertaken primarily for education and pleasure. They were accompanied by a mentor and a guardian and were expected not only to observe the arts, science, music, literature, and culture of Europe but to apply the knowledge gained, on their return. The purpose of the tour eventually evolved from one of learning for the young to one of sensual pleasures for all ages. Diplomats, scholars, and businessmen undertook the grand tour. The duration of the tour was generally three years.

The origins of the modern tourism industry are believed to have begun with the grand tour. Lodging facilities and hotels made their appearance during this period. Superior hotels and services were provided in some of the major cities of Europe such as Paris, Milan, and Rome.

In 1640 AD, horse-drawn coaches were used to transport people and goods from one city to another over long distances. The stagecoach was a popular mode of road travel amongst the elite. As the journey was completed in stages, the wagon was called a stagecoach (see Fig. 2.10). Teams of pack horses were used to transport heavy goods while stage-coaches carried the rich. In 1720, turnpike trusts were set up to charge toll to maintain the roads which were in a poor state.

Fig. 2.10 Stagecoach

The grand tour for the English elite reached its peak in 1700 and ended after the French Revolution in 1789 and the wars in the 1800s.

Modern-day grand tours are now undertaken after the last year of schooling and are an enriching experience of exploring the way of life and prevalent cultures of other countries. They are exclusively educational tours.

The Industrial Era

The only source of energy in the pre-industrial era was human or animal power, which was replaced by steam power in the industrial era, created by burning coal as a source of power.

The Industrial Revolution, which occurred in the late eighteenth and early nineteenth century, was a period when major changes occurred in agriculture, manufacturing, and transportation. It started in Britain and subsequently spread throughout the world. The manual labour-based economy began to be replaced by one dominated by machinery. One of the first products of the Industrial Revolution to affect tourism was the development of the steam engine. Steam engines were used in the industries for manufacturing and also for transportation. Steam-powered ships and railways hastened the speed of travel. The internal combustion engine and electrical power generation were developed. People migrated to towns to work in factories. Rail locomotive with a steam engine was used for transport of passengers and goods in 1825–30 AD (see Fig. 2.11).

Rail travel initiated the first form of mass travel, as a large number of people could be moved around at a relatively low cost. In 1841, Thomas Cook, the pioneer travel agent organized a special train to carry 570 passengers from Leicester to Loughborough to attend a meeting (see Fig. 2.12). In 1843, he took nearly 3000 school children on a trip from

Fig. 2.11 Steam engine

Fig. 2.12 Thomas Cook

Leicester to Derby. He introduced the concept of chartered transport and package tours which resulted in a spurt in pleasure travel. People began to travel to visit pleasure spots like beaches and spas.

Advent of Technology

Automobiles with internal combustion engines were developed in 1860 AD. The invention of the automobile and their mass production in 1903 is regarded as a technological advance which allowed people to move at their will. It is the most widely used mode of transportation in terms of passenger miles as compared to any other form of transportation. Henry Ford launched the people's car, the Ford model 'T' in 1908 (see Fig. 2.13). Also known as the 'tin lizzie', it was comparatively low-priced, economical, and changed the face of travel worldwide (see Fig. 2.14).

An extensive network of roads was laid and food and lodging facilities were developed on main routes. The present day motels and hotels have evolved from these early tourist courts of 1920s–30s.

The Industrial Revolution was a great turning point in the history of the world. It created a working class and most workers lived and worked under miserable conditions. Although the Industrial Revolution mobilized people to work in cities, it was the improvement in work conditions which gave people the time and money to travel. Working hours reduced from 70 hours a week to 40 hours a week; wages were increased with the Ford Motor Company paying USD 5 a day which was one of the highest wages paid to workers; weekly offs were declared, and the Labour Act was enforced. The greater disposable incomes led to the formation of a middle class in society. It is this middle class who constitute the majority of tourists today.

Fig. 2.13 Henry Ford

Fig. 2.14 The Ford-T model

Before World War I, the privileged class of society led an enviable lifestyle with ample servants, comforts, and plenty of leisure time. The opulence and grandeur of the luxury liners which crossed the Atlantic in those days, was unmatched in terms of services and comforts offered to passengers and even surpassed those services offered by many of the finest resorts of today. The Quaker City journey was the first transatlantic pleasure party voyage. Many notable personalities including Mark Twain embarked on this voyage from New York in 1867 (see Fig. 2.15). He later published his experiences in *The Innocents Abroad*. Twain's story of the adventure aboard, gave a boost to transatlantic steamship travel and shows us the importance of familiarization tours and travel writers in promoting tourism (refer to Chapter 12). Transatlantic cruises received a setback when the luxury ocean liner, Titanic, struck an iceberg in the North Atlantic Ocean and sank in 1912, with only 711 of its 2224 passengers surviving the tragedy.

Fig. 2.15   Mark Twain

Air travel has its origin with the use of the hot-air balloon in 1783 by the French. The Wright brothers, Orville and Wilbur, succeeded in sailing their prototype airplane in December 1903 near Kitty Hawk, North Carolina (see Fig. 2.16). The plane flew 120 feet at about 48 kilometres per hour. Air travel became commercial in 1919, shortly after World War I offering daily flights between London and Paris.

Fig. 2.16   The world's first successful airplane—
The Wright Brothers' 'Flyer'

Impact of the World Wars

The rivalry over trade and colonial possessions, and the assassination of Archduke Franz Ferdinand of Austria in June 1914, triggered World War I. The war resulted in massive destruction of human life and property, while all resources were used for producing materials required for the war. This period witnessed technological advancements in radio communication, land, and air transport, which were later made use of by the developing tourism industry.

The end of World War I ushered in prosperity throughout Europe and the USA. This period is called the 'roaring twenties' as wealth and leisure time was in abundance. Pleasure travel and luxury liners regained popularity, there were marked improvements in automobile transportation and infrastructure, and camping grounds with lodging facilities became popular. Resorts were developed along beaches, mountains, and lake areas near major cities and people had the leisure time and money to indulge in pleasure tourism.

In 1930, the collapse of the financial markets brought the tourism of the roaring twenties to an abrupt halt as the Great Depression set in. People migrated in search of employment, leaving families and friends behind. This resulted in travel to return to ones roots and visit friends and relatives in the near future.

While measures to restore the economy were still in process, World War II was declared in 1939. The six year period of World War II witnessed a sharp rise in technology with the beginning of the nuclear age and the detonation of the nuclear bomb at Hiroshima in 1945. World War II ended the Great Depression throughout the Western world. The industry expanded to produce weapons for war and continued expansion even after the war shifting to production of consumer goods. This marked the beginning of the consumer age. The growing industrialism and prosperity led to mass tourism, making the USA the largest producer of tourists.

TOURISM IN INDIA—POST INDEPENDENCE

In India, tourism got further impetus during the British rule. During the British Raj, hill stations and beaches were developed as destinations for the elite. All these destinations were connected by a railway network and *circuit houses* and *dak bungalows* were constructed to provide high quality accommodation, suitable for the British officers (see Fig. 2.17). The catering and entertainment facilities provided there were of the highest standards. Recreation facilities such as cricket, golf, clubs, and libraries were also provided at these destinations.

Fig. 2.17   A circuit house

When India became independent in 1947, the facilities which were already in existence were used for domestic as well as international tourists. They were easily accessible because of the vast railway network introduced by the British, making tourism affordable to the masses. The rich legacy of British hotels in India was taken over by enterprising hoteliers such as the Oberoi and the Taj Group of Hotels who expanded them into chain hotels. In the early 1960s the India Tourism Development Corporation (ITDC) was established to provide western comforts to international visitors at major tourist attractions in the country. Tourism was further promoted by establishing tourist offices abroad and by forming a separate tourism department. The private sector was encouraged to develop high-class infrastructure and superstructure to attract high-spending tourists. India's tourism policy was first formed in the late 1960s. In the 1970s tourism was separated from the Ministry of Civil Aviation, and state tourism development corporations (STDCs) were set up in every state. Tourism organizations had been formed to guide tourism industry professionals. In 1980, institutes to train tourism professionals had been set up and are still being promoted. Recently since 2006, the Ministry of Tourism is conducting short programmes under the scheme— Capacity Building for Service Providers (CBSP) in various hotel management institutes throughout the country to train tourism service providers.

MODERN TOURISM

Early air travel was not affordable to the masses and was for the rich and famous only. Cost of air transportation and travel time was reduced with

Fig. 2.18 A modern airplane

the use of jet engines and larger aircrafts in 1958. The airline industry has steadily grown from a single-engine airplane to the first jumbo jet Boeing 747 in 1970 and the first supersonic passenger plane in which passengers enjoyed safe, fast, and comfortable travel and a variety of in-flight services. Air travel became commercial in 1919. The late 1950s was the beginning of space travel. Air travel has become affordable to the masses and with the numerous international flights available, the international tourist arrivals have shown a steady increase (see Fig. 2.18).

Tourism, both domestic and international, is growing at a rapid pace in India. The air-transport network is expanding with new players entering the competition and airports with modern facilities are being constructed in major cities. The development of labour unions and government legislations brought about a reduction in work hours and paid vacations which prompted people to travel. Though the average work hours are once again on the rise, the increase in disposable income, and the realization of the need to de-stress, has people planning weekend getaways at the first opportunity.

Table 2.1 sums up the important milestones in the history of travel and tourism.

Table 2.1

Year	Milestones in travel
10,000 BC	People travelled on foot, carried their own load and developed settlements
5000 BC	Rafts and canoes propelled by paddles used in rivers, lakes, and streams
5000 BC	Donkeys and oxen used for transporting goods over rough terrains
3500 BC	First wheeled vehicles built by the Mesopotamians (Mesopotamia is now a part of modern Iraq)
3200 BC	First sailboats invented by the Egyptians
1000–400 BC	First merchant fleets developed
776 BC	First Olympic games held in Greece; beginning of organized sports tourism
100 BC–400 AD	The first paved road network was built by the Romans throughout the Roman empire
100 AD	Religious travel; beginning of pilgrimages
1215	King John signs Magna-Carta; foundation for justice system, includes right to travel
1400–1500	Long voyages by ships with a rudder, sail, and mariners' compass
1492	Columbus discovers West Indies, route to America established
1640	Horse-drawn stagecoaches used to transport goods and people
1700	Industrial Revolution
1758	Cox & Kings Tour Company formed
1783	Hot-air balloon successfully used in France
1800–07	Steam engines used in steamboats
1804	Hotels, guest houses developed at seaside resorts
1825	Rail locomotive used to transport goods and passengers
1830	First passenger train introduced
1838	Peninsular & Oriental Steam Navigation Company (P&O) introduced long distance sea voyages to North America and the Far East
1841	Thomas Cook founds the first travel agency
1869	Hotels developed at railway stations
1870	Telegrams introduced
1890	Gasoline engines with automobile bodies introduced
1891	American Express introduces travellers' cheques and money orders
1900s	Luxury liners, travel for the wealthy
1903	Mass production of automobiles
1903	Wright Brothers develop the aeroplane
1912	Titanic sinks; setback in luxury ocean travel
1914	Passports introduced
1919	Air travel begins between London and Paris; first international flight
1920	Automobiles become the main mode of transport in USA
1950	International air travel open to public; the first commercial jet airlines service
1951	The first motor inn or motel constructed outside Memphis, Tennessee
1958	Boeing 707 introduced
1960	India Tourism Development Corporation (ITDC) established
1970	Licencing of tour operators
1970	Jumbo jets with more travellers per plane and lower fares, major growth in international air travel
1976	Concorde, the first supersonic passenger airliner, begins service between Europe and the USA

The modern-day tourist has thus evolved from the explorer, the farmer, the merchant, the pilgrim, the conqueror, the student, the worker, and the cure seeker. Knowledge about the development of tourism over the ages is essential for tourism professionals to understand and plan tourism for the future. The chapter which follows will focus on the forms and types of present-day tourism around the globe.

SUMMARY

The present tourism industry is an outcome of various historical events which occurred worldwide. Travel developed from the need to survive, the desire to expand trade, and the quest to conquer new lands. The driving forces behind the development of tourism were an innate curiosity about the world and a desire to escape from the routine. Throughout history, people have shown an unquenchable thirst to travel. People travelled on foot in search of food and shelter and moved on when food supplies were exhausted. Various modes of transportation developed gradually to travel on land, on water, and by air. Tourism has thus evolved from the early man travelling for survival to the modern man travelling for business or leisure, in comfort and safety.

KEY TERMS

Automobile A passenger car, usually four wheeled, with an internal combustion engine meant for travelling on roads.

Canal An artificial waterway for transportation.

Caravan A large covered van or a trailer with facilities for passengers to live in. Also called a recreational vehicle.

Caravanserai A kind of inn with a large central court where caravans stop for the night.

FAM (familiarization) tour A free or reduced-rate trip offered to travel professionals to experience first-hand what a destination, attraction, or supplier has to offer.

French Revolution The revolution of the French people against the monarchy in France, 1789–99.

Grand Tour A tour of the European continent formerly taken by young men of the British aristocracy to complete their education.

Hospices A shelter for travellers, maintained by monks.

Industrial Revolution The change in social and economic organization resulting from replacement of hand tools with machines and power tools in manufacturing units and large scale production of goods.

Luxury Liner A passenger ship offering superior comfort likened to a 'Resort at Sea' mainly designed for affluent passengers.

Passenger mile It means one passenger carried one mile. It is calculated as a product of number of vehicle miles travelled and number of passengers transported.

Renaissance The great revival of art, learning, and literature in Europe from the fourteenth to sixteenth century which began in Italy and gradually spread to other countries, marking the transition from the medieval period to the modern world.

Thomas Cook Pioneer of modern mass tourism who organized the first package tour for a group of 570 people from Leicester to a rally in Loughborough 18 kilometres away.

Transatlantic Crossing or spanning the Atlantic Ocean or on the other side of the Atlantic.

CONCEPT REVIEW QUESTIONS

1. Discuss the significant developments which contributed towards tourism during the following periods:
   (a) World Wars I and II
   (b) European Renaissance
   (c) The Imperial Era
2. In the context of tourism, explain the following terms:
   (a) Tin lizzie
   (b) Roaring twenties
   (c) The Great Depression
3. Briefly explain how the Industrial Revolution has influenced the growth of the tourism industry.
4. Write short notes on:
   (a) The Silk Route
   (b) Industrial Era
   (c) The Grand Tour
5. Which factors, do you feel, have had a major impact on the growth of tourism?

CRITICAL THINKING QUESTIONS

1. It is said that the British left behind a strong foundation for setting up a tourism industry in India. Justify this statement?
2. Explain how the various modes of transportation developed from the beginning of the human race.

PROJECT/ASSIGNMENT

Collect pictures of ancient tourist attractions and find out how many still exist as attractions today. Prepare a scrap book and give a brief write-up on each.

REFERENCES

Andrew, S. 2007, *Introduction to Tourism and Hospitality Industry,* Tata McGraw-Hill , New Delhi.

Bhatia, A.K. 2001, *International Tourism Management,* Sterling Publishers Pvt Ltd, New Delhi.

Gartner, W.C. 1996, *Tourism Development Principles, Processes, and Policies,* Van Nostrand Reinhold, USA.

George, R. 2007, *Managing Tourism in South Africa,* Oxford University Press Southern Africa, Cape Town.

Ghosh, B. 2000, *Tourism and Travel Management,* Vikas Publishing House Pvt Ltd, New Delhi.

Guralink, D.B. 1972, *New World Dictionary of the American Language,* Second College Edition, Simon and Schuster, New York.

Kaul, R.N. 1985, *Dynamics of tourism: A Trilogy Vol. III Transportation and Marketing.* Sterling Publishers Pvt. Ltd, New Delhi.

Keyser, H. 2002,*Tourism Development,* Oxford University Press Southern Africa, Cape Town.

Seth, P.N. and S.S. Bhat 1993, *An Introduction to Travel and Tourism,* Sterling Publishers Pvt Ltd, New Delhi.

The World Book Encyclopedia, 1991, Vol. 1, 16, World Book Inc, A Scott Fetzer Company, USA.

CHAPTER 3

Types of Tourism

Learning Objectives

After reading this chapter, you should be able to:
* appreciate the pace of growth of the tourism industry
* understand the different travel motivators
* know the various types of tourism
* differentiate between needs of the leisure traveller and business traveller
* describe the various types of tourism available to the tourist
* appreciate the need to develop alternative forms of tourism

INTRODUCTION

The last decade has witnessed an increase in tourism activities. Globalization, modernization, increase in disposable income, and awareness created by the media have contributed to the growth of the tourism industry. Due to the growing awareness and tourism promotional activities by various governments, large numbers of people are now visiting various places. The movement of people is not only within their own country but also to neighbouring and distant countries. The motivation behind travel varies widely from person to person depending on the nature of the tourists.

Tourism presently is recognized worldwide as an industry due to the vast economic benefits it delivers to the host country. The two major economic benefits of tourism are earning foreign exchange and generation of employment at all levels in the society.

Most professionals, especially in the information technology (IT) field, have a hectic schedule and often feel the need to take a break. They may go for weekend tours, short tours for a few days or a week, or longer tours during vacations. Some examples of specially designed tour programmes are educational tours for students, senior citizens tours, and tours for women only. For example, Kesari Travels, Pune has designed a special package tour called 'My Fair Lady' for women only.

For many people work is not the sole aim in life and this has definitely encouraged tourism. Tourism helps people to get a better understanding of social and cultural values and helps create a better life and a better society.

PURPOSE OF TOURISM

Why do people travel? The answer to this question varies according to the psychological and sociological make-up of the tourist and his/her cultural background.

Tourism has witnessed considerable changes in the twenty first century from its previous motivations of travel, which were mainly visiting places of religious interest or travel for trade purposes. In the developed countries like Europe and the USA, tourism is not only a part of the lifestyle of the upper income group or high-class society any longer but has come within the reach of industrial workers as well. In American parlance the 4 'S' formula—Sun, Sea, Sand, and Sex is what motivates a tourist to travel. Bathing and water sports at the seashore, warm sunny beaches with ample sunshine and clean sand is what tourists look forward to. A pleasant escape from the temperate to the tropical climate to acquire a sun tan which is more fashionable today than a fair, pale complexion is one of the reasons for travel.

The tourism industry will not survive if people are not motivated to travel. The basic question of motivation as applicable in different fields can similarly be applied to travel. Why do some people travel and not others? Why does only one family member go on a tour? Why are a larger number of people in a particular country or region engaged in tourism activity than in another country? Many studies related to the psychology and motivations for tourism have been conducted. These studies show that tourists normally travel for more than one reason.

TRAVEL MOTIVATORS

Travel motivators can be defined as those factors that create a desire in people to travel. Motivators are the internal psychological influences affecting individual choices. McIntosh and Goeldern have mentioned four categories of motivators. These are as follows:

Physical motivators   These are related to physical rest and relaxation, sport activities, and health purposes.

Cultural motivators   These are identified by the desire to know and learn about other cultures, lifestyles, folk art, music, dance, etc.

Interpersonal motivators   These are related to a desire to meet new people, visit friends or relatives, seek new experiences. People undertake travel simply to escape from their mundane day-to-day routine.

Status and prestige motivators   These are identified with one's personal esteem and status symbol. These also include travel for business, education, or pursuit of hobbies.

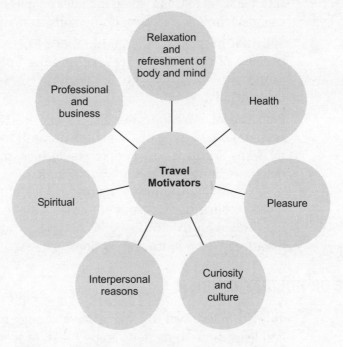

Fig 3.1   Travel motivators

Robinson's Classification

Robinson further classified the above four categories of travel motivations into seven groups (see Fig. 3.1). According to Robinson, the main motives for travel are as follows:

Relaxation and refreshment of body and mind   Due to the increased industrialization and hectic modern lifestyle, there is a need for rest and relaxation, to de-stress the body and mind. This desire for relaxation varies from individual to individual.

Health   Since the medieval days, people have been visiting spas and bathing in hot sulphur springs for specialized medical treatment. Several spas and health resorts have developed over time in most of the countries which attract visitors because of their curative aspects.

Pleasure   Satisfying an individual's need for pleasure is the most predominant of all individual travel motivations. A person's need for pleasure is very deep-rooted and travel can satisfy this desire.

Curiosity and culture   People are curious and eager to learn about other countries, their people, and their culture. Tourists visit places of historical interest, fairs, festivals, museums, dances, etc. to know more about the lifestyle of people from different countries.

Interpersonal reasons   This includes people's desire to visit their relatives, friends, families, ancestral homelands, and also for meeting new people.

Spiritual purpose   A large number of people are motivated to travel because of spiritual motives, i.e. visiting holy places, shrines, etc. The number of people who seek solace in such places is increasing dramatically.

Professional or business reason   People need to travel for business-related reasons and this type of travel both domestic and international is growing by leaps and bounds. People travel to expand their business, attend meetings, conferences, and exhibitions.

These different motivators or purpose of travel have led to different types of tourism. The types of tourism can be categorized on the basis of their travel motivations (see Fig. 3.2). The different types of tourism are discussed in the following section.

LEISURE OR HOLIDAY TOURISM

Tourists may travel to experience a change in climate and place, to see and learn something new, enjoy pleasant scenery, or to learn and know more about the culture of a destination.

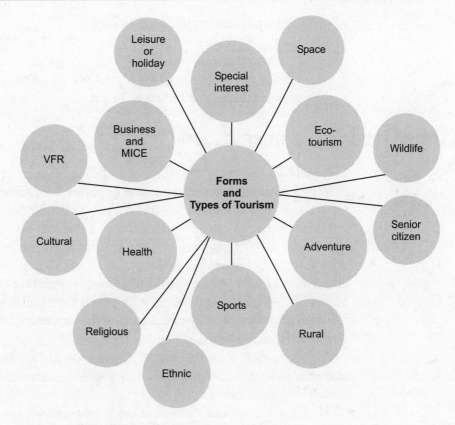

Fig. 3.2   Different forms and types of tourism

Tourists who seek respite from the stress of day-to-day life, devote their holidays to rest and relaxation, and refresh themselves when tired are included in the category of leisure, holiday, or recreational tourists. These tourists prefer to stay in some quiet and relaxed destination preferably at a hill resort, beach resort, or island resort. Nowadays, many resorts offer complete health packages or health benefits as extra facilities to the tourist in the form of a body massage, steam and sauna bath, yoga, facials, etc.

Industrialization and long working hours have created a lot of pressure on people today. Due to the stress and strain of urban city life, people are opting for relaxed, healthy, and peaceful holidays.

We have already read in Chapter 1 that there are many reasons why people seek leisure tourism such as:

- long and stressful working hours per week;
- working couples trying to find time for each other or the family;

- good pay packages and travel benefits;
- liberalization, privatization, and rise of the IT and BPO sectors; and
- awareness created by print and electronic media about various travel destinations; brochures of travel agents and hotels which focus on the pleasure aspect of holidays and weekend packages

VISITING FRIENDS AND RELATIVES (VFR)

This includes visiting one's relatives and friends for interpersonal reasons. A large number of Americans visit European countries in order to see their families or because they feel they are visiting their homeland.

This particular type of tourism is very common in India. Many people take time out of their busy schedules to visit their friends and relatives during school vacations or during major festivals and to attend weddings and other rituals. While visiting friends or relatives, people also visit tourist attractions in and around the city. These tourists do not have the freedom to choose their destinations, but they show an interest in shopping and visiting tourist attractions.

In India, due to leave travel concession (LTC) facility and travel allowances by private firms, many people are now visiting their native places in their holidays.

Hotels and restaurants benefit the least by this type of tourism as the tourists' board and lodging is taken care of by the hosts. However, these tourists are of benefit to other sectors such as transport, local transport, attractions, entertainment, and shopping.

CULTURAL TOURISM

People are always curious to know more about foreign lands, their people, and their culture. Culture is one of the most significant factors, which attracts tourists to a destination. Culture in terms of tourism gives the tourist an insight into the

- way of life or lifestyle of the people which one can experience;
- dress, jewellery, dance, music, architecture, and painting; and
- customs and beliefs, fairs and festivals, and religion practised in the region.

Cultural tourism covers all those aspects of travel whereby people travel to learn about each other's ways of life, their beliefs and thoughts. The food, beverages, hospitality, crafts, etc. appeal to the travellers.

Tourism is an important tool for promoting cultural relations and international cooperation. The way in which a country represents itself to tourists can be considered as its cultural factors.

Thus, cultural tourism includes widening one's knowledge about other places and people, their ways of life, their culture and includes journeys to places of art and heredity treasures, religious shrines and other civilizations, interest in religion, philosophy, history, etc. to participate in cultural events such as art festivals and celebrations—music, theatre, dance, folklore, festivals, etc. such as the Ellora festival, Elephanta festival, Khajuraho festival, Malaysia festival, Dubai festival, etc.

Fairs and festivals are one of the main reasons of travel as these are based on the culture of a country. They are not only popular with foreign tourists but also with modern Indian youth. Cultural tourism is one of the most significant reasons for travel in India because not only does culture differ from state to state, but also from region to region. For example, there is a marked difference in the culture of people residing in the different regions of Maharashtra namely Vidarbha, Marathwada, Konkan coastline, and the rest of Maharashtra.

Every state uses fairs and festivals to attract tourists. For example, during *Dussehra* and Diwali in Goa, *Narkasurs* or demons are paraded down the streets and prizes are awarded to the best *Narkasur* procession. Fairs and festivals are marked by colours, lights, traditional fare, games, races, new attire, religious celebrations, and festivities and a huge gathering of hosts and tourists. *Ganesh Chaturthi* or Lord Ganesh festival or Pune festival is celebrated for 10 days in September every year (see Fig. 3.3).

Fig 3.3 *Ganesh Chaturthi*

Cultural tourism can offer the tourist an original and unique destination experience especially in India because of the ethnic diversity, which India has to offer.

ADVENTURE TOURISM

Adventure tourism is a different type of tourism. It is more challenging because it takes the tourists into regions which are less frequently visited and may not have easy access. These regions may offer minimal facilities and comforts. For example, going on a trek through dense forests and pitching a tent to live in with a camp fire for cooking and light, may expose tourists to some risks along with the excitement.

Adventure tourism is a package of recreation, enjoyment, education, and the thrills of participating in an adventure.

Travelling to participate in adventurous feats is a popular form of modern tourism. Young people are attracted to this form of travel because of the excitement and risks involved.

Adventure tourism is a form of travel, wherein recreation has a revitalizing effect because all adventure activities are outdoor recreational activities with the unpredictability of nature adding thrill and spice to the tour. It fascinates people who want to live life in the fast track.

Adventure tourism has various forms, which can be broadly categorized as follows:

Adventure on Land

Adventure on land is available in many forms, which may be natural or man-made. Natural landforms include jungles, deserts, hills, and mountains covered with their natural flora and fauna or snow.

Adventure on land could be in the form of a safari travelling caravan style over a long specified distance or a wildlife excursion, or travelling through a desert or jungle where the elements of adventure could be experienced.

Motorcar racing is also an adventure sport, testing the navigation skills and endurance of man and machine. All terrain vehicles (ATVs) are an added attraction at many tourist destinations (refer to Chapter 5).

Other popular forms of land-based adventure sports are mountain or wall climbing, trekking and camping, mountain biking, and rock climbing. Mountaineering institutes have been set up by the government in a few states to promote these sports. Trained instructors, safety measures, and equipment necessary for adventure sports are available at these centres.

Motorcar racing, skiing, and heli-skiing are popular amongst both domestic and international tourists. Annual competitions for various adventure sports are an added attraction for the daring and adventurous tourists.

Land-based adventure sports are popular in India in the states of Himachal Pradesh, Jammu and Kashmir, Uttar Pradesh, and Sikkim. Large virgin forest tracks, untouched by formal transportation are available in the Sahyadris, Nilgiris, and Himalayas, while rock climbing is popular in Maharashtra, Karnataka, Haryana, and Rajasthan.

Water Adventure

Water or aqua adventure sports are available at seashores, gushing waterfalls, springs, glacial lakes, and man-made water parks. Diving is the most popular water adventure sport especially in areas with coral reefs like the Andaman and Nicobar Islands and at Lakshadweep. Scuba diving and snorkelling are popular underwater sports to observe the beautiful creatures of the water world on the ocean floor. Deep-sea diving is also gaining popularity. Parasailing and water scooters are available at almost all beaches as a tourist attraction for the less adventurous tourist.

Flatwater adventure sports, such as water skiing and wind surfing, and whitewater rafting and canoeing through rapids are some of the popular water adventure sports.

Rivers originating from glaciers of snowcapped mountains, crash on boulders and caverns to create swirls of whitewater and lots of rapids before they reach the plains. This makes whitewater rafting more challenging and exciting.

Aerial Adventure

This form of adventure helps people realize their dream of flying without wings and has gained popularity ever since the invention of the aircraft. With the aid of modern materials and established training methods, some forms of aerial sports are relatively inexpensive and safe.

The oldest form of aerial adventure is ballooning. Balloons are filled with a light gas like either hydrogen or helium gas or with hot air and can accommodate two or more people depending on the size of the balloon and basket. These colurful balloons are a major attraction at some destinations. Other adventure sports like parachuting and skydiving are costly and require prior training. Paragliding is a simpler sport, similar to parachute jumping except for the shape of the canopy.

Parasailing, gliding or soaring, hang gliding, and bungee jumping are also forms of aerial adventure.

SPORTS TOURISM

The concept of sports tourism has become more prominent in the current decade. People have been travelling to participate or watch sporting events for centuries. Today, sports tourism is considered as one of the most sought after leisure experiences. Sports and travel share a symbiotic relation, whereby people are attracted to a particular destination for active or passive participation. Sports tourists may be participants or spectators, who have travelled to enjoy the sport.

Standeven and De Knop (1999) have defined sports tourism as 'all forms of active and passive involvement in sporting activity, participated in casually or in an organized way for non-commercial or business/commercial reasons that necessitates travel away from home and work locality.'

The concept of sports tourism started with British nationals travelling abroad for winter sports. The first such sports tourism package can possibly be traced back to 1898 when Sir Henry Lunn, a British travel agent, organized a 10-day skiing holiday in the Alps for a group of 10 for a then princely sum of USD 15.

Sports tourism today is a worldwide phenomenon billed in several billions of dollars. According to Sports Tourism International Council (STIC), sports tourism could well account for 32 per cent of the total tourism market in the coming years.

Interest in sports among Indians, till recently, was generally restricted to cricket, but now other sports have also started gaining popularity. India is fast becoming a destination for sports tourists from all over the world. For example, an adventure sports such as whitewater rafting on the river Ganga at Rishikesh is popular among tourists, both foreign and domestic.

The counter trend of Indians travelling abroad extensively has, to an extent changed perceptions about their compulsion to travel; one of them potentially being for active and passive sports.

Sports tourism has also given an impetus to tourism in India. The Ministry of Tourism has set up a National Institute of Water Sports in Goa to promote water sports throughout the country. The state governments assist in procuring water sport equipment for canoeing, kayaking, hovercrafting, wind surfing, yachting, river rafting, etc.

Sports tourism is a small segment in India, but it ensures higher returns since a sports traveller is a high spender. Some of the popular tour operators and travel agents who specialize in dealing with sports packages are

SOTC Sports Abroad, specializing in cricket, golf, Formula 1 racing, tennis, and soccer (FIFA World Cup);

Sports Services Pvt Ltd, Bangalore, specializing in cricket, golf, Formula 1 racing, and soccer;

GET Lionel India, specializing in cricket, tennis, Formula 1, and soccer.

Active sports tourism, where tourists indulge in activities like adventure sports or golfing apart from sightseeing, is still a largely untapped segment, which shows tremendous potential. Many tourists visited Pune, India in October 2008 to witness the Commonwealth Youth Games (CYG). Tourists from all over the world attended the 2008 Beijing Olympics and many are expected to attend the 2010 Commonwealth Games to be held in Delhi.

RELIGIOUS TOURISM

Religious tourism is also known as pilgrimage or spiritual tourism. The evolution of tourism could also be attributed to journeys undertaken since ancient times to places considered as sacred. People travelled singly or in groups for the purpose of spiritual benefit or to attain salvation or *moksha.*

Religious tourism is a journey, undertaken for the sake of worship and/or to pay respect to a site of special religious significance.

In India, since time immemorial, tourism has been associated with places of religious significance. These destinations are scattered all over the country.

Varanasi in Uttar Pradesh is amongst the oldest living cities in the world. It is also the holiest of Hindu pilgrimages. Thousands of pilgrims come to Varanasi daily to take a ritual dip in the sacred river Ganga, as it is believed that it will cleanse their souls of sins, and to worship God at its many temples. Varanasi is so old that it is a part of Indian mythology and finds mention in the epics Ramayana and Mahabharata. Varanasi has nearly hundred *ghats.* Many are bathing *ghats* but at the others, cremations are conducted. According to Hindu belief, dying at *Kashi* or Varanasi ensures release from the eternal cycle of birth and rebirth.

Another important city of religious importance is Haridwar which is also known as the Gateway of the Gods. Two great events that take place here are the memorable Kumbh Mela, which happens once every 12 years and the Ardh Kumbh Mela, which comes once every six years. Haridwar stands as the gateway to the four pilgrimages of Uttarakhand also known as the *Char Dhams* of Uttarakhand—Gangotri, Yamunotri, Kedarnath, and Badrinath.

Another important Indian Hindu pilgrimage is visiting the *Char Dhams* of India which were founded by Shankaracharya. These are located at the four corners of the country namely at Rameshwaram in the south, Puri in the east, Dwarka in the west, and Badrinath in the north (see Fig. 3.4).

Vaishnodevi temple and Amarnath caves in Jammu and Kashmir, Mathura in Uttar Pradesh, the 12 Jyotirlingas, 51 Shaktipeeths, Shri Sai Baba temple at Shirdi, Anand Sagar at Shegaon, Maharashtra, etc. are some other important pilgrim centres (see fig. 3.5). The Balaji temple at Tirupati in Andhra Pradesh is considered as one of the world's richest temples.

For the Muslims, a visit to Mecca is sacred. Every Muslim wishes to visit Mecca, Islam's holiest city, once in lifetime. The annual religious

Fig. 3.4 Char Dhams of India

Fig. 3.5   Anand Sagar, Shegaon

journey to Mecca is known as Hajj and the pilgrims are known as Hajis. As part of the Hajj, pilgrims perform several rituals including praying at the *Kaaba* shrine located at the centre of the *Masjid al-Haram* or the *Grand Mosque*. The Sufi Saint Khwaja Moinuddin Chisti's *dargah* at Ajmer and Haji Ali at Mumbai attracts devotees of all faiths from all over.

For the Christians, a visit to Jerusalem and Bethlehem is considered very auspicious. Rome is recognized as the holy city for the tombs of St Peter and St Paul and so is the Vatican City. In India, the Church of Basilica of Bom Jesus at Goa and the church at Velankanni, Tamil Nadu are considered holy by Christians.

Buddhist pilgrims from Japan, China, and other places visit Sarnath, Bodhgaya, Rajgir, Sravasti, and Nalanda, places connected with events of the life of Buddha. Tourists from all over visit the world famous Stupas at Sanchi, and the Ajanta and Ellora caves at Aurangabad.

The Golden Temple at Amritsar in Punjab is the most sacred place for Sikhs. Anandpur Sahib or the holy 'City of Bliss' founded by Guru Teg Bahadur and Takhat Sachkhand Sri Hazoor Sahib, a shrine on the banks of the river Godavari in Maharashtra are popular Sikh pilgrimage sites.

For the Jains, Dilwara temples at Mount Abu, Girnar temples in Gujarat, Ranakpur, and Shravanbelagola are auspicious places. Thus, India has many pilgrimage centres and holy places of interest to all the major religions of the world.

BUSINESS TOURISM

Travel is not always undertaken for pleasure or leisure. The business traveller's main motive for travel is work. He/she visits a particular destination for various reasons pertaining to his/her work such as attending a business meeting, conference, convention, trade fair, selling products, meeting clients, etc.

Many travel and tour operators specialize in business tourism. About 80–85 per cent of all air travel is business related. Business travel is recognized as the most important segment for revenues for the hotel industry. More than 50 per cent of occupancy of a large majority of hotels in many countries comes from the business travel segment. The business traveller is the lifeline of the tourism industry.

Out of 2.8 million tourists visiting India, the majority are business travellers. According to the Federation of Hotel and Restaurant Association of India, 60 per cent of all guests in the Indian hotel industry comprise of business guests. Many convention centres have emerged in keeping up with the growing demand of business travellers. Similarly, the hotels target business travellers and have modern day facilities of arranging meetings and conferences. The airline and hotel industry have recognized the monetary worth of business travellers and, therefore, have directed a lot of their services towards them.

A business traveller looks for the best and not the cheapest, as he/she is not worried about the cost, for most travel expenses of the business traveller are borne by his/her company, which he/she is representing. Sometimes a business traveller decides his/her trip at the last minute. He/she has less time and needs comfort during his/her travel. The needs of a business traveller are, therefore, different from those of a regular tourist.

Unlike the leisure traveller, the business traveller does not choose his/her destination. Business trips are also shorter in duration. Most business travellers are frequent and experienced travellers and, thus, more demanding customers. Their expectations and demands are also more than that of an average tourist.

Sometimes the services used by both business and leisure tourists are similar such as hotel rooms and airline seats. At other times the services are specially designed for business travellers such as provision of convention facilities, etc. Special facilities are often made available in existing rooms for the business traveller like Internet access points in guestrooms and facsimile machines on board an aircraft.

Many countries are witnessing the revolution in business tourism, as a large numbers of corporate employees are travelling round the globe. Many IT and BPO companies send their executives abroad for projects and new assignments.

The city hotels in major metros find the business–leisure ratio to be 3:1. Travellers from China, Taiwan, Hong Kong, and Singapore visit India mainly for business purposes. Business travellers coming from western countries and those from the eastern part of the globe have different needs. For example, a survey showed that the Chinese usually need a tour escort, who may also be the interpreter or a designated interpreter. The interpreter is expected to travel with the group at all times and be part of the cost of the tourist group. They prefer staying in three or four star hotels with big impressive lobbies (implying quality) and large clean rooms. They are very particular in regards to maintaining their Chinese food and eating styles (there should be Chinese snacks and teas available), while pubs, dancing bars, karaoke, and shopping is what they look for as entertainment in the evenings.

Likewise, people from other countries would have their own likes and dislikes, which service providers must be aware about.

Meetings, Incentives, Conventions, and Exhibitions (MICE)

Business tourism involves meetings, conferences, and conventions where information is exchanged, lavish events are organized to launch new products, incentive travel is offered to motivate or reward staff, exhibitions are organized to promote corporations, etc. This is popularly called meetings, incentives, conventions, and exhibitions/expositions or MICE tourism, the four most important aspects of business tourism.

MICE has often been confused as mainstream business travel but the demarcation is now getting more defined as both corporate and service providers have begun realizing MICE's significance and potential.

MICE, a subset of business travel has become the buzzword in the travel industry. This was evident when the Indian Association of Tour Operators (IATO) convention identified MICE tourism as the upcoming tourism product.

MICE including small meetings, training courses, seminars, and workshops have gained special significance as a type of tourism throughout the world. Many hotels, resorts, and countries have developed facilities that are uniquely devoted to this form of tourism.

Some examples are Trade and Convention Centre at Vancouver in Canada and the Conference Centre at Manila in the Philippines. These centres are recognized internationally for the services and facilities offered by them. Pragati Maidan, New Delhi is a major exhibition centre. It hosts one of the largest annual domestic fairs—the India International Trade Fair in the month of November.

India ranks a distant 28 in the MICE chart and gets just 0.92 per cent of the total 10,000 conferences and meetings held globally every year. This is due to the simple reason that there is little infrastructure to cater to MICE traffic. The decision makers of international conferences will not select a venue on the basis of a country's scenic beauty, cultural heritage, or wildlife. An event planner looks for meeting facilities, accommodation, world-class airports, connectivity, transportation facilities, and competitive prices. Day trips and sightseeing can also be

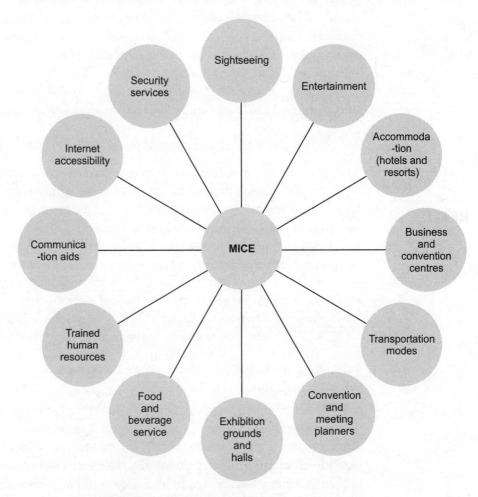

Fig 3.6 Infrastructure required for MICE

offered as incentives to MICE tourists as additional benefits so that they may also come back as repeat visitors, and bring their families along.

MICE travellers expect a high level of comfort, hassle-free movement, and value for money experience. MICE planners do not go by brochures, but their own experiences and feedback from colleagues in the industry.

Many countries have developed MICE as their primary activity of tourism interest. Countries such as Singapore, Thailand, South Korea, South Africa, Malaysia, New Zealand, Australia, Spain, and even Nepal, etc. are trying to promote themselves as MICE destinations. Similarly, places like Dubai are projecting themselves as major exhibition and event centres.

Planning for MICE requires a lot of coordination, perhaps more than the tourism industry (see Fig.3.6). The areas that require a special planning for MICE are as follows:

Venues   There should be enough space for international delegations to hold meetings, conventions, and exhibitions.

Transport   Air and ground transport.

Accommodation   Preferably near their meeting/conference/exhibition venues and should be equipped with fax machines, laptops providing internet connections, telex, videoconferencing facilities, etc.

Other support services   Catering, shopping, and entertainment.

HEALTH TOURISM

People have been travelling for centuries to improve and rebuild their health and stamina.

During the Roman empire the visit to spas, which was mainly for health reasons, became a pleasure activity as more number of spas, both warm and cold, came into existence. In Europe, the subsequent establishment of many sanatoria was the result of an awareness of the various benefits of good health. These sanatoria laid the foundations for future resort development. Today, there is a growing increase in the travel to spas and health clinics for curative baths and medical treatment. Hotels and resorts offer health services because in spite of busy schedules, people take time out to relax and de-stress. People all over the world are seeking good health through the various techniques offered by yoga and other alternative therapies and a lot of foreigners are coming to India for learning more about them.

The term 'spa' stands for *sanus per aquam*, which means in good health through water. A spa is a place where one can find time to relax, reflect, revitalize, rejoice, and discover one's inner self.

The history of spas can be traced as early as 500 BC amongst the Egyptians, Romans, and Greeks, when social bathing was an important aspect of their culture. Today's spas are an interesting combination of ancient traditions and modern mechanical wonders through the use of thermal and mineral water treatments. The unique selling proposition (USP) of many hotels and resorts is their spa.

Spas offer relaxing massages, pedicures, manicures, body scrubs, deep cleansing facials, and other healing therapies such as yoga and reiki.

They are gaining popularity because they are natural stress relaxants. They not only change the way you look but they also change the way you feel about yourself and everything around you.

People visit spas for many reasons. A business traveller comes to a spa to minimize his/her jet lag, an old lady seeks back pain relief, a teenager comes looking for a cure for acne and pimples while leisure tourists want to pamper their senses and gain peace of mind. Some of the world's finest international spas are the Cinq Mondes spa in the Beau Rivage Palace in Switzerland, the spa suite at Wildflower Hall, a resort in Shimla (see Fig. 3.7), and the Ananda Spa in the Himalayas which also offers Ayurvedic treatment.

To the tourists, India and other Asian countries offer the best attractions and at prices which few destinations can match. So is the case with medical tourism. It offers some of the best facilities for general medicine as well as specialized care, state of the art technology, and professional care.

Thus, health tourism covers regaining one's health or recovery from ailments through one or more of the following aspects:

Fig. 3.7   Spa suite at Wildflower Hall resort, Shimla

Change of climate   A change of climate from cold to warm or wet to dry helps one regain health during convalescence.

Alternative therapy   Destinations are popular because of alternative health therapies available in the form of ayurvedic treatment popular in Kerala and other states. Hot sulphur springs at Manikaran in Kulu for treatment of skin problems, the use of therapeutic mud from the Dead Sea in Israel, naturopathy and art of living courses, *yogasanas* at the Swami Iyengar Institute in Pune are some examples.

Medical tourism   Some tourists visit a destination because of the medical treatment available at the destination.

Medicare is on the upfront and is one of the motivational factors for tourism. Medical tourism is the most sought after term in the tourism industry today. It is more so in the Asian countries keeping in view the gains associated with this emerging area of tourism. India is working hard to establish itself as the number one country for medical tourism. Large numbers of international visitors come to India for medical treatment. This has become possible only because of the emergence of the private health care sector.

India is an ideal stop for medical treatment because it has world class hospitals, state-of-the-art technology, competent doctors, professional management, top quality nursing, and paramedical staff. All this is on offer at comparatively lower prices making it economical to the tourists as well.

Half a million annual tourists come to India with the chief purpose of either treating or enhancing their health. Two external agencies, Mc Kinsey and Messe Berlin have revealed that a 25 per cent growth in India's medical tourism segment could render the players richer by Rs 5000–10,000 crores. Messe Berlin feels that India can expect to earn USD 1 billion in foreign exchange from medical tourism by 2012. India's main USP is the low-cost treatment by highly skilled and qualified professional doctors. A large population from the Middle East comes to India for gynaecological treatment and abortions (abortions are considered illegal in their country).

The Ministry of Health of the Sultanate of Oman has signed a contract with a leading state-of-the-art hospital in Pune for treating patients with orthopaedic and spinal cord related disorders.

In India, the cost of treatment is between one sixth to one tenth of the cost incurred in the USA or Europe. Visitors from western countries find medical treatment in India cost-effective and less time consuming as compared to their own homeland. For instance, a heart surgery that costs about Rs 20 lakhs abroad would cost Rs 2 lakh (approx) even if it is performed in the topmost hospitals in India. The low-cost treatment is feasible and also a reality in India because of the low value of the rupee and low cost of labour. In addition, in India, waiting time is minimal which is proving to be a major attraction particularly for patients coming in from the UK or USA.

With its numerous other attractions, one can come here with the family and combine the medical check up with a pleasure trip for the family. The traveller, who visits India, can also look for a holistic package that includes a refreshing or relaxing tour. The traveller can choose from various systems of alternative medicine too, such as acupuncture, aroma therapy, meditation, ayurveda, unani medicine, mud therapy, physiotherapy, reiki, etc. In addition most hotels and resorts in India have their own spas and ayurvedic centres that further encourage such alternative forms of medical tourism.

To ensure standardization in health care it is necessary that hospitals offering medical tourism need accreditation from the Confederation of Indian Industry (CII), National Accreditation Board for Hospitals and Healthcare providers (NABH).

ALTERNATIVE FORMS OF TOURISM

Alternative tourists are different from the regular tourists. Alternative tourism aims at seeking a transition from impersonal, traditional mass tourism to establishing cordial rapport between visitors and the local hosts. These tourists normally avoid the services that are used by tourists such as accommodation, transport, and other services. They prefer to use or share the services of the local people. Their main motive is to experience and get an insight into their way of living.

Alternative tourism is nowadays regarded as a key to sustainable development. While mass tourism can have a negative impact on a destination, alternative tourism promotes a balanced growth form, more in line with local environmental and sociocultural concerns. Tourism development activities such as building of infrastructure, etc. are not only costly but also affect the environment and are minimal in this form of tourism.

Many of the western travellers have expressed their dissatisfaction towards the sun-based holidays. In fact many of the tourists are looking for a change. These tourists want tour packages comprising of wildlife, cultural sites, local tribes, whitewater rafting, etc.

This interest in alternative tourism has, thus, led to the emergence of travel agents and tour operators who specialize in these different interests of the tourists. Alternative tourism is not a type of tourism but is rather a guiding principle involving ecotourism, heritage tourism, cultural tourism, etc.

Special Interest Tourism

Special interest tourism has evolved from a search for new avenues, which are likely to attract and add value to conventional tourism. The tourism industry has felt the need to expand the destination experience beyond pleasure tourism and give the tourists a completely unique experience in an area, which is of special interest to the tourist.

The special interest tourist looks for the unusual and not for the routine itineraries, which include attractions, which cater to the needs of the mass tourist.

Special interest tourism can be defined as people travelling to a particular destination with the purpose of fulfilling a particular interest, which can be pursued only at that destination.

Special interest tourism offers many alternative forms. It is developed keeping tourist preferences in mind. It covers diverse market segments and equally diverse tourism products ranging from historical, culinary, archeological, and other interests such as golf, fishing, etc.

In India, from the special interest point of view, culture is the most popular of a range of special interests that a tourist may pursue. A large number of tourists visit cultural sites in India such as the Red Fort, the Taj Mahal, temples, and palaces to understand their historical value. Although a majority of mass tourists in India travel to these historical sites, a large number of tourists nowadays are looking at these sites with a different perspective, keeping their special interests in mind. This is how special interest tourism has developed.

Special interest tourism could be visiting Mughal architecture, gardens of India, textile centres of India, gourmet tours to learn about various kinds of foods in India, rail tours—travel by different types of railway systems, especially steam locomotives, Darjeeling toy train (see Fig. 3.8), Palace on Wheels, Deccan Odyssey, etc. The interests also include visiting tribal areas, wildlife safaris, camel safari, elephant safari, horse safari, walking safari, cycling safari, jeep safari, camping safari, etc.

Fig 3.8 Darjeeling toy train

Special interest tourism also includes sports tourism such as golf tours, polo, car racing, cricket, football, and hockey matches. Some tour operators sell package tours to coincide with sports events such as the football World Cup, the Olympic games, and the Commonwealth games.

Ecotourism

Ecotourism is one of the popular forms of alternative tourism. It is often defined as sustainable nature-based tourism. However, ecotourism also incorporates social and cultural dimensions where visitors interact with local residents. Ecotourism is usually used to describe tourism activities which are conducted in harmony with nature. This form of tourism fosters environmental principles with an emphasis on visiting and observing natural areas. It ensures that the impacts from the tourism activity are controlled.

Thus, ecotourism can be defined as 'purposeful travel to natural areas to understand the cultural and natural history of the environment, taking care not to alter the integrity of the ecosystem, while producing economic opportunities that make the conservation of natural resources financially beneficial to the local citizens'.

Due to the large movement of people and unplanned tourism development, the environment, ecology, and the people at a destination are greatly affected. The environment is the most fundamental ingredient of the tourism product and needs to be preserved.

It is generally agreed that unregulated tourism tends to destroy forests, consume firewood, create pollution and over crowding, and threaten the floral and faunal diversity. It also produces garbage trails, overburdens environment with tourist structures and roads, and at times causes hazards. There is massive reduction in forest cover in the hills and mountains. The rich forested slopes have been converted into barren rocks due to the development activities such as roads, hostels, and trekking trails. In Uttarakhand, the soils, biomass, flora and fauna, and water bodies have suffered a lot due to unplanned encroachment. Waste generation, especially solid waste by the hotels such as food waste, vegetable scraps, paper, rags, plastic, bottles, etc. is causing damage to the local ecosystems. While some wastes are biodegradable others such as soft drink bottles and polythene are not and cause immense harm to the environment.

Many of the tourist attractions have been damaged to a great extent due to increased human presence. The intrusion of humans has led to the decline of forest cover and damage to the precious ecosystem and biodiversity. It can also upset the living habitat of wildlife, forcing them to unusual diet and habitat. The unplanned growth of tourism can have an adverse effect on agriculture, forest, local people, and their way of living.

Many wildlife sanctuaries and national parks have been established, partly to promote tourism, the main aim being to protect and preserve the natural landscape, flora, and fauna. Tourism should be developed within the carrying capacity of the park and not at the cost of park and its resources.

Rural Tourism

Tourists nowadays are shifting their interest of travel to new destinations to explore and experience the destination and have first-hand knowledge of the local people, their cuisine and actual way of living.

Of late, rural tourism has gained importance in India. The Indian government is marketing rural tourism through its 'Incredible India' promotional campaign.

Fort Jadhavgarh near Pune has recently been renovated and taken over by the Kamat Group of Hotels, India which is known for its green policy.

In the European countries, the tourism infrastructure is quite strong in the rural areas, for example, in France and Germany when tourists visit vineyards which are quite famous there, or go for sightseeing to historical buildings they prefer staying in the countryside. In Scotland and Wales as well as other parts of the UK, tourists prefer the bed and breakfast motels and lodges where they can stay in comfort. More than 50 per cent tourists visiting Ireland stay on farms. The board and lodging is looked after by the farm's management. Special entertainment programmes are arranged for the visitors depicting the life lived by aristocrats and the landlords some 500 years ago.

In India, states like Rajasthan, Gujarat, Madhya Pradesh, Uttar Pradesh, Himachal Pradesh, and Maharashtra have heritage hotels. Many of the forts, *havelis* (old palatial bungalow houses), and palaces have been converted into hotels and they provide accommodation, food, and other basic facilities needed by the tourists. The entertainment programmes provided by these heritage hotels give an insight into the rural culture of the place.

Ethnic Tourism

Ethnic tourism involves travel for the purpose of observing the cultural expressions of lifestyles and customs of the indigenous and exotic people. This type of tourism focuses directly on the local people. It involves direct intimate contact with the authentic culture of the indigenous people. The tourists visit the local homes, observe, and participate in their traditional rituals, ceremonies, dances, festivals, etc. This type of tourism is also referred to as a combination of culture and nature tourism. In ethnic tourism, the tourist is mainly interested in having direct contact with the local people. The tourist's main aim is to gain first-hand experience of the way of life and cultural artifacts of the local people, whereas in cultural tourism the contact with the local people is done indirectly, i.e. these tourists will view the culture but not experience it. Some examples of ethnic tourism are the Pushkar fair, Bikaner fair, and Nagaur fair of Rajasthan.

Senior Citizen Tourism

This is a fairly new emerging trend in tourism meant for the senior citizens or old people. Many tour operators nowadays specialize in package tours specially designed for the elderly. They provide them with a tour escort or tour leader who keeps them occupied with entertainment and activities suitable for their age and at the same time making sure they do not get tired. Extreme care has to be taken while planning their tour. Due to their age factor and other health problems they should have a relaxed and enjoyable tour.

This type of tourism is common in the West, because of the nuclear family concept. It is now gaining popularity in India.

World over, the number of senior citizens is on the rise because of a longer lifespan attributed to developments in medicine and technology.

Wildlife Tourism

Wildlife is a term used to refer to both the floral and faunal components of a natural environment. Wildlife tourism has gained popularity in the last decade. Many young enthusiasts and nature lovers as well as adventure seekers are exploring this new area of tourism. Realizing the economic benefits of tourism, the governments of many countries are promoting wildlife tourism in a big way. Wildlife tourism is also considered an important element in wildlife protection. On one hand, the tourists can help in the conservation of wildlife while on the other conversely their presence can affect the wildlife (see Fig. 3.9). Thus, each area has to be assessed according to the number of people it can sustain. Disruptive human presence in the parks can have a negative impact on the number of wildlife and, thus, cause a drop in the number of tourists also. Due to the increased poaching and hunting activities many wildlife species are

Fig 3.9   Wildlife

on the verge of extinction, like the Asiatic Lion at Gir National Park in Gujarat.

Many tour operators specialize only in wildlife tourism. Luxury safaris, wilderness backpacking, zoos, aquaria, and safari parks all form part of the increasingly successful wildlife tourism industry.

Examples of well known wildlife sanctuaries and national parks are Corbett National Park in Uttarakhand, Bandhavgarh and Kanha National Park in Madhya Pradesh, and Kaziranga National Park in Assam, etc.

Space Tourism

Space tourism is the term broadly applied to the concept of paying customers travelling beyond the earth's atmosphere.

This is a new upcoming form of tourism where ordinary people will buy tickets to travel to space and back. The limitless resources in space are soon going to become profitable business. Virgin Galactic is all set to launch its first space tour with four Indians on board and has also booked twenty people for 2009 (refer to Chapter 16).

Tour operators and destination planners have realized the need to motivate people to travel and are seeking novel ways to attract tourists. Destinations are being developed keeping the travel motivators or needs of the tourists in mind. There is a visible shift from mass tourism to special interest tourism. The next chapter focuses on the infrastructural facilities which are necessary at the destination.

SUMMARY

The tourism industry has witnessed a large scale movement of people for various tourism related activities. Today, people are more aware of destinations and attractions, have money to spend, and need a break from their routine stressful life. They take short or long breaks to refresh and relax or may travel to fulfil some psychological and/or social needs. Sometimes travel may be related to business.

Tourism service providers need to understand what motivates a person to travel. Various travel motivators have been categorized and these have led to different types of tourism. The popular types of tourism are leisure or holiday tourism, visiting friends and relatives (social tourism), cultural tourism, adventure tourism, sports tourism, religious tourism, health tourism, and business tourism.

Mass tourism has led to dissatisfaction among some tourists and they now look forward to alternative forms of tourism. Many of them are looking for a change and wish to learn more about the local culture of a place. Special interest tourism adds value to conventional tourism by offering the tourists what they are especially interested in. Ecotourism is one of the alternative forms of tourism, where only those activities, which are in harmony with nature, will be undertaken. These alternative forms of tourism help preserve the environment for the future generations. Rural and ethnic tourism help the tourist to understand the way of life of the host population.

KEY TERMS

Carrying capacity Carrying capacity of a destination or attraction is the maximum number of tourists acceptable at any given time that can enjoy the attraction without harming the physical environment.

Convention An assembly of people meeting formally to discuss common issues and formulate policies. Conventions are normally annual events and attended by large number of people.

Convention centre A venue for hosting large conventions; located centrally in pleasant surroundings, accessible to airports with ample parking facility.

Corporate sector It consists of companies, business houses.

Exhibition or trade fair It is the display and sale of products or services to an invited audience or to the general public, with an aim of creating awareness and promoting products. They are of importance to the tourism industry because buyers, sellers, and exhibitors travel long distance to visit them.

Heritage tourism A type of tourism which covers the cultural heritage of the past.

Kayaking It means sailing in a kayak or canvas covered lightweight canoe.

Meeting In the context of tourism it may be defined as an organized event, which brings people together to discuss a topic of common interest which may last for a few hours or few days and which utilize services of the tourism industry.

Potential tourist A person who is likely to purchase a tourism product or can possibly become a tourist is known as a potential tourist.

Resort Generally located in hill stations or on beaches which provides built in recreation and sports facilities along with food and accommodation.

Sauna A steam bath available at spas and health centres.

Scuba A self contained underwater breathing apparatus.

Snorkelling It means to swim just below the surface of the water with a breathing apparatus called a snorkel which is held in the mouth and is fitted with a long tube which projects above the surface of water.

CONCEPT REVIEW QUESTIONS

1. What is alternative tourism and why is it gaining popularity?
2. Why does the VFR tourist not require accommodation for his/her stay?
3. Write a note on cultural tourism.
4. Discuss how sports are gaining importance with respect to tourism. What is the significance of religious tourism?
5. List the various land- and water-based adventure sports.
6. Discuss the requirements of a special interest tourist.
7. Name the tours related to special interest tourism.
8. Write a note on ecotourism.
9. Name four wildlife sanctuaries in India.

CRITICAL THINKING QUESTIONS

1. Discuss the significance of MICE to the tourism industry.
2. How does medical tourism help the economy of a country?
3. How does rural tourism help in the development of a region?

PROJECT/ASSIGNMENT

Visit the tourist spots in and around your city and find out the types of tourism which your city offers.

REFERENCES

Bhatia, A.K. 2001, *International Tourism Management,* Sterling Publishers Pvt Ltd, New Delhi.

Davidson, R. 1994, *Business Travel*, Pitman, London.

Goswami, B.K. and G. Raveendran 2003, *A Textbook of Indian Tourism*, Har-Anand Publications Pvt Ltd, New Delhi.

Hinch, T. and J. Higham 2006, *Aspects of Tourism: Sport Tourism Development*, Viva Books Pvt Ltd, New Delhi.

Kamra, K.K. and M. Chand 2004, *Basics of Tourism: Theory, Operation and Practice*, Second Edition, Kanishka Publishers, New Delhi.

Lundberg, D. 1985, *International Travel and Tourism*, John Wiley and Sons Inc Publishers, New Delhi.

Negi, J. 1997, *Travel Agency and Tour Operation: Concepts and Principles*, Kanishka Publishers, New Delhi.

Pearce, D. 1987, *Tourism Today: A Geographical Analysis*, Longman, New York.

Ritchie, B.W. and D. Adair 2006. *Sport Tourism: Interrelationships, Impact and Issues,* Viva Books Pvt Ltd, New Delhi.

Sethi, P. 2000 *Business Tourism*, Rajat Publications, New Delhi.

Singh, R. 1998, *Dynamics of Modern Tourism,* Kanishka Publishers, New Delhi.

Standeven, J. and P. De Knop 1999, *Sport Tourism*. Human Kinetics Publishers, Champaign, Illinois.

CHAPTER 4

Tourism Infrastructure

Learning Objectives

After reading this chapter you should be able to:
- understand the meaning of the term tourism infrastructure
- explain the relationship between infrastructure and tourism
- know the importance of telecommunication and essential services to tourists
- identify the main aspects of transport infrastructure

INTRODUCTION

The popularity of any destination depends to a great extent on the tourism infrastructure at the destination. Since the terms tourism and tourism product are complex and without any well-defined boundaries, the term tourism infrastructure too is vast and includes much more than just the basic infrastructure, i.e. the facilities located below the ground which complement those which lie above the ground such as water, street lights, power, drains, sewage, buildings, roads, etc.

An integrated package of infrastructural facilities such as water, waste disposal, roads, airports, railways, accommodation, transportation, attractions, etc. is the basic need of any destination. Destinations with excellent infrastructure are most popular and pose few or no barriers to travellers. This is because they are easily accessible, transport facilities are comfortable and affordable, accommodation standards are high, and food and beverages offered suit every palate. The environment is clean and hygienic and there is ample choice of attractions for all age groups at the destination. Singapore and Malaysia are examples of destinations with excellent infrastructure and it is no wonder that the number of tourists visiting these places is on the rise. Tourist traffic to any destination largely depends on the extent to which minimum infrastructural facilities are provided.

Tourism infrastructure covers two aspects. The first aspect being easy accessibility and freedom to travel, this means good international relationships amongst nations with minimum barriers to enter a country in terms of permits, visas, language, currency, etc. The second aspect of infrastructure is the level of development of facilities for tourists and hosts. These facilities include water supply, sewage disposal, energy sources, electricity, and drainage, well developed roads, designated parking areas, open spaces for parks, street lights, airports, railway stations, local transport, bus terminals, marine and dock facilities, communication facilities, security, etc. Infrastructure for tourism and infrastructure at the destination is for use of the resident community or the locals or hosts, as well as the tourists. This is because there is an overlap between tourist-oriented products and resident-oriented products.

The government provides the basic infrastructure at any destination and encourages the private sector to invest in superstructure such as accommodation, restaurants, catering, shopping malls, amusement parks, etc. by providing tax incentives. The tourism industry is witnessing joint ventures (JV) and public–private partnerships (PPP). Facilities such as catering, entertainment, and shops are provided by commercial entrepreneurs.

Tourism should be viewed as a national asset. Since infrastructure has a direct bearing on the quality of the tourism product, it should be optimally developed. Figure 4.1 shows the major components of the tourism infrastructure.

DEFINITION

Tourism infrastructure can be defined as the tourism policies and international relationships that remove barriers or obstacles and give the tourist freedom to visit a destination. It also includes developmental facilities and amenities such as water, electricity, roads, transport,

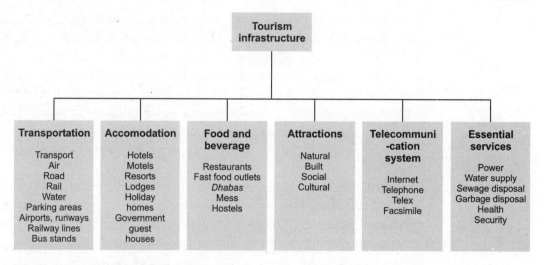

Fig. 4.1 Tourism infrastructure

construction, taxation policies, communication networks, and institutions that improve the quality of life of both the guests and hosts.

Although some infrastructure is developed specially to promote tourism at the destination, there is no line of demarcation and all facilities at the destination are for use by both the locals and the tourists. This clearly shows that planned tourism is a developmental activity which can bring revenue for destination development. India has a variety of attractions and does not use its tourism potential to the fullest extent; the reason being poor infrastructural facilities which create obstacles to international travellers.

Infrastructure for tourist transportation includes vehicles, network of roads and railway tracks, terminals, and parking areas.

Vehicles

Different types of aircrafts, trains, automobiles, and ships are used to transport tourists to and within the destination. These are discussed in detail in Chapter 5.

Network of roads and railway tracks

A well developed public transportation system or mass transit is necessary at the destination to give a boost to tourism as it is economical. It includes rapid rail, metros, subways, buses, tramcars, ferries, etc. For example, the mass rapid transit (MRT) in Singapore and mass transit rail (MTR) along with ferries in Hong Kong, connects the entire city making travel very simple. Fast, clean, efficient, and inexpensive local transport attracts tourists from all over the world.

Roads Roads which tourists use once they land at a destination and which connect important destinations should be in a state of good repair, with signage boards in English as well as the local language and street lighting in cities. The network of roads includes national highways, state highways, district roads, and village roads.

National highways are arteries of road transport, running through states, major industrial areas, capitals of states, and major ports. Expressway and freeway are other terms for a national highway. These roads should have well-maintained petrol pumps, food malls, and rest-rooms at regular intervals, for the convenience of the travelling public. Directional boards indicating the distance and location of these facilities along with helpline numbers, should be clearly visible to the motorist.

State highways connect state capitals with district headquarters, main cities, and towns in a state and with the highways of neighbouring states.

District roads and village roads connect towns and villages. They are interior roads often inaccessible during monsoons.

Railway tracks Like roads these are also permanent ways for trains with a route length of approximately 62,000 kilometres in India and are divided into nine zones namely the Central, Eastern, Northern, North Eastern, North East Frontier, Southern, South Central, South Eastern and Western, and Konkan Railways. There are three gauges (distance between the two rails) namely:

1. Broad gauge (1.67 metres), operating on main trunk routes
2. Meter gauge (1 metre), operating on feeder lines
3. Narrow gauge (0.76 and 0.61 metres), operating only in difficult terrain

The largest rail networks are in the USA, Canada, China, India, and Russia which link remote areas. Local trains have their own network in the city which is used by both the local people as well as the tourists.

Terminals

Terminals form an important part of transportation systems. They facilitate the movement of passenger and freight traffic. Terminal facilities of airways, roadways, railways, and waterways are discussed as follows:

Airways Airports should have all basic facilities for international and domestic carriers to land and take-off such as:

- Air Traffic Control (ATC) tower to monitor the movement of aircraft in the air and on the ground;
- runways for planes to take-off and land and taxiways or roads which connect to the runway;
- hangars or sheds for repair and maintenance of aircraft;
- loading aprons or overhead bridges for passengers and cargo to be loaded;
- designated parking zones for all types of private cars, coaches, and taxis; and
- cargo terminals, baggage claim areas, ticketing counters, etc. as well as passenger facilities.

Some international airports, such as Changi Airport, Singapore, and Schiphol Airport, Amsterdam are beautiful destinations offering all tourist facilities.

Roadways   Interstate bus terminals, bus stands, taxi stands with timetables and fares and basic facilities should be developed and maintained. Tourist coaches for sightseeing and open top buses are available at popular destinations.

Railways   Railway stations with retiring rooms and up-to-date information on arrival and departure schedules of all trains is necessary along with basic facilities for travellers. The Indian Railway Catering and Tourism Corporation Ltd (IRCTC) is working towards improvement of all services at railway stations.

Waterways   As sea and rivers are provided by nature, there is no building cost except for construction of terminals like docks for receiving ships, ports to load and unload cargo, jetties or piers for ferries to land which are to be built. For this reason cost of transportation is low compared to other modes of transport.

Parking areas   There should be adequate parking space provided especially at all tourist attractions, accommodation, restaurants, etc. All vehicles should be parked in the designated parking areas to prevent traffic congestion and road blocks, which influence not only the tourists' movements but are a nuisance to the local people as well.

ACCOMMODATION

Travellers and tourists need lodging for rest, sleep, luggage storage, etc. while they are on a tour. Roadside inns were built for weary travellers during the primitive times. Today, the hospitality industry is one of the top 10 largest industries and is growing by leaps and bounds to meet the demands of the increasing volume of tourists. Accommodation in the form of low budget lodges to world-class luxury hotels is available at all major tourist destinations to provide a home away from home to the travelling public. Exhibit 4.1 shows some important facts regarding tourist accomodation.

There are various types of accommodation which are being used by tourists regularly. Figure 4.2 lists the different types of accommodation

Exhibit 4.1   Some important facts regarding tourist accommodation

Tourist Accommodation: Some Important Facts
• All tourists do not pay for their accommodation, for example, tourists staying in private homes with friends and relatives save on accommodation expenses.
• Some tourists own the accommodation, for example, second homes, caravans, and timeshare apartments.
• Sometimes accommodation is mobile and can be moved from one place to another, for example, caravans, tents, and houseboats.
• Accommodation not built for tourists is used as tourist accommodation, for example, rooms in school and university campus, hostels during midterm breaks or vacations, paying guest accommodation in the host population's homes.
• Providing extensive services are not an essential part of the accommodation, for example, holiday homes, camps, caravans, etc. are forms of non-serviced accommodation.
Source: Adapted from Accommodation Classification, Keyser (2002).

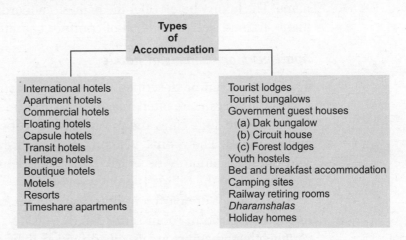

Fig. 4.2   Types of tourist accommodation

available for tourists. A brief description of various types of accommodation is given as follows:

Hotels

Hotels are a vital and essential part of the tourism and hospitality industry. Due to the increasing volume of tourists travelling, government should provide proper infrastructure to boost tourism. More hotels must be built to keep up with demand.

The dictionary defines hotel as 'a place supplying board and lodging'. Today, the hotels provide not only accommodation and meals but also various other services as per the needs of the guests such as massage parlours and cultural programmes.

International or star category hotels

These are the modern western style hotels, which are mostly found in the metropolitan cities, major tourist centres, and large cities at prime locations. These hotels have been classified on the internationally accepted star grading which ranges from five star deluxe to one star grade depending on the services and facilities provided by these hotels. Some of the facilities provided by five star hotels include information desks, conference rooms, travel desk, restaurants, banquet halls, room service, swimming pool, gymnasium, health clubs, shopping arcades, beauty parlours entertainment programmes, etc. Many of the hotels are luxury hotels and owned by public companies and controlled by a board of directors. Some hotels are chain hotels operating under a common brand name. The luxury hotels offer the highest standards of excellence through highly trained staff, high level of comfort, and efficient service.

Apartment or residential hotels

These hotels can be described as residential homes with hotel services and for this reason are often referred to as apartment hotels. These hotels are situated in large cities and mostly have European plan, i.e. only room and no meals. The rooms, which may be furnished or unfurnished are sold out on a monthly or yearly basis. The rents are usually collected monthly while the billing is done weekly.

The concept of apartment hotels started in America. A maid, clean linen, dining room, room service and, possibly, a cocktail lounge and certain other amenities are usually provided at the apartment hotel. These hotels are very popular in the USA and Europe and are gaining popularity in India as well. One example of an apartment hotel is Seasons, An Apartment Hotel, in Pune.

Non-star or commercial hotels

These hotels cater to the individual tourists for business purpose, the middle budget tourists, and their repeat guests. The location of these hotels is mainly near the business or commercial centres. Besides accommodation these hotels provide parking space, restaurants and, sometimes, business facilities for their guests.

Floating hotels

These hotels are mainly located on the surface of the water, which can be on seawater or river water or even on a lake. The facilities and services of these hotels are similar to those of a regular hotel. At many places the old ships have been converted into floating hotels and are very popular with the tourists. For example, Queen Elizabeth II, a cruise ship, is now being brought to Dubai as a floating hotel.

In India, houseboats at Kashmir and Kerala are quite popular with the tourists. Figure 4.3 shows houseboats floating on the picturesque Dal lake at Kashmir. The houseboats have elegantly furnished rooms with wall-to-wall carpeting, hot and cold water, and exquisite crockery and cutlery.

Fig. 4.3   Houseboats

Capsule hotels

A capsule hotel was first opened in Osaka, Japan in 1979. These are budget hotels present not only in Japan but also in other major cities of the world. These hotels cater primarily to the business tourists.

The capsule is a box made of glass reinforced plastic or cement, which is open either at one side or one end to provide facilities similar to a traditional hotel such as bed, television, flexible lighting, a box for valuables, and a table for writing. The rooms in a capsule hotel are lined up similar to that of a double decker, along with a central aisle comparable to a sleeping compartment of a second class AC train. Toilets, washrooms, vending machines, and lounge area are located on each floor close by. A central computer system monitors its functioning. Close circuit TV cameras are also installed for security purpose.

Transit hotels

These hotels are located near the airports. These hotels are also called airport hotels. They cater specially to the transient passengers and airline crew who are waiting for a connecting flight and need a place to rest or stay for a few hours to a few days. The transit hotels provide temporary accommodation to passengers who need not wait at the airport because of delayed or cancelled flights. Centaur Hotel in Mumbai is an example of a transit hotel.

Heritage hotels

Many of the old properties of the royal and aristocratic families like castles, palaces, forts, and *havelis* have been converted into hotels. These properties are renovated and the majestic grandeur and splendour is recreated for the tourists' experience. In the Indian states of Rajasthan and Gujarat these heritage hotels are an attraction, for example, Lake Palace, Udaipur, and Umaid Bhavan Palace, Jodhpur. Other examples of heritage hotels are castles such as Paradors in Spain, Posadas in Portugal, Chauteaux in France, and Schlosse in Australia. The guests are treated as nobles or members of a royal family at these heritage properties.

Boutique hotels

These are designer hotels based on a theme which provide luxurious personalized services and facilities to their clientele. They are generally smaller in size than the branded hotels and have thirty to hundred rooms.

These hotels appeal to the aesthetically inclined, sophisticated, modern international traveller, who chooses a hotel based on attitude, values, and lifestyle.

Rooms and guest areas are designed by contemporary designers for an innovative hotel experience.

Motels

Motels are generally located along busy highways and cater primarily to the transient, cost conscious travellers. Earlier the motels used to provide only parking space but now with the changing time many motels provide extra amenities such as restaurants, television, swimming pool, business facilities, etc. These motels also attract pleasure tourists who are on vacation.

Resorts

Resorts mainly cater to tourists for rest, relaxation, and recreation. Resort hotels are mostly located near the seaside, at hill stations, in wildlife sanctuaries or national parks. These resorts provide indoor recreation activities as well as other amenities such as swimming pool, tennis court, skiing, boating, surfing, etc. The rooms are generally larger than the other type of hotels and often provide kitchen facilities since most families may stay for several weeks.

The resorts are classified on the basis of climate and topography, which are as follows:

1. Summer resorts
2. Winter resorts
3. Hill resorts
4. Health resorts
5. All seasons resorts

Timeshare apartments/condominiums

The concept of timeshare originated in the 1960s and has been popular since the 1980s and 1990s. The timeshare offers the consumer stay in an apartment, resort or any type of hotel for a fixed period of time, each year with various facilities and amenities. It is the advance purchase of time in holiday accommodation. The period of time usually sold is for a week, 15 days or even a month.

The timeshare concept of holiday has now become a global product. Consumers have the option of more than 5000 worldwide timeshare resorts to choose from. For example, Club Mahindra Holidays offers timeshare holidays to Indian customers.

Supplementary Accommodation

Supplementary accommodation includes accommodation for tourists, but not necessarily hotel service.

A large proportion of the hospitality operations is not yet organized or categorized and does not have any grading also. Supplementary accommodation is of importance to the tourism industry and a large number of tourists prefer this kind of accommodation since it is economical.

Tourist lodges

The rooms in these lodges are moderately furnished. These lodges provide simple accommodation at a reasonable price with facilities such as an attached bath with hot and cold running water, dining room, laundry, parking, room service, etc. and at some places, bar and car rentals. These are generally located at railway stations, bus stands, etc.

Tourist bungalows

This is another inexpensive supplementary accommodation at important but out of the way places. Tourist bungalows are situated at tourist centres and are moderately maintained. These bungalows cater normally to middle class, budget travellers, and youth.

Government guest houses

These are government run and offer inexpensive accommodation and at times free or minimum priced accommodation for government employees. The guest houses are moderately furnished and available at a very low cost. There are also *dak bungalows, circuit houses,* PWD houses, and forest lodges which are run by the government. The *dak bungalows* are small rest houses, having limited number of rooms. These bungalows are only for the bona fide travellers or government officials. The *circuit houses* are superior as regard to the facilities offered. They are meant for high level government officials and run by the respective state governments, for example, Jodhpur Circuit House is run by the Rajasthan State Government.

The guest houses, dak bungalows, and circuit houses provide the services of a cook and attendant. *Forest lodges* are located inside or near the wildlife sanctuaries and national parks. For example, the Bharatpur Forest Lodge, Rajasthan.

Youth hostels

Youth hostels offer clean, simple, and inexpensive accommodation to the youth travelling independently or in groups for holiday or educational purpose. Youth hostels are controlled by non-commercial organizations, whose basic objective is the development of youth tourism. Here, the young people of different social backgrounds and nationalities meet and come to know each other. The facilities provided are very basic. There are dormitories and double rooms for a limited stay and at a very low price. The guests share a common washroom and can prepare their own meals. Youth hostels are very popular with students and budget travellers. They function at the national and international level. For example YMCA, YWCA, and Yatri Niwas.

Bed and breakfast (B&B) accommodation

This type of accommodation has its origin in Europe where families let out their extra rooms to tourists to supplement hotel accommodation during the peak season. The facilities include comfortable rooms and a complete English breakfast which could sustain the traveller for the full day. Many of the private households now offer bed and breakfast to the tourists. In India, the India Tourism office has a list of people who provide these services. The guests get a full breakfast, a room, and an attached or shared bathroom at a price. Bed and breakfast is very common in Kerala where foreign tourists stay with a family at a given price and also learn and enjoy the culture of the host.

Caravans/camping sites/camping grounds/tourist camps

These provide facilities such as parking, tents, water, electricity, common toilets, and washroom, etc. In some camps, there are cooking facilities also. Read about recreational vehicles in Chapter 5 for further detail.

Railway retiring rooms

The railway retiring rooms are provided by the railways to their bona fide railway passengers holding confirmed and current tickets. The rooms are moderately furnished and reasonably priced. Dormitories are also available. The meals are served from the railway canteen. The retiring rooms are situated within the railway station premises.

Dharamshalas

This accommodation is available for pilgrims and low-budget travellers at religious sites. Simple meals are also provided.

Holiday homes

They provide furnished apartment type accommodation along with cooking facilities to tourists who would like to prepare their own meals, at a reasonable price. This type of accommodation is available at popular tourist destinations especially in hill stations and is preferred by families on short holidays.

FOOD AND BEVERAGE

All tourists and travellers require catering services at the destination. Catering outlets to suit all budgets and levels of tourists ranging from food stalls and *dhabas* to fine dining restaurants are seen at all destinations. Most residential commercial establishments like hotels, motels, resorts, etc. have their own specialty restaurants and 24-hour coffee shop in the premises and may also offer room service facilities. They provide a variety of cuisines depending on the profile of the guests and the specialty restaurants in the hotel. High standard of cleanliness and hygiene are expected from star category hotels, and restaurants are graded on the basis of the hygiene and sanitation they follow. Figure 4.4 shows various

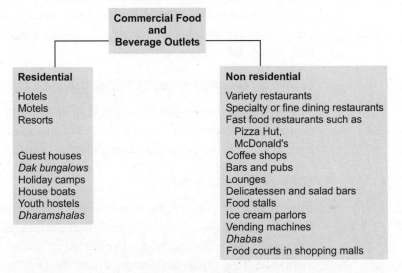

Fig. 4.4 Types of commercial food and beverage outlets

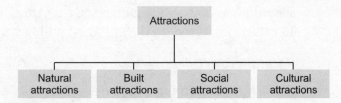

Fig. 4.5   Types of attractions

outlets where tourists can get their meals. The food vendors are also required to have a licence issued by the government and are subjected to stringent checks on quality of food being served. International fast food restaurant chains such as Pizza Hut, Kentucky Fried Chicken, Mc Donald's, etc. offer quick service and takeaway options to tourists.

ATTRACTIONS

In Chapter 1, we have broadly classified attractions into four basic categories namely natural attractions, human-made or built attractions, cultural attractions, and social attractions (see Fig. 4.5). In this chapter we will further elaborate on this classification.

Detailed classification of various types of attractions is as follows:

1. Natural attractions
2. Built attractions
3. Business attractions
4. Relatives and friends
5. Historic attractions
6. Cultural or ethnic attractions
7. Special events such as Commonwealth Youth Games
8. Medical attractions
9. Religious attractions
10. Government attractions

Attractions or the fourth 'A' of tourism forms the core of the tourism experience and the reason people travel to a particular destination. The other constituents of the tourism industry such as accommodation, transport, food and beverage, etc. depend on the existence of attractions at the destination for their survival. The main attraction may be a stand-alone unit or a cluster of many smaller attractions and activities at one place.

It is not easy to categorize attractions and there is likely to be some overlap. Almost anything can be an attraction, and appeal to a person according to his/her age, interests, etc. Attractions can be grouped into 10 categories based on the strongest pull factor or motivator.

Natural attractions

These include dominant land or water features, flora, fauna, climate, etc. that may form the main attraction or provide supporting features of most attractions. Tourists from all over the world flock to the Mediterranean region to enjoy the pleasant climate all year round. The Alps in Switzerland is another world famous natural attraction. People view the Niagara Falls from Buffalo, USA or flock to Niagara Falls, Ontario state, Canada to view the magnificent Horseshoe Falls which does not freeze even in the coldest winter months.

Built attractions

This is a very large category which includes resorts, amusement or theme parks, etc. for example, the Ocean Park at Hong Kong, Sentosa Island Resort at Singapore, Disney World at Orlando, USA, etc. These attractions are beautifully developed and spread over hundreds of acres of land and water. The Ocean Park uses natural attractions such as land features for the rope car, flora and fauna from water and land as attractions as well as a built environment and manmade rides and shows, making it a very popular theme park. These attractions are commercially profitable and have great appeal because of excellent planning and wide range of services, which they offer.

Built attractions require facility construction and complement the already existing tourism in the area. They include zoos, aquariums, sports stadiums, etc. The Butterfly Conservatory at Niagara Falls, Canada is a built attraction, which complements the Horseshoe Falls.

Business related

Metropolitan areas are centres of business activity, complete with information technology, manufacturing, finance and government offices, which attract business tourists for launching new products, MICE activities, etc. Resorts in hill stations and rural areas are developing conference facilities to attract business tourists especially during the lean season.

Friends and relatives

This is a major attraction or travel motivator especially in our country. Friends and relatives draw people to visit them along with their guests, especially if they live in the vicinity of another attraction. People travel to reinforce personal relationships and tourism professionals do not need to put in special efforts for this type of attraction.

Historic attractions

Heritage buildings, remains of old civilizations, monuments, and places where significant events occurred in the past are major attractions specially if accompanied by interpretation which creates interest by informing, entertaining, educating, and explaining the significance and relationship of the attraction with our daily life. The Government of India is restoring and preserving relics of the past to keep history alive, for example, the Cellular Jail at Port Blair has a sound and light show where historical events come alive through interpretation and visitors get the feel of the freedom struggle.

Cultural attraction

These depict the way of life of people from different cultures, i.e. how people live, their customs and traditions, fairs and festivals, food habits, etc. which may seem unique for visitors from other cultures. These attractions need to be preserved and sentiments of the host culture should be respected, as these are sensitive issues. For example, the northeastern states of India attract many tourists interested in the culture of the tribes.

Medical attractions

Preserving one's health has been a popular reason to travel with the discovery of the curative powers of mineral springs. Health spas, health resorts, or sanatoriums for convalescents and famous spas using ayurveda and herbal oil massages are now popular at many destinations. Specialized diagnostic and treatment centres at renowned hospitals are attracting patients from all over the globe.

Special events

Special events for short duration held annually or at regular intervals act as attractions during that period. These are specially organized and may be international mega-events such as the Olympic Games, Commonwealth Youth Games (CYG), etc. Specially organized festivals, such as the Pune festival in September every year draws thousands of visitors from all walks of life and showcases community values and the culture of Maharashtra.

Religious attractions

Religion has been a strong travel motivator since ancient times. The element of faith is what attracts tourists to pilgrim sites more than the tourism facilities present in the area. Some of the famous religious attractions are Vatican City, Rome; Jerusalem; Mecca, the birth place of Prophet Mohammed; and the Buddhist circuits in India.

Government attractions

National capitals and state capitals have government headquarters, monuments, and museums that serve as tourist attractions, for example, the White House in Washington DC, the Parliament House in New Delhi.

TELECOMMUNICATIONS

Telecommunications or communication by transmission of signals by transmission towers through various networks is necessary at the destination. This is because communicating to our near and dear ones practically every day is the modern way of life. Satellite communication has improved the speed and quality of our communication and has made it possible for us to connect even to remote villages. Telephones form the backbone of modern communication and are now an affordable means of communication. They are reliable for long distance communication and with the advent of technology, the clarity of voice is excellent even if the caller is halfway across the globe.

Telecommunication networks at the destination should include the following:

- Public telephones—ISD, STD, and PCO booths
- Mobile phones and calling cards
- Internet cafes
- Computers and videoconferencing
- Television
- Radio
- Telex, facsimile

ESSENTIAL SERVICES

Every destination should have adequate water supply and drinking water should be potable to prevent the spread of water borne diseases. Drinking water fountains are conveniently located for the locals as well as the tourists all over the USA while water needs to be purchased in Europe. Water bodies should be cleaned regularly to prevent breeding of mosquitoes and pollutant levels should be checked. At some destinations where drinking water is inadequate, it is imported and sea water is treated and used for other purposes. Water desalination plants, recycling, and purification plants are set up to provide sufficient water to the people.

Electricity

A continuous supply of power or electrical energy is needed with a back up system for all the constituents of the industry to perform efficiently. Other alternative sources of energy like solar energy should be used wherever possible.

Waste disposal and sewage treatment plants

These are necessary to prevent solid wastes from building up in the vicinity and untreated sewage (liquid waste from the toilets, bathroom, and kitchen drains) from getting into our water supply.

Health facilities

These should be easily available at any tourist destination. Hotels and other tourist accommodation should have care centres to provide medical care. For specialized care, tourists have to visit clinics or hospitals located in the area.

Security

It is another prerequisite at a tourist destination. Tourists would avoid visiting a particular place unless they feel that they would have a safe stay there. Hence, security arrangements in terms of police or security guards patrolling the area, etc. are essential to ensure safety of the tourists and also the local people.

OTHER SERVICES

This would include shops and emporiums as well as duty-free shops to attract tourists, foreign exchange money changers, banks, etc. Under the Global Refund GST Scheme, many shops at popular tourist destinations, offer tax-free shopping to tourists only. Duty-free shops, which sell goods free from local taxes and duties, are located mainly at important airports, train and ship terminals, etc. Foreign exchange money changing services are available for tourists to meet their foreign exchange requirements.

Automated teller machines (ATMs) are placed in easily accessible locations, enabling travellers to withdraw cash, check balance, etc.

The state tourism departments in India have offices and counters at important entry points or transportation terminals such as airports, railway stations, bus stands to guide tourists. Information brochures, road and rail maps, etc. are distributed free of cost at many destinations. Also available are tour guides or escorts who take the tourists for sightseeing (refer to Chapter 7).

Adequate infrastructural facilities are thus necessary at the destination. Destinations having excellent facilities in terms of accessibility and ease in crossing borders, as well as developmental facilities and amenities will receive more tourists than destinations with poor facilities. If tourism is to be promoted it is necessary to check that tourists have no hassles in reaching the destination and can stay in a clean, safe, and secure environment with good food and accommodation.

SUMMARY

Tourism infrastructure includes a vast number of structural elements—visible and invisible which are interconnected and which make it simpler for a person to travel. Some of these elements are located below the ground such as pipelines transporting water, sewage, under ground cables while others such as buildings which house hotels, restaurants, etc. are above the ground. Tourism infrastructure includes all facilities which will make the trip comfortable and memorable without any barriers or obstacles while travelling. It includes easy accessibility, well-developed roads with wayside facilities, clean environment and accommodation, variety of attractions, safety and security, excellent communication networks, choice of cuisine, shopping facilities, etc.

Infrastructure needed for all types of transportation is covered in this chapter.

KEY TERMS

Hotel chains Many hotels providing the same level of service in terms of accommodation and catering under a common brand name, located in various locations of the country or region.

Infrastructure The basic public services such as roads, water, electricity, sanitation, health, security, communication, airports, railways, public transportation, etc. needed for developing tourism.

Interpretation Explaining the significance of the attraction to visitors so as to enhance visitor appreciation, stimulate a desire to learn more and enjoy resources with minimal impact. The purpose of interpretation is to inform, entertain, educate, and provide a frame of reference for the site.

Motel Accommodation located on a highway which provides basic facilities.

Restaurant A commercial food and beverage service facility.

Supplementary accommodation Various types of accommodation for travellers such as lodges, government guest houses, youth hostels, camping grounds, etc. excluding conventional hotels.

Tourism infrastructure A complex system of all interconnected structural elements and policies which makes travelling easy.

CONCEPT REVIEW QUESTIONS

1. Classify the various types of hotels.
2. Briefly discuss the infrastructure needed for communication, purchasing souvenirs, and preventing water borne disease at a destination.
3. Discuss the important tourist attractions in your city.
4. Explain the following:
   (a) Role of youth hostels
   (b) Government guest houses
   (c) Natural attractions

CRITICAL THINKING QUESTIONS

1. List the names of and the type of accommodation available to high-spending tourists in your city.
2. Comment on the transportation infrastructure in your city. As a tourism planner, what steps would you take to improve on the same.
3. List any 10 food outlets in your city and mention which category they belong to.

PROJECT/ASSIGNMENT

Visit any four or five star hotel in your area and prepare a detailed report on the different facilities offered to the guests. On the basis of your findings, categorize the hotel.

REFERENCES

Andrews, S. 2007, *Introduction to Tourism and Hospitality Industry*, Tata McGraw-Hill, New Delhi.

Bhatia, A.K. 2001, *International Tourism Management*, Sterling Publications Pvt Ltd, New Delhi.

Brochures of National Tourism Boards.

Gartner, W.C. 1996, *Tourism Development: Principles, Processes, and Policies*, Van Nostrand Reinhold, USA.

George, R. 2007, *Managing Tourism in South Africa*, Oxford University Press Southern Africa, Cape Town.

IGNOU Schools of Social Sciences TS-1 Foundation Course in Tourism 1994, *Tourism Marketing and Communications*, Berry Art Press, New Delhi.

Keyser, H. 2002, *Tourism Development*, Oxford University Press Southern Africa, Cape Town.

Kotler, P., J. Bowen, and J. Makens 2005, *Marketing for Hospitality and Tourism*, Third Edition, Pearson Education, Delhi.

Negi, J. 1990, *Tourism and Travel: Concepts and Principles*, Gitanjali Publishing House, New Delhi.

Weaver, D. and M. Opperman 2004, *Tourism Management*, John Wiley and Sons Inc.

CHAPTER 5

Tourist Transport

Learning Objectives

After reading this chapter you should be able to:
- understand the importance of transport in the tourism industry
- know the various modes of transport available to tourists
- understand the importance of transport as an attraction
- know the advantages and disadvantages of different modes of transport
- appreciate the efforts taken by the public sector in promoting tourism in India

INTRODUCTION

We have already read about the basic infrastructure needed for transport in the previous chapter. This chapter introduces the various modes of transport available to reach the destination and to see the various attractions at the destination. It highlights the regular and unique vehicles used for transportation in the tourism industry.

The transport industry has gained a vital place in the global network system and is one of the most important components of the tourism infrastructure. It has now become easier for people to travel from one place to another because of the various modes of transportation available. As we have already read in Chapter 2 the earliest forms of transport in the ancient times were animals on land and sails at sea. Travel developed from the need to survive, to expand and develop trade to far off countries, and the hunger to capture new lands and territories. This was followed by the use of steam and electricity in the nineteenth century followed by internal combustion engines. Aircraft with jet engines were introduced in the 1950s. With the development of technology, travel became faster and more and more people could travel around the globe.

Since tourism involves the movement of people from their places of residence to the places of tourist attractions, every tourist has to travel to reach the places of interest. Transport is, thus, one of the major components of the tourism industry. To develop any place of tourist attraction there has to be proper, efficient, and safe modes of transportation. Transportation is vital to tourism. Studies have shown that tourists spend almost 30–40 per cent of their total holiday expenditure on transportation and the remaining on food, accommodation, and other activities. This aspect once again highlights the importance of transportation.

A tourist can travel by a variety of means. The tourism professional as well as the tourist should be aware of the various modes of transport available to reach the destination and at the destination.

The various modes of transport can be broadly divided into the following three categories:

1. Air transport
2. Land transport
3. Water transport

AIR TRANSPORT

Due to the growth of air transport in recent years, long distance travel has become much simpler and affordable. Distance is now measured in hours and not in kilometres. The world has indeed shrunk and become a small village.

The development of air transport mostly occurred after World Wars I and II. Commercial airlines were created for the travellers. Because of the increasing air traffic, the commercial sectors also grew rapidly. Before World War II, Swissair already was carrying around 14–16 passengers between Zurich and London. The first commercial service was introduced by KLM, the Dutch Airlines, in 1920 between Amsterdam and London. Commercial air travel grew mostly after World War II. More facilities were introduced and there was more comfort in travel. Jet flights were inaugurated by Great Britain in the year 1952. In the year 1958, Pan American introduced the Boeing 707 service between Paris and New York. Due to the introduction of jet flights, the year 1958 onwards saw a tremendous increase in air traffic. The concept of chartered flights was also introduced during this period.

Jumbo jets have revolutionized travel. A large number of people travel by air because of the speed, safety, comfort, and economy in terms of time saved.

The modern era, thus, is the era of mass air travel. After road transport, air travel is the most popular mode of travel particularly for international travel. For the business travellers, air transport is more convenient as it saves their precious time and offers a luxurious and hassle-free travel. Many airlines nowadays offer special facilities to the business tourist such as Internet on board.

There are two types of airlines—scheduled and chartered. Scheduled airlines operate as per the regular schedules. Chartered airlines or the non-scheduled airlines operate only when there is a demand, mainly during the tourist season. The chartered flights work out cheaper than the scheduled carriers as they are operated only when there is high load factor. Chartered flights provide cheaper packages to destinations such as Portugal and Spain. India receives more than 200 chartered flights, especially to Goa. Goa has maximum number of chartered flights coming in during the months of December to January.

The International Air Transport Association (IATA) regulates international air travel. IATA has more than 105 major airlines of the world as its members. IATA regulates the prices of tickets on different sectors of travel in the world. The concerned governments decide the domestic fares. The airfares are normally determined on the volume and the air travel demand in an area. For example, the airfare of London–New York is lower in terms of mileage compared to the same distance between London–Delhi because of high traffic between London and New York.

The International Civil Aviation Organization (ICAO) is an intergovernmental organization established in the year 1945. Only the government of a country can become a member. The governments have to enter into a bilateral agreement for the frequency of flights for operating commercial airlines between them.

Airlines are classified into two broad categories namely small carriers and large carriers. The small carriers also known as commuter airlines have less than 30 seats. The larger carriers, also known as major airlines fly direct routes between the major cities and seat 100 to 800 passengers.

The recent boom in the aviation technology has certainly brought some new developments to the airline industry. There has been a major change in size of the aircrafts. Singapore Airlines Airbus 380 is a double decker aircraft which seats approximately 800 passengers on flights from Singapore to Sydney.

Every year there are a growing number of new airlines being introduced. Because of the growing number of new private airlines there is stiff competition among them. This has resulted in a considerable reduction in air fares and has boosted the growth of air traffic. To woo and attract customers, many airlines offer cheaper promotional fares such as excursion fares, group fares, and apex fares.

Millions of tonnes of cargo and mail are also handled by the air transportation industry.

Frequent Flyer Programmes

The frequent flyer programme (FFP) was introduced by a group of American Airlines in North America as a marketing tool and to foster brand loyalty among people who fly frequently. This programme was mainly targeted for the business travellers. The passengers were given mileage points for travelling every 1000 kilometres. If they travelled more with a particular airline they earned more points. The frequent (loyal) user of the company's services earns free or discounted travel such as a free upgrade in the plane or a free ticket for the traveller or his/her spouse or even a free fly-cruise package, hotel stays, or other benefits in exchange of the points. FFPs may be operated by a single airline or jointly by airlines having an interline agreement. Air India has a FFP called 'Flying Returns' in which members can accrue mileage points while flying on Air India, Air France, and flights of Air India's code share partners, and redeem them for award tickets on Air India or Air France. Apart from airlines, Air India has tie-ups with leading hospitality service providers and members can earn additional mileage points to redeem their tickets faster.

AIR TRANSPORT IN INDIA

The first scheduled airlines service in India was started by the Aviation Department of Tatas on 15 October 1932, which was renamed as Tata

Airlines. After World War II, it was closed down in 1945 and around 21 airlines started operation in India. In July 1946, Tata Airlines was renamed as Air India. In 1952, after the government's decision to nationalize air services, all the existing airlines were merged to build two national carriers—Air India for international services and Indian Airlines for domestic services.

Air India

Air India is India's national flag carrier and finest flying ambassador. Air India inaugurated its first international service to London in June 1948. The corporation was first set up on 15 October 1953 under the Air Corporation Act 1953. Its main objective was to provide adequate and efficient air transportation service covering international routes except in countries such as Afghanistan, Myanmar, Sri Lanka, and Nepal. Domestically, it connects major metropolitan cities to provide international connection. It is one of the 20 largest IATA international airlines of the world.

The National Aviation Company of India Limited (NACIL) is the entity into which Air India and Indian Airlines have been amalgamated. The merged entity has a fleet of 148 aircraft, offering passengers seamless travel across domestic and international routes and is called Air India Limited.

Air India operates around 38 weekly services to four destinations in the USA—New York, Newark, Chicago, and Los Angeles. The airline also offers a daily nonstop flight between Mumbai–New York and Delhi–New York after the introduction of brand new Boeing 777–200LR in its fleet from August 2007.

The B777–200LR is technologically the most advanced aircraft in the world today. Passengers who travel on this aircraft have access to 400 hours of video and audio entertainment-on-demand

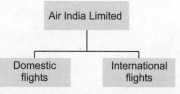

provided in every seat—first, executive, or economy class, by Thales, world leaders in digital in-flight entertainment.

Flights to the UK have also been increased from 10 to 30. Out of these 25 flights are for London and five for Birmingham. Similarly for the South-East Asia and Far East sectors the airline has increased the frequency of flights. Air India has also revamped its first class on all its long haul aircrafts—Boeing 747–400s, for the India–London–New York/

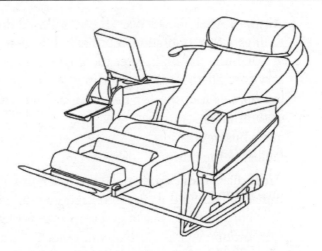

Fig. 5.1   Executive class seat in a Boeing

Chicago, India–Frankfurt–Chicago/Los Angeles and India–Paris–Newark sectors by retrofitting 180-degrees flatbed seats in the first class. The executive class of Boeing 747–400s and Boeing 777 have slumberettes—160-degree recline seats, thus providing more comfort (see Fig. 5.1).

The cabins have been upgraded with new seats in the economy class; state-of-the-art i4000 in-flight entertainment system, with audio-video on demand, gaming and other interactive entertainment, has been installed on every seat back.

Air India Express

To offer air travel options to passengers on a low budget, Air India has introduced Air India Express, in April 2005. It offers 140 international flights to 12 stations in the Gulf, including Dubai, Sharjah, Abu Dhabi, and Al Ain in the UAE, Muscat, and Salalah in Oman, Doha in Qatar, Bahrain, Singapore in South-East Asia, and Colombo in Sri Lanka.

Air India network

Air India now provides direct services from various points in India. It operates flights from Mumbai, and 12 other Indian cities, viz. Ahmedabad, Amritsar, Bangaluru, Chennai, Delhi, Goa, Hyderabad, Kochi, Kolkata, Kozhikode, Lucknow, and Thiruvananthapuram. Now passengers from these cities need not travel to Mumbai or Delhi, the traditional gateways, for taking international flights. Passengers boarding or deplaning in these cities can now complete their immigration and customs formalities at their city airport, both at the time of departure and arrival. Additionally,

Air India has increased its market access through code-sharing arrangements with other international carriers such as Air France, etc.

Facilities on the ground

Air India's lounge for transit passengers at Mumbai Airport provides shower facilities, specially designed slumberettes, Wi-Fi, a gymnasium, and a business centre. First and executive class passengers can use Internet facility at the business centre, which is located in the Maharajah Lounge while waiting for their flight to depart. There is a lounge for unaccompanied minors as well. Air India has its own exclusive lounges at Delhi, London, Hong Kong, and New York in addition to the one in Mumbai. At other international airports, Air India has tie-ups with other international airlines or local airport authorities for lounge facility.

Booking

The procedure for booking tickets has been simplified. For *online booking*, passengers visit http://www.airindia.in/ and click on 'Book Tickets Online Now!' and check schedules, ascertain the availability of seats and fares, make reservations and pay by credit card. For online destinations, electronic tickets or e-tickets are available for travel between certain online points in India like Mumbai, Delhi, Hyderabad, Bangaluru, Ahmedabad, Kolkata, Chennai, Kochi, and Thiruvananthapuram; and online points in the USA—New York, Newark, Chicago, and Los Angeles. Figure 5.2 shows an electronic ticket.

Fig. 5.2   An electronic ticket

Air India reservations can also be accessed from MTNL/BSNL land-lines within India on the common toll free no. 1600 22 77 22, and from mobile and private landline phones on Air India call centre numbers at Mumbai, Delhi, and Bangaluru.

Hand baggage

For security reasons the Bureau of Civil Aviation Security, Government of India, has banned passengers boarding an Air India aircraft from carrying liquids, gels, or aerosols, which include beverages, sun tan lotions, creams, toothpaste, hair gels, hair sprays, liquid cosmetics or any other item of similar consistency, exceeding 100 millilitres, except medicines, inhalers, or baby food in their hand baggage or on person from 29 September 2006. This rule has been recently relaxed in certain sectors.

Similarly, to ensure safety of aircraft and passengers as well as the convenience of fellow passengers, only one piece of *cabin baggage* of specified dimensions can be carried in the cabin (see Table 5.1).

Air India holidays

Air India holidays are very popular and cover a wide range of destinations in India and abroad. The latest being the Overseas LTC holiday packages designed for people availing of the leave travel concession (LTC). The Overseas LTC packages offer a combination of international and domestic destinations.

Air India offers over 400 comprehensive package options covering 150 cities in 22 Indian states and ten international destinations including London, Hong Kong, Shanghai, Singapore, Dubai, and Kuala Lumpur. The Mainland China package introduced in April 2008 takes the traveller to Shanghai, Beijing, Suzhou, and Hangzhou.

A package normally includes return airfares, airport transfers, and accommodation in standard three to five star hotels, meals, and local sightseeing, all at economical prices.

Table 5.1 Baggage specifications by an airline

Particulars	No. of pieces	Size	Weight
Checked in Baggage	2	Max.158 cm each (L × B × H)	46 kg (23 kg each)
Hand Baggage	1 + 1 personal brief-case, purse or laptop	56 cm × 45 cm × 25 cm	7 kg
Note: Specifications vary from one airline to another and depend on the class of travel			

Air India's logo

The earlier logo 'The Maharajah' of Air India has been changed to a red coloured flying swan with the 'Konark Chakra' inside it.

Indian Airlines

Indian Airlines was established on 1 August 1953 and was given the responsibility of providing air transportation within the country as well as to the neighbouring countries. Indian Airlines, together with its fully owned subsidiary Alliance Air, has a fleet of 93 aircrafts.

Indian Airlines is fully owned by the Government of India and has a total staff strength of around 19,300 employees including that of Alliance Air. Its annual turnover, together with that of its subsidiary Alliance Air, is well over Rs 6000 crore (around USD 1.4 billion).

Indian Airlines network

Indian Airlines operates its flight from Kuwait in the west to Singapore in the east and covers 76 destinations; 58 within India and 18 abroad. The Indian Airlines international network covers Kuwait, Oman, the UAE, Qatar, and Bahrain in West Asia; Thailand, Singapore, Malaysia, and Myanmar in South East Asia; and Pakistan, Afghanistan, Nepal, Bangladesh, Sri Lanka, and Maldives in the South Asia sub-continent.

Now Indian Airlines has been merged with Air India and the new company is called Air India Limited. Indian Airlines takes care of domestic flights while Air India handles international flights.

SECURITY OF AIRCRAFT AND PASSENGERS

To ensure the security of aircraft and passengers, security regulations have been made more stringent than before. The passengers may have to face some inconvenience during security checks. These security regulations are framed by the Bureau of Civil Aviation Security and have to be implemented by all operators.

Some of the security procedures are listed as follows:

- The passenger's ticket is checked at the time of entering the terminal building.
- At major airports, the checked baggage is passed through X-ray machines and a 'security checked' sticker affixed before entering the check-in area.

- Passengers are checked through personal frisking, and/or doorframe metal detectors and hand held metal detectors.
- The cabin baggage is either checked through X-ray machines or physically examined.

Security personnel put a security stamp on boarding passes and cabin baggage labels. In case of a 'red alert', a secondary security check is also carried out near the stepladder before embarkation. Checked baggage has to be personally identified by the passengers before it is loaded on the aircraft. Wherever the boarding is through aerobridges, passenger and baggage reconciliation is done through an internal matching system instead of physical baggage identification. Ten per cent of the checked baggage/cabin baggage is usually physically checked at random. If the passenger wishes to come back from the security hold area after the completion of security check, he/she has to get a fresh boarding pass in place of the old boarding pass from IA check-in counters. The passenger also has to undergo the security check again. This facility is available only in extreme emergency.

Passengers need to report at the airport only 60 minutes prior to the departure of any domestic flight. However, airports like Jammu, Srinagar, and Leh require reporting time of 120 minutes before departure.

For international flights, passenger should report 150 minutes prior to the departure for completion of immigration formalities.

Most of the airports are managed by the Airports Authority of India (AAI) and a few are under the control of the defence authorities. The maintenance, including upgradation of facilities of navigational aids, extension of runways, expansion of terminal buildings, etc. is under the jurisdiction of the AAI. Indian Airlines pays various charges such as landing, parking, and route navigation fee, etc. to the airport controlling agencies for using the airport.

Indian Airlines offers special fares to travellers such as Discover India fares, India Wonder fares, youth fares, and ship crew fares. These fares are applicable for foreign nationals and Indians settled abroad.

Special fares offered by Indian Airlines on Indian rupee fare are categorized under the following heads:

Armed forces and associated personnel discount   Under this category, a discount of 50 per cent on economy class Indian rupee fare is given to armed forces personnel belonging to the Indian Army, Navy, and Air Force. Ex-armed forces personnel, recipients of the National Bravery Award, personnel from General Engineering Reserve Force, officers disabled during war, and war widows.

Discounts offered on humanitarian grounds Discounts are offered to visually challenged persons, cancer patients, persons suffering from 80 per cent or more locomotive disability, and passengers on stretcher.

Concessional fares These are offered to senior citizens, students, civilian citizens, and recipients of gallantry awards.

Promotional fares These are offered to families travelling to Port Blair, Andaman and Nicobar islands.

Return fares These are meant for executive class passengers.

Night fares These are specially discounted fares for travel during night time.

Excursion fares These are promotional fares usually for a round trip and for a specified period of time.

Visit Taj fares These are special fares to promote Taj Mahal, Agra.

Easy fares These are promotional fares offered on specified domestic sectors of Indian Airlines. These fares are lower than the normal published fares.

Apex fares These are lower fares which are available for sale up to 21 days prior to the date of departure on specified domestic sectors. Only confirmed tickets can be booked under apex fare.

Bookings can be done online by visiting IA website www.indianairlines.in or calling their call centre at 1800 180 1407.

Vayudoot

Vayudoot was established on 26 January 1982, as a subsidiary of Air India and Indian Airlines. This airline was originally conceived to connect inaccessible areas of the North-East and other regions and stations not served by the Indian Airlines, which are important centres of trade or commerce or from the point of tourism.

It had a fleet of one helicopter and 16 aircrafts. Vayudoot's financial performance was not satisfactory which led to its dissolution and merger of its assets into Indian Airlines.

Pawan Hans Limited

Pawan Hans Limited, formerly known as Helicopter Corporation of India, was incorporated on 15 October 1985 as a government company. The corporation had been set up to provide helicopter services in India, initially to the oil industry including ONGC. Now, it also provides services to backward areas and remote tourist places, for example, the northeastern states in India.

Pawan Hans is India's largest helicopter operator. It has a fleet of 36 helicopters. It is the first ISO 9001:2000 certified aviation company in India.

Functions

The functions of Pawan Hans are to

- plan, promote, develop, organize, provide, and operate air support services to meet the requirements of the petroleum sectors including ONGC;
- provide scheduled and non-scheduled services by helicopters to inaccessible areas for the carriage of passengers, mail, and freights; and
- operate tourist charters by helicopters and to undertake any other operations that may be directed or requested by the government at Jammu.

The corporation also started its own helicopter services on the Jammu, Sanj, and Chhatkatra sector from 12 November 1987. The introduction of this service has been welcomed, especially by the old and disabled. Thousands of pilgrims have utilized this service to visit Vaishnodevi temple at Jammu.

Private Airlines

In recent years, the Government of India has allowed private airlines to operate and import aircrafts. Some of the popular private airlines are Jet Airways, Kingfisher Airlines, Spice Jet, Go Air, and Indigo, which operate hundreds of flights daily to over 59 destinations within India and overseas including New York (both JFK and Newark), Toronto, Brussels, London (Heathrow), Singapore, Kuala Lumpur, Colombo, Bangkok, Kathmandu, Dhaka, Kuwait, Bahrain, Muscat, and Doha. Private airlines offer electronic ticketing service which allows passengers to book tickets to any destination on the airlines' route network through the Internet.

Jet Airways (India) Ltd. has received the IATA Operational Safety Audit (IOSA) Registration.

INTERNATIONAL AIR TRAVEL CLASSES

Airlines normally have three travel classes. Nowadays, more long haul airlines are introducing the premium economy concept. The classes are

- first class, the highest quality of accommodation available;
- business class, high quality, traditionally purchased by business travellers and sometimes called executive class;
- premium cconomy, slightly better economy class seating as seats are not so cramped and there is greater distance between rows of seats; the seats themselves may or may not be wider than regular economy class; and
- economy class, also known as coach class, basic accommodation, commonly purchased by leisure travellers.

On airlines used for short flights, there are only two cabins—business and economy class cabins. The short-haul business class cabin is usually designated as 'first class' in North America (domestic).

Some airlines merge their international first and business classes into a premium business product (for example, Continental Airlines have a business first class), whereas others supplement the business class cabin with a premium economy class cabin. Some flights operated by Singapore Airlines (using their Airbus A340–500 aircraft) offer only business and premium economy class service. Some airlines, such as Japan Airlines and Lufthansa, offer flights with only a business class service.

Most low-cost carriers only provide an economy class. The costs of extra services and amenities offered in premium cabins are eliminated, and more seats can be installed in the aircraft.

Fare Class

Within each travel class there are often different fare classes, relating to ticket or reservation restrictions and used to enhance opportunities for price discrimination. Passengers within the same travel class receive the same quality of accommodation and may indeed sit next to each other; however, the price or restrictions they face for that accommodation will vary depending on the fare class.

Airline fare classes are commonly indicated by letter codes, but the exact hierarchy and terms of these booking codes vary greatly from carrier to carrier.

First class codes

A, F, P, R, Z

On domestic flights, F commonly indicates first class on a two-cabin plane. If a three-cabin aircraft is used, P (premium) may be used to distinguish the higher level of service in first class. The R code indicated supersonic transport and is no longer used with the retirement of the Concorde. The A and Z codes may indicate a first class ticket whose fare is reduced due to restrictions on refunds, advance reservation requirements, or other terms. A lowercase 'n' after any class code indicates night service.

Business class codes

C, J, D, I

On many airlines, C or J indicates full fare business class, whereas discounted and, thus, restricted and un-upgradeable fares are represented by D or I.

Economy class codes

Full fare: Y, B, H; Standard fare: M, N
Special or discount fares: G, I, K, L, O, Q, S, T, U, V, W, X

On most airlines, unrestricted economy ticket is booked as a Y fare. Full fare tickets with restrictions on travel dates, refunds, or advance reservations are commonly classed as B, H, or M although some airlines may use S, W, or others. Heavily discounted fares, commonly T or W, will not permit cabin upgrades, refunds or reservation changes, may restrict frequent flyer program eligibility, and/or impose other restrictions. Other fare codes such as X are restricted for use by consolidators, group charters, or travel industry professionals.

Most low-cost carriers have greatly simplified the fare classes and use few codes only.

ROAD TRANSPORT

We have read in Chapter 2 how humans travelled from place to place in search of food in the primitive era. They tamed animals such as the dog, ox, horse, camel, reindeer, elephant, etc. for carrying loads and travelling. After the discovery of the wheel, humans developed the cart, the chariot, and the carriage. Until the seventeenth century, horses were used for travelling. Later on better roads were constructed and some of these roads developed into trade routes, which linked many countries. One of them is the Silk Route, which was used for transporting silk from China to Persia and the Blue Gem road from Iran to Afghanistan and India. The road systems of the Roman empire developed an efficient transport network covering almost all of the Mediterranean and Western European countries. These roads were constructed with the main motive of military use besides trade and sightseeing. The Chinese roads were magnificent with many bridges. Most of the roads constructed were crooked to give a slip to evil spirits. Ancient India also had a vast and developed road network, which linked the administrative cities and religious places. There were *sarais* and *dharamshalas* offering rest, food, and water facilities en route. In the sixteenth century, the coach was introduced which was drawn by horses.

Today, the most popular and widely used mode of road travel is the automobile or the car. Road transport is dominated by the automobile, which provides views of the landscape and the freedom to travel. Tourists often travel with their entire family for holidays.

To promote tourism, the vehicles required are coaches and tourist cars. Tourist coaches or buses are preferred for large tourist groups travelling together on a specified tour itinerary. Coaches are of different types, with seating capacity ranging from a 14-seater minibus/tempo traveller, to a 35-seater bus and 50–55-seater bus used for sightseeing. Special motor coaches equipped with large glass panes, guides, public address system, and many other amenities such as washroom facilities are used for tourist buses, for example, in Greyhound buses.

Many tourists prefer to travel in comfort and privacy and hire cars. Cars of various makes and standards are available on rental basis. Air-conditioned luxury cars are required for meeting the requirements of sophisticated foreign and business tourists. The state tourism development corporations (STDCs), travel agents, tourist transport operators, and hotels operate such coaches and cars.

Tourists also use their own motorcar when holidaying. 'Motorail', i.e. cars and coaches carried over long distances by train facility is also available in some countries.

The car rental segment of the tourism industry is in a very advanced stage in foreign countries. The client can book a car, himself or through agents, and make it wait at the desired place at the destination. The client can then drive the car himself/herself on reaching the destination. On releasing the car on his/her return trip, he/she can make the payment along with the fuel charges. In some cases, he/she makes the payment to the suppliers through the travel agencies. In India, this particular segment is not so common with the tourists. The car is provided along with the driver who in turn takes the client around as per the client's wish. Though the self-drive option is being recently introduced in cities, in most parts of India the system of chauffeur driven cars is prevalent. Inadequate road directional signs, narrow and poorly maintained roads may be some of the reasons.

Some of the worldwide car rental agencies are Hertz rent-a-car, Euro car, Budget rent-a-car, Aloma rent-a-car, Avis, etc.

Recreational vehicles (RVs) have become popular in the recent decade, especially so in the USA. The cost of travel is very less as the travellers have their own services such as meal preparation and accommodation. The tourists travel with their families in their vehicles to get a break from their daily lifestyle. They look at it as a form of vacation despite the fact that they have to make their own beds and wash their own dishes. The money saved on accommodation can be spent on shopping and visiting places of attraction.

Table 5.2 Various Modes of Transport at a Glance

Form of transportation	Brief description and examples
Road Transport	
Buses or motor coaches	35–55 seaters of state transport undertakings or privately owned AC deluxe, AC semi-deluxe, non-AC buses. Shuttle buses for passengers in transit. For example, shuttle buses ply transit passengers from Changi Airport to Singapore city and back. Visa free transit facility helps in attracting tourists to see Singapore and also promotes the destination. Open top double decker buses which give passengers a panoramic view of the city are most popular for tours at many destinations.
Minibuses, maxicabs and matador vans	Small passenger vans where routes may or may not be fixed. Maxicabs are popular in South-East Asia. These have a smaller capacity and are used for sightseeing. They also include recreational vehicles (caravans/vans furnished with basic living amenities).
Cars	AC and non-AC taxis or cars on rent which may be chauffeur driven or self driven. A wide choice of automobiles of various makes and models is available to suit all budgets and includes luxury cars/limousines. Taxies are the most popular mode of transport at all destinations.
ATVs	All terrain vehicles—two, three, and four wheelers to travel over difficult terrain.
Other forms	Auto rickshaw—three wheeler transport, carries two to three passengers in towns and cities. Snow mobile—land vehicles designed to move on snow or ice. Motor cycles—popular in Goa. Pillion rides are given to tourists at nominal charges.

Contd

Table 5.2 Contd

Form of transportation	Brief description and examples
Animal power	Bullock carts in rural India, sledges, horse carriages. Mules at Vaishnodevi Temple, Jammu, and Yaks at Sikkim.
Human power	Cycle rickshaws and hand-pulled rickshaws in Nagpur, India.
Rail Transport	
Super fast trains	TGV (World's fastest passenger train).
Express trains	Fast trains with superior dining car facility and comfortable seats/berths which halt at very few stations, for example, the Rajdhani Express (India), Shatabdi Express (India).
Mail	Fast trains which halt at select stations only, for example, Punjab Mail.
Passenger	Trains which are slow and halt at all stations en route, for example, Solapur Passenger, underground tube.
Local	Mass rapid transit and local trains offer swift, convenient and economical transportation. For example, the underground subways at Hong Kong and Singapore. They link nearby cities and suburbs to metros. Frequency may be as often as every few minutes in peak hours. They ply throughout the day.
Toy train	Operate in hilly areas on narrow gauge, for example, Kalka-Shimla toy train.
Trams or street cars	Move on rails, laid on city streets and are electrically powered. Seen in Kolkata.
Luxury Tourist Trains	Luxurious fully furnished coaches fit for royalty with exquisite cuisine and facilities of a five star hotel, for example, Place on Wheels, Deccan Odyssey.
Air Transport	
Aircraft	To transport up to 400, in some aircrafts up to 800 passengers at a time.
Types	Airbus, Boeing, and jumbo jet, Concorde: Supersonic passenger airliner, helicopters.
Water Transport	
Ocean liners	Passenger ships for long distance travel from port to port. For example, P & O, MV Tipu Sultan, MV Nicobar.
Cruise liners	Special luxurious holiday ships for long distance. For example, Carnival cruises, Star cruises.
Ferry ships	Used for shorter trips. Scenic mode of transport to various islands and are popular worldwide.
Launches	A large motorized boat at all tourist places near rivers and seas.
Boats and canoes	Transport for short distance.
Hover craft and Hydrofoil	Fast communication over sea routes and difficult terrain.
Sea planes	They can land or take-off on water. They include float planes, flying boats, and amphibians.

Due to the growth in the number of recreational vehicles more RV camp grounds are being built. Private and government camping grounds provide easy access from major highways and tourist attractions. Some of the better camp grounds offer water, electricity, and sewage disposal facilities for the RV travellers. For example, Kampgrounds of America (KOA).

Car rentals and RVs have helped in the development of road transport. RVs offer the tourist both driving and camping facilities. The USA has more than 14,000 public and private parks and camping grounds for tourists.

Automobile Associations

Automobile associations are present in almost all the countries. These associations give emergency services to the car owners in case they have a problem on the road. They also publish road maps and help in providing other facilities to the motorists. For example, the American Automobile Association (AAA). India has regional automobile associations such as Upper India, Eastern India, Western India, Southern India, etc. The Upper India Association trains new drivers and teaches them safe driving practices. There is an apex organization called the Federation of Indian Automobile Associations (FIAA).

Inter-city and Inter-state Bus Service

In India, this is a very popular mode of transport because of its economical price and speed. Most of these buses are operated by the public sector state transport corporations. The budget tourists usually use coaches for inter-city travel. Many tourists nowadays prefer travelling by modern buses such as Volvo because of comfort. Transport operators also use Volvo for their conducted group tours.

The inter-state bus system in India is fully developed and provides different categories of buses. Many state transport corporations have ordinary buses, semi-deluxe, deluxe, and air-conditioned coaches. Reservation facility is also available for these buses at the bus stands and other reservation counters.

Greyhound and Trailways are the major bus companies of the USA. Greyhound offers highly discounted tickets to foreign tourists visiting the USA under various schemes.

Permits for Tourist Vehicles

Road transport operators have to comply with Motor Vehicles Act 1988 and Central Motor Vehicles Rule 1989. There is also, Maharashtra Motor Vehicles Rule 1989. The objectives of all these are to regulate motor transport and to develop it on healthy lines. Under Motor Vehicles Act 1988, with a view to developing tourism, the state transport authority is empowered to issue tourist permits to tourist vehicles to be effective throughout India and its neighbouring states. For encouraging long distance inter-state road transport, national permits irrespective of goods carriage are also issued by the appropriate authority. If tourism is to be promoted, it is necessary to remove all possible constraints for making smooth movements of road transport between the states within India.

In respect to road transportation in India, taxation policies, licencing systems, etc. differ from state to state. Motorists complain about time wasted at state boundaries and check posts in connection with paying of octroi, etc. Such restrictions should be removed and movement of vehicles from state to state should be made smooth. In foreign countries such restrictions do not exist, hence car rentals are a preferred option.

Road transport is most suitable for short and medium distances. It has an important role in the opening up of interior and remote areas and is comparatively cheaper than other forms of transport.

RAIL TRANSPORT

Railways are the most economical, convenient, and popular mode of travel especially for long distance travel all over the world. The railroad was invented in the seventeenth century in Germany with wooden tracks. The first steel rails were developed in the USA during the early 1800s. The railways revolutionized transportation and mass movement of people was seen in the nineteenth and twentieth centuries.

In India, the railways serve as the most important means of inland transport. The Indian Railway is Asia's largest, and world's second largest railway system under one management. It has a total route length of 62,000 kilometres. It was in April 1833 when the first train steamed out of Bombay (Mumbai) to Thane, a stretch of 34 kilometres. Today, it is India's largest public sector undertaking employing more than 20 lakh people. The Indian Railways is owned and managed by the Government of India. It operates around 11,000 trains everyday, of which 7000 are passenger trains.

The broad gauge lines account for more than 55 per cent of the total network and carry 85 per cent of the total traffic. The steam engines have been replaced by diesel and electric engines which has helped in increasing the speed.

There are different classes of travel—air-conditioned first class, first class, air-conditioned two-tier, air-conditioned three-tier, AC chair car, second class, and general class. The railways have promoted tourism in India by introducing special trains such as the super fast Rajdhani Express, super fast Shatabdi Express making rail journey faster and comfortable. Toy trains at Kalka and Shimla, New Jalpaiguri, Darjeeling, Matheran, and Udhagamandalam are major attractions for the tourists. The exotic 'Palace on Wheels' of Rajasthan (RTDC) and 'Deccan Odyssey' of Maharashtra (MTDC) are attractions for the foreign tourists.

The countries Europe and Japan have developed some very high-speed trains. France operates its TGV (Train de Grande Vitesse, or very high speed train) service between Paris and Lyon at a speed of 380 kilometres an hour. The Japanese Bullet train travels at a speed of 225 kilometres an hour. The speed of many of the Japanese trains has also been increased up to nearly 300 kilometres an hour.

In Europe, the railway systems of six European countries have been clubbed to make rail travel easier for the people of Europe. A rail passenger can buy a ticket in any one country of Europe and travel through six countries. For the foreign tourists, Eurail Passes offer unlimited discounted travel in express trains for periods ranging from a week to three months. The Eurail Youth Pass offers more discounts for young people below the age of 26 years in express trains.

In the USA, AMTRAK (National Railroad Passenger Corporation) operates trains.

Indrail pass

The Indian Railways has introduced Indrail passes for foreign tourists. The Indrail pass allows unlimited travel during the validity of this pass. Travel agents usually get a 10 per cent commission on the sale of Indrail passes.

To explore the beauty of multi-faceted India, Indrail passes provide excellent value and adds to the charm of holidays from abroad. Indrail passes offer visitors on a budget, the facility of travel, as they like, over the entire Indian Railways system, without any route restriction within the period of validity of the ticket. These passes can only be purchased by foreign nationals and NRIs on payment of US dollars, pound sterling and other convertible foreign currencies. The pass holder is not required to pay any reservation fee, super fast charges, or surcharge for the journey. The Indrail passes are more attractive for transit and short stay visitors. The passes are also available for half day, two days, and four days for the benefit of visitors arriving by international flights and visiting only one or two connecting destinations. Indrail passes are sold through general sales agents (GSA) abroad, Indian Airlines and Air India's overseas outlets at Oman, Australia, Malaysia, UK, Germany, Finland, UAE, Bangladesh, South Africa, Kuwait, Bahrain, Thailand, Myanmar, Singapore, Nepal, and Sri Lanka.

In India, Indrail passes are available for sale in tourist bureaus at major railway stations. Certain recognized travel agents are also authorized to sell these passes in Delhi, Mumbai, Kolkata, and Chennai. One can refer to the website www.indrail.gov.in/intert.html for information on the fare structure of Indrail passes.

Tatkal Scheme Facility by Indian Railways

The Tatkal or immediate booking scheme opens at 8 a.m. five days before the actual date of journey excluding the date of journey. For example, if a train is leaving on the sixth day of the month, tatkal booking will start at 8 a.m. on the first day of the month. No proof of identity is required for reservation under tatkal scheme neither at the time of booking nor during the journey.

The Indian Railways has a tatkal quota in each train in 2A, 3A, AC chair car, and sleeper classes. Under this scheme passengers are required to pay full fare from the starting point till the end destination, even if they board or get off the train at any in between station on the route plus the tatkal charges as applicable.

Circular Journey Tickets

Indian Railways provides the facility of booking circular journey tickets for pilgrimage or sightseeing trip to many destinations. These tickets offer unique travel flexibility, as they are issued for all journeys (other than regular routes), which begin and complete at the same station. Circular journey tickets can be purchased for all classes of travel. A maximum of eight break journeys are admissible on these tickets. Standard circular journey tickets are also offered by zonal railways. These cover popular destinations for the convenience of tourists. The details of route, fare, etc. for these tickets can be obtained from nominated stations in each zonal railway.

Circular journey tickets give the passenger benefit of telescopic rates, which are considerably lower than regular point-to-point fare. With these tickets, the passenger not only saves time but also the inconvenience of booking a ticket at each leg of the journey.

The Indian Railway Catering and Tourism Corporation Limited

The Indian Railway Catering and Tourism Corporation Limited (IRCTC) is a public sector enterprise under the Ministry of Railways, Government of India. IRCTC provides complete travel and tourism solutions for the various customer segments and also catering on trains and at stations over the Indian Railway network.

IRCTC provides the following range of products and services:

- luxury tourist trains
- exclusive steam and hill charters
- chartering of special trains and coaches over the Indian Railway network
- tour packages—Bharat Darshan—special tourist trains for the budget travel
- hotels—near important railway stations all over India
- car rentals
- e-ticketing for travel over Indian Railways
- call centres—for rail and tourism related information
- on-board catering on trains all over the IR network
- multi-cuisine food plazas at important railway stations
- packaged drinking water—Rail Neer

With the availability of such wide range of services under one umbrella, IRCTC is, thus, able to offer readymade as well as customized packages to meet the requirements of all segments of the travel and tourism industry.

Luxury tourist trains

IRCTC works with Indian Railways and other public and private organizations in the tourism sector, for running of luxury trains over the Indian Railways network. These include Palace on Wheels, Deccan Odyssey, Heritage on Wheels, and Fairy Queen.

Mountain railway steam/diesel charters

IRCTC offers charters on a number of scenic mountain railway sections, which includes:

- Darjeeling Hill Railway—UNESCO World Heritage railway (steam/diesel)
- Nilgiri Mountain Railway (steam/diesel)
- Kalka–Shimla Railway (steam/diesel)
- Kangra Valley Railway (diesel)
- The Neral–Matheran Railway (diesel)

Tourist cars

IRCTC offers luxury tourist cars for smaller groups. These tourist cars are air-conditioned cars with kitchenettes and modern comforts providing the luxury of a hotel on wheels.

Train and coach charters

IRCTC organizes train and rail coach charters for the convenience of tourists travelling in large groups.

Tour packages

IRCTC provides tour packages, covering a variety of tourist interests and requirements. These packages are all-inclusive, including rail travel, road travel, and hotel accommodation, sightseeing as well as onboard and off board hospitality.

Bharat Darshan

These are special tourist trains for the economy traveller, which have customized itineraries covering places of cultural, historical, and religious interest.

The Bharat Darshan tour package costs Rs 500 per person per day, and includes travel by train in second class sleeper coaches, along with the following:

- hall accommodation at places of night stay/morning freshening up
- vegetarian meals
- tourist buses for sightseeing
- guides/tour escorts
- security at each coach
- a railway staff on train as train superintendent

Toy Trains

Several toy trains operate in India. They are discussed as follows:

New Jalpaiguri–Darjeeling

The toy train on the Darjeeling Himalayan section represents the engineering skills of the highest order. This 83 kilometre long section connecting Darjeeling with the railhead at Siliguri is of great importance and has been given the status of World Heritage Site.

In 1999 UNESCO declared Darjeeling Himalayan Railway (DHR) as a World Heritage Site. After the Austrian Alps, DHR is the second railway system in the world to be accorded the world heritage status.

Kalka–Shimla Railway

This railway line is one of the most popular hill railways in India. The trains running on these tracks are popularly called 'toy trains'. A journey on this railway is a unique experience as one can view the majestic Himalayas, through tunnels and over bridges; amid the lush green valleys of pine and oak trees.

The Kalka–Shimla railway line was inaugurated by the then British Viceroy, Lord Curzon in November 1903, covering the distance of 96 kilometres from Kalka, up to Shimla hills. The toy train passes through 102 tunnels (originally 103), 969 bridges, 919 curves, and 20 railway stations in its entire journey. The Guinness Book on 'Rail Facts and Feats' included Kalka–Shimla Railway as the greatest narrow gauge engineering achievement in India.

The KS toy train has about seven coaches that can seat around 200 passengers in a single trip. The train runs through hazardous and adverse weather conditions with temperatures ranging from 0 to 45°C, heavy snowfall (average recording two feet during winters), and the annual rainfall of 200–250 centimetres. The train travels with a moderate average speed of 25–30 kilometres throughout its journey. It has been included as a World Heritage Site since July 2008.

Nilgiri Mountain Railway

The Nilgiri Mountain Railway is 46 kilometres long and runs on a 1000-millimetre gauge railway connecting Mettupalayam to Ooty. The first section of the Nilgiri Railway up to Coonoor was completed in 1899 by the Nilgiri Railway Company and was extended to Ooty in 1903.

This Nilgiri rail system is unique as it is the steepest one in Asia.

Neral–Matheran Railway

Matheran Railway links Neral, which lies on the Mumbai–Pune route, to the beautiful hill station of Matheran. The route, covered in a time period of one and half hours, is full of beautiful scenic views of the region.

The Matheran Hill Railway is a heritage railway in Maharashtra, built between 1901 and 1907 by Abdul Hussein Adamjee Peerbhoy, at a cost of Rs 16,00,000. The railway covers a distance of 20 kilometres (12.67 miles), connecting Neral to Matheran in the Western Ghats hills near Mumbai. The railway is a two feet (610 millimetre) narrow gauge railway and is being promoted as a future World Heritage Site.

Pathankot–Joginder Railway

The Kangra toy train links Pathankot and Joginder Nagar through hills and valleys, offering the travellers beautiful scenic views. The work on this line started in 1926. Three years later, this 163-kilometre route was opened to traffic.

The entire route gives beautiful views of Kangra valley, hills on the sides, streams, and the Dhauladhar range. It travels past the ruins of the old Kangra fort.

Luxury Tourist Trains

Luxury tourist trains operating in India include the Fairy Queen, Deccan Odyssey, and Palace on Wheels. They are discussed as follows:

Fairy Queen

The Fairy Queen was built for the erstwhile East Indian Railways (EIR) in 1855. Its steam engine is the oldest working engine in the world. It has the prestige of having a place in the Guinness Book of World Records and also winning the National Tourism Award. It has also graced the National Rail Museum, New Delhi. The Fairy Queen starts from Delhi and reaches the picturesque town of Alwar in Rajasthan the same day, from where the guests are taken to Sariska Tiger Reserve for an overnight stay. Indian Railways offers a unique two days all-inclusive package on the Fairy Queen.

The Fairy Queen has a 60-seater specially designed air-conditioned chair car with a large glass window from where the passenger can have a frontal view of the locomotive, with a well-maintained pantry car for on board catering. The coach also has a beautiful lounge in the front, which provides scenic beauty of the countryside. For the passengers' enjoyment numerous cultural programmes are organized on the evening of the first day at the hotel Sariska Palace. For tour itinerary refer to Chapter 10.

Deccan Odyssey

Maharashtra Tourism, Development Corporation Ltd (MTDC) in association with Indian Railways, Ministry of Tourism has launched a super deluxe luxury train—The Deccan Odyssey. The train has been associated along with the best luxury trains in the world such as the Blue Train of South Africa, the Orient Express of Europe, and the Eastern and Oriental of South-East Asia.

The train reflects the ways of Indian royalty. Each coach is named after some of the best tourist places and forts of Maharashtra. The train has 21 coaches, out of which 13 are passenger cars and can accomodate eight people per coach. Eleven passenger cars, two presidential suites, one conference car, two dining cars, two generator cars with luggage store, one staff, spare car, one spa car, and one bar car.

The train has on-board facilities such as air-conditioning, business centre with Internet, FAX, ISD, and STD in the conference car, LCD TV in eleven lounge cars, plasma TV with allied equipment, one health spa car with steam, beauty parlour and gymnasium, music channel, cell phone on demand, foreign exchange facilities, laundry services, 24-hour room service, valet attendant, special assistance for physically challenged people, luggage collection facility, guests are provided with arrival kits, fully stocked bar, daily newspapers and magazines, packaged drinking water, and mail box facility. Bookings can be made through agents/Internet, and assistance is provided for travel arrangements on completion of tour.

The route for the train has been fixed as Mumbai–Ratnagiri–Sindhudurg–Goa–Kolhapur–Pune–Nasik–Aurangabad (Ajanta–Ellora)–Nasik and Mumbai. The itinerary is of seven days round trip starting every Wednesday from Mumbai. Refer to Chapter 10 for the tour itinerary of the Deccan Odyssey.

Palace on Wheels

The Palace on Wheels has been rated as one of the 10 best luxurious train journeys in the world. Originally the train had 12 fully furnished non-air conditioned saloons, which were once owned by the former maharajas, governor generals, and viceroys of the British period. The

Palace on Wheels initially started as a unique holiday concept hauled by a steam engine on 26 January 1982.

In 1991, a new air-conditioned meter gauge—Palace on Wheels, on the lines of the old heritage train, was launched. The interiors of the current 14 saloons have authentic replicas of the historic coaches. Each salon is equipped with twin-bedded cabins, channel music, and intercom facility.

The coaches are named after the princely states of Rajasthan. Everything matches with the colourful tradition of Rajasthani art. Panels and ceilings are covered with miniature and traditional motifs reflecting the pageantry of courtly life.

Each saloon has a mini pantry and a lounge with beverages and refreshments and a place to relax, two exquisite restaurants, the Maharaja and the Maharani, with opulent draped curtains, elegantly crafted lights. Apart from the chef's special of the day there is delicious choice of local Rajasthani, Chinese, and Continental cuisine. Refer to Chapter 10 for the tour itinerary of the Palace on Wheels.

Tariff for 2007–08 and 2008–09 per person per night (off season/season) varies from USD 322 to USD 560 depending on occupancy.

WATER TRANSPORT

Humans have been travelling through water since time immemorial and carried goods and people from one place to another. The boats progressed from the simple raft with some modifications and improvements and were first used around 6000 BC.

Travel by ship was the only means for travelling overseas till the middle of the twentieth century. The Cunard Steamship Company was formed in 1838 with regular steamship services operating on the North Atlantic. During World War I, in 1914 the operations of the steamship company had to be suspended. After World War I, the steamship luxury liners were back to business till World War II. After World War II, large luxury liners again started their operations all over the world and carried passengers and holiday makers. Some of the liners were very large accommodating up to 1000 passengers and had facilities like swimming pools, cinema halls, shops, casino, etc. SS France and SS Queen Mary II are two great Atlantic luxury vessels, still operating. The cruise lines are the new attractions among the tourist. The cruises are booked several months in advance for trips into the tropical and sub-tropical waters of the Hawaii, Caribbean, Mediterranean, etc.

Water transport today plays two main roles in travel and tourism namely ferrying and cruising.

Ferry ships are comfortable and have an extensive network throughout Europe. They are widely used on shorter crossings in many parts of the world. The demand is highly seasonal because of holidays.

Hydrofoils and Hovercrafts

Modern vessels such as the wave-piercing catamaran, the hydrofoil, and the hovercraft are the over-the-water transport and used for short distance routes.

Hydrofoils are lifted by foil action through the water and are comparatively faster. There is a 35–40 minute hydrofoil service between Copenhagen (Denmark) and Malmo (Sweden). Hydrofoils connect some of the Hawaiians islands and also Hong Kong and Macau.

Hovercrafts are lifted by propeller induced pressure and run on a cushion of air, eight feet above the water with a speed of 125 kilometres an hour. Hovercrafts operate on short routes between Dover and Boulogne on the English Channel. A giant hovercraft can carry 30 passenger cars and upto 250 passengers at one time.

Riverboat Travel

The Mississippi river has been a popular tourist river since the first settlers came to the USA. Today, tourists enjoy two or three-day luxury trips along the river. In Europe, the Rhine, winding through the grape growing areas of Germany, offers similar leisurely tourist trips.

Motorized ferries and launches are used over rivers to transport tourists and locals, to transport vehicles, and offer facilities such as car parking, restaurants, viewing decks, etc.

Cruise Ships

A cruise ship or cruise liner is a passenger ship used for pleasure voyage or travel where the voyage itself and the amenities offered onboard the ship are an attraction and part of the experience. Every year more and more newly built ships are added for the benefit of North American and European clientele. The Asia Pacific region has a smaller market and is usually serviced by older vessels displaced by new ships.

Cruise ships operate mainly on circular routes where the passengers return to their originating port. In contrast, ocean liners do 'line voyages' and normally transport passengers from one point to another, rather than on round trips. Some ocean liners also have longer trips that may not return back to the same port for some months. A river cruise is shorter, narrower with a shallower draft to allow it to travel in inland waterways but has similar amenities as a cruise ship.

The first cruise ship vessel Prinzessin Victoria Luise, commissioned by Albert Ballin (Director of Hamburg–America line) was completed in 1900. To attract more passengers the ocean liners added more amenities such as fine dining and well-appointed staterooms for example, the Titanic. In the late nineteenth century, Albert Ballin sent his trans-Atlantic ships out on long southern cruises to North Atlantic.

The 1960s experienced a decline in the growth of ocean liners. With the advent of the jet aircraft the international travellers shifted from ships to airlines. The cruising voyages gained popularity from 1980 onwards as compared to ocean liners. Initially, the small redundant liners were used and the cruise ships built were also small. But after the success of the SS Norway (SS France re-launched in 1980) the Caribbean's first 'super-ship', large passenger cruise ships were built.

Earlier the cruise ships centred around Caribbean, Alaska, and Mexico but now they move all around the globe. Today, several hundred cruise ships, some carrying over 3000 passengers and over 1,20,000 gross tonnes of cargo; move on the world water transport route.

The cruise ships function with a complete hospitality staff in addition to the ship's crew members similar to a floating hotel. Sometimes the staff of the luxurious cruise ships outnumber the passengers.

The inland waterway cruise ships or river cruise have similar luxury as that of a cruise ship with some differences. The ships are much smaller and carry around 20–240 passengers. The size of these ships allows movement through locks. For example, Moonlight Lady travels through the locks of the Chamblay Canal between the USA and Canada. The advantages are to visit more destinations ashore, possibility to leave and catch the boat later using some other mode of transportation. The inland waterway cruises are more common than the ocean cruises and destinations available are also more.

In 2005, 14 million cruise tourists travelled worldwide. The main regions for cruising were North America (70 per cent of cruises), Caribbean, Continental Europe (13 per cent), Mediterranean Sea, Baltic Sea. The Caribbean cruise lines are very popular. They include Royal

Caribbean International, Princess Cruises, Carnival Cruise Line, Disney Cruise Line, Holland America, Cunard, Norwegian Cruise Line, etc. The cruises travel on itineraries depending on the port of departure and the duration of the cruise. A majority of the major cruise lines also stop at their own 'private islands'. Many of the private resorts are reserved for the passengers of some selected cruise lines. These resorts offer features such as aqua park, kayaking, snorkelling, parasailing, and private cabanas.

Many of the International cruise ships have been developed and converted into 'floating holiday resorts', which are self contained in terms of the various visitor attractions on board. The cruising experience thus can also be termed as 'transport tourism'.

The cruise liners have the advantage of combining accommodation and transportation along with excursions at the different ports they visit. Thus, water transport is important; not only as a means of transportation, but also as a visitor attraction.

The 'Freedom of the Seas' of the US–Norwegian company Royal Caribbean Cruises is the world's biggest cruise liner. It is four times heavier than the Titanic and with decks that would accommodate 25 football pitches. It weighs 158,000 tonnes and can accommodate 4375 passengers and 1365 crew. The ship has a kitchen staff of 240 and is 339 metres long, 56 metres wide and 72 metres high. The ship offers amenities such as a pool with artificial waves big enough for surfing, a 135-square-metre shopping centre, and a rock climbing wall, a mini golf course, and a casino. The ship also has three F-16 fighter jet replicas and a Morgan sports car for decoration.

India has around 300 million middle class citizens and according to a recent survey, Indians rank third in travel spending in the world. Most Indians travel by air, rail, and road for holiday. Since the screening of the Hollywood movie *Titanic*, Indians have been fascinated by the concept of holidaying on ships. Since then, many cruise lines have visited the Indian ports, including Queen Elizabeth II. The response of Indian travellers has been overwhelming. Many upper class Indians are keen on travelling by luxurious cruise lines across the world. There are more Indians travelling on international cruises. Most of them prefer a one-week or ten day cruise rather than long voyages. Cost is also a major factor. A week long cruise in Caribbean or Alaska costs around USD 600–700, while the long voyages of more than 100 days cost a minimum of USD 40,000 on a luxury liner.

MS Amsterdam, Aurora, and Oriana are some of the major cruise lines which have visited India. The major ports of call for cruise lines in India are at Mumbai, Goa, and Kochi. India is emerging as a major destination for cruise tourism. Cruise terminals of international standards are being built at major ports on the western coast. The tourist traffic, both inbound and outbound, is growing. Tour operators offer special packages and incentives. Also with the launching of India-based cruising by Star Cruises from Mumbai, many tourists are going in for local cruises. The Star Cruise offers corporates special packages for on-board conference and seminars and also to families. The packages offered are Mumbai to Goa, to Lakshadweep and an overnight sail in Mumbai. Kadmat Island (Lakshadweep), Goa, Kochi, and Chennai are the destinations offered by Super Star.

Cruises are still a developing concept in India as Indians are generally not inclined towards long sailing and a four to five nights package is more popular. The major drawback for cruise operations in India is the passenger amenities, which are very poor at all port terminals.

A number of passenger ships operate between Kochi, Chennai, Kolkata, and Andaman and Nicobar Islands and Lakshadweep. The journey from Kochi to Lakshadweep takes 18 to 20 hours. The passenger ships which are all weather ships and ply on this route are MV Bharat Seema, MV Tipu Sultan, MV Amindivi and MV Minicoy. The Andaman and Nicobar islands comprise 572 islands in the Bay of Bengal, 1200 kilometres off the east coast of India. Only 38 islands are inhabited and offer a 700-kilometre stretch for sailing. The Shipping Corporation of India plies four ships a month from Kolkata and Chennai and once a month from Vishakhapatnam. The sailing time is 66 hours, 60, and 56 hours respectively. However, the services are subject to weather sea conditions. Various packages are offered by the Tourism Department of Andaman and Nicobar islands in semi-deluxe liners. Some of the ships which ply on these routes are MV Nicobar, MV Nancowry, MV Akbar, etc. Many private operators offer a variety of packages on different classes of cruise ships.

Tourists have a wide variety of transport options available today. The essential features which tourists look for while selecting a mode of transport are given in Fig. 5.3.

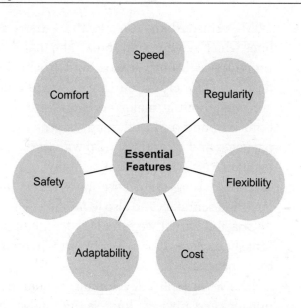

Fig. 5.3 Essential features of tourist transport

There are several advantages and disadvantages of all the modes of transport. They are presented in Table 5.3.

Table 5.3 Advantages and Disadvantages of Various Modes of Transport

Mode	Advantage	Disadvantage
Air	Direct route, high speed, quick service, social and political significance, luxurious travel	High cost, jet lag, unsuitable for heavy bulk cargo, accidents always fatal, international rules to be observed
Road	Flexible, reliable, door to door service, economical, supplements other modes of transport, quick transit for short distances	Slow speed, carrying capacity limited, accidents, non-AC coaches not so comfortable, comfort depends on condition of road
Railways	Long distance travel cheaper, carrying capacity large, dependable service, quicker than road transport, personal comfort in AC class, ability to view scenery en route,	Inflexible, unfit for hilly regions, difficulties in rural areas, dining car facility not always available

Contd

Table 5.3   Contd

Mode	Advantage	Disadvantage
	abilty to move around the coach, arriving at the destination point rested and relaxed (AC coach), environmentally friendly mode of transport	
Ropeways	Quicker and easier transport in hilly areas	Maintenance
Waterways	Economical, carrying capacity enormous, develops international, and coastal trade	Slow speed, zig-zag route, observe international routes, difficulties in operation because of weather

TRANSPORT AS AN ATTRACTION

To attract customers as well as take them around an attraction, destination developers have used many forms of transport to move people around. These novel modes of transport ensure that major exhibits are viewed in a certain sequence and ensure that the crowd moves through at a reliable pace. Overcrowding should be avoided at all costs to prevent untoward incidents and to maintain the beauty of the place.

Tourists can cover the entire park in a shorter duration with the help of these modes of transport. Table 5.4 shows how the mass movement of tourists at an attraction can be controlled using these novel modes of transportation. These vehicles help tourists enjoy the exhibits and displays without tiring out.

Table 5.4   Transportation at the destination

Transport	Examples where it is used
Cable cars	At ski resorts, hill stations, and theme parks.
Helicopters	To take tourists to the top of the hill at Mata Vaishnodevi temple, Jammu.
'Pitthus'	Children carried piggy back over long terrains by humans.
Mules	Mule ride to the hill top at Jammu.
Yaks	In hilly terrain at Gangtok.

Contd

Table 5.4 Contd

Transport	Examples where it is used
All terrain vehicles (ATV's)	Can ride over mountainous terrain, sandy, rocky, or slushy areas and used as recreational vehicles for trail rides at Phuket.
Travelator or walkalator	Used in theme parks, museums, or art galleries horizontally or on an incline, where people can stand or walk.
Cycle rickshaws	Trishaw tour in decorated cycle rickshaws on the streets of Singapore.
Shuttle buses	For passengers in transit, for example, visa-free transit facility helps in attracting tourists to Singapore and promoting the destination. Shuttle buses ply transit passengers from Changi airport to Singapore city and back.
Dark rides	Is an indoor amusement ride where riders in guided vehicles travel through specially lit scenes that contain animation, sound, music, and special effects, e.g. Pirates of the Caribbean at Disneyland.
Panorail	Air conditioned, comfortable train leisure ride with commentary which gives a panoramic view at a theme park Jurong Bird Park, Singapore.
Tram ride	Popular for distances of a few kilometres. For example, during the night safari in Singapore tourists are taken for a 45 minute ride of 3.2 kilometres to view wild animals and birds in natural surroundings. Meals are served on board moving trams.
Balloon tours	Offer panoramic views from a height of 150 metres as you float and observe the sky line.
Amphibian vehicle	These are boats-on-wheels which can travel on both land and sea and are used for both city and harbour tours without passengers having to change the vehicle. For example, a duck tour at Singapore. Similar tours are available at other destinations such as Japan and Toronto.
Boats, canoes, kayaks, rafts, barges	Used to leisurely cruise down rivers or streams and enjoy scenic views.
Limo-buggy	Semi-covered sightseeing tourist four wheeled vehicle. Safe, comfortable tours of attractions with guide services for a smaller group.
Funicars	Used for climbing steep slopes, these vehicles travel on the ground and are pulled by cables on the surface of steep hill slopes, for example, the Peak tram at Hong Kong takes tourists up the peak quickly.
Steamboats	To traverse crashing waters and massive rock formations, for example, the 'Maid of the Mist' cruises to the base of the American Falls and Horse shoe falls at Niagara, Canada.

As we have read, transportation is by far the most crucial component of the tourism infrastructure. It is required not only for reaching the destination but also visiting the site and moving about at the destination. Variety in modes of transportation adds colour to the overall tourism experience. Unusual forms of transportation are also an attraction such as the cable cars in hilly terrain, the funicular railway, or jet boating. The choice of mode of transport is vast and tourists can choose a mode to suit their budget. They can opt for scheduled or non-scheduled transport such as hiring of vehicles, boats, coaches or trains so that they can travel with their group.

SUMMARY

This chapter has highlighted the vital necessity of transport for the growth of tourism. It is of prime importance for a tourist and the tourism professional needs to be familiar with the different modes of transport. The airline industry is growing by leaps and bounds every year. Many new airlines have been introduced in the market. The frequencies of flights have been increased in all the major sectors of the tourist places. The railway is still considered the most economic of all the modes of travel. Luxury trains, such as Palace on Wheels, Deccan Odyssey, and toy trains are not only a mode of transport but also are an attraction for the tourists. Tourist coaches and cars are considered for quicker transit for short distances. The cruise lines are an attraction in itself as they offer the advantage of accommodation and transportation along with the excursion at different ports. These luxury liners offer some of the finest facilities on board. Transportation also plays an important role in moving people around the attraction, preventing overcrowding and ensuring that tourists do not tire out. Unusual forms of transportation serve as an attraction at the destination.

KEY TERMS

Apex fares Advanced purchase excursion fare, purchased in advance, non-refundable, conditions apply.

Blue skies policy Permission given to the private sector to enter domestic airline business.

Budget airlines No-frills airline, i.e. minimum services offered on board, hence cheaper airfares.

Cable cars Mode of transport at attractions with hilly terrains, ski resorts which travel along overhead cables

Chartered flights Special flights booked exclusively for a specific group of people who belong to the same organization or who are guests of a particular host. Even scheduled airlines offer chartered flights.

Code sharing Use of same airline identification code for two or more sectors which may be operated by different airlines. Promoting use of different airlines for connecting flights.

Cruise ships Transport passengers on round trips, in which the trip itself and the amenities of the ship and ports visited are an attraction.

Cruises Sea voyages in luxurious liners very popular amongst the rich and elite.

Cruising It is a lifestyle that involves stay for extended time on a boat while travelling from place to place for pleasure.

Domestic airlines Connects principal cities of a country and even upcountry locations through feeder services

Duck tour or boat-on-wheels Amphibian vehicle which can travel on both land and sea, is used for touring at Singapore, Toronto, and Japan.

E-tickets Tickets procured via the Internet.

Excursion fares Promotional fares usually for a round trip and for a specified period of time.

Ferry A ferry is defined as a form of short-distance water-borne transport.

Fly-cruise Travel plan where to board a cruise ship travellers have to fly to the port of embarkation.

Funicars Mode of transport for tourists to travel over steep hill slopes. Funicars travel on the ground pulled by cables on the surface of a slope. For example, the tram service to reach the peak at Hong Kong.

Group fares Discounted fares for a group of 14 or more individuals. One ticket is free or group leader/tour escort may travel free.

General sales agents (GSA) General sales agents are agents appointed by an airline or any other organizations in a particular territory to handle their bookings, inquiries, etc.

Hydrofoil A vessel raised partially above the surface of water using fins and foils. It travels very fast as there is no friction and drag caused by immersion in water.

Interline agreements Agreements between two or more transportation line.

IOSA Is a quality audit programme under the continuing stewardship of International Air Transport Association (IATA). It is a globally recognized and accepted benchmarking and evaluation system for assessing the operation management and control systems of an airline.

Liner A large ocean sailing vessel or aircraft used to transport passengers belonging to a regular line and observing maritime regulation.

LTC Leave Travel Concession. In many organizations the employees are given the LTC facility to travel for self/family when on leave.

Ocean liners Are passengers or passenger-cargo vessels transporting passengers and sometimes cargo on longer line voyages.

Passenger ship Is a ship whose primary function is to carry passengers.

Port of entry The official port for entry of passengers and goods.
River cruise Is a voyage along inland waterways, often stopping at ports.
Toy trains Trains run at tourist places and are one of the attractions for the tourist visiting these places.

CONCEPT REVIEW QUESTIONS

1. What services do the Indian Railways offer foreign tourists?
2. Explain in brief the role of railways in promoting tourism. What are the features/significance of (a) Indrail pass, (b) Eurail pass?
3. What is the primary mode of transport used by the inbound tourists to come to India? Why is it so popular?
4. Explain car rental services.
5. What are recreational vehicles?
6. Give the importance of airlines in the tourism industry.
7. What are promotional fares? Name three such fares.
8. What is the role of Air India Limited in tourism development in our country?
9. What kind of mode of transport are hydrofoils and hovercrafts? Where are they mostly used?
10. Write a note on (a) Palace on Wheels, (b) Deccan Odyssey.
11. How is road transport an important element of tourism infrastructure? Discuss its role and importance.
12. Discuss the revolutionary impact of air travel on international tourism. Give its significance.
13. Explain in brief the role of transport at a theme park.
14. Explain how the travel and tourism industry is dependent on transport industry.

CRITICAL THINKING QUESTION

A group of foreign tourists want to visit an ecotourism project in a village in Maharashtra. What various modes of transport would you recommend throughout their tour. Give reasons for your choice of transport.

PROJECT/ASSIGNMENT

Visit a travel agent and collect information about the different types of road and rail transport available and cost of travel from Pune to Mumbai. Highlight the advantages and disadvantages of each category of transport.

REFERENCES

Andrew, S. 2007, *Introduction to Tourism and Hospitality Industry,* Tata McGraw-Hill, New Delhi.

Bhatia, A.K. 2001, *International Tourism Management*, Sterling Publishers Pvt Ltd, New Delhi.

George, R. 2007, *Managing Tourism in South Africa*, Oxford University Press Southern Africa, Cape Town.

Ghosh, B. 2000, *Tourism and Travel Management*, Vikas Publishing House Pvt Ltd, New Delhi.

Kaul, R.N. 1985, *Dynamics of Tourism: A Trilogy Vol. III Transportation and Marketing*, Sterling Publishers Pvt Ltd, New Delhi.

Keyser, H. 2002, *Tourism Development*, Oxford University Press Southern Africa, Cape Town.

Seth, P.N. and S.S. Bhat 1993, *An Introduction to Travel and Tourism*, Sterling Publishers Pvt Ltd, New Delhi.

www.railtourismindia.com, accessed on 29 May 2008.

www.indianrailways.gov.in, accessed on 29 May 2008.

www.tourindia.com, accessed on 29 May 2008.

www.airindia.in, accessed on 29 May 2008.

www.maharashtratourism.gov.in, accessed on 29 May 2008.

www.indianairlines.in, accessed on 11 June 2008.

www.thepalaceonwheels.com, accessed on 11 June 2008.

www.deccan-odyssey-india.com,accessed on 11 June 2008.

www.rajasthantourism.gov.in, accessed on 20 June 2008.

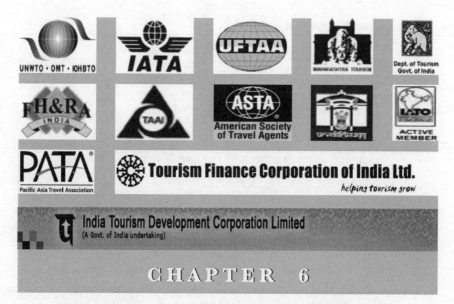

Tourism Organizations

Learning Objectives

After reading this chapter you should be able to:
- understand the need for tourism organizations
- know the different levels of tourism organizations—private, national, and international
- learn about various functions performed by these organizations
- understand the role played by organizations for the benefit of travellers
- know the role played by international, national, regional, and local organizations for their members

INTRODUCTION

The development of any industry needs an organization to plan, develop, and monitor its progress and growth and the tourism industry is no exception. Organizations are formed when groups of people come together for a common purpose or interest. They work together to achieve the purpose, i.e. the aims and objectives, which the organization has laid down. These can be best achieved when there is unified action through a formal structuring of its members so that the organization can work effectively and efficiently as a team and develop the industry. Tourism organizations thus play an important role in

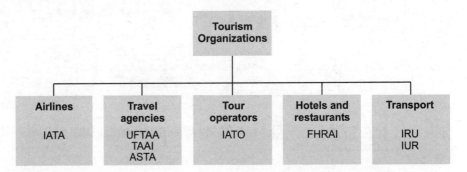

Fig. 6.1 Classification of tourism organizations based on different sectors

marketing destinations and managing a country's tourism industry. Figure 6.1 shows the classification of tourism organizations based on different sectors.

We read in Chapter 1 that the travel and tourism industry is composed of different sectors such as transport, accommodation, and intermediaries. Each of these sectors has different interests which can be discussed and resolved on a common platform, if these sectors are grouped together into 'organizations' and 'associations'. For example, the United Federation of Travel Agents' Associations (UFTAA) represents associations of the national travel agents of more than 100 countries and the Travel Agents Association of India (TAAI) is a member of UFTAA. Both these organizations look after the interests of all travel agents. Since tourism plays a crucial role in a country's economy, it is necessary that tourism develops in a sustainable manner as it should be economically, socially, and environmentally sustainable. Unplanned growth of tourism may be detrimental to the destination and can have negative impacts on the environment, society, and the economy. This makes it imperative that the government and the tourism organizations be actively involved in tourism-related activities and developments.

Tourism organizations exist in the public sector as well as private sector at different levels. The levels of organizations are mentioned below, as shown in Fig. 6.2.

1. International level
2. National level
3. State level
4. Local level

Many organizations have been established at all these levels and in all sectors, in the past few decades.

Fig. 6.2   Classification based on levels of organization

NEED FOR TOURISM ORGANIZATIONS

Tourism organizations are essential for the following reasons:

- Different sectors of the industry are interdependent on each other. For example, for a tour to be successful, many sectors such as transport, accommodation, transfers, and entertainment need to work in harmony.
- Many of the vendors/operators are small-scale operators and need an association to defend and protect their rights.
- The tourist market is fragmented and organizations help in reaching the potential customers.
- Destinations can be located far apart, especially in case of international tourism.
- Tourism has to develop in a planned manner if it is to remain sustainable.

The tourism industry has recognized the fact that successful tourism can be best achieved through a consolidated effort of the government and private organizations. These organizations need to coordinate with the various sectors of the tourism industry to ensure that they function harmoniously and with maximum profits. At the same time these organizations should ensure easy accessibility, adequate facilities, safety, and value for money for the tourists, leading to customer delight.

INTERNATIONAL ORGANIZATIONS

There are several international tourism organizations which are discussed in the following section.

World Tourism Organization

The World Tourism Organization (WTO) was founded in the year 1975. It was formerly known as International Union of Official Travel Organization (IUOTO). Since December 2006, the WTO has been renamed as the United Nations World Tourism Organization (UNWTO) so as to clearly distinguish it from the World Trade Organization. The UNWTO is a specialized agency of the United Nations. It is the leading international organization in the field of tourism. The headquarters of UNWTO are located in Madrid, Spain.

Aim

It serves as a global forum for tourism policy issues and practical source of tourism know-how. The UNWTO plays a central and decisive role in promoting the development of responsible, sustainable, and universally accessible tourism, with an aim to contribute to the economic development, international understanding, peace, prosperity, and a universal respect for as well as observance of human rights and fundamental freedom. In pursuing this aim, the organization pays particular attention to the interests of developing countries in the field of tourism.

Activities

The UNWTO performs many activities. All these activities are related to its members and development of tourism in general. The activities performed by the UNWTO are as follows:

- It conducts research studies for the tourism market for various purposes such as promotions and marketing, area development, and physical planning.
- It organizes seminars and conferences on issues such as aviation, infrastructure development, planning, and marketing that are shared by many countries. The member countries can exchange expertise, experiences, and work towards a common goal.
- It gathers information on tourism, which includes statistical data, facilities, special events, regulations, and legislations.
- It collects, analyses, and disseminates information on various aspects of tourism.
- It prepares drafts for international agreements on tourism.
- It provides updated information and supply of studies on tourism trends in the various fields of tourism to its members.

- It constantly reviews tourism trends and developments and exercises vigilance over the changes in world economics and the social conditions affecting tourism. It also reviews the market fluctuations and maintenance of standards within the tourism sectors.

The permanent activity of UNWTO is to collect and update the available information on training needs and special activities, which includes participation in technical cooperation projects for vocational training.

The UNWTO provides vocational training through its Centre for Advanced Tourism Studies. It also provides permanent education programmes by correspondence and residential study circles. The regions of the world—Africa, the Americas, East Asia and the Pacific Europe, the Middle East, and South Asia—have regional representatives based at the headquarters in Madrid. These representatives pay special attention to their regions and act as travelling ambassadors. The regional representatives meet with the top tourism officials from each of the countries to analyse problems and offer solutions.

They represent UNWTO at national and regional tourism events.

Membership

UNWTO offers three types of memberships. They are: *full membership*, open to all sovereign states; *associate membership*, open to territories that are not responsible for their external relations (for this, a prior approval of the government is required, which should mention the responsibility for the external relations); and *affiliate membership*, open to a wide range of organizations and companies, working directly in travel, tourism, and related sectors. These include airlines and other transport, tour operators, travel agents, banking sectors, hotels, restaurants, publishers, travel insurance companies, etc.

The UNWTO is the only international organization which works as an inter-governmental organization. It offers membership to the operational sector and is the only contact point for discussions between government officials and industry leaders.

A number of publications of UNWTO on topics, such as tourism statistics, world tourism forecasts, tourism carrying capacity, development of resorts and national parks, sustainable development, education, and training institutions, are published regularly.

International Air Transport Association

In 1919, when the world's first international scheduled services started, the International Air Traffic Association (IATA) was founded in the Hague. It has changed its name to the International Air Transport Association (IATA) which was founded in Havana, Cuba, in April 1945.

The IATA is an international trade body formed by a group of airlines. It is a non-governmental, voluntary, and democratic organization. It is the prime vehicle for inter-airline cooperation in promoting safe, reliable, secure, and economical air services for the benefit of the world's consumers. IATA specializes in standards, practices, and procedures for the airlines.

When IATA was established it had 57 members from 31 countries, mostly from Europe and North America. Today it has around 240 members from 126 countries. IATA is closely associated with International Civil Aviation Organization (ICAO).

The headquarters of IATA are in Montreal, Canada. IATA has its main office in Geneva also. Regional technical directors are based in Bangkok, Geneva, London, Nairobi, and Rio-de-Janeiro and regional director (special assignments) in Singapore and Buenos Aires. IATA traffic service offices are in New York and Singapore.

Aims

The aims of IATA are to

- promote safe, regular, and economical air transport for the benefit of the people of the world, foster air commerce, and study the problems connected therewith;
- provide means for collaboration among the air-transport enterprises, engaged directly or indirectly in international air-transport service;
- cooperate with the newly created ICAO, the specialized United Nations agency for civil aviation and other international organizations.

The IATA's mission is to represent, lead, and serve the airline industry. Its members are the world's leading passenger and cargo airlines which represent 94 per cent of scheduled international air traffic.

Services

The IATA provides a wide range of services. These are as follows:

- It helps in global planning of international timetables
- It has formulated a single formula for tickets and airway bills

- It helps in international coordination of telecommunication networks and computer systems
- It, as a leader organization of scheduled airlines, examines and solves the problems raised by tourism, the movement of passengers and cargo at airports, and it also establishes the procedures and technical norms.
- It helps in training of travel and freight agents.
- It also helps in standardization of inter-company communications and reservation system.
- It helps to regulate legal questions of general concern in order to develop security measures.

Activities

The main purpose of IATA is to ensure that all airline traffic moves anywhere with the greatest possible speed, safety, convenience, and efficiency and with utmost economy. To achieve this, IATA performs a wide range of activities, for the benefit of its consumers and member airlines, which are as follows:

- It simplifies the travel and shipping processes, while keeping costs down. Passengers can make a single telephone call to reserve a ticket, pay in one currency and then use the ticket on several airlines in several countries.
- It allows them to operate safely, securely, efficiently, and economically under clearly defined rules.
- It seeks to ensure they are well informed about the complexities of the aviation industry; to ensure better, long-term decisions.
- IATA also serves as an intermediary between airlines and passengers as well as cargo agents via neutrally applied agency service standards and centralized financial systems.
- A large network of industry suppliers and service providers gathered by IATA provide solid expertise to airlines in a variety of industry solutions.

Membership

IATA's membership is open to any airline, scheduled or non-scheduled, which has been licensed to provide scheduled air service, by governments eligible for membership of ICAO. Other industry partners can also participate in different IATA programmes and benefit from a wealth of resources to carry out their operations.

IATA regularly organizes international conferences, exhibitions, and industry meetings. This provides members, who are active in all sectors of the air transport industry, with a platform for discussion and cooperation, on new technologies and industry-related issues, on topics such as pricing, ground handling, e-ticketing, legal issues, fuel, etc. Thus such events benefit airlines, travel and cargo agencies, service providers, and governments. Many IATA conferences are now considered premier world events.

United Federation of Travel Agents Association

United Federation of Travel Agents Association (UFTAA) was earlier known as Universal Federation of Travel Agents Association and was created on 22 November 1966 in Rome. It was founded by the merger of two large world organizations, International Federation of Travel Agencies (IFTA) and Universal Organization of Travel Agents Association (UOTAA), in recognition of the need to unite travel agencies and tour operators into one international federation. UFTAA's General Secretariat is in Monaco.

UFTAA represents travel agencies and the tourism industry all over the world. It effectively represents travel agents' and tour operators' views on both inbound and outbound travel by keeping continuous contact with other international organizations, such as the IATA, the International Hotel and Restaurant Association (IH&RA), the International Chamber of Commerce (ICC), the International Union of Railways (IUR), and the International Road Union (IRU), to name a few.

UFTAA works closely with world bodies such as the United Nations Educational, Scientific and Cultural Organization (UNESCO), the World Health Organization (WHO), etc. for sustainable and responsible tourism. UFTAA has a consultative status in the UN and is an affiliate member of the UNWTO.

Aim

The aim of UFTAA is to act as an international forum where matters affecting the world travel industry are addressed, representing and defending the interests of inbound and outbound tour operators, travel agencies before the governmental bodies, suppliers, and other entities of international scope. It also aims at strengthening its members' image and enhances the world travel and tourism industry, and sustainable tourism. Some of the key functions of UFTAA are to

- act as the negotiating body with the various branches of tourism and travel industries on behalf of travel agents and the interest of the public;
- ensure for all travel agents, through their national association, the maximum degree of cohesion and understanding, prestige and public recognition, advancement of members interest, and protection, from legislation and from other legal points of view; and
- offer its members all the necessary material, professional and technical advice, and assistance to enable them to take their proper place in the economy of world tourism.

Functions

UFTAA performs the following functions for the interest of its members.

- It unites and consolidates the Federation of Travel Agent's National Association, to enhance and promote the interest of the members.
- It represents the travel agents' activities before the various world bodies, government authorities, and suppliers.
- It adopts new measures to ease travel for the consumer and to offer services to its members.
- It acts as an information and investigation centre, to offer information for technological development.
- It organizes a world congress of travel agents. It also organizes meetings, seminars, and conferences, for exchange and transfer of knowledge.
- It lobbies to oppose legislations which are directly harmful to tourism and for free movement of citizens of any country.
- It works to reduce bureaucratic obstacles in travel and to seek greater transportation safety.
- It assists through its education committee, so that travel agents become better qualified through the IATA/UFTAA training programmes.

Overall, UFTAA's primary goal is to develop, promote, and assist in the professional training of travel agents.

Membership

UFTAA's membership includes a large group of travel partners including major airlines, hotels, tourism boards, shipping companies, car rental companies, and many other operators allied to the tourism industry. It comprises 80 national associations.

UFTAA provides various benefits to its members such as a copy of its annual directory, a monthly UFTAA information bulletin courier, access to publish particulars of agency in the UFTAA annual directory, a discount in the registration fee of the UFTAA annual world congress, free-of–charge assistance by the UFTAA legal department for the recovery of outstanding debts, and most importantly, the UFTAA's symbol on letter heads and in all literature, giving the agency a professional and ethical standing.

Pacific Asia Travel Association

The Pacific Asia Travel Association (PATA) was founded in Hawaii, in 1951, with 44 members. PATA is a non-profit travel industry association which promotes the Pacific Asia areas as travel and tourism destinations. PATA focuses its attention on travel opportunities in the member countries and develops awareness among the travel trade in tourism originating countries.

The headquarters of PATA are in Bangkok. It maintains divisional offices in Sydney, Singapore, Monaco, and San Francisco.

Aims

The main aim of PATA is developing, promoting, and facilitating travel, to and within the Pacific areas and South-East Asian regions. It primarily operates in the USA which is the world's biggest travel market. The organization provides a meeting point for the people involved in all aspects of the travel trade from a large number of countries. It focuses its attention on travel opportunities in member countries and builds up greater awareness and specific contacts among the travel trade in countries from where the tourists originate.

PATA serves as a central resource for information and research, travel industry education and training, and quality product development, with sensitivity for culture, heritage, and environment.

Activities

The activities performed by PATA are as follows:
- It provides information and practical assistance in the field of tourism
- It assists upcoming destinations to develop their infrastructure by providing expertise.

- It serves as a central source of information and guidance through its research, development, education, and marketing council.
- It helps the members in marketing their destination and products through training and educational programmes for human resource development.
- It organizes an annual travel mart.

Membership

There are over 2100 PATA members worldwide, working as travel industry organizations. It includes 101 government, state, and city tourism bodies; 76 airlines and cruise lines, and 2060 industry members from the Pacific Asia region.

The memberships are divided into the following nine different categories.

Active government members These are primary government organizations designated by the government of any nation.

Associate government members The membership is given to organizations that are responsible for the domestic or overseas promotion of tourism. These are designated by the government of any nation.

Active carrier members These are any government recognized or certified airlines, ship lines, etc. which provide scheduled passenger service in Pacific areas.

Associate carrier members The membership is for any government recognized passenger carrier. This does not provide common carriage as prescribed for active carrier members.

Active industry members This membership is for the hotel industry.

Allied members Allied members consist of travel agencies, tour operators, hotel representatives, and firms, representing the various segments of Pacific travel industry.

Affiliated allied members These are the branch offices of an allied member, i.e. travel agencies or tour operators.

Associate members These are individual operating organizations such as communication media, advertising, public relations, and research agencies. All of them must have an interest in Pacific travel.

Sustaining members These are the organizations or individuals with cultural or commercial interest in tourism of Pacific region.

PATA functions through Pacific travel conference and workshops, marketing, and research and development.

PATA chapters

There are two types of chapters—area chapters and promotional chapters. The chapters located within the PATA region are referred to as *area chapters*. The chapters outside the PATA region are termed as *promotional chapters*. The chapters arrange meetings, seminars, conferences, and travel marts to promote tourism in Pacific region. The travel mart is an annual event which brings investors and sellers together for tourism development.

The PATA chapter membership provides a wide range of services and opportunities such as:

- information on new trends
- help in conserving the region's heritage, culture, and environment
- improvement in travel trade and destination marketing skills through education programmes

PATA's India chapter is one of the area chapters. The chapter undertakes promotional work for promoting India as a destination. PATA promotion is done through *Pacific Travel News*, *Pacific Area Destination Handbook* and *Hotel Directory* and *Travel Guide*.

American Society of Travel Agents

The American Society of Travel Agents (ASTA) is the world's largest professional travel trade association. The ASTA was established in New York in 1931. It was earlier known as American Steamship and Tourist Agent's Association (ASTAA).

It aims to foster programmes for the advancement of the travel agency industry and to promote ethical practices in tourism industry. The headquarters of ASTA are located in New York City, USA.

Aim

The ASTA's basic aim is the promotion and advancement of the interests of the travel industry and the safeguarding of the traveller against fraud, misrepresentation, and unethical practices.

Services

The services which ASTA offers to travel agents are also beneficial to the traveller. They are

- sponsorship of conferences on tourism-related matters;

- discussion with airlines on fare construction/structure and travel destinations;
- travellers' preferences research;
- assistance to all agencies in travel-oriented matters; and
- cooperation to other agencies, states, and government.

Membership

ASTA offers two different categories of memberships, namely, active and allied.

Active membership   Active members are year round travel agents or tour operators.

Allied membership   It includes airlines, steamship companies, railroad, bus lines, car rental firms, hotel resorts, and government tourist offices.

The society also has separate membership for students, travel schools, retail travel sellers, retired travel professionals, and others.

Members get education and training in ASTA travel courses and seminars, and guidance for business and trade. They also get a newsletter and a monthly magazine which is a great source of information.

ASTA World Congress

The ASTA World Congress is the most important meeting held annually. It includes tourism and related workshops, seminars, business meetings, film presentations, and social events. Members from all over the world participate in this congress. It acts as an educational programme for travel agents. The *ASTA Travel News* is the monthly magazine of ASTA.

GOVERNMENT ORGANIZATIONS IN INDIA

There are several government organizations working in the field of tourism in India. They are discussed in the following section.

Dept. of Tourism
Govt. of India

India Tourism

India Tourism was formerly known as the Department of Tourism. It functions under the auspices of the Ministry of Tourism and Culture. It is the nodal agency for the development and promotion of tourism in India. The administrative head of the Department of Tourism is the secretary (tourism). The department is assisted by an attached office headed by the director general and ex-officio additional secretary to the Government of India. The office of the directorate general of tourism provides executive directions for the implementation of various policies and programmes. The directorate general of tourism has a network of 20 offices within the country and 13 offices abroad. One subordinate office/project—the Indian Institute of Skiing and Mountaineering (IISM)/Gulmarg Winter Sports Project (GWSP), is located at Gulmarg in Kashmir.

Its regional offices are at New Delhi, Mumbai, Kolkata, Chennai, and Guwahati. Other offices are at Patna, Jaipur, Bangaluru, Varanasi, Agra, Bhubaneshwar, Port Blair, Imphal, Shillong, Hyderabad, Kochi, Goa, Aurangabad, Khajuraho, Naharlagun, and Itanagar. The field offices in India provide facilitation services to tourists and coordinate with the state governments on tourism infrastructural development.

The Ministry of Tourism is the nodal agency for the formulation of national policies and programmes and for the coordination of activities of various central government agencies, state governments/union territories (UTs), and the private sector for the development and promotion of tourism in the country. The ministry is headed by the union minister of tourism.

The administrative head of the ministry is the secretary (tourism). The secretary also acts as the director general (DG) of tourism (see Fig. 6.3). The office of the director general of tourism (now merged with the office of the tourism secretary) provides executive directions for the implementation of various policies and programmes. The overseas offices are primarily responsible for tourism promotion and marketing in their respective areas, while the field offices in India are responsible for providing information service to tourists and to monitor the progress of field projects. The activities of IISM/GWSP have now been revived and skiing and various other courses are being conducted in the Jammu and Kashmir valley.

The Ministry of Tourism has under its charge a public sector undertaking, the India Tourism Development Corporation (ITDC) and the following autonomous institutions:

- The Indian Institute of Tourism and Travel Management (IITTM) and the National Institute of Water Sports (NIWS)
- The National Council for Hotel Management and Catering Technology (NCHMCT) and the institutes of hotel management

The Ministry of Tourism has six international offices or regional offices overseas which are located at Sydney, Frankfurt, Tokyo, Dubai, London,

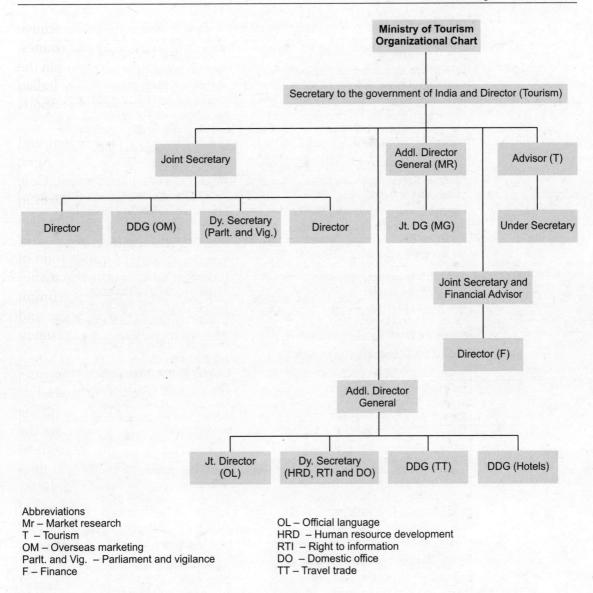

Abbreviations

Mr – Market research
T – Tourism
OM – Overseas marketing
Parlt. and Vig. – Parliament and vigilance
F – Finance

OL – Official language
HRD – Human resource development
RTI – Right to information
DO – Domestic office
TT – Travel trade

Fig. 6.3   Ministry of Tourism Organizational Chart
Source: India Tourism Office, Mumbai

and New York headed by officers of different ranks (see Table 6.1). There are seven sub-regional offices located at Toronto, Paris, Milan, Amsterdam, Los Angeles, Johannesburg, and Singapore.

The main functions of these 13 overseas offices are to

- carry out overseas marketing

Table 6.1 India Tourism overseas offices

Sydney (Australia)	Dubai—Regional Office
Level 5, 135 King Street, Glasshouse Shopping Complex, Sydney, New South Wales - 2000. Phone : 61-2-92219555, Fax : 61-2-92219777, E-mail : info@indiatourism.com.au	Post Box 12856, NASA Building, Al Maktoum Road, UAE. Phone : +971-4-2274848, 2274199. Fax : +971-4-2274013, E-mail : goirto@emirates.net.ae
Toronto (Canada)	**London (UK)**
60, Bloor Street, West Suite 1003, Toronto, M4 W3, B8,Canada. Phone : +1-416-962-3787/3788, Fax : +1-416-962-6279, E-mail : indiatourism@bellnet.ca	London WIS 3LH, U.K. Phone : +44-207-4373677(Gen.) +44-207-7346613 (Direct line). Fax : +44-207-4941048, E-mail : info@indiatouristoffice.org
Paris (France)	**Los Angeles (USA)**
11-13, Bis Boulevard Haussmann, F-75009 Paris, France. Phone : +331-45233045, Fax : +331-45233345, E-mail : indtourparis@aol.com	3550 Wilshire Boulevard, Suit 204, Los Angeles, California 90010 2485 USA. Phone : +1-213-380-8855. Fax : +1-213-380-6111, E-mail : indiatourismla@aol.com
Frankfurt (Germany)—Regional Office	**Johannesburg (South Africa)**
Basler Strasse 48, D-60329, Frankfurt, AM-MAIN 1, Federal Republic of Germany. Phone : +49-69-2429490, Fax : +49-69-24294977, E-mail : info@india-tourism.com	P O Box: 412452 Craig Hall 2024, Johannesburg-2000 Tel : +27-11-3250880 Fax: +27-11-3250882 E-mail : goito@global.co.za
Milan (Italy)	**Singapore**
Via-Albricci 9, Milan 20122, Italy. Phone : +39-02-8053506. Fax : +39-02-72021681, E-mail : info@indiatourismmilan.com	20 Kramat Lane, #01-01A United House 228773 Singapore Singapore Tel : +65 6235 3800 Fax : +65 6235 8677 E-mail : indtour.sing@pacific.net.sg
Amsterdam (Netherlands)	**New York (USA)—Regional Office**
Rokin 9-15, 1012 KK Amsterdam. Phone : +31-20-6208991, Fax : +31-20-6383059, E-mail : info.nl@india-tourism.com director.nl@india-tourism.com	1270 Avenue of Americas Suite 1808, 18th floor, New York – 10020, USA Tel : + 1 212-586-4901/4902/4903 Fax : +1 212-582-3274 E-mail : ny@itonyc.com
Tokyo(Japan)—Regional Office	
Art MastersBuilding, 6-5-12 Ginza, Chuo-Ku-Tokyo 104-0061, Japan. Phone : +81-3-3571-5062/63, +81-3-3571-5196/97, Fax : +81-3-3571-5235, E-mail : indtourt@smile.ocn.ne.jp	

- position India as a preferred tourism destination
- promote various Indian tourism products

The overseas offices are in constant touch with tourists, travel intermediaries, and the media to promote tourism in India.

The function of India Tourism, both organizational and promotional, is performed by the following seven divisions:

1. Planning and programming
2. Publicity and conference
3. Travel trade and hospitality
4. Accommodation
5. Supplementary accommodation and wildlife
6. Market research
7. Administration

Functions/activities of India Tourism offices in India

The function/activities performed by India Tourism offices are as follows:

- Collection, compilation, and dissemination of tourist information in India and abroad, and attending to enquiries of international tourists, tour operators, and members of the travel industry such as airlines, steamship companies, and hotels.
- Cooperation with international travel and tourist organizations at government and non-government levels.
- Development of tourist facilities of interest to international tourists.
- Publicity at home and abroad with the object of creating an overall awareness of the importance of tourism.
- Simplification of frontier formalities in respect of international tourists.
- Regulation of activities of the various segments of the travel trade such as hotels, youth hostels, travel agents, wildlife, guides, etc. catering to tourist needs.
- Compilation of statistics and market research on international tourist traffic to India and their utilization for more effective tourist promotion.

As part of its marketing/publicity activities, India Tourism, Ministry of Tourism brings out brochures, leaflets, maps, films, CDs, etc. on various topics. In the case of the destination folders, the leaflet/folder/brochure gives the information about the place or the destination with various facets of the facilities available, places of sightseeing around the destination, important telephone numbers, and the contact points of India

Tourism offices. Similarly, the films deal with the subject in its entirety covering all destinations of the country.

Following are the various types of publicity material produced by India Tourism.

- The 'Incredible India' theme brochures
- Destination leaflets
- Heritage destination leaflets
- North East brochures
- Maps
- Films
- CDs

As the organization representing the central government, India Tourism plays an important role in development of tourism in India and promoting India as a tourist destination in overseas market.

India Tourism Development Corporation

The India Tourism Development Corporation (ITDC) is the second most important organization after India Tourism. It works as a public sector organization. The main purpose of ITDC is to promote India as a tourist destination. This organization came into existence because the private sectors in India were hesitant to invest in tourism infrastructure as the profitability was doubtful. Although ITDC is a public sector organization, it works on a commercial level.

The organization came into existence in October 1966 by merging the Hotel Corporation of India Ltd, the India Tourism Corporation Ltd, and the India Tourism Transport Undertaking Ltd. The main objectives and functions of the corporation are to

- construct, take over, and manage existing hotels and to market hotels, beach resorts, travellers' lodges, and restaurants;
- provide transport, entertainment, duty-free shopping, and convention services;
- produce, distribute, and sell tourist publicity material;
- render consultancy-cum-managerial services in India and abroad;
- work as full-fledged money changers (FFMC), restricted money changers, etc; and
- provide innovative, dependable, and value for money solutions to the needs of tourism development and engineering industry, including consultancy and implementation of projects.

ITDC, as the name suggests, is aimed at setting up a sound base for the development of tourism infrastructure. It has been the prime mover in the progressive development, promotion, and expansion of tourism in the country. ITDC works in close cooperation with India Tourism and the Central Ministry of Tourism.

'The Ashok' is the brand name of ITDC's products and services. The Ashok International Trade Division of ITDC offers world-class duty-free shopping facilities to international travellers at its 38 outlets, earning crucial foreign exchange for the country and showcasing Indian products to the world. The Ashok Travels and Tours (ATT) handles work relating to domestic and international ticketing, hotel booking and tour packages, car and coach rentals, money changing services, money transfer services, overseas insurance, and organizing exhibitions. The Ashok Hospitality and Tourism Management, New Delhi, imparts training and education in the field of tourism and hospitality. The Ashok Reservation and Marketing Services (ARMS) division of ITDC, which is mainly responsible for marketing of Ashok Group of Hotels, participates in national and international events such as ITB Berlin to ensure direct interaction with foreign tour operators, to promote various services of ITDC. Besides this, ITDC is also managing a hotel at Bharatpur and a restaurant at Kosi on behalf of India Tourism. In addition, it manages catering services at Western Court, Vigyan Bhawan, Hyderabad House, and the National Media Press Centre at Shastri Bhawan, New Delhi.

Presently, ITDC has a network of eight Ashok Group of Hotels, six joint venture hotels, two restaurants (including one airport restaurant), 12 transport units, one tourist service station, duty-free shops at international, as well as domestic customs airports, one tax-free outlet, one sound and light show, and four catering outlets.

In a nutshell, the achievements of ITDC are—promoting the largest hotel chain in India and providing all tourist services, i.e. accommodation, catering, transport, in-house travel agency, duty free shopping, entertainment, publicity, consultancy, etc. under a single window. It also offers consultancy services in the tourism field both for private as well as public sector.

State Tourism Development Corporation

India is famous for its variety of attractions, which are spread over its different states. India Tourism and Central Government Tourism Department looks after all this in general.

ITDC is an autonomous body whose main function is commercial part of promoting tourism in the country. But for the proper development of the destination and its promotion as a tourist attraction, almost all the states and union territories have their own tourism corporations. State tourism development corporations (STDCs) concentrate largely on the domestic tourists. For this, STDCs are involved in construction of low-income rest houses, development of tourist centres, publicity, guide provision and arrangement of sightseeing tours, establishment of art galleries, and provision of shopping and wayside amenities to name a few.

STDCs have their information centres located at entry points like railway stations, airports and bus stands to facilitate the incoming tourists. The main functions of STDCs are listed in Fig. 6.4.

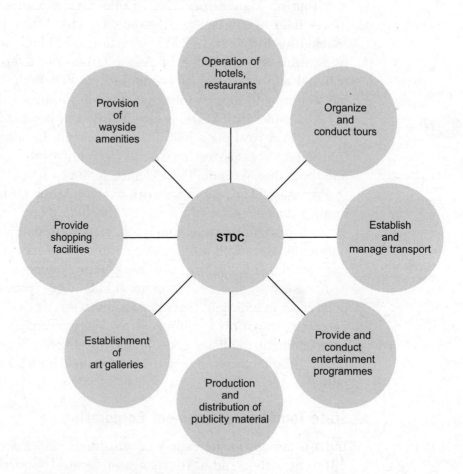

Fig. 6.4   Main functions of STDCs

Maharashtra Tourism Development Corporation

The Maharashtra Tourism Development Corporation (MTDC) is an example of an STDC. It has its main office at Mumbai, and regional offices at Pune, Ratnagiri, Nashik, Nagpur, Amravati, and Aurangabad. MTDC works in the following ways:

- It looks after the construction of new resorts or public amenities related to tourism.
- It supervises the existing properties regarding their occupancy, housekeeping, suggestions, and complaints from the tourists.
- It updates the product from time to time.
- It advertises the activities in the media to create awareness about the product.
- It organizes fairs and festivals at various places of historical importance to promote tourism and culture.
- It introduced the Deccan Odyssey, a tourist train, to showcase a variety of attractions in Maharashtra.

Tourism Finance Corporation of India

The Tourism Finance Corporation of India (TFCI) was formed by the Government of India after the recommendation of the National Committee on Tourism. TFCI was sponsored by IFCI Ltd, and other all India financial/investment institutes. This is a separate all India institute that caters to the needs of tourism and related projects. TFCI became operational from 1 February 1989.

TFCI's registered office is situated in IFCI Towers, New Delhi. It holds shares with IFCI, State Bank of India, Canara Bank, Bank of India, Life Insurance Corporation of India, National Insurance Co Ltd, etc.

Objectives

The main objective of TFCI is to provide financial assistance to various enterprises who are setting up and developing tourism-related activities and facilities. These include hotels, restaurants, holiday resorts, amusement parks, entertainment complexes, tourist emporia, convention centres, transport operators, and travel and tour operating agencies. TFCI coordinates and forms guidelines and policies to finance them. It organizes seminars, and participates in tourism-related activities organized by the Ministry of Tourism and by other travel-related organizations.

TFCI provides all forms of financial assistance for new ventures, expansion, diversification of projects in tourism industry, and other related activities. It provides assistance in the form of

- loans
- equipment
- finance and leasing
- underwriting of public issues of shares/debentures and direct subscription of such securities, etc.

Activities

The activities centre on tourism promotion in India. It is in the form of

- financial assistance for setting up or development of tourism related activities
- tourist-flow survey
- facilities and services for tourists
- preparation of tourism master plans
- planning for amusement/nature parks
- undertaking environmental/carrying capacity studies

In a nutshell, TFCI provides financial assistance for various tourism-related activities such as vehicle purchase for tour operators, office equipment, equipment for adventure sports, and working capital for the industry. TFCI provides finance to the private and public sector also.

The Archaeological Survey of India

The Archaeological Survey of India (ASI), under the Ministry of Culture, is the premier organization for the archaeological researches and the protection of the cultural heritage of the nation.

The objective of the ASI is to maintain the ancient monuments, archaeological sites, and remains of national importance. Besides this, it regulates all archaeological activities in the country. For the maintenance of ancient monuments and archaeological sites and remains of national importance, the entire country is divided into 24 Circles.

The ASI has a large work force of trained archaeologists, conservators, epigraphists, architects, and scientists for conducting archaeological research through its circles, museums, excavation branches, prehistory branch, epigraphy branches, science branch, horticulture branch, building survey project, temple survey projects, and underwater archaeology wing.

There are at present more than 3650 ancient monuments and archaeological sites and remains of national importance. These monuments belong to different periods, ranging from the prehistoric period to the colonial period and are located in different geographical settings. They include temples, mosques, tombs, churches, cemeteries, forts, palaces, step-wells, rock-cut caves, and secular architecture, as well as ancient mounds and sites, which represent the remains of ancient habitation.

These monuments and sites are maintained and preserved through the various circles of the ASI spread all over the country. The circles look after the research on these monuments and conservation activities; the science branch, with its headquarters at Dehradun, carries out chemical preservation, and the horticulture branch, with its headquarters at Agra, is entrusted with laying out gardens and environmental development.

PRIVATE SECTOR ORGANIZATIONS IN INDIA

There are several private sector organizations operationg in the field of tourism in India. Some of them are discussed in the following section.

Travel Agents Association of India

The Travel Agents Association of India (TAAI) was formed in the year 1951 by 12 leading travel agents who felt the need to create an association, to regulate the working of the travel industry in an organized manner, based on sound business principles.

Purpose

The primary purpose of TAAI is to protect the interest of its members. TAAI promotes the orderly growth and development of tourism. It also safeguards the rights of the travellers by preventing exploitation by unscrupulous and unreliable operators.

The TAAI symbol is a guarantee for reliable and professional service. TAAI has been recognized as the 'voice of travel and tourism' in India as it represents all that is professional, ethical, and dynamic in the nation's travel-related activity. It is a professional body which coordinates different sectors of the tourism industry.

It is a non-political, non-commercial, and non-profit making organization.

Objective

TAAI aims at the development of travel and tourism in India, by constantly improving the standards of service and professionalism in the industry, so as to cater to the needs of the travellers and tourists, within India and overseas. TAAI is also engaged in promoting mutual cooperation among TAAI members and different segments of the travel and tourism industry, by contributing to the sound progress and growth of the industry as a whole.

TAAI aims to safeguard the interest of the travelling public and maintain high ethical standards within the travel trade.

Activities

The activities of TAAI are as follows:

- TAAI functions as a powerful platform for exchange of thought and experiences.
- It helps to promote and maintain the growth of travel and tourism in India.
- It organizes seminars and conventions, and educates the members about upcoming trends in the industry.
- It maintains close contact with world tourism bodies and represents India for matters affecting the travel and tourism industry.
- It offers membership under different categories through which it develops better understanding among the different segments of the travel industry.
- It acts as an information dissemination centre for its members.

Membership

TAAI offers different categories of membership. They are as follows:

Active members   A TAAI approved head office of a travel agent providing comprehensive services.

Associate members   Branch office locations of an active member.

Allied members   Organizations engaged in allied business, i.e. various segments of the travel and tourism industry such as excursion agents, tour operators, hoteliers, airlines, general sales agents (GSA) of airlines, visa handling agents, travel writers and computer reservation systems (CRS), companies providing services to airlines and agents.

Government members   Central and state government departments, and public sector organizations.

Non-resident members   Overseas travel agents, tour operators, hotels, etc.

Indian Association of Tour Operators

The Indian Association of Tour Operators (IATO) was established in the year 1981.

Purpose

IATO was established to promote international understanding and goodwill. It is a joint forum of tour operators which promotes and helps the development of tourism in India. For promotion it organizes discussions and meetings with other tourism-related agencies.

Objectives

The main objectives of IATO are as follows:

- It aims to promote national integration, international welfare, and goodwill.
- It helps to promote, encourage, and assist in the development of tourism throughout the country.
- It communicates with the Chamber of Commerce, mercantile and public bodies in India, government departments, IATA, and various foreign associations, for the interests of travel trade and nominates members to act on them.
- It aims to setup and maintain high ethical standards in the tourism industry.
- It aims to encourage and promote friendly feelings among the tour operators and travel agents.
- It protects the interests of the members from malpractices of foreign tour operators.
- It undertakes activities which the members cannot undertake individually.
- It promotes equal opportunities for all visitors to enjoy tourism and travel, without distinction of race, creed, colour, and nationality.
- It organizes tours to foreign countries with the help of airlines and Government of India's tourism offices and other organizations.
- It conducts and helps in seminars, group discussions, courses of studies, and cultural meetings.
- It assists students in the field of development of tourism through scholarship, to pursue higher education, study, and research.
- It collects information and publishes it for the benefit of its members.

Membership

IATO offers different categories of membership. These are as follows:

Active members   This membership is given to any company or firm in India, recognized by Ministry of Tourism as a travel agent/tour operator for at least two years. The main activity of the company should be tourism promotion and foreign exchange earning.

Associate members   This membership is given to any other office of an active or allied member.

Allied members   This category of membership is for the firm or company engaged or associated with tourism industry such as carrier companies, hoteliers, restaurateurs, excursion agents, transport contractors, shipping companies, state tourism corporations, trade publications, etc.

International (allied) members   Any international firm engaged with tourism in India.

Honorary members   This is offered to the persons who are Hall of Fame awardees and the persons who have rendered services to tourism in national or international field.

The IATO publishes a newsletter called *IATO Imprint* to update its members on developments in tourism and achievements of its members. It is also involved in taking promotional tours abroad in collaboration with Air India Ltd, the flagship carrier of our country.

Federation of Hotel and Restaurant Association of India

The Federation of Hotel and Restaurant Association of India (FHRAI) is an apex body of four regional associations, representing the hospitality industry. FHRAI was established in the year 1954 and incorporated as a company under the Indian Companies Act in 1955. It was formed by the Hotel and Restaurant Association (HRA) of North India, New Delhi; HRA of Eastern India, Kolkata; HRA of Western India, Mumbai; and South India Hotels and Restaurants Association, Chennai. FHRAI is sponsored by these four regional associations. FHRAI is committed to provide and protect the interest of the hospitality industry by giving concessions to the industry.

The FHRAI is a member of the International Hotel Association (IHA). Its head office is the Federation Secretariat in New Delhi. The office bearers are a secretary general, joint secretary, deputy secretary, and other staff.

It provides a link between the hospitality industry, political leadership, academicians, international associations, and stake holders. It also helps the hospitality industry to grow, prosper and keep pace with the development of the international scenario.

FHRAI has more than 3300 members. They are 2052 hotels, 1016 restaurants, 105 associate members, and four regional associations. It employs more than fifteen million direct employees. It also has a hospitality management institute under it, the FHRAI Institute of Hospitality Management.

Objectives

The objectives of FHRAI are to

- unite the four regional associations and work towards encouraging, promoting, and protecting by lawful means the interest of the hotel and restaurant industry and raising the standards of the industry both at home and abroad;
- consider policies, guidelines, legislations, by-laws, and regulations that affect the industry and discuss with the government authority and initiate, support, or oppose by lawful means such legislation or regulation by various means;
- advise and inform members about national/international matters pertaining to the industry and disseminate statistical and commercial information through surveys and research;
- print, publish, and circulate, papers, periodicals, books, and other literature, conducive to advance the interests of the industry;
- assist in affording training facilities for the hospitality personnel and for promoting and running a hotel institute; and
- convene national and international conferences in the interest of the hospitality industry and organize meetings to encourage friendship between members, and discuss questions of current importance.

Activities

The activities of FHRAI are

- dissemination of information to the members;
- organizing conventions and seminars which are an ideal forum to exchange experiences and ideas;
- conducting research on the hotel and restaurant industry and updating members on the latest developments;

- training human resource in different spheres of the hotel and restaurant activities; and
- conducting regular professional development programmes to develop and update the knowledge and skills of hotel professionals.

Membership

The FHRAI offers different categories of membership which are as follows:

The FHRAI hotel membership This is offered to a hotel who is a member of one of the regional associations. The hotel should have at least ten rooms which should be functional, and a restaurant in the hotel is mandatory.

The FHRAI restaurant membership The restaurant, seeking the membership, must be operational and must be a member of one of the regional associations. It should have a minimum of 25 covers.

The FHRAI associate membership It is offered to companies and firms. The companies or firms must be a member of a regional association. It should be associated with the hospitality industry. Institutes of hotel management can avail of this membership.

The federation works in close coordination with the government keeping the government informed about the problems faced by the hotel and restaurant sectors. This has helped the industry through tax reliefs and fiscal incentives, for the hotel industry. The FHRAI hosts an annual four days All India Hotel and Restaurant Convention, in which state and union government representatives are invited to participate in discussions pertaining to problems and their solutions, developmental plans, and promotional activities.

FHRAI Institute of Hospitality Management

The FHRAI Institute of Hospitality Management (IHM) was established in the FHRAI's golden jubilee year, 2005, and today offers undergraduate and postgraduate degree/diploma programmes in hospitality management, for top, middle, and entry level professionals under one roof. A new three year graduate programme in hospitality, catering and tourism with the Sikkim and Manipal University, a one year programme in various hospitality operations, and a four-year international programme in hospitality and catering with the EHL, Switzerland are being offered at present.

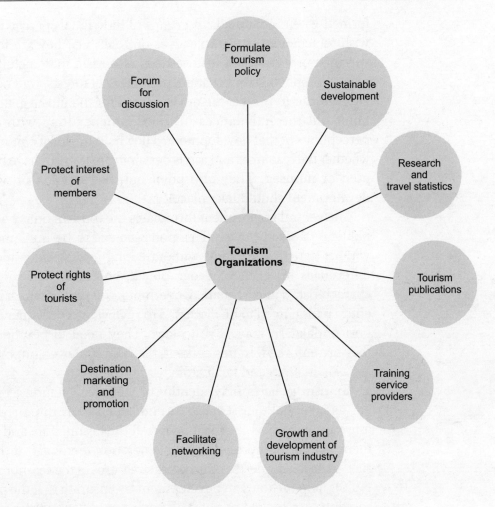

Fig. 6.5   Activities undertaken by various tourism organizations

The Rural Bharat Certification Scheme is a unique training programme, provided to uneducated youth from villages and the remote areas of the country, who are trained to become globally marketable; corporate culture is inculcated in them through FHRAI IHM.

The FHRAI has formed an educational trust and publishes the bimonthly FHRAI magazine.

NON-GOVERNMENT ORGANIZATIONS

Non-government organizations (NGOs) play an important role in the socio-economic development of the nation. These organizations are formed when individuals or groups of individuals perceive an idea and wish to achieve certain objectives or goals, i.e. they are formed with a specific purpose which with respect to tourism may include issues such as environmental conservation, protection of forests, water conservation, etc. in order to protect the environment for the future generation. They point out the imbalances in development along with the people's perceptions of that development. They help the local community realize whether the resources and assets pertaining to tourism have been correctly used or misused. They also point out the direction in which tourism development should take place.

The central government formulates the tourism policy along with the political party in power. This policy needs to be implemented by the various state governments without taking into consideration the major differences in terms of geographical, cultural, economic, and social characteristics in each state. Government directives which can affect the entire nation need to be discussed to review the consequences which the host population may have to face. They need to be approved before they are enforced. In this context, the NGOs play an important role and act as mediators and facilitators.

Tourism policies may identify beaches, hill stations, religious sites, etc. as potential tourist spots, but unilateral tourism policies, which are imposed, can affect the local people at the destination, and may deprive them of their traditional income generation methods. At the same time such polices may destroy the natural treasures of the seashores and forests. NGOs help the tourism development by ensuring that the problems and solutions are looked at not only from the policy makers' point of view but also from the locals' viewpoint who bear the brunt of such unilateral decisions.

Many NGOs work dedicatedly towards protecting the environment, such as the Kerala Sastra Sahitya Samiti (KSSP), which initiated a public campaign against the 'Silent Valley' project that was about to destroy a large forest. The Orchid Hotel in Mumbai, which is Asia's first certified five star ecotel (eco-friendly hotel), promotes eco-friendly practices and equations, and was established for carrying out research, training, and promotion of holistic tourism policies. It questions the real benefits of tourism to the host communities and studies the social, cultural, and economic impacts of tourism. Its aim is to minimize the negative impacts of mass tourism.

Problems Faced by NGOs

Voluntary organizations that come forward to assist the locals in solving certain issues are likely to face certain problems such as:

- suspicion towards the NGOs' motive to work; locals feel that such organizations must be having their own vested interests;
- limited funds to carry out work; and
- indifference shown by the locals towards the NGOs, often dampens their interest.

NGOs thus play a vital and challenging role in tourism development by acting as mediators and facilitators between the local population and the policy decision makers. In spite of the problems faced by them, they work for saving the planet.

OTHER IMPORTANT TOURISM ORGANIZATIONS

Some other international and Indian tourism organization are discussed as follows.

World Travel and Tourism Council (WTTC)

WTTC is a high-level private sector organization. The membership comprises Chief Executives of multinational accommodation companies, catering, cruises, entertainment, recreation, transportation, and other travel related companies.

International Hotel and Restaurant Association (IH&RA)

IH&RA represents the interest of the world's hotels and restaurants.

International Airline Passenger Association (IAPA)

This association represents the views of passengers in issues regarding aviation.

International Congress & Convention Association (ICCA)

This association specializes in managing international conferences and events, and trains professionals at all levels through its academy which has been specially founded as a training organization.

International Civil Aviation Organization (ICAO)

It is a specialized agency of the United Nations with a common purpose of promoting civil aviation on a global scale.

Travel Agents Federation of India (TAFI)

This organization's membership includes tour operators, non-IATA agents, hotels, taxi operators, foreign exchange agents, GSA (general sales agents), and GDS (global distribution systems).

IATA Agents Association of India (IAAI)

The only national association representing IATA's accredited travel agents in India with membership limited to them.

Indian Tourism Infrastructure Ltd (ITIL)

It is a newly formed tourism infrastructure company looking after tourism infrastructure.

Poona Hoteliers Association (PHA)

This is a local association of hotels in Pune and its members include luxury as well as mid-sized hotels. It is affiliated to the Hotel and Restaurant Association, Western India (HRA WI).

Indian Railway Catering and Tourism Corporation Limited (IRCTC)

This is a Government of India enterprise, which is responsible for catering at the railway stations and in the pantry-cars on the trains. Other functions performed by the corporation are e-ticketing, tourist trains, booking of cabs, hotels, various tour packages and loyalty programmes for the travellers of the Indian Railways network.

This chapter shows us that the number of organizations working for the betterment of tourism as a whole as well as the tourism industry is as vast as the number of activities undertaken by them. Organizations are actively working to create awareness about our environment and its conservation at all levels, keeping the negative impacts of tourism in mind and making efforts to minimize them.

SUMMARY

Tourism organizations have been formed to plan, develop, and monitor all tourism-related activities around the globe. They play an important role in marketing destinations and managing a country's tourism industry. Unplanned tourism activities can have a detrimental effect on the destination. These organizations help in promoting sustainable tourism development.

Many tourism organizations exist in both the private as well as public sectors, at the international, national, state, and local level. Tourism organizations are essential. The UNWTO is a specialized agency of the United Nations and is the leading organization in the field of tourism. It plays a central and decisive role in promoting the development of responsible, sustainable, and universally accessible tourism. It performs many activities. Many other organizations such as ASTA, PATA, UFTAA, etc. work on an international level. National organizations such as TAAI, FHRAI, and TFCI, which feel the need to protect the members and regulate the working of their sectors, have formed associations. TFCI provides financial assistance to various enterprises that are setting up and developing tourism-related activities and facilities.

IATA is one of the oldest air-transport organizations formed by a group of airlines which works to promote safe, reliable, secure, and economical air services for the benefit of all air travellers.

Government organizations working for tourism in India are India Tourism, ITDC, and STDCs. These organizations have a network of offices which promote various tourism products in India and abroad. Non-government organizations view tourism activities in terms of benefits to the locals and the environment. They discuss the policy decisions which the government plans to implement and point out the pros and cons of such decisions. Organizations, such as the ASI and the NGOs, help in preserving the national and cultural environment of our country.

KEY TERMS

Carrier Any public transportation company such as an airline, ship, rail, bus, etc.

Clients The individuals or organizations who are customers of a travel agency.

Conference A meeting of people for discussing formal matters which are of common interest. It involves planning, solving problems, etc.

Congress These are usually general sessions of delegates belonging to a particular organization or a body engaged in special studies.

Customer Here it refers to the consumer of tourism services; a person who purchases and/or enjoys the tourism services. A customer becomes a passenger when he boards any means of transport. Also referred to as clients.

Infrastructure These include facilities such as roads, railways, airports, electricity, drainage systems, water supply, buildings, etc. at the destination.

Package A prepaid travel plan sold at a fixed price which includes constituents such as transport, accommodation, meals, transfers, sightseeing, etc. The price of the package is lower than the price of its individual components taken together.

Private sector Entrepreneurs or business houses, which provide facilities and services such as hotels, restaurants, transport, etc., with a main motive of making profit on their investment. Includes large and small operators like MNC hotels, travel agents, tour operators, etc.

Promotion All activities such as advertising, publicity, personal selling, and public relations which are carried out to enhance sales.

Public sector Public sector or the government, whose primary role is governance, enactment, and implementation of policies and regulations, and in the context of tourism, providing basic infrastructure, promoting and marketing destinations, providing and maintaining attractions and monuments, etc.

Travel agent An individual or a firm who is authorized by the airlines, hotels, etc. to enhance the sale of all travel related services.

Tourist board An office maintained by a government to promote tourism in a particular area.

Tourist market The sum of actual and potential buyers for a tourism product or service in a specified geographical location, at a given point of time.

Tour operator A company or a firm which designs tour packages and makes them available to customers through travel agents.

Unethical Unprincipled/wrong practices followed in the industry.

CONCEPT REVIEW QUESTIONS

1. Explain the need for organizations in the tourism industry.
2. How does IATA help the airline industry?
3. Explain the role of UNWTO in tourism promotion.
4. Explain how STDCs help to promote tourism in India.
5. How does the organization PATA benefit its members?
6. What do the following abbreviations stand for?
   (a) UNDP   (b) SIHRA   (c) IUOTO   (d) ICCA
   (e) IRU   (f) IRCTC
7. Fill in the blanks:
   (a) _____ is the annual event of PATA.
   (b) The head office of FHRAI is located in _____.
   (c) The monthly magazine of ASTA is the _____.
   (d) The headquarters of UNWTO is located at _____.
   (e) _____ looks after travel agents in India.
   (f) _____ is the newsletter of IATO.
   (g) _____ provides financial assistance to various enterprises developing tourism-related activities.

CRITICAL THINKING QUESTION

What activities, do you feel, NGOs should take up in your city pertaining to tourism development?

PROJECT/ASSIGNMENT

Visit the STDC office in your state and find out which are the ongoing activities. Collect handouts and brochures and prepare a detailed report.

REFERENCES

(*Note:* All websites mentioned below were accessed between 20 June 2008 and 12 July 2008.)

Bhatia, A.K. 2002, *International Tourism*, Sterling Publishers Private Ltd, New Delhi.

Gupta, S.P., K. Lal, and M. Bhattacharya 2002, *Cultural Tourism in India*, Indraprastha Museum of Art and Archeology, New Delhi.

IGNOU 1994, Schools of Social Sciences TS-1 *Foundation Course in Tourism*, New Delhi.

IGNOU 1994, Schools of Social Sciences TS-2 *Tourism Development: Products, Operations and Case Studies*, New Delhi.

IGNOU 1994, Schools of Social Sciences TS-6 *Tourism Marketing*, New Delhi.

IATA, Foundation, January 2004, *International Travel and Tourism Training Programme*, Montreal.

IATA Book—Module one 2004 IATA Training Institute Montreal.

http://en.wikipedia.org/wiki/world_Tourism_organisation

http://www.iato.in

www.travelagentsofIndia.com

www.fhrai.com

www.world-tourism.org

www.PATA.org

www.TATA.org

www.asta.org

www.uftaa.org

www.asi.nic

www.maharashtratourism.gov.in

www.incredibleindia.org

www.tourisminindia.com

www.theashokgroup.com

CHAPTER 7

The Travel Agent and the Tour Operator

Learning Objectives

After reading this chapter you should be able to:
- explain the need for intermediaries in the tourism industry
- define the terms travel agent and tour operator
- describe how the distribution system in tourism functions
- describe the functions performed by a travel agency and a tour operator
- differentiate between a travel agent and a tour operator
- appreciate the liaison between the travel agents/tour operators and the travel suppliers
- understand the contents of a package tour
- define the role of guides and escorts
- know the various sources of income for a travel agency

INTRODUCTION

As we have read in the earlier chapters, tourists require a wide range of tourism-related services, ranging from assistance in procuring a passport, visa, airline tickets, accommodation, information about the destinations and attractions, local transport, and other services. Tourism suppliers or the primary and secondary constituents of the tourism industry need to approach their potential customers and meet their needs effectively and efficiently. However, this task is not so simple because of the vast geographical distance between the suppliers and the consumers, as consumers are spread all over the globe. The task of the intermediary is to link the suppliers of tourism services to the consumers so that the demands of both the suppliers and the consumers are fulfilled. This link in the tourism system is the intermediary, i.e. the travel agent or tour operator, and it forms the primary means through which the tourism product is sold to the consumer or tourist. They form the channel of distribution or the place from where the tourism offerings are made available to the consumer. Their role is to bring the consumers or buyers and the suppliers or sellers together. Distribution plays an important link in the tourism system, linking tourism supply and demand. Tourism offerings have been traditionally distributed either directly or indirectly through the travel agents and the tour operators (see Fig. 7.1). However, recent technological developments have revolutionized the distribution channels and today consumers are dealing directly with the suppliers to get the best deals. We will read about the influence of information and communication technology later in Chapter 16.

Travel agents; either working for a travel agency or individuals working on their own; assist their clients in planning their trips, planning the tour itineraries, making reservations for airlines, hotels, and other services. They act as intermediaries between the customers and the principal suppliers. They sell a variety of travel products and services and help their clients in turning their dreams into reality.

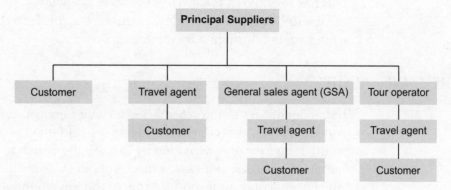

Fig. 7.1 Distribution channels used by suppliers
(The longer the distribution channel the higher the cost of the tourism product.)

The term 'travel agent' was coined in the early years of the eighteenth century. Travel in the old days was very simple with no travel formalities that exist today. The different modes of transport available today were also not present in those times. People were more motivated to travel only after the transportation systems such as railroads developed and organized travel came into picture. The rising income due to the industrialization and urbanization is another factor that has helped in the growth of organized travel.

The development of organized travel can be associated with Thomas Cook, the founder of Thomas Cook Group Limited, who was not only the first organized travel agent in the world but also the inventor of the travel and tourism business as it is today. Thomas Cook, as discussed in Chapter 2, persuaded a railway company to carry passengers at a very cheap fare, to attend a quarterly delegate meeting from Leicester to Loughborough in England. His idea was put into operation and around 570 travellers travelled by the Midland Counties Railway at a specially reduced fare. After this success, Thomas Cook organized excursions to various other places. In 1843, around 3000 school children were taken on a trip from Leicester to Derby in England, which was supposed to be the largest group of the time.

Much has changed on the tourism scenario since Thomas Cook chartered a train at a reduced fare. The introduction of jet travel has given a boost to the business of travel agencies. The improved living standards and the improvements in technology and transportation system have also motivated people to travel. Earlier, the travel agents were mainly into arranging some forms of transport reservations for tourists. But today, they have to perform many functions. People are travelling in large numbers both in their own countries as well as to foreign destinations. This has resulted in the growth of travel agencies all over the world.

Due to hectic life schedules, tourists today prefer to book their travel arrangements through a travel agent.

THE TRAVEL AGENT

Travel agents act as intermediaries serving between the various service providers and travel consumers. They sell and may, at times, market the products and services provided by the suppliers such as hotels, transport operators, airlines, railways, cruise operators, tour operators, etc. The travel agents play an important role in the development and promotion of travel sales. They put together all the components of the tourism product and sell them to the tourist.

The travel agent thus organizes the travel for the consumer. Travel agents are also referred to as 'travel consultants', 'travel counsellors', and sometimes even 'tour operators'. Travel agents serve as a link between the travel suppliers and the tourists. Hence, a travel agency is like a retail store, with a uniqueness; that it serves on behalf of both the suppliers and the consumers. For example, a client walks into a travel agency for booking a tour. The travel agency after getting an initial booking amount from the client will book the air tickets/rail tickets, arrange for a pick-up from the airport/railway station, make reservation at the hotel, book a vehicle for sightseeing, etc. Thus, the travel agent has not only served the tourist but also given business to the airlines/railways, transport operator, hotel, etc. Each and every tourist does not have the time to book and arrange for the travel and the suppliers also cannot get in touch with every potential customer. That is why the services of a travel agent are considered important (see Table 7.1).

Table 7.1 Benefits of intermediaries

Benefits to suppliers	Benefits to customers
Financial: Saves cost of setting up office and employing sales personnel to deal with customers. Travel agents collect their own payments.	Convenience: All travel arrangements are organized under one roof by an expert. Amount of effort spent making bookings with different suppliers is reduced.
Retail outlets in different cities are not required.	Provide expert knowledge: Intermediaries have thorough knowledge about tourism products/destinations, travel formalities, etc. and can advice customers accordingly.
Minimizes risk: Intermediaries increase the number of distribution channels and reduce the supplier's risk of loss of revenue due to unsold rooms, seats, etc.	Saves money: Tour operators get hotel rooms, airline seats, etc. at a discounted rate because they purchase in bulk and in advance.
Bulk purchasing by tour operators ensures minimum occupancy levels in hotels, number of seats booked on a flight, etc.	They offer packages at a cost lower than what the consumer would pay if he were to make all arrangements on his own.
	Greater variety and choice, latest information and brochures on all products and services is available.
	Minimizes risks and uncertainties about quality product as intermediaries are well informed and can recommend good products.

Definition

A travel agency may be an individual, a business firm, or company which acts as an intermediary in the sales and promotion of different travel-related services, such as accommodation, airlines, railways, road transport, cruises, etc. and earns commission received on selling services to its clients (see Fig. 7.2).

A travel agency can also be referred to as a retail travel agency since it sells the various services offered by the travel suppliers directly to its customers.

TYPES OF TRAVEL AGENCIES

In the earlier days travel was mainly by sea and railways; tickets were sold directly at the offices of the steamship companies and the railway stations. But when the airlines and the transport operators started operating, they were unable to earn profit, as they could not sell enough tickets through their own offices. The airlines, therefore, were forced to identify sales outlets and thus started the concept of retail travel agencies. To boost their sales, the airlines offered higher commission to the travel agent.

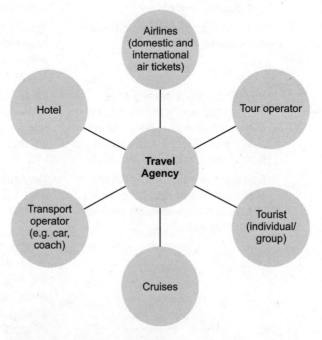

Fig. 7.2   Principal suppliers for a travel agency

Retail Travel Agency

A retail travel agency is one which sells the different travel-related services directly to its clients on behalf of the principal service providers/suppliers, i.e. hotels, airlines, cruises, railways, coach operators, etc. and in return earns a commission from them. The retail travel agency may add a mark up cost on these travel services. Thus, it earns its income from the commission earned from suppliers as well as from the mark up.

Definition

According to Airlines Reporting Corporation (1987), 'a retail travel agency is defined as a business that performs the basic functions of quoting fares and rates, books seats for airlines, railways, coaches, makes reservations for hotels, arranges for passport, visa, and other documentation services, and acts on behalf of the tourism vendors'.

The services performed by a retail travel agency are as follows:

- preparation of tour itineraries
- transportation—air, rail, and road
- accommodation
- insurance services
- foreign exchange
- travel documentation
- special interest tours.

Wholesale Travel Agency

A wholesale travel agency plans, organizes, develops, and sells package tours through a network of travel agencies or directly to the clients if it operates as a retail travel agency. Some travel agencies operate as both retail as well as wholesale travel agency, for example, Thomas Cook, Travel Corporation of India, etc.

The wholesale travel agency purchases the various travel products and services in bulk from the principal suppliers and sells to the retail travel agency or to the clients directly. Thus, the wholesale travel agency acts as a medium or a link between the principal suppliers and the retail travel agency.

Definition

A wholesale travel agency is one which assembles the different components of travel and forms a package to suit the needs of tourists. A wholesale travel agency thus designs package tours and sells them under its agency's name.

Features

The features of a wholesale travel agency are as follows:

- It serves as a link between the principal travel suppliers and the retail travel agency.
- It negotiates with the travel suppliers for best possible rates on bulk booking.
- It assembles the various travel components such as hotel, airlines, rail, and ground transport to form a package tour.
- It conducts research to know the changing preferences of tourists.
- It markets and promotes its products through advertising, etc. to increase sales volume.

There are many ways in which travel agencies can be further classified. Travel agencies are generally classified as follows:

Full Service Agency

A full service agency organizes and handles all types of tours for leisure, free individual travellers (FITs), group individual travellers (GITs), corporate travellers, etc. for inbound, outbound, and domestic destinations. Individual departments work on the different functions of travel agency, for example, leisure department, inbound department, outbound department, trade fairs, accounts, etc.

Commercial Agency

Commercial agencies are specialized for meeting the requirements of corporate travellers. Such agencies are mainly located at the business centres and cater only to the business travellers. Walk-in or individual travellers are not served by these agencies. The airline, hotel, car/coach, documentation, etc. are all looked after by the trained staff.

Implant Agency

It is a branch office of a full-fledged travel agency/tour operator functioning on the premises of a corporate office. It handles all the travel arrangements of the corporate office.

Table 7.2   Different bases for classification of travel agencies

Services offered	Generalist travel agent—Offers a wide range of services for all types of leisure and business travel. Specialist travel agent—Sells only special products to niche markets.
Geographic presence	Multiples—Large organizations with many retail outlets in major cities. Miniples—Number of branches located in a particular region. Independents—Generally small family-run agencies which are not part of any travel agency chain.
Purpose	Leisure travel agents—Deal with all travel arrangements for the leisure travellers. Business travel agents—Offer services to business travellers. Some corporate travel agencies are housed within the company.
Type	Traditional travel agents—They include all of the above types of electronic travel agents or online travel agents (OTA)—allow consumers to access information and make online bookings.

Special Interest Travel Agency

Specializes in creating tour programs for special interest groups, such as adventure, wildlife, religious, etc. For example, Pug Marks, Pune.

E-travel Agents or Online Travel Agents (OTA)

Also known as virtual/online travel agents (VTA's) or e-retailers, they are the new generation travel agents such as MakeMyTrip.com, Yatra.com, ezeego1.com, Travelguru.com, and lastminute.com. These web portals allow consumers to access information and make online bookings. Chapter 16 elaborates the concept further.

There are many ways in which travel agencies can be classified. They may also be classified as given in Table 7.2.

FUNCTIONS OF A TRAVEL AGENCY

The travel agency being an intermediary has an active role in providing quality services to the tourists (see Exhibit 7.1).

The travel agency performs a number of functions such as:

1. Providing travel-related information
2. Planning tour itineraries
3. Liaisoning with the tourism suppliers/vendors
4. Tour costing
5. Ticketing—domestic/international
6. Reservations

Exhibit 7.1   Role of the travel agency in the tourism industry

- Travel agents play an important role in promoting and developing any new tourist destination.
- They have contributed significantly to the growth of domestic, inbound, and outbound tourism.
- Foreign exchange earnings from inbound tourists have boosted the economy of the country.
- More than 70 per cent of tourist traffic is generated by the travel agents.
- The travel agents give around 60–80 per cent business to the airlines.
- The travel agency serves as a convenient location for the tourists in meeting and purchasing their travel requirements.
- It also helps in providing ancillary services such as passport, visa, insurance, foreign exchange, etc.
- The travel agent, while selling travel products, promotes tourism in the country.
- Domestic tourism not only helps in revenue earnings but is also important for national integration. Tourism is also promoted within the country.

7. Documentation
8. Settlement of accounts
9. Trade fairs/business tours/meetings, incentives, conferences, and exhibitions (MICE)
10. Foreign exchange (Forex)

Figure 7.3 shows the various departments in a large-scale travel agency.

Providing Travel-related Information

This is one of the most important and basic functions of a travel agency. The tour professionals should have detailed knowledge of the tourist destinations, distance from the airport/railway station, different categories of hotels and the services provided by them, etc. The staff should be fluent in the local language, English, and foreign languages, if dealing with foreign countries.

Planning Tour Itineraries

The tour professionals after receiving the client's preference of destinations to be visited, his/her approximate date of travel and duration, the mode of transport, hotels, etc. has to plan the itinerary to suit the client's needs. The itinerary is a tour programme in sequential order which is designed day wise to identify the origin points, destinations en route points, hotel, meals, mode of transport, sightseeing, car/coach and other relevant details related to the tour. Chapter 10 discusses the concept in detail.

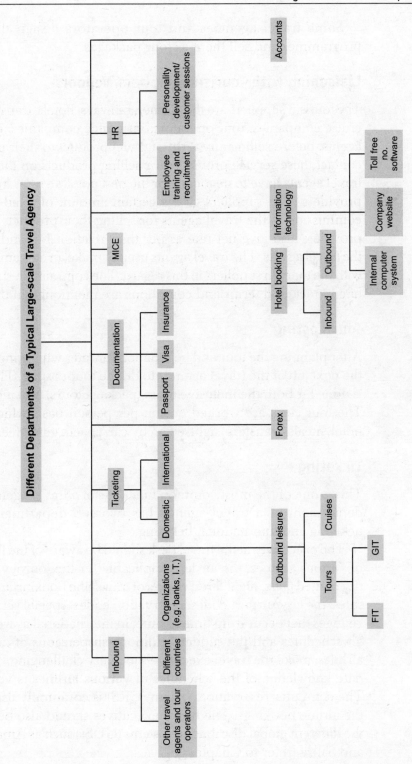

Fig. 7.3   Different departments of a typical large-scale travel agency

Some travel agencies and tour operators design their own tour programmes and sell them as tour packages.

Liaisoning with Tourism Suppliers/Vendors

The tourism suppliers are the airlines, railways, hotels, transport operators, cruise companies, tour operators, insurance companies, etc. The travel agents, before selling any form of travel product to their clients, have to contact these service providers for selling products on their behalf. The travel agents have to negotiate for the best possible rates from the service providers. The suppliers give a certain amount of fixed percentage as commission to the travel agents for selling their products. Some service providers also give net rate as per their relationship and business with the travel agents. The travel agents usually make an agreement or contract with the tourism suppliers in this regard. The commission structure, period of contract, and terms and conditions are mentioned in the agreement.

Tour Costing

After planning the tour and negotiation for rates with principal suppliers, the next job of the travel agent is to do the tour costing. The tour costing is done for both the inclusive tours (package tours) and individual tours. The tour costs are worked out on per person basis which include the hotel, meals, transfers, sightseeing by car/coach, guide fees, and airfares.

Ticketing

This is one of the most common functions of a travel agency. The travel department of a travel agency has two sub departments—domestic ticketing and international ticketing.

The executives at the travel desk should be aware of the flight schedules of various airlines, the air fare applicable for the journey, special fares, discounted fares, night fares, classes of travel, the booking and cancellation rules, the city/airport codes, reservation codes, special services, etc. The changes that occur from time to time, in international as well as domestic air schedules and the sudden additions/suspensions of new flights and airlines, make the travel executive's job very challenging. Thus an up-to-date knowledge of the schedules of various airlines is very important. The computer reservation system (CRS) is commonly used for making the airline bookings. The travel executives should also be familiar with the different global distribution systems (GDSs) such as Amadeus, Galileo, and Sabre (refer to Chapter 16).

Settlement of Accounts

Settlement of accounts with the tourism suppliers is one of the major functions of a travel agency. The executives working in the accounts department should be familiar with and have thorough knowledge of foreign currencies, their cross value, exchange regulations, etc.

Documentation

This department helps its clients in providing facilitation services such as passport, visa, health certificates, insurance, customs regulations, immigration and permits required for restricted areas, baggage allowed, etc. for travelling abroad. Chapter 8 elaborates the concept further.

Business Tours/Trade Fairs

Apart from handling the leisure tourists and arranging domestic, inbound, and outbound tours, another major and much-in-demand job for the travel agent is the handling of business tours.

The travel agent has to meet the different demands of the business tourists. The business tourists may visit a particular destination for various reasons pertaining to their work such as to attend a business meeting, conference, convention, travel fair, selling products, meeting clients, etc. The travel agent has to work in coordination with the internal departments such as ticketing and documentation for the air booking and for arranging services such as passport, visa, insurance, etc. The travel agent has to arrange venues for meetings, conventions, and exhibitions; transport, accommodation, and sightseeing facilities, required at these venues and business centre facilities such as fax machines, laptops, video conferencing, etc.

Reservation

The travel agent after getting confirmation and initial payment from the clients has to book airline seats, hotel rooms, transport arrangement, and other services as per the requirements of the client. The tour professional should thus be familiar with the terms and abbreviations used for reservation procedure for airlines and hotels. The phonetic alphabet is preferably used for making reservations on telephone (refer to Chapter 13). Once the booking has been confirmed and payments made, the confirmed tickets, itinerary, and travel vouchers have to be handed over to the client.

Forex

Providing foreign currency, travellers' cheques, etc. to tourists and getting it endorsed on the passport is yet another important function performed by the travel agencies. This saves the tourist the trouble of visiting a bank or an exchange bureau.

SETTING UP A TRAVEL AGENCY

A lot of planning goes into starting and setting up of a travel agency. Any kind of business is risky and the person involved should have proper knowledge of the product he/she is selling. Similarly, for a travel agency business, the person should have good product knowledge and presentation skills. He/she should be clear about the product which he/she wishes to sell. For example, whether the travel agency wants to handle domestic tours, inbound tours, outbound tours, or all of these, has to be decided in advance. This has to be decided by the travel agent at the initial planning stage. The staff to be employed should be trained properly to handle the queries asked by tourists. Qualified and trained staff should be hired by the employer to handle the clients.

Requirements of a Travel Agency

The travel agency can be successful if it meets the following minimum requirements:

- enough finance to run the business;
- a centrally located premises or near a business centre;
- qualified and trained staff;
- approvals from government and other organizations, such as India Tourism Office, Ministry of Tourism, IATA, and TAAI; and
- authorization to sell on behalf of principal suppliers, such as hotels, transport operators, etc.

Infrastructure, location, and adequate finance

For a setting up travel agency, the financial requirements are not very high. Investments are mostly needed for the following areas:

- buying or hiring of space for office
- furniture
- computers
- laptop
- telephones, fax machine, photocopying machine, etc.

- office stationery
- promotional material (brochures, etc.)
- salary for the employees

While setting up the travel agency, proper thought needs to be given to the location of the travel agency. It should be near a business or industrial area, centrally located, or in areas where there is demand for travel. Hence, some research should be done on this.

Approvals by concerned organizations

A travel agency should have the necessary approvals from the concerned organizations. For example, if the agency is into selling air tickets, it has to get approval from International Air Transport Association (IATA), which is the world organization of scheduled airlines. Commission is paid only to the approved travel agents by the airlines. The travel agency has to submit the application form along with other required documents. The travel agency has to fulfill the following conditions:

- ability to generate and procure air passenger transportation;
- adequate financial status;
- location of the travel agency near to business area; and
- qualified and experienced staff.

IATA gives an approval only after an inspection by the concerned authorities. The travel agency should also have recognition from India Tourism Office, Ministry of Tourism, and licences from the industry suppliers such as airlines, Reserve Bank of India, Passport Office, and recognition from the hotels. This is essential for earning commission from the suppliers. The travel agency should be registered under the Shops and Establishment Act.

SOURCES OF INCOME FOR A TRAVEL AGENCY

The travel agency and tour operator's main source of income is from the commission, which they get from the various travel service providers. The travel agency sells the airline seats, railway seats, hotel rooms, cruise packages, car rental services, etc. and in return are paid a commission for each travel product sold by them for the respective airlines, railways, hotels, cruise line companies, transport operators, and tour operators (see Fig. 7.4). The commission structure differs from supplier to supplier and also as per the business given by the travel agency and tour operator to these service providers. It ranges from five per cent to 20 per cent.

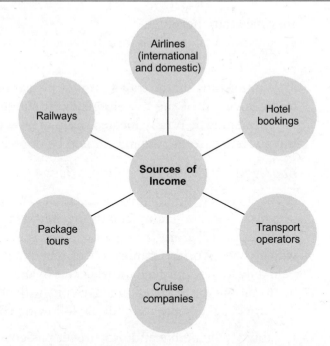

Fig. 7.4 A travel agency earns revenue from these principals

Commission on selling their products to the clients

The industry suppliers pay these approved agents a commission on the services sold on their behalf. The commission is usually a fixed percentage of the sales prices of the service or the product sold, and is paid to the travel agent/tour operator after the sale of the service or product. The commission is deducted from the final payment and the balance is forwarded to the principal. For example, a client purchases a tour worth Rs 20,000. If the commission for that tour is 10 per cent for the tour operator then the travel agent will retain Rs 2000 and forward the tour operator the net amount of Rs 18,000.

Some service providers such as airlines give commission only to officially appointed travel agencies. Officially approved agencies are those agencies which are approved by IATA. To be an IATA approved agency it is necessary that the staff working in the agency is IATA qualified. Non-IATA accredited agents work as subagents for IATA accredited agents and earn a commission of around 4.5 per cent of the basic fare. Commission received from principal suppliers is shared by non-appointed or non-IATA travel agents who obtain tickets from IATA appointed travel agents. Such commission is called *split commission* or *shared commission*.

Incentives or overrides

In addition to the commission, some service providers may pay incentives to the travel agents who have given large amount of business in terms of sales volume to them. These incentives are referred to as overrides or bonuses.

The commissions given by the principal suppliers are normally fixed, but some suppliers offer the agency an override, i.e. higher the sales, higher will be the commission rate. Sometimes a part of this commission may be passed on to the customer as a discount rate.

Service charges

Service charges are another source of revenue to travel agents which are charged for services rendered to the clients. For instance, for getting a passport or a visa the travel agency charges the client as they do not receive any commission on selling these services. Some service providers may give the travel agent very less commission which is insufficient to cover the expenses of the travel agency. In such cases the travel agent charges the client for services rendered. The service charges differ from travel agency to travel agency and on the nature of service provided.

Apart from the commission and service charges, the agency gets additional income from other sources. They are as follows:

Mark up on tours

A travel agent buys the travel products from the principal suppliers in large volume, at a net rate or discounted rate, and creates his/her own package tour. The travel agent tries to get the best prices for each component of the package tour and then adds a mark up to the tour cost for selling it to the clients directly or through other travel agents.

Wholesale fee

Some wholesalers may not pay the usual 10 per cent commission to the travel agents for selling their tours. Instead, they will pay a flat fee for each reservation made.

Representation fee

The tour operators or airlines may not have their branch offices in all cities of the country or world. In this case, the tour operator or the airline may appoint a general sales agent (GSA), who could be a travel agent, to handle their business in these cities, so as to generate higher sales. The GSA will handle the services of the tour operator or principal service provider to promote the sales. The tour operator will pay a fixed fee or commission and a budget for advertising and promoting their product to the GSA.

THE TOUR OPERATOR

The roles and functions of a tour operator are different to that of a travel agency. A travel agency may work as or offer the services of a tour operator.

Tour operators are professionals who should have all the required skills, expertise, and knowledge of organizing travel. The tour operator assembles all the different components of travel and sells it as a package tour, to and from a destination, with complete ground arrangements. Most of the tour operators have their own fleet of vehicles to cater to the transport segment. The tour operator offers different kinds of package tours as per the requirements of individual travellers, groups, retail travel agencies, business firms, etc. These package tours may be escorted or unescorted as per the need.

Planning and organizing package tours is a time consuming process. Many tourists and individual travel agencies do not want to bother themselves with planning, booking the airline, and hotel rooms, etc. They want this to be arranged by someone else. This demand has thus led to the origin of package tours. The tour operator sells the package tours as per the interests and needs of the tourists. The tour costs of these package tours are different for different class of tourists, as per their budget. The package tours include the transportation (air, rail, or road), accommodation, tour escort/guide, etc. The individual who puts together all these different services into a package is called a tour operator.

To be more precise, a tour operator is an individual who provides information, and plans and organizes the travel with various service providers to create a package tour. The tour operator also ensures that the tour runs smoothly without any hassles. A tour operator is sometimes also referred to as a tour consultant or a tour coordinator.

Definition

'Tour operator is one who has the responsibility of putting the tour ingredients together, marketing it, making reservations, handling all financial and accounting aspects, and selecting as well as managing tour managers' (Poynter 1993).

Responsibilities of a tour operator include the following:

- Providing information of the tourist destinations, different kinds of accommodation available, transport facilities, any entertainment, etc.
- Planning the tour effectively.
- Coordinating and liaisoning with the service providers or principal suppliers.
- Monitoring the entire operation of the tour. In case of any problem, providing some alternative arrangements with least inconvenience to the tourist.

TYPES OF TOUR OPERATORS

A tour operator specializes in the planning and organizing of prepaid, preplanned tours and sells these directly either to the tourists or to the retail travel agency. The tour operator may target market some specific areas to sell the tours. The tour operator may be international, domestic, or specialized in a region or continent. Some tour operators cater to international as well as domestic markets. The tour operator can be an individual/independent tour operator or a travel agency functioning as both.

Tour operators are broadly classified into the following as per the functions performed.

Inbound Tour Operator

Inbound tour operators operate and handle the inbound tourists coming into the country from overseas. The tourists are provided various services right from their arrival such as airport transfers, accommodation, car/ coach for sightseeing, entertainment, etc. till their departure. The inbound tour operators get their business either directly from individual inbound tourists or through the foreign tour operators. The inbound tour operator helps in boosting the economy of the host country by contributing to the valuable foreign exchange earnings.

Outbound Tour Operator

Outbound tour operators operate tours to foreign countries, which can be either to a single country or for more than one country. The tour operators design and market package tours for outbound tourists for a specific predefined period. All the necessary arrangements for documentation such as passport, visa, insurance, etc. are also taken care of by the outbound tour operators. These operators work in coordination with the foreign tour operators for the accommodation, transfers, ground arrangements, sightseeing, etc.

Domestic Tour Operator

Domestic tour operators conduct tours within the country and cater to the needs of individual and group travellers. The domestic tour segment has witnessed a phenomenal growth in the recent years as many large tour companies have entered the market. For example, Thomas Cook, Cox & Kings, Kesari Tours, etc.

PACKAGE TOURS

The various components of travel, such as accommodation, transportation (air, water, rail, and road), attractions, etc. are combined and sold as a package tour to the tourist by the tour operators and travel agents. A package tour is thus a single product which is planned, organized, combined, and sold as an 'all inclusive tour' at a specified price by the tour operators.

Package tours are in use since the 1600s. Thomas Bennet organized the first inclusive tour in the year 1821. He set up his business as a tour operator in 1850 and made the first individual tour itinerary and booked the hotel and other arrangements. But the credit for the concept of package tours goes to Thomas Cook. In 1855, Cook planned and organized all the different components of a tour package and sold it as an inclusive tour to the tourists. After the success of his tour, other travel agents and tour operators also started operating similar tours to other tourist destinations.

Definition

A tour package is a total tourism product which is planned and operated for either independent travellers or for groups, to a single destination or to multiple destinations. It consists of air travel (generally) and land arrangement segments for a specified number of days, with a set of tangible and intangible features for a set price.

A package tour is thus a programme which is organized for an individual or for group travellers having all the necessary tour ingredients such as accommodation, transportation, sightseeing, and also, if required, guides/escorts, entertainment, etc.

Different people have given different definitions, as tour package is a broad concept.

Holloway (1992) defines the tour package as, 'A tour package is a total tourism product as it generally consists of transport from the generating area to the destination, accommodation at the destination and possibly some other recreational or business tourist services.'

'A tour package is an advertised journey including specific features, arranged and promoted with tour literature by a tour operator and paid for in full by the tourists before starting on the tour.' (Gregory 1985).

A package tour is thus a product which is planned, organized, operated, and sold at a set price to individual tourists or groups, to a single or multiple destinations, usually involving air travel, accommodation, and land arrangements for the number of days specified.

Some experts have defined package tours based on

1. Destinations and
2. Interests of the tourists

Destinations

The destinations are further classified into single country, area tour, single city tour, and two city tour.

Single country package tours   Organized for only one country, for example, China.

Area tour package tours   Organized for visiting more than one country, belonging to a common area. For example, tours to the South-East Asian countries such as Singapore, Thailand, and Malaysia; and tours to Europe and America.

Single city tour package tour   Organized for only a single city, for example, Aurangabad, Hyderabad, etc.

Two city tour package tour   Organized for two cities. For example, Delhi–Agra tour, Jodhpur–Udaipur tour, etc.

Interests

Some package tours are designed and organized as per the different needs and interests of the tourists. Tourists may visit certain destinations for different purposes including

- cultural sites/historical sites such as Taj Mahal, Agra; Lake Palace, Udaipur; and Pushkar Fair, Pushkar
- special interest tours, for example, rail tours, such as Kalka–Shimla toy train, Palace on Wheels, etc.

- adventure tours designed for adventure activities such as trekking, mountaineering, wildlife sanctuaries, hang gliding, paragliding, etc.
- sports tours, for example, Olympics, golf tours, car racing, cricket, football, etc.

Advantages

Advantages of package tours are as follows:

- Package tours save time, as the tour operator plans and organizes the travel details with the principal travel suppliers, for the tourist.
- Unnecessary correspondence is also reduced.
- They work out to be cheaper than the other tours.

Disadvantages

Disadvantages of package tours are as follows:

- Package tours are planned well in advance and do not have personal choice of destinations for the tourist.
- The tourist cannot change the itinerary as per his/her choice as it is already preplanned and prepaid.
- Some tourists may not be interested in visiting all the places mentioned in the package tour.

Components of a Package Tour

A package tour consists of the following components/elements:

- accommodation
- travel by airline/railway
- transfers to and from airport/railway, and hotels
- sightseeing
- guide/escort

The above components can be broadly classified into two parts:

1. Travel arrangements
2. Ground/land arrangements

Travel arrangements

Travel is related mainly to the air transportation in the tour itinerary. The tour operator negotiates with the airlines for group bookings and also bulk purchase, and combines it with the land arrangements to sell it as a package tour. Some tour operators also coordinate with air charters, which work out to be cheaper than the regular scheduled airlines. Air travel is one of the core elements for the inbound and outbound tour package.

Ground/land arrangements

It includes the transfers, i.e. pick-up and drop from the airport/railway station and the hotel, accommodation, meals, car/coach for sightseeing, guides/tour escorts, entertainment, shopping, and other special requirements or services for the tourist. Ground arrangements are looked after by the ground handlers.

Ground handlers are agents that work on behalf of international and domestic tour operators, travel agents, and principals. They look after all ground arrangements, once the tourists reach the destination, such as transfers from airport to hotel, booking of hotel, car rentals, excursions, entry tickets for attractions and activities, restaurant bookings, shopping, etc. The tour operators coordinate and negotiate with the hotels and transport operators for discounts or special rates.

TYPES OF PACKAGE TOURS

Tour operators nowadays offer a wide variety of tour packages as per the needs of the tourists. These are discussed as follows:

Independent Tours

Independent tours are specially designed or tailor-made as per the requirements of the individual tourist. Such tours are not published in the company's tour brochure. The travel agent/tour operator combines all the travel and land arrangements and coordinates with the principal suppliers for special or net rates. A mark up is usually added to the price to cover his/her expenses. Such tours are also known as foreign independent tours (FITs) and domestic independent tours (DITs), depending on the location of the destination of the package tour.

Inclusive Tours

For inclusive tours, the tour operator purchases all the different components of the tour package in bulk from the principal suppliers at a special or group rate. The package is advertised, and sold to the tourists at an inclusive price by the tour operator. The inclusive tours work out to be cheaper than the independent tours for the tourists, as the tour operator gets it at a group rate. However, the tour members have to travel in a group for the entire tour.

Sometimes tour operators incur a loss for inclusive tours if they are unable to sell the required seats and rooms, which are usually purchased one year in advance from the suppliers.

Escorted Tours

The tours which include the tour escorts or group leaders are known as escorted tours. The tour escort is present right from the commencement of the journey upto the return of the tour. The tour escort assists the travellers throughout the entire tour. His/her function is to receive the tour members at the airport/railway station and help them through customs clearance and other airport formalities both at the time of arrival and departure. Such tours are also known as *conducted tours* or *hosted tours*.

Business Tours

The business tours are specially designed and packaged as per the requirements of the clients. People travel for business for various reasons and for varying durations. The tour operator arranges the accommodation, facilities/services required, transport, and sightseeing as per the schedule of the business visit. Some tour operators also arrange conference tours and incentive tours.

Conference tours require special skills, as special arrangements have to be made for such tours. The tour operator has to look after the conference arrangements right from the initial stage of organizing, selecting the venue, marketing the conference, booking of accommodation and transport, secretarial services, conference equipments, conference facilitation such as registrations, interpreters, special events, entertainment, local sightseeing, and other facilities.

More recently, incentive tours have also appeared and companies are offering incentives to their dealers or employees in the form of additional payments, gifts or some kind of a holiday. The incentive tours are very popular and are usually of shorter duration. Such tours are a motivational factor for the employees and the dealers. The tour operators have to pay attention to details such as size of the group, the cuisine preferred, gifts, theme parties, baggage handling, etc. The size of the group for incentive tours varies from one company to another.

GUIDES AND ESCORTS

Guides and escorts have gained importance ever since tourism has been recognized as a great economic activity. Guiding and escorting tours are now being considered as highly professional business activities. Special skills and qualities are required by the guides and escorts if they are to be successful in this field.

Guides

A guide serves as a public relations representative for his/her particular site, city, region, and country. A guide should therefore be knowledgeable about history, geography, sociocultural practices, etc. related to his/her area of concern, so as to inform the tourists accordingly. In India, the India Tourism Office, Ministry of Tourism regularly conducts courses to train new guides. The guides are given licences and are approved by the Ministry of Tourism to work as freelancers. The fees are decided upon by the India Tourism Office depending on half day, full day, or overnight charges and also for foreign languages as required.

Definition

'A professional guide is in varying degrees a business person—often freelance, sometimes an employee; a travel industry representative; a public relations representative for his or her site, city, region, and country—as well as an educator, an entertainer, and a public speaker, among other roles.' (Kathleen Lingle Pond, The Professional Guide, New York 1993).

Location guides

In India location guides can be categorized into the following different categories depending upon the locations.

Monument guides   The monument guides are specialized in describing the history of the monumental heritage of India. The monument guides should have proper historical knowledge of the monument and the region so as to describe the same to the tourist. They should be aware of all historical facts of the monuments like the date and time taken for construction, the architect, and the purpose of constructing the monument. The guides should be able to make the entire particulars interesting to the tourists in the form of fables and anecdotes.

Museum guides   The museum guides should have knowledge about the various artifacts/exhibits displayed at the museum. They should know the area of interest of the tourists. This will help the guides in deciding to curtail or extend the time spent in visiting the museum. The tourists might also appreciate the varieties and the artistic merits of the artifacts, in which case more time should be spent in the museum.

Wildlife guides   The guides located at wildlife sanctuaries should be familiar with wildlife tourism. Many tourists visiting any wildlife reserve are at times not familiar with the wildlife they are visiting and thus it becomes important for these guides to instruct them and give proper information.

City guides

The city guides should be able to profile the tourists visiting the city and their purpose of travel. The city guides should be aware of the opening and closing timings of the tourist attractions and also on which particular day the attractions are closed. They should pay detailed and careful attention on the commentary of the tour. The guide should see that the tour does not physically tire the tourists. There should be enough and adequate stops during the tour along with sufficient time for shopping.

Skills required for guiding

Leadership   A tour guide should have good leadership qualities such as decision making, flexibility, enthusiasm, confidence, sensitivity, and should have a good sense of humor.

Factual knowledge   The guide should have knowledge about the topography, geography, history, culture, religion, folk art, folklore, economy, etc. related to the city, region, state, or country.

Presentation skills   The guide should have good presentation skills such as a clear voice and good body language. The voice should be lively and the guide should be able to explain the site in simple language.

Grooming   Personal hygiene, positive attitude, good manners, and politeness are the other qualities which are desirable in guides and escorts.

Escorts

An escort has to accompany the tourists right from commencement till the end of the tour. He/she has to perform the role of a tour leader or a tour manager. The escort may accompany the tourists to historical sites, rural areas, pilgrimage places, shopping, museums, etc. The escort has also to look after the facilitation of the tour such as the check-in formalities, customs clearances, etc. The escorts have to take care of the tourists, throughout the tour and at the destination.

The tour escort has to plan the tour properly with a schedule of events and live the tour day by day. He/she has to be prepared with alternative arrangements incase of any unforeseen circumstances due to weather, transport strike, accident, etc. The tour escort should be well prepared in advance with all the travel arrangements such as checklists, tour itinerary, commentary of tour, and travel tips. The tour escort should also be able to handle the tour in case of special unforeseen situations. Some frequently encountered problems during a tour which may arise are loss of money, loss of passport, sickness of any tour member, missing tour members, etc. The tour escort should be able to handle the tour members in an effective way and advise them accordingly so that time schedules are maintained and there are no missed trains or flights.

The travel agent and the tour operator, thus form the two main intermediaries in the tourism distribution chain. They play a vital role in not only providing various services to the traveller, but also in promoting destinations and in the overall growth of the tourism industry. Guides and escorts at the destination or accompanying the group, are an essential part of the tourism experience. Intermediaries thus form a vital link between the tourism supply and demand in the tourism system. Tour operators and travel agents too have to keep pace with the technological advances and changing scenario of the tourism industry and offer value added services and professional services.

SUMMARY

Travel agents and tour operators are the main intermediaries in the tourism industry, serving both the suppliers of tourism products and services as well as the tourists or customers. Principal suppliers, such as hotels, airlines, transporters, etc. need a distribution channel so that their products reach the customers. Because of the perishable and intangible nature of the tourism products they play a very important role in ensuring that the products produced by the suppliers, are consumed.

A travel agency is a retail outlet for the promotion and purchase of different travel-related services. A tour operator is a person who assembles all the different components of travel and sells it as a package tour to and from a destination with complete ground arrangements. These package tours may be escorted or unescorted depending on the needs of the customer. Travel agents perform many functions such as providing travel information, planning itineraries, ticketing, reservations, documentation, tour costing, and Forex- and MICE-related services. Their source of income is mainly from commissions received from the various suppliers and service charges from the customer. They are a vital link between suppliers and customers. They offer a wide variety of tours to suit the needs of tourists both for independent and group tours.

KEY TERMS

Commission A payment made by a supplier to an agent for services rendered. It is generally calculated as a percentage of the value of the transaction and percentage varies between products and services and differs from one country to another.

General sales agent (GSA) An agent generally appointed by an airline or other principal in a particular territory to look after inquiries, reservations, ticketing, and promotional campaigns for the airline or other principals. Also called sole agent.

Ground handlers Agents who work on behalf of tour operators, travel agents, and principals and look after all arrangements once tourists reach their destination.

Hotel voucher Coupon issued by a tour operator or travel agent to the tourist, which covers prepaid elements of a trip like accommodation and meals. It is surrendered by the tourist on arrival at the hotel, which later claims payment from the issuing authority.

Intermediary An intermediary in tourism is any third party or organization between the supplier and customer who facilitates the purchase of the tourism product.

Mark up The extra amount added to the per person cost of a tour to get the final cost and one of the main source of income for travel agents and tour operators.

Miscellaneous charges order (MCO) An all purpose voucher issued by an airline and drawn on any organization such as accommodation, food and beverage, sightseeing, transfers, etc. which is willing to accept it in prepayment for services or charges.

Overriding commission An additional commission paid by a principal such as an airline or a tour operator, to a travel agent as a bonus or an incentive to generate high sales.

Principal A provider of travel-related products and services.

Tour operator or tour wholesaler Tour operator or tour wholesaler is a person or organization who buys individual travel services in bulk from principal suppliers and combines them into a package tour which is sold to travellers directly or through travel agents.

Transfer Transport service for arriving and departing passengers to take them from one transport terminal to another or to hotels, usually free between airport terminals, as a hotel courtesy service or as part of an inclusive tour.

Travel agent An intermediary between the principals and the customer who sells travel services and provides travel-related information. Its main function is that of a retailer for principal suppliers and customers.

Travel voucher An all purpose voucher issued by a tour operator to cover the prepaid elements of a package tour such as meals, local transport, entrance fees for attractions, etc. It is given to the ground handling agent.

CONCEPT REVIEW QUESTIONS

1. Define travel agency and tour operator.
2. Mention the different types of travel agencies and tour operators.
3. What are the different kinds of package tours?
4. Briefly describe the functions of a travel agency.
5. Explain the role of guides and escorts.
6. Give the sources of income of a travel agency.
7. Describe the role of travel agency in tourism industry.
8. What are the minimum requirements for setting up a travel agency?

PROJECT/ASSIGNMENT

Visit an IATA approved travel agency in your city and study the different departments and their functions and prepare a detailed report.

REFERENCES

Bhatia, A. K. 1997, *Tourism Management and Marketing: The Business of Travel Agency Operations,* First Edition, Sterling Publishers, New Delhi.

George, R. 2007, *Managing Tourism in South Africa*, Oxford University Press Southern Africa, Cape Town.

Gregory, A. 1985, *The Travel Agent: Dealers in Dreams*, Fourth Edition, The Prentice Hall International Ltd, USA.

Holloway, Christopher J. 1992, *The Business of Tourism*, Third Edition, Pitman Publishing, London.

Kamra, K.K. and Mohinder Chand 2002, *Basics of Tourism Theory, Operation and Practice*, First Edition, Kanishka Publishers, New Delhi.

Keyser, H. 2002, *Tourism Development*, Oxford University Press Southern Africa, Cape Town.

Middleton, V.T.C. 1994, *Marketing in Travel and Tourism*, Butterworth Heinemann, Oxford.

IGNOU 1994, Schools of Social Sciences TS-1 *Foundation Course in Tourism,* New Delhi.

IGNOU 1994, Schools of Social Sciences TS-2 *Tourism Development: Products, Operations and Case Studies,* New Delhi.

IGNOU 2003, Schools of Social Sciences MTM 13 *Tourism Operations,* New Delhi.

Negi, J. 1998, *Travel Agency and Tour Operation, Concept and Principles,* First Edition, Kanishka Publishers, New Delhi.

Poynter, James M. 1993, *Tour Design, Marketing and Management*, Prentice Hall, London.

CHAPTER 8

Travel Formalities and Regulations

Learning Objectives

After reading this chapter you should be able to:
- understand why travel documents and regulations are necessary
- know the different types of travel documents and understand the travel they are required for
- know how to fill application forms for obtaining various documents
- understand the procedure to be followed for obtaining the various documents
- understand the significance of laying down different travel regulations

INTRODUCTION

Many rules and regulations affect tourism both directly and indirectly and tourism professionals should be aware of the latest rules and travel formalities which need to be completed before undertaking any outbound travel. All travellers are governed by the rules and regulations which are in force in the country which is being visited.

Travel regulations are necessary for the security of the country being visited. They protect the country from the entry of illegal migrants, terrorists, and criminals, and illegal traffic of banned goods such as narcotics and drugs, animal hides, explosives, arms, etc.

Certain formalities need to be completed by tourists before they can leave their country or enter another country. This is in the interest of the tourist as well as the country being visited. These formalities are in the form of official documents and endorsements which need to be procured well in advance. Completing the necessary formalities in the form of obtaining a valid passport or getting a visa should be completed before finalizing other details of travel, as these processes are time consuming and may take a couple of weeks. Without the requisite documents, travel is not possible abroad. Generally there is no restriction on Indian and foreign nationals visiting any state in India except for the border states and islands, for which a special entry permit is required.

Most travel formalities are compulsory while others are desirable. The travel agent should discuss the benefits of completing all formalities before the client embarks on a trip. Travel formalities which need to be completed before undertaking any travel abroad are as follows:

1. Passport
2. Visa
3. Compulsory vaccinations
4. Travel insurance
5. Foreign exchange
6. Restricted area permits

Tourists should be familiarized with customs regulations, baggage allowed, and goods permitted to be carried in their hand baggage to avoid offloading of items at the airport.

PASSPORT

A passport is an official document issued by a competent public authority of a country to its nationals, to help the holder to cross any border or port of the country, without any hindrance or delay. It is issued only when the government does not have any objection for the person to leave his country. It is also a document of the highest legal order.

The passport is issued in the name of the country, i.e. the president/chancellor/king, etc. It is a booklet issued to the holder by the Ministry of External Affairs with the help of the Ministry of Home Affairs. The passport is the holder's international identity which shows the holder's national status in the world.

Every passenger going abroad must possess a passport or other official documents of identity. These documents establish the bearer's identity and nationality and authorize them to travel outside their own country. It is a permission to pass the port.

To be valid for international travel, a passport must be used within the period of validity specified on it. It contains a photograph of the holder, and bear endorsements and visas/tourist permits required for the journey. It is on the basis of this document with its endorsements that a national of a country is permitted to leave his/her country for a certain period of time, for an entry into a foreign land for various purposes. It does not ask for religion, caste, or creed but only for the place of origin of the individual.

Passports usually indicate the countries for which they are valid, or that they are valid for all countries. If a passport is valid for most countries, excepting a few, the latter will be listed separately.

The public authorities competent to issue passports and other documents of identification vary from one country to another. Outside the country of residence, these documents can be issued by the diplomatic or consular offices representing the country concerned. Any citizen of the country can apply for a passport and if the government has no objection to issue him/her the same, then the External Affairs Ministry will issue him/her a passport. To apply for a passport, the holder must be enjoying the citizenship of the country whose passport has been applied for.

Citizenship

The Oxford dictionary defines the term citizen as 'a member of a state or Commonwealth, either native or naturalized' or 'an inhabitant of a city' or 'a free man of a city'. A person can get only one citizenship and can hold only one passport at a time. However, some countries nowadays are offering dual citizenship, for example, India.

Citizenship can be awarded to a person on the basis of the following six conditions:

By birth   By being born in a particular nation or a country, a person is entitled to receive that country's citizenship. For example, if Mrs X, who is an Indian citizen, gives birth to a child in the USA, then the child would automatically get American citizenship.

Through parents   One can get the citizenship of parents by natural course.

By normalization or by application   If a person is settled in a particular country for many years and then wishes to have citizenship of that country, he/she would receive citizenship, only after fulfillment of all government procedures. For example, a person enters the USA on a student visa and continues his/her studies. After his/her stay in the USA for 10 years, he/she applies for a green card and then applies for a citizenship.

Political asylum   Political asylum is given only in extraordinary situations, especially to those who have become victims of political/social problems. For example, during the Fascist regime many Jews fled from Germany and took shelter in the USA and were given political asylum. Salman Rushdie, a famous writer has been given political asylum by the UK. Even Bangladeshi writer Taslima Nasreen is under political asylum in India. As these people's lives are in danger in their respective countries, they are being given political asylum by other countries.

Through marriage   If one of the spouses holds a different citizenship then if the other spouse wishes, he/she can get the spouse's citizenship. For example, Mr. X from India goes to the USA and then marries Ms. Y, who is an American citizen, then if Mr. X wishes he could get American citizenship or vice versa.

Citizenship by honour or invitation   This is given only to very extraordinary persons. For example, when Neil Armstrong returned from the Moon, many countries honoured him by giving their citizenship.

Definition

A passport can be defined as an official document which is issued by a government or competent public authority, identifying a traveller as a citizen or a national of a country, giving particulars about him/her (with his/her photograph), and recognizing his/her right to return to that country. The word passport has originated from the French meaning, passer, i.e. to pass through any port, or harbour.

Apart from bearing details of the national identity of the passport holder, the passport generally requests that he/she be allowed to pass the port (border) freely without any hindrance and that he/she should be given protection and assistance, when necessary. A passport entitles or authorizes a citizen or national to leave a country and the right to return to it.

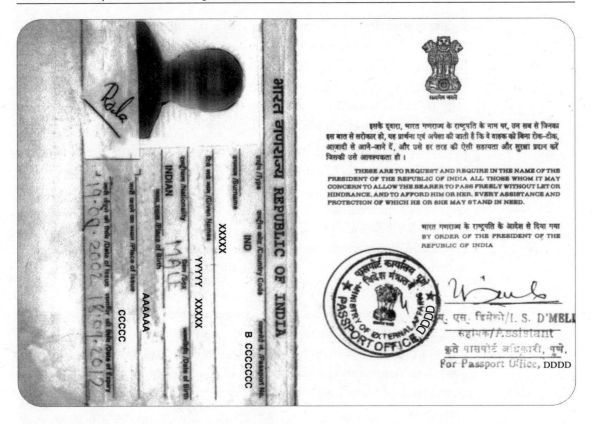

Fig 8.1   A passport is used as a proof of identity

Figure 8.1 shows the identity of a passport holder. A passport can be used as the following:

- means of access to another country
- means of identification (nationality)
- evidence of legal entry into another country.

Some countries still allow joint passports. That means that two or more people travelling together can hold a single joint passport. Spouses and/or their children may obtain a joint passport. The passport holder may also travel using the passport without being accompanied by those who are included on the passport, provided that they remain at their country of residence.

All passports generally bear the following information of the passport holder, which may vary from country to country.

- Family name/surname
- Given name

- Nationality
- Place of birth
- Date of issue
- Holder's signature
- Name of father/legal guardian
- Name of spouse
- Validity period (expiry date)
- Endorsement
- Emigration status
- Date of birth
- Gender
- Place of issue
- Holder's photograph
- Name of mother
- Address
- Children
- Validity for certain countries as well as restrictions to travel to others

Types of Passport

Three types of passports are currently issued in India. They are as follows:

Ordinary or normal passport   This dark blue coloured passport is issued to any ordinary citizen of India.

Official passport   This white/grey coloured passport is issued to government officials or other persons travelling on government missions. The request to issue such a passport has to be made by the concerned person's department along with personal information of the applicant.

Diplomatic consular passport   This red coloured passport is issued to persons holding diplomatic or consular status as per international law and custom.

Although most people will travel with a passport, it should be noted that other travel documents can also be used in lieu of a passport. These documents are valid only for limited countries and purposes. Therefore, it is always necessary to check carefully whether such documents are recognized by the country of the passenger's destination and transit, even if such documents bear an endorsement for such countries. The travel agent should contact the issuing authority to check that it can be used for any travel arrangements being organized by him.

Other Documents Required to Pass a Port

The following are special kinds of documents, issued in special circumstances that can be used instead of a passport.

Bona fide certificate   Issued to domiciles for travel to Nepal or Bhutan.

Pilgrim pass   This is issued by the Hajj Committee for Hajj, Umma, and Zirat pilgrims. Every year approximately 21,000 such passes are issued by the Hajj Committee. Every state of India has a quota for such passes.

Continuous discharge certificate (CDC)   It is issued to those seamen who have to join on duty or go off duty. It is issued by the directorate general of shipping.

Military I-cards   These are issued to defence personnel. For example, for goodwill visits of naval ships.

The status of the passport is much higher than the above mentioned papers. The basic difference in this is that, while the holder of any type of passport can travel anywhere and for any purpose, the documents mentioned above are special documents which are issued for specific travel only.

Responsibility of Travel Agent

It is the responsibility of the travel agent to ensure that the passport is valid for

- the country to which the client is travelling and
- the period of time for which the client intends visiting a country.

A passport is normally issued for 10 years and is usually valid for all countries of the world. If the passport is not valid in a specific country it is mentioned in the passport. However, the agent can also get detailed information in the Travel Information Manual (TIM).

An agent may be confronted with several passports from various countries and should always check the validity because it may vary. The expiry date of the passport is very important, and can be located in different places within the passport according to the country of issue. It must never be assumed that all passports are the same as those issued in one's country, and the validity of the passport should be checked with regard to which countries it covers, and that it has not, or will not, expire during the course of travel. It should be noted that some countries demand that a passport has a minimum validity available after the client intends to leave a country. Therefore, this also needs to be checked. For example, India requires six months validity. The agent on checking the passport should be able to determine the client's nationality. A person is considered to be of the nationality of the passport he/she is travelling on, regardless of where he/she was born or if he/she holds dual citizenship. In this regard, it is wise to ensure that a client who has dual nationality travels on the passport which the agent has actually seen.

The travel agent should carefully check all travel arrangements and intentions of those travelling on a joint passport to see that they intend to stay together. The agent should recommend separate passports if he feels that a family may split.

The agent should also check if the child included on a joint passport qualifies for such passport. Some countries will only allow children less than 16 years of age to be included. A child over 16 years of age or those turning 16 during the intended travel will require a separate passport. The joint passport will have to be returned to cancel the child's name from that passport before a separate passport is issued.

The travel agent should always inform the passport holder or his/her client the following:

1. The passport is a valuable document. It should always be either in a person's own custody or in the custody of a person duly authorized by him/her. It must not be altered or mutilated in any way (see Example 8.1). If lost or destroyed it should be immediately reported to the nearest Indian Mission and to the local police.

2. It is an offence under the Indian Passports Act 1967 to give false information in the application. Passport facilities can be denied on grounds of suppression of factual information, submission of false particulars, willful damage of passport, and for making unauthorized changes in the passport.

3. A photocopy of the passport should be kept in a safe place. Without this, relevant issuance of a duplicate passport in case of loss/damage/theft may be delayed.

4. The expiry date of the passport should be checked on receiving it for the first time and one should remember to get the passport renewed well in advance of the expiry date.

Example 8.1

On an Air India flight, a passenger travelling from Dubai to Trivandrum decided to take a dessert—gulab jamun—served on the flight to him, home. He put the sweet in a plastic bag and put the bag in his pouch. On arrival, to his dismay, he found that the sugar syrup had got into his passport. One must remember that a passport is an identity. One should keep it safe and away from food and drink.

If the passport is lost/stolen locally, the passport holder should inform the nearest police station, register a complaint and then inform the passport office.

While travelling abroad if a passport is lost then the holder should take the following steps:

- inform the embassy immediately;
- register a police complaint and inform the issuing passport office; and
- obtain a certificate or travel document from the consulate which would enable the holder to travel.

One should remember the exact name that has been mentioned in the passport and the method of writing the name should not be changed.

In the countries where India does not have an embassy, one needs to enquire about the embassy, through which the citizens of India are being looked after. Normally, it is the British High Commission who takes care of the Indians in absence of Indian Embassy, as India is a member of the Commonwealth.

Documents Required while Applying for a Passport

Applicants can apply for a passport through online registration and get printouts of the application form. Apart from this, they can submit the form directly in the respective passport office/district passport centres/ speed post centres. A sample passport application form is enclosed in Appendix 8.1.

Along with the application form, one needs to submit the following:

Photographs Three recent passportsize photographs in colour showing frontal view of full face are required. Black and white photographs, photographs with coloured or dark glasses or in uniform, polaroid prints, or computer prints are not accepted.

Address proof Photocopies of the first and last page of the ration card, election card, telephone bill, electricity bill, bank account statement, certificate from employer of a reputed company on the official letter head, gas connection bill, or water bill, that bear the applicant's address details.

Date of birth proof Photocopies of the birth certificate or school leaving certificate.

Citizenship document This is required if the applicant is a citizen of India by registration or naturalization.

Identity certificate Government, public sector, and employees of statutory bodies should submit their identity certificate in original.

No objection certificate This should be submitted in original, if the person applying is a government employee.

Affidavit/marriage certificate For change of name on passport after marriage.

Letter of authority Required for travel agents.

Supporting documents These are needed as a proof for Emigration Clearance Not Required (ECNR) status.

In case of minors, copies of the parents' passports, and a consent letter from both parents are required.

Various Services Offered by the Passport Office

The passport office offers the following services on payment of fixed fee.

1. New passport, thirty six pages (also for renewal after expiry of ten years)
2. New passport jumbo, sixty pages (also for renewal after expiry of ten years)
3. New passport for minor children (under 18 years of age), five years' validity
4. Additional booklet, thirty six pages
5. Additional booklet jumbo, sixty pages
6. Duplicate passport (in lieu of lost/damaged passport)
7. Change of name—maiden to married, or otherwise (issue of a new passport booklet)
8. Extension of short validity passports (in lieu of lost/damaged passport)
9. Emergency travel document
10. Renewal of emergency travel document
11. Identity certificate
12. Renewal of identity certificate
13. Endorsement on identity certificate
14. Issue of duplicate identity certificate
15. Tatkaal scheme (out of turn passport issue)

Relevant documents should be submitted for the above passport services as per the guidelines available with the passport office.

New passport or renewal after 10 years

Passports are valid for 10 years. The application for a new passport has to be made when the applicant's old passport has completed 10 years. It can also be renewed one year before the expiry of the passport. This service can be rendered on passports only up to a total of 10 years, which is the prescribed life of an Indian passport booklet, after which the validity cannot be extended on the same booklet, and therefore a new booklet needs to be issued and applied for. Also, in case of possession of a duplicate passport, 10 years have to be counted from the date of issue of the original passport, in lieu of which the duplicate passport has been issued.

The application needs to be made on the application form for an Indian passport. Other requirements are as follows:

1. Old passport (in original)
2. Passport size photographs showing frontal view of full face
3. Photocopy of the first four and last four pages of the old passport, including ECR/ECNR page
4. Pages indicating visa

Duplicate passports (in lieu of lost/damaged passports)

The applications for duplicate passport are not accepted by post and neither are the passports dispatched by post. The applicant has to go in person for filing the application for a duplicate passport. Exceptions can be made with prior approval of the passport officer or the consular officer only under special circumstances.

The application form should be submitted along with the following documents:

1. Copy of police report or complaint number with date
2. Photographs
3. Copy of personal verification form in 'prescribed proforma'
4. Required fee
5. In case of a student, a letter from the school/college is required
6. Photocopy of the previous (lost) passport
7. Photocopy of driving licence/a letter by the employer, if applicable
8. Address proof
9. An application on a plain paper giving reasons for the loss of passport.

It is important to furnish full, accurate, and truthful information on the form. Misrepresentation of facts may entail denial of passport facilities.

Applications which are received with incomplete details are not processed by the passport office. A duplicate passport may not be issued for the second loss/damage of passport. People who habitually lose their passports are subjected to enquiry.

It normally takes three months in completing the process and duplicate passports are issued only on receipt of clearance from the concerned authorities. In case the passport is required urgently for personal or business travel, a special request can be made to the passport officer or the consular officer for a one year validity passport.

Change of name

The change of name service is restricted to change of name in the passport. For change of name a new booklet is issued and the old booklet cancelled and returned to the applicant. Application has to be made in the application form for new passport. Photographs have to be submitted and a fee as applicable is charged.

In case of change from maiden name to married name, substitution of father's name with the husband's name, or in case of divorcees applying for change of name or for substitution of husband's name with father's name in existing passport, the following documents have to be submitted.

1. Original passport
2. Attested copy of the marriage certificate along with original or copy of the divorce deed duly authenticated by court along with the original as applicable
3. Husband's passport
4. In case of remarried ladies (married ladies applying for change of name/husband's name in case of remarriage after divorce or death of husband), divorce deed or death certificate as the case may be in respect of her first husband

In all other cases, change of name is to be advertised in a daily newspaper (circulation in the area of permanent and present residence); submission of original newspaper clippings; and an affidavit on change of name, duly notarized in the prescribed proforma has to be submitted in addition to the above.

Tatkaal scheme (out of turn issuing of passport)

If an applicant desires to obtain his/her passport under the tatkaal scheme, a verification certificate and standard affidavit should be submitted along with the tatkaal fee. No proof of urgency is required for out-of-turn issue of passport. Post police verification is done for all passports issued under this scheme.

A passport may also be obtained on submission of only three documents provided. A photo identity document, at least one identity proof such as ration card, pan card, etc. as well as a standard affidavit on non-judicial stamp paper duly attested by a notary are required.

The charges for a fresh passport are as follows:

Days	Tatkaal charges (Rs)	Passport fee (Rs)
1–7	1500.00	1000.00
8–14	1000.00	1000.00

VISA

Visa (visitors intended stay abroad) is a permit which allows a citizen of one country to enter into another country for a designated period and for a specific purpose. The visa is issued in the form of an endorsement or rubber stamp on a passport. Therefore, it is necessary to submit the passport at the time when the visa is applied for. Some countries do not stamp visas into the passport, but issue them in loose form. In this case, no record appears in the passport.

A visa is normally obtained from the embassies and consulates of the country to where travel is intended. If there is no representative in the country to issue a visa, it may be essential to send the passport abroad in order to obtain it. In this case, the applicant should have legal status in the country from which he/she applies. If the person who requires the visa is not a resident or citizen of the country, then it may be necessary for that person to obtain the visa on arrival.

For some countries it is essential that the citizens of other designated countries obtain a visa prior to arrival in their country. In some countries, such as Hong Kong, Malaysia, and Mauritius, the visa can be obtained on arrival in the country.

The travel agents should check the citizenship of their clients and the visa requirements for the countries they intend to travel.

Definition

'A visa is an entry made by a consular official of a government in a passport or other travel document, which indicates that the bearer has

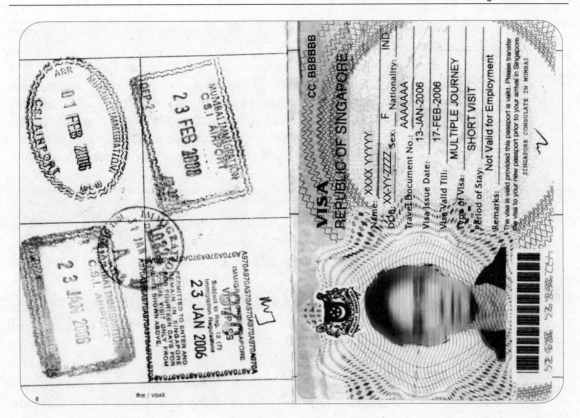

Fig 8.2   Visa stamped before departure for Singapore

been granted permission to enter or re-enter the country concerned. It generally mentions the authorized length of stay, the period of validity and the number of times a person is allowed entry (single or multiple entry), during that period.'

Visas are issued for single entry or multiple entries. A single entry visa will not be valid if it has been used once, even when the validity date has not expired. In the case of multiple entry visas, its validity expires on the date of its expiry. The date of the entry stamp is imprinted on the passport when a person arrives in the country concerned (see Fig. 8.2). This stamp can be placed on the page bearing the visa or on another page. It shows that the visa has been used.

Entry is normally granted to a foreigner after the visa has been issued. However, the final decision regarding entry into any country rests with the immigration officials at the entry point. They may deny entry to any visitor (see Example 8.2).

Example 8.2

A fellow passenger on-board was quite excited as he was flying for the first time. He was going from Mumbai to Singapore. On arrival at Singapore, when the immigration official asked him the purpose of his visit, he confessed that he had come to see the city for two/three days and would buy a dozen cell phones, a few cameras to cover his expenses and go back. He was refused entry on the spot, his visa was cancelled and he was sent back on the first available flight.

The visa system is important as it helps the immigration officials in keeping a tab on the number of visitors that are likely to travel to and from a country. The visa regulations are usually the bilateral agreement between two countries.

Visas are also required for children. If a child travels on an adult passport, the visa in that passport must mention that it is valid for both the child as well as the adult concerned.

Travel Information Manual

The travel agents should keep themselves updated and give accurate information to their clients. This information is available in the Travel Information Manual (TIM). The main purpose of TIM is to provide airlines, their agents, and other businesses in the travel industry with up to date, official information on government travel regulations. It is published in English by the IATA Netherlands Data Publications in a book form, every month and can also be accessed via the computer reservation system (CRS). TIM is updated each month and provides a valuable source of information regarding government requirements for international air travel to more than 200 countries worldwide. It contains detailed information related to passports, visas, health, airport tax, customs, and currency.

Information regarding checking of documents at the time of departure, while in transit and on arrival at the destination is given in TIM for each country, as rules differ from one country to another for all essential documents and procedures.

An agent should never assume that a traveller, regardless of how well travelled he/she may be, knows all the regulations. Example 8.3 and Example 8.4 give some important information to a traveller.

Example 8.3

This may sound weird, but it is true. An Air India flight from Kuwait which was going to Mumbai was re-routed via Chennai. About six passengers requested that as they planned to go to Chennai by train after reaching Mumbai, they should be allowed to deplane at Chennai. They also did not have any check-in baggage.

So what was the hurdle? Well, the fare between Kuwait to Chennai was Rs 4500 more than the Kuwait–Mumbai fare and they would be required to pay the difference if they wanted to get off at Chennai.

Fares depend on point to point destination and convenience.

Example 8.4

If you are planning a flight from Mumbai to Singapore and have an onward connection to Australia, book your ticket as Mumbai–Australia.

In case your initial flight from BOM–SIN (Mumbai–Singapore) is delayed, then getting you a timely connection, food, and hotel accommodation becomes the airline's responsibility.

Most of the travel agencies offer a visa service, and charge a fee for this. The agent must first find out the nationality of the client by checking the passport on which he/she intends to travel. Once the nationality has been identified, the agent must then look at the visa regulations which can be checked from TIM. TIM relates to air travel and if a client is travelling by land, different regulations may apply. The agent should check the complete passport and see what other visas are contained in it. Many countries have strict rules regarding some of the 'controversial areas' because of racial or political unrest. The travel agent should concern himself/herself with visas for business or tourist purpose. Clients who want to travel abroad with the aim of settling there or immigrating should be referred to the country concerned which will have the necessary related rules and regulations. A tourist's visa is stamped in the passport on arrival at a country (see Fig. 8.3).

When the agent has obtained a visa on behalf of a client, it is the responsibility of the travel agent to check that the visa has been issued correctly along with its validity and as per the client's requirements. The visas will indicate the number of entries permitted, the validity period and the maximum period that a client can stay in the country. If the visa

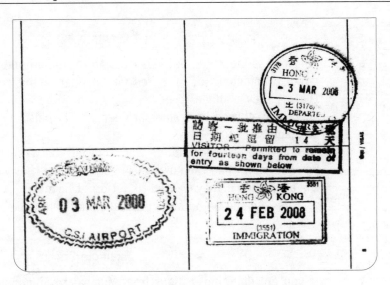

Fig 8.3   Visa stamped on arrival in Hong Kong

Exhibit 8.1

Some important facts regarding visas
• Visa and immigration laws vary from one country to another.
• One must check the validity and correctness of the visa stamp before embarking on the journey.
• Having a visa does not guarantee an entry to the host country. The border-crossing authorities take the final decision to allow entry and may even cancel a visa if they are not satisfied with the visa status.
• Entering a country without a valid visa or visa exemption may result in detention and deportation.
• After entering the country, the validity period of a visa can often be extended for a fee at the discretion of the immigration authorities.
• The validity of a visa is not the same as the authorized period of stay in the issuing country. For example, if a visa has been issued on 1 January 2008 and expires on 30 March 2008 (authorized period of stay 90 days), then the 90 day authorized stay starts from the date of arrival which has to be between 1 January and 30 March 2008. If the person reaches on 1 March, he/she could stay in the issuing country until 30 May 2008.
• A single entry visa gets cancelled as soon as the holder enters the issuing country. For example, a single entry visa may be granted for six months, but if the holder enters the country after 50 days the visa becomes invalid.

is in a foreign language or is not clear, then the agent should check with the authorities concerned, if the client has any queries. Exhibit 8.1 shows some important facts regarding visas.

Types of Visas

Visas are also referred to as permits by some countries. There are many types of visas and different countries may call these by different names.

Table 8.1 briefly describes the different types of visas, some of which are discussed further in detail.

Table 8.1 Types of visas

Type of Visa	Description
Transit visa	Usually valid for three days or less, for passing through the country to a third destination.
Tourist visa	For a limited period for leisure travel, no business activities allowed. Some countries do not issue tourist visas. Saudi Arabia introduced tourist visas only in 2004 but issues pilgrimage visas for Hajj pilgrims.
Business visa	For engaging in commerce in the country. A work visa is required for permanent employment.
Temporary worker visa	For approved employment in the host country. Generally more difficult to obtain but valid for a longer period of time than a business visa. Examples of such visas are H-1B and L-1 visas in the USA.
On-arrival visa	Granted immediately on entering a country at the airport or border control post. This is different from not requiring a visa at all. Visa is in the form of an entrance fee and is required before they can pass immigration.
Spousal visa	Granted to the spouse of a resident or citizen of a given country, to enable the couple to settle in that country. Examples include the EEA family permit of the UK.
Student visa	Allows its holder to study at an institution of higher learning in the country of issue. However, some countries such as Algeria, issue tourist visas to students.
Working holiday visa	For individuals travelling between nations offering a working holiday programme, allowing young people to undertake temporary work while travelling.
Diplomatic visa	Sometimes called an official visa, it is available exclusively to diplomatic passport holders. It confers the diplomatic status on its holder.
Courtesy visa	Issued to representatives of foreign governments or international organizations who do not qualify for diplomatic status but do merit expedited, courteous treatment. A courtesy visa does not normally confer privileges or immunities.
Journalist visa	Some countries, such as Cuba, Iran, North Korea, Saudi Arabia, Zimbabwe, and the USA, insist that journalists when travelling for their respective news organizations have a valid visa.
Fiancee visa	Granted for a limited period prior to marriage based on a proven relationship with a citizen of the destination country. For example, an Indian woman who wishes to marry an American man would obtain a fiancee visa (K-1 visa) to allow her to enter the USA.
Immigrant visa	Granted to those intending to migrate to the issuing country. They are usually issued for a single journey as the holder may be issued a permanent resident identification card permitting him unlimited entry in the issuing country.

Entry/visitor visa

This is also referred to as entry visa, entry permit, tourist visa, business visa, travel pass, etc. This visa allows a foreign national the right to enter the country for a short stay.

The conditions regarding the entry visa normally require that the traveller should possess sufficient funds for the duration of stay and proof of prepaid onward travel. It is the agent's duty to check and advise the traveller accordingly.

The validity of an entry visa is for six months to five years stay with multiple entries. The USA issues a visa for up to 10 years.

Transit visa

It authorizes the holder the right to temporarily enter into another country for the purpose of making travel connections, onward to a third country. This is normally required for people travelling through a country to another, in some cases even when continuing their journey on the same flight. The regulations vary from country to country and these should be checked in TIM. For example, some countries may demand that passengers, who transit within eight hours, do not need a visa, whereas some countries may require a passenger to obtain a transit visa even if they arrive and leave, all within a four-hour period.

If the time permitted is hardly sufficient to allow flights to connect, then it is probably wise to obtain an alternative visa that would allow for unforeseen circumstances such as flight delay or cancellation, especially as this can sometimes require an overnight stay.

Without a proper visa, a client can be put under supervision by the immigration authorities if the transit visa expires, and the majority of passengers find this uncomfortable. The best thing is to explain the situation to a client and allow him/her the choice of a transit visa or some other type of visa which allows a stay if necessary. As the cost will probably be more to obtain a visitor's visa, some passengers may prefer to take the risk. The validity is usually for 15 days only.

Transit without visa

A transit visa is not normally required for a passenger (except as specified) who has to spend a few hours in the transit zone of the airport to change flights. This exemption will come under the heading transit without visa (TWOV). Many countries have certain agreements which will allow the citizens of other countries to transit their country without the need to obtain a visa.

The period of validity of a TWOV will vary from one country to another.

In certain cases, transit passengers are permitted to leave the airport for a short period, for example, 24, 48, or 72 hours, provided they hold tickets with confirmation and other reservations for onward or return travel. For example, at the Changi Airport, Singapore, short city tours are arranged by shuttle bus for transit passengers to see Singapore instead of waiting in the transit lounge. Similar facilities are also available at other airports, for example, at the Schiphol Airport, Amsterdam.

Re-entry permits

Where necessary, these permits allow travellers to return to their country of domicile.

Exit visa

Exit visa gives the right to a traveller to leave a country. These permits or visas may be necessary for citizens to leave their own country of domicile. Exit visa may be required by foreign nationals to leave a country through which they had been travelling, or by expatriates.

Schengen visa

The Schengen states comprise Austria, Belgium, Denmark, Finland, France, Germany, Greece, Iceland, Italy, Luxembourg, Netherlands, Norway, Portugal, Spain, and Sweden. The Schengen is an agreement between these member states of the European Union (EU), to remove immigration controls for travel within and between these countries. This borderless region is known as *Schengen Area*. The Schengen Agreement was created on 26 March 1995. There are four types of Schengen visas:

Type A: Airport transit visa   This is required for those nationals who cannot use the TWOV facility at all, as they are in direct transit in a Schengen country when arriving and are departing from/to non-Schengen countries. The passengers in general, cannot leave the airport.

Type B: Transit visa   This is required for passengers who are making a transit in the Schengen territory, exceeding the allowed transit time, and for passengers who are transiting in more than one Schengen country.

Type C: Short period visa   (Maximum three months) This is the common Schengen visa, issued by any one of the fifteen states and is valid for all others.

Type D: Long period national visa This visa is issued in case of a longer period or for other special cases which is issued by an individual Schengen state on a national basis. This particular visa is valid for the country of issue only.

When applying for either a Type B or Type C visa for visiting/transiting for only one Schengen state, then an application should be made at the consulate or the embassy of that country. When the passenger has to apply for several Schengen states, the application should be made at the consulate or the embassy of the country which is the main destination of visit. In case of application of several Schengen states and not having a main destination, the application has to be made at the consulate or embassy of the country which is the first point of entry into the Schengen states. If the above regulations while applying are not complied with, then there is a possibility of refusal of entry and also investigation by the immigration officers.

Requirements for Visas

Many travel agents offer visa services to their customers. A fee is normally charged for this service. The procedure for applying for a visa is usually same when the travel agent applies on his client's behalf and also when the client applies directly. Visa forwarding services (VFS) is an organization available in major cities in India for the convenience of travellers. VFS provides its services with the official approval of the government of the country for which a visa is required. VFS fee has government approval. The VFS is a completely different organization operating under Indian law and is not an agent of the government. It is not mandatory to go through VFS and the visas may be obtained directly by applying for the same through the embassy, high commission, or the consulate; or through a travel agent.

Given below are the general requirements of documents, applicable for obtaining a visa.

1. Original passport valid for minimum six months from the expiry of the visa
2. Latest passport size photographs (as per the requirement of the country of travel)
3. Visa form duly filled and signed as per the signature in the passport by the applicant
4. Overseas mediclaim policy valid for the total period of travel

5. Foreign exchange, to be endorsed in the passport, or a copy of an international credit card
6. Covering letter on company letterhead mentioning the applicant's name, designation, purpose, and duration of visit (for business purpose)
7. Covering letter from the applicant stating purpose and duration of visit (for tourism purpose)
8. For partnership companies, partnership deed to be enclosed
9. For Pvt Ltd Co, the memorandum and articles of association
10. Original income tax papers for last three years
11. Original bank passbook/bank account statement for minimum three months
12. Property papers
13. Fixed deposit certificates
14. No objection certificate if working in a government organization
15. Form 16A, salary slip, or TDS for salaried persons
16. If retired then retirement letter and/or pension proof
17. Marriage certificate, wedding card, or photograph of marriage for newly wedded couples
18. No objection certificate from parents if a minor accompanying other than parents
19. Bona fide certificate/identity card from the school if students
20. ECNR status
21. No objection certificate letter from husband/father for ladies travelling alone

Fee as applicable needs to be paid. If a person is travelling for the first time, consulate may insist for personal interview. The visa regulations differ from country to country. These should be checked by the travel agent from the embassy/consulate.

Visa Refusal

An applicant may be denied a visa if he/she

- has committed fraud or misrepresentation in the application;
- does not have a legitimate reason for the journey;
- does not have lodging in the destination country;
- has no visible means of sustenance;
- has not arranged his/her transportation;
- does not have a valid health/travel insurance for the destination and the duration of stay;

- has a criminal record or has criminal charges pending;
- is considered to be a security risk;
- has had his/her prior visa applications rejected;
- is a citizen of a country with whom the host country does not have an amicable relation;
- has previous immigration violations;
- has a communicable disease such as tuberculosis; and
- is in an advanced stage of pregnancy (see Example 8.5).

Example 8.5

A family of three was denied entry to the USA at Chicago airport, as the lady was seven months pregnant and the immigration officer suspected that she had come to the USA to her sister-in-law's place to deliver her baby and get American citizenship for the child. She had not declared that she was pregnant when she had applied for a visa a month ago in India.

The visa requirements for some major countries are given in Appendix 8.2.

HEALTH REGULATIONS FOR INTERNATIONAL TRAVEL

The World Health Organization (WHO) prepares and reviews the international sanitary regulations and proposes measures to prevent the spread of epidemic throughout the world. As per the WHO norms, vaccination of persons who arrive from infected areas, against certain diseases such as plague, cholera, yellow fever, hepatitis etc. is compulsory. A valid immunization certificate as approved by WHO should be completed and signed by a competent authority.

Travellers should acquaint themselves with the health regulations in force for the country of origin, country of transit, and the destinations they propose to visit, to avoid inconvenience. The travel agents should advise the travellers on the vaccinations and preventive health precautions to be undertaken while travelling. A sample health questionnaire format is enclosed as Appendix 8.3.

The WHO collects and publishes the health requirements of individual countries in the form of a booklet called 'International Travel and Health'. TIM can also be used as a source of reference on health as it describes exactly what is required at the airports. The Official Airline Guide (OAG)

Health Supplement Guide, which is published quarterly by OAG worldwide, also gives information on passports, visas, and vaccinations that are necessary or recommended.

The required vaccinations can be given by a family doctor or an official health authority as per the regulations, which are in force in the country of departure, and the destination country. A health certificate is given by the doctor to the travellers when they receive the compulsory vaccinations. Other vaccinations, which are not compulsory, do not need a health certificate. But these may be recommended for travel to certain countries, such as the tropical regions of Africa and South America.

Compulsory Vaccinations

There are two types of immunizations, which are compulsory and recommended. The compulsory vaccinations are required only by certain countries. Some countries may recommend certain immunizations, especially when the travellers normally travel outside the urban areas.

The travellers should therefore be advised to obtain a health certificate, proving that they have been vaccinated for a specified infectious disease (either yellow fever or cholera). If they are not able to produce the same, they could be deported back out of the country or they could be detained and kept in quarantine.

An internationally recognized certificate is generally required by travellers if they have to be vaccinated against certain diseases. The certificate has to be produced by the traveller at the point of entry into the country.

The WHO international certificate of vaccination can usually be obtained from health clinics, doctors, and health authorities. In order for the certificate of vaccination to be valid, it must bear the name of vaccination, the date, and should be signed by the concerned authorities in the country of issue. Cholera and yellow fever are the only vaccinations which are normally required for travelling to certain countries.

When yellow fever and cholera vaccinations are taken together they require up to twenty days to become effective. Yellow fever vaccinations are valid for ten years, beginning ten days after the vaccination, whereas cholera vaccinations are valid for six months, beginning six days after the first injection. Travellers should therefore plan their vaccinations accordingly. Some vaccinations can be obtained up to a month before departing on a trip abroad. Travellers should thus keep a record of their vaccinations along with the date as the period of protection offered by vaccinations differs widely.

Travellers should also be advised to take out travel insurance before they embark. Medical insurance companies provide coverage for certain expenditure incurred on accidents, medical treatment, etc. In certain countries medical insurance is compulsory.

SPECIAL PERMITS FOR RESTRICTED AREAS

Domestic and foreign tourists normally do not have restrictions for movement within India. But a special entry permit is required for tourists for the border states and the islands of Andaman, Nicobar and Lakshadweep. In some areas, only foreigners are required to obtain a permit. This permit is valid for fifteen days only and should be applied for at least two weeks in advance. This permit can be issued by either the Ministry of Home Affairs or the Foreigners Regional Registration Offices (FRRO), located in New Delhi, Mumbai, Chennai, and Kolkata, or the Indian Diplomatic Missions abroad.

The tourist groups should consist of four to 20 people. Special permits are required for the following areas:

Assam

Kaziranga National Park, Manas National Park, Guwahati, and Kamakhya temple. Permits are issued for a stay of 10 days to those travelling in groups.

Meghalaya

Shillong. Permits are issued for a stay of seven days to those travelling in groups.

West Bengal

1. Darjeeling and adjoining areas (Tiger Hill, Lebong Race Course, Jorabunglow, Ghoom, and Kurseong). Permits are issued (also by Home Department of West Bengal) for a stay of 15 days to those travelling individually or in groups.
2. Sandakphu and Phalut areas in Darjeeling and wildlife sanctuaries at Mahananda and Simchal, and Jaldapara, Chapramari and Goruari in Jalpaiguri district. Permits are issued for a stay of seven days only to those travelling in groups (protected area).

Sikkim (protected area)

1. Gangtok, Rumtek, and Phodang. Permits for seven days are issued to those travelling individually or in groups.
2. Zongry and West Sikkim. A 15-day permit is issued to groups coming for trekking.
3. Pomayangtse. A two-day permit is issued to groups coming for trekking. Permits are issued only by the Ministry of Home Affairs.

Manipur (protected area)

Imphal, Loktak Lake, Moirang, INA Memorial, Kaibil Deer Sanctuary, Waillye Lake, and Konyom War Memorial. Permits for three days are issued to groups only and exclusively by the Ministry of Home Affairs.

Andaman and Nicobar Islands

1. Municipal area of Port Blair and Havelock Island. Permits for 15 days and night visits are issued to those travelling individually or in groups.
2. Jolly Buoy, South and North Cinque, Red Skin, and Neil. Permits for day visits only are issued to those travelling in groups. Permits are also issued by the immigration officer at Port Blair.

Lakshadweep

Bangaram, Suheli, and Tilkam Islands. Permits for a stay of seven days are issued to those travelling in groups only, by the Ministry of Home Affairs and the administrator of Lakshadweep.

CUSTOMS REGULATIONS

In the olden days, a trader was free to bring in goods and exchange them for local products which he could take back to his country. In the medieval and later ages, however, the traveller had to undergo a customs check and a duty was imposed which differed from country to country. In the nineteenth century, many countries formulated their frontier regulations due to the increasing number of travellers.

World Wars I and II witnessed an even larger number of people crossing their national borders. The customs checks became stricter and the collection of duty helped the countries to earn revenue. The tourist was treated like any other visitor by the customs authorities even when his motive was not for trade, employment, or permanent stay. The situation improved a little in the post-war period, but the tourist still had to undergo the customs checks and duties. In 1949, a multilateral convention was signed by nine European nations to grant special facilities to tourists from their countries under the UN Economic Commission for Europe, one of the ECOSOC subordinate commissions. Due to the success of this convention, ECOSOC convened in 1954, the General Customs Conference in New York. Two conventions were adopted as a result of this conference which were the '1954 Convention Concerning Customs Facilities for Touring' and the 'Customs Convention of the Temporary Importation of Private Road Vehicles (1954)'.

The conventions agreed that a tourist was entitled to bring in his 'personal effects' which should be allowed free and treated as a duty-free allowance, provided, none of the items listed in personal effects was supposed to be used for commercial purposes. The personal effects were listed and included one still camera, a movie camera, one portable gramophone, one sound recorder, one radio set, a portable typewriter, sports equipment, fixed quantities of cigarettes, cigars, or tobacco, a bottle of wine, and a quarter litre of spirits and perfume. The 1963 International Tourism and Travel Conference, however, recommended more liberalization of the above allowance.

Many countries have now established their own individual frontier regulations. The regulations of each country can be obtained from the travel agents, information offices of governments, public carriers, TIM, etc.

Customs regulations relate to the rules and regulations of the transport of articles and species from one country to another. The import and export of certain articles are prohibited and the rules differ in each country. A duty has to be paid if the traveller exceeds the limit for permitted items. This duty collected by the customs officials is a source of revenue for the country. Most countries allow concessions on certain items.

Clearance of Incoming Passengers

For the purpose of customs clearance of incoming passengers, a two channel system is adopted by the customs officials. They are

1. Green channel for passengers not having any dutiable goods
2. Red channel for passengers having dutiable goods

However, all the passengers have to file correct declaration of their baggage. The passengers at the green channel have to deposit the customs portion of the disembarkation card with the customs official at the gate before leaving the terminal. Foreign exchange/currency also has to be declared before the customs officers in the following two cases:

1. Where the value of foreign currency notes exceed USD 5000 or equivalent
2. Where the aggregate value of foreign exchange including currency exceeds USD 10,000 or equivalent

If passengers walk through the green channel with dutiable/prohibited goods they are liable to prosecution/penalty, and confiscation of goods. Trafficking of narcotics and psychotropic substances is a serious offence and is punishable with imprisonment.

Table 8.2 shows articles which are allowed duty free. A tourist arriving in India shall be allowed clearance of duty-free articles in his/her bona fide baggage to the extent as mentioned below.

Table 8.2 Articles allowed free of duty for tourists

Type of tourist	Articles allowed free of duty
1. Tourists of Indian origin other than those coming from Pakistan by land route	(i) Used personal effects and travel souvenirs, if: (a) These goods are for personal use of the tourist. (b) These goods, other than those consumed during the stay in India, are re-exported when the tourist leaves India for a foreign destination. (ii) Up to Rs 25,000 worth of goods is duty-free allowances applicable to Indian residents.
2. Tourists of foreign origin other than those of Nepalese origin coming from Nepal or of Bhutanese origin coming from Bhutan or of Pakistani origin coming from Pakistan.	(i) Used personal effects and travel souvenirs, if: (a) These goods are for personal use of the tourist. (b) These goods, other than those consumed during the stay in India, are re-exported when the tourist leaves India for a foreign destination. (ii) Articles up to a value of Rs 8000 (Rs 2500 for tourists of Indian origin) for making gifts.
3. Tourists of Nepalese origin coming from Nepal or of Bhutanese origin coming from Bhutan.	No free allowance.

Contd

Table 8.2 Contd

Type of tourist	Articles allowed free of duty

4. Tourists of Pakistani origin or foreign tourists coming from Pakistan or tourists of Indian origin coming from Pakistan by land route	(i) Used personal effects and travel souvenirs, if:
	  (a) These goods are for personal use of the tourist.
	  (b) These goods, other than those consumed during the stay in India, are re-exported when the tourist leaves India for a foreign destination.
	(ii) Articles up to a value of Rs 6000 for making gifts.

In the context of baggage rules for tourists, personal effects would include the following:

1. Personal jewellery
2. One camera, with film rolls not exceeding 20
3. One video camera/camcorder with accessories and with video cassettes not exceeding 12
4. One pair of binoculars
5. One portable colour television (not exceeding fifteen centimetres in size)
6. One music system including compact disc player
7. One portable typewriter
8. One perambulator
9. One tent and other camping equipment
10. One computer (laptop/notebook)
11. One electronic diary
12. One portable wireless receiving set (transistor radio)
13. Professional equipment, instruments and apparatus or appliances including professional audio/video equipments
14. Sports equipments such as one fishing outfit, one sporting fire arm with fifty cartridges, one non-powered bicycle, one canoe or ranges less than 51 metres long, one pair of skids, two tennis rackets, one golf set (14 pieces, with a dozen golf balls).
15. One cell phone

Tourists, whether of foreign or Indian origin, are allowed the following items duty free but within their free allowance

Alcoholic drinks/cigarettes (as baggage)

(a) Fifty cigars, 200 cigarettes, or 250 grams of tobacco.
(b) Alcoholic liquor or wine up to two litres each.

Gold Any passenger of Indian origin or a passenger holding a valid passport, issued under the Passport Act 1967 (who is coming to India after a period of not less than six months' stay abroad), can import gold, to be carried as baggage. The duty has to be paid in convertible foreign currency. The weight of gold (including ornaments) should not exceed 10 kilograms per passenger. Ornaments studded with stones and pearls are not allowed to be imported.

Silver Any passenger of Indian origin (even if a foreign national) holding a valid passport issued under the Passport Act 1967 can import silver. The weight of silver (including ornaments) should not exceed the quantity of 100 kilograms per passenger.

The passenger has to obtain the permitted quantity of silver and gold from customs bonded warehouse of the State Bank of India and the Mineral and Metals Trading Corporation. A declaration has to be filed in the prescribed form before the customs officer at the time of arrival in India stating the passenger's intention to obtain the silver from the customs bonded warehouse and pay the duty before clearance.

One laptop computer (notebook computer) over and above the free passenger allowances is also allowed duty free if imported by any passenger of the age of 18 years and above. The free allowance cannot be pooled with the free allowance of any other passenger.

Foreign exchange/currency

Any person can bring into India, from a place outside India, foreign exchange, without any limit. However, declaration of foreign exchange/currency is required to be made in the prescribed currency declaration form in the following cases:

1. Where the value of foreign currency notes exceeds USD 5000 or equivalent
2. Where the aggregate value of foreign exchange, in the form of currency notes, bank notes, travellers' cheques, etc. exceeds USD 10,000, or equivalent

Indian currency

Import of Indian currency is prohibited. However, in the case of passengers normally resident of India who are returning from a visit abroad, import of Indian currency up to Rs 5000 is allowed.

Firearms

Import of firearms is strictly prohibited. Import of cartridges in excess of fifty, is also prohibited.

Import of pet animals

Domestic pets such as dogs, cats, birds, etc. are permitted to be imported. Import of pets, dogs and cats, is allowed only up to two numbers per passenger, at one time, subject to production of required health certificate from country of origin and an examination of the said pets by the concerned quarantine officer.

Outgoing Passengers

All the passengers leaving India by air are subject to clearance by customs authorities. Only bona fide baggage is allowed to be cleared by passengers. There is a procedure prescribed whereby the passengers leaving India can take the export certificate for the various high value items as well as jewellery from the customs authorities. They are required to enter the costly items on a tourist baggage re-export (TBRE) form. Such an export certificate comes handy while bringing back the things to India so that no duty is charged on such goods exported by the passenger. This form is filled by incoming tourists as well, which ensures that the costly articles are taken back on departure. Sample customs declaration form is enclosed as Appendix 8.4.

Tourists should also note the following rules while travelling.

- Export of most species of wild animals and articles made from wild flora and fauna such as ivory, musk, corals, reptile skins, furs, shahtoos, etc. is prohibited.
- Trafficking of narcotic drugs and psychotropic substances is prohibited.
- Export of Indian currency is strictly prohibited. However, Indian residents when they go abroad are allowed to take with them Indian currency not exceeding Rs 5000. Carrying Indian currency notes in the denominations of Rs 500 and Rs 1000 to Nepal is prohibited.
- Tourists while leaving India are allowed to take with them foreign currency not exceeding an amount brought in by them at the time of their arrival in India. As no declaration is required to be made for bringing in foreign exchange/currency, which does not exceed USD 10,000, or its equivalent, tourists can take, foreign exchange/currency

not exceeding the above amount, out of India with them at the time of their departure. The export of foreign currency is otherwise prohibited.

Basic Travel Quota

Under the basic travel quota (BTQ) scheme, resident Indian citizens are permitted to purchase foreign exchange up to USD 5000, or its equivalent, for undertaking in a calendar year, one or more private visits to any country abroad (except Nepal and Bhutan). The foreign exchange can be purchased directly from any branch of an authorized dealer or from a full-fledged money-changer (FFMC).

Travel under BTQ can be combined with visits for business, conference, seminar, training, study tour, Hajj pilgrimage, and employment. Persons emigrating from India and drawing foreign exchange for that purpose cannot, however, draw additional exchange under BTQ.

EMIGRATION AND IMMIGRATION

The procedure for going out of the country is called emigration. The procedure followed while entering a particular country is called immigration. The prime duty of the immigration department is to check whether the person is holding the correct documents such as passport, health documents, visas, etc. Police personnel do the immigration check. Except for Pakistan and Bangladesh, one must have immigration clearance. Sample departure and arrival forms which tourists have to fill before going out of the country (departure) or while entering a country (arrival) are enclosed as Appendix 8.5.

Emigration check is carried out at the office of protectorate of emigrants (POE) in India. Hence before one leaves the country it is necessary to have the emigration check suspended. If not, one will not be allowed to leave the country. Emigration check is not required for graduates, minors, income tax payers, doctors, or for females whose husbands are employed on ships, etc. ECNR is stamped on their passport.

Often people go out of the country and have no means of livelihood and are cheated abroad. The office of the POE is established so that these people are protected and do not fall prey to cheating. Therefore, a return ticket is required to suspend emigration check.

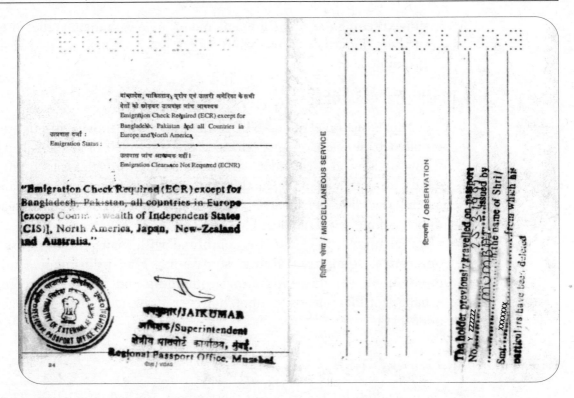

Fig 8.4 ECR stamped on a passport

The duty performed by the airport emigration is different from that of the emigration protectorate. The personnel at airport authority, who do the emigration check, are the police officials. They check for convicts, fraud cases, etc. The procedure is the same all over the world.

But if one has an airport emigration check but no POE office emigration check suspended, one will not be able to travel.

In the case of an emergency, where the office is closed and one needs to travel immediately, for example, in case of serious illness, then one can approach the assistant commissioner emigration or DCP emigration and convince them of the emergency. If the authority is convinced of the case being genuine, onewill be allowed to travel. The airlines staff does not require emigration check. Figure 8.4 shows emigration check required (ECR) stamped on a passport.

TAXES PAID BY TRAVELLERS

Travellers have to pay several taxes which are discussed as follows:

Airport Taxes

All airport taxes are generally included in the cost of the ticket and are not to be paid separately. Example 8.6 shows the total fare of a passenger flying from Mumbai to New York and back to Mumbai, via London.

Example 8.6

Break up of cost of ticket	INR
The basic fare from Mumbai to New York via London	31,390
Mumbai airport departure tax	225
London airport tax	3,198
(This is charged as the passenger is transiting through London and using the airport facility)	
US tax immigration	1,300
YC tax (customs)	233
XY tax (federal inspection fee)	296
XA tax (animal and plant health inspection services (APHIS user fee)	211
AY tax	106
YQ tax (fuel surcharge)	18,906
XF tax (US tax for pollution and congestion)	190
Total cost of ticket	Rs. 56,055

Discounts, if any, by the travel agent can only be given on the basic fare. All taxes have to be paid in full. If there is a hike in the fare for any reason such as hike in fuel prices, this fare hike is applicable only for blocked tickets and not for tickets which are already issued.

Taxes charged by the Indian Government

Travel taxes charged by the Indian Government are given below.

1. Inland Air Travel tax (IN) in India is 15 percent of basic fare amount and is applicable for all cases of purely domestic tickets when payment is made in INR.
2. Foreign travel tax (FT) for passengers departing on international flights of INR 500.
3. Passenger service fee (WO) of INR 200. For tickets issued outside India passenger service fee of USD 5 will be collected per departure.

Port Taxes

Port charges are the taxes charged to the cruise liners using the port to be docked, to avoid congestion. The amount charged depends for how long the ship will be docked. These charges are collected by the travel agent when the traveller pays for the cruise in full.

Example 8.7 shows port charges in the USA.

Example 8.7

Taxes for a cruise from Los Angeles to Cabo San Lucas to Mazatlan to Puerto Vallartra and back to Los Angeles.

Port taxes	:	USD 160
Gratuity	:	USD 73
Fuel Surcharge	:	USD 49
		USD 282

Charges are USD 350 for up to 4 days + USD 6 per night per electrical outlet.

Some of the other taxes levied are: *luxury tax on room tariffs*—up to 10 per cent on Rs 1200 and above, and four per cent on Rs 200–Rs 1199, *service tax, excise, customs, local levies,* etc. Chapter 14 provides additional information on different types of taxes.

Tax structure differs widely from one country to another. For example, in Hong Kong, fine dining restaurants add seven per cent as gratuity to the restaurant bill if there are more than six people at a table.

TRAVEL INSURANCE

Tourists going abroad need to insure themselves against any sudden and unexpected mishap, such as sickness, accident, or death, which may arise when the insured person is outside his country of origin. This is especially true for tourists visiting countries such as the USA, Europe, and Australia, where medical expenses are so steep that they can lead one to bankruptcy.

Travel insurance is needed even if one already has life insurance policies. Travel insurance or overseas mediclaim insurance policy is not a general health insurance policy, but is an insurance against any untoward incident pertaining to the health and well-being of a person which requires prompt medical attention. Apart from impairment of health it may also cover any one or all of the following clauses depending on the insurance company and the insurance plan selected.

- medical expenses cover
- total loss of checked in baggage
- loss of passport
- personal accident
- financial emergency assistance
- burglary (home contents)
- missed connections
- bounced bookings of hotels and airlines
- dental treatment
- delay of checked in baggage
- personal liability
- hijack distress allowance
- fire and allied perils (home building and contents)
- trip cancellation and interruption
- travel delay

Insurance companies offer various plans for travel to different destinations. Most insurance companies offer a comprehensive travel insurance specially designed for travellers, which covers the most likely contingencies that may occur. The insurance premium which needs to be paid by the traveller depends on the following criteria:

- destination
- purpose of visit (business/holiday)
- present state of health
- duration of journey
- age of the traveller
- number of clauses/benefits opted for

The average traveller is unaware of the costs which could be incurred or the discomfort that would be caused if one does not have a comprehensive travel insurance. It is the travel agent's duty to advise travellers of the unforeseen risks involved. They should ensure that travellers are given complete information and guidance in selecting the insurance plan, at the same time highlighting the benefits of the particular plan and what all it covers.

The following clauses are usually included in most policies.

Medical expenses cover

- This clause covers expenses incurred for availing immediate medical assistance required on account of any illness or injury sustained or contracted whilst on a trip abroad but not exceeding the sum insured for. The policy will normally cover all reasonable medical, surgical, hospital, and nursing fees incurred overseas, as a result of bodily injury, illness, or disease, to relieve pain.
- Related expenses cover travel and accommodation expenses for another person, to escort the client or patient home, or, in the event of death, to cover the cost of returning the body or ashes home.

- Careful attention needs to be paid to exclusions because some policies do not cover pre-existing illnesses whilst others will cover them, provided a doctor's certificate of fitness to travel is issued.
- Other exclusions can relate to the age of the client or pregnancy, to name a few.
- Travellers may be concerned not only with medical attention in specific diseases at the destination, but also for pre-existing health problems. Private medical insurance companies are generally used to provide coverage for such expenditure.
- In commercial contracts, difficulties may arise due to the exclusion of pre-existing medical conditions, or insurance may not be available to senior citizens who are in the high risk category.
- Lack of medical insurance can be an obstacle to the movement of both international and domestic travellers.

The insurer will pay or reimburse the costs to the insured during the policy period as per the guidelines mentioned in the policy. Sample insurance claim form is enclosed in Appendix 8.6.

Dental treatment

This clause covers expenses incurred on acute anaesthetic treatment of a natural tooth or teeth during a trip abroad but not exceeding the sum insured for.

Total loss of checked-in baggage

This clause covers the total loss of checked-in baggage on a trip abroad. The payment for this benefit will be limited to the travel destinations specified in the main travel ticket purchased from the Republic of India and return trip back to India during the trip abroad. All halts and via destinations included in this main travel ticket will also be considered for payment under this benefit.

Delay of checked-in baggage

This clause covers the temporary delay of checked-in baggage being transported during a trip abroad. The payment for this benefit will be limited to the travel destinations specified in the main travel ticket from India and return trip back to India during the trip abroad. All halts and via destinations included in this main travel ticket will also be considered for payment under this benefit.

This includes costs of necessary emergency purchases of toiletries, medication, and clothing in the event of the insured suffering temporary delay of his/her checked-in baggage while being transported during the trip. However, the delay of checked-in baggage should be more than 12 hours from the actual arrival time of the common carrier at the destination and relate to delivery of baggage that has been checked in by the common carrier. Receipts for the necessary emergency purchases of toiletries, medication, and clothing that the traveller needed to buy should be submitted along with the claim.

Loss of passport

This clause covers the loss of passport during a trip abroad but not exceeding the sum insured for the coverage. In the event that the passport belonging to the insured is lost, the company will reimburse the insured for actual expenses necessarily and reasonably incurred in connection with obtaining a duplicate or fresh passport.

No payment will be made under this benefit in connection with or in respect of any expenses whatsoever incurred by the insured for the following reasons:

- The loss of the passport is due to a delay, confiscation, or detention by the customs, police, or public authorities.
- The loss is due to theft, unless it has been reported to the police authorities within 24 hours of the insured becoming aware of the theft and a written police report being obtained in that regard.
- The loss is due to carelessness on part of the traveller.

Personal liability

This clause covers the insured in the event if the insured becomes legally liable to a third party under statutory liability provisions in private law for an incident which results in death, injury, or damage to the health of such third party, or damage to their properties.

Personal accident

This clause covers the insured for personal accident suffered during a trip abroad. An accident is considered to have occurred if

- the insured suffers involuntary damage to his/her person as a result of an event that suddenly acts on his/her body from outside; and

- due to excessive exertion, a joint is dislocated or muscles, ligaments, or tendons are strained or torn.

If the insured meets with an accident, which leads to death or disablement of the insured, the company will provide insurance coverage to the insured for

- death of insured
- permanent disablement of the insured

However, it does not cover the following:

- Accidents due to mental disorders or disturbances of consciousness, strokes, fits, or convulsions which affect the entire body and pathological disturbances caused by the mental reaction to the same.
- Damage to health caused by curative measures, radiation, infection, and poisoning, except where these arise from an accident.

Hijack distress allowance

This clause covers compensation in the event of hijack of a common carrier in which the insured is travelling on a trip abroad.

However, the following are not included.

- Expenses incurred in the first 12 hours of the hijacking.
- Any incident where the insured is suspected to be either the principal or an accessory in the hijacking.
- Any change in the regular routes of travel/journey of the common carrier due to traffic, weather, fuel shortage, and technical snag or security reasons.

Financial emergency assistance

This clause covers compensation of the insured in the event of a financial emergency arising due to theft, mugging, robbery, or dacoity of the funds of the insured. 'Financial emergency' means a situation wherein the insured loses all or a substantial amount of his/her travel funds due to theft, robbery, mugging, or dacoity, such that there is a detrimental effect on his/her travel plans.

It does not cover a shortage or loss of funds due to currency fluctuation, errors, omissions, exchange loss, or depreciation in value. This includes any loss not reported to the police authorities having jurisdiction at the place of loss within 24 hours of the occurrence of the incident and a written report being obtained for the same.

Fire and allied perils (home building and contents)

This clause covers the home or any part of the property where the traveller is residing abroad. One receives compensation if after payment of the premium the property insured described in the said schedule or any part of such property is destroyed or damaged by any of the perils, such as fire, lightning, explosion/implosion, damage caused by aircraft, riots, strikes, and other malicious damage excluding direct or indirect loss or damage by an act of terrorism.

This clause excludes loss, damage, cost, or expense of whatsoever nature directly or indirectly caused by, resulting from, or in connection with any acts of terrorism or natural calamities such as storms, cyclones, typhoons, tornados, and floods.

Burglary (home contents)

This clause covers compensation for any loss or damage sustained by the insured during the stay abroad caused by burglary and/or attempted burglary, to the contents of insured's dwelling.

Trip cancellation and interruption

This clause covers compensation if a trip is delayed, cancelled, or interrupted due to any of the following reasons:

- unforeseen serious illness, injury, or death of the insured or insured's family member;
- termination of employment or layoff, affecting the insured or the travelling companion(s) of the insured;
- inclement weather conditions causing delay or cancellation of the trip;
- any fire, flood, vandalism, burglary, or natural disaster, making the insured's intended place of occupancy, at the destination, uninhabitable;
- abduction or quarantine of the insured;
- the insured or a travelling companion being the victim of a felonious assault within ten days prior to the departure date; and
- a terrorist incident in a city/destination listed on the insured's itinerary within 30 days of the insured's scheduled arrival.

Missed connections

This clause covers compensation in the event that inclement weather causes cancellation or a delay of all regularly scheduled airline flights on which the insured is or would be travelling, for three to twelve hours from the scheduled departure time.

This clause covers the following:

- Additional transportation costs to join the trip (must be same class of original tickets purchased).
- Reasonable accommodations and meals up to USD 50 per day.
- Non-refundable, unused portion of the prepaid expenses as long as the expense is supported by a proof of purchase and is not reimbursable by another source; the common carrier must certify the delay of the regularly scheduled airline flight.

Travel delay

This clause agrees to reimburse the insured for the reasonable additional expenses, incurred by the insured up to USD 100 per day, if the insured's trip is delayed for more than six hours from the scheduled time until travel becomes possible. Incurred expenses must be accompanied by supporting receipts. This benefit is payable for only one delay per insured per trip on account of the unforeseen reasons mentioned in *trip cancellation and interruption* clause as well as delay by the common carrier, lost or stolen passport, travel documents, or money.

Bounced bookings of hotel and airlines

This clause agrees to reimburse the insured if the hotel booking/airline ticket bounces due to over booking. To claim this benefit under non-availability of accommodation on account of over booking by the hotels or airlines, the insured should have reconfirmed the booking in advance and should have written proof of the same. Wait listed booking will not be compensated for. The compensation will be reimbursed for reasonable additional cost incurred in staying at a similar hotel or buying a new ticket, less the refund/compensation given by the airline or hotel.

Some general conditions

Travel insurance applies to sea/cruise travel as well. However there are age restrictions that apply. Minimum age of the insured should be six months and maximum age should be 70 years. The maximum number of travel days in a travel insurance policy is 180 days and some companies may extend the same for an additional period of 180 days, maximum. The policy comes into effect from the commencement of the trip or when the traveller boards the carrier.

Most policies do not cover potentially dangerous sports such as mountaineering, skiing, underwater sports, etc. Professional and semiprofessional sportsmen may need to pay an additional premium.

Refund of premium

Some amount may be refunded after deducting cancellation charges, if the policy is terminated at an earlier date because the insured returns back to India. However, this is applicable only if the number of days for which refund is asked is minimum 30.

The travel agent should advise the tourist to preserve original tickets and boarding passes as well as original bills and vouchers, reports, prescriptions, etc. In the event of any unforeseen circumstances, these documents will need to be submitted for claiming settlement. The helpline numbers (toll free) and fax, and e-mail identity of the party to be contacted in an emergency should be noted. The travellers should ensure that they carry the insurance policy as well as claim form along with them, and have emergency numbers handy.

Careful attention needs to be paid to exclusions and travellers should familiarize themselves with the policy document by reading it before departing on their trip. Exclusions may relate to pre-existing illnesses, state of health, age, pregnancy, etc. Each clause covered is likely to have some exclusion. Once again the travel agent must ensure that the maximum contingencies are included in the policy, and advise the traveller accordingly.

Travel involves certain formalities which must be completed before one sets course on a journey if it is to be smooth and hassle free. Without the necessary official documents and endorsements, as well as desirable formalities like travel insurance and prophylactic medication, which need to be completed, one must not venture crossing borders and ports. Tourism professionals should be up-to-date with the latest rules and regulations in force and should be aware that some of the procedures are time consuming. The regulations vary from one country to another and are framed keeping the interests of the country and the tourist in mind. They need to be completed by the tourist before they can leave their own country or enter another country.

SUMMARY

Travel formalities are regulations which are necessary both in the interest of the tourist and of the country being visited. They affect tourism both directly and indirectly. Certain formalities need to be completed by tourists before they leave their own country and some regulations come into force en route. They include possessing a valid passport which shows the holder's national status and allows the person to pass the port or border without any hindrance, entitles a person to seek assistance in a foreign country and gives a person the right to return to his country. It contains personal information and is used for identification.

A visa is a permit which allows a citizen of one country to enter into another country. It is issued by embassies and consulates of the countries to which travel is sought. It may be endorsed on the passport, issued separately, or given on arrival into a country.

Health regulations are in force to protect the health of the tourist and prevent the spread of communicable diseases. Special permits are issued to travel to the border states of India. These permits are generally valid for up to 15 days.

Customs checks are enforced at all entry/exit points and customs duty is charged on goods as per rules. Forex rules need to be followed which includes foreign exchange to be carried, spent, or kept in one's custody after the trip. Duty-free shops at ports, offer a wide array of gifts and goods which are available at a rate lower than the local market.

The travel agent should advise customers to get travel insurance before undertaking a foreign tour because of exorbitant medical expenses charged abroad. Travel insurance covers many benefits in addition to health or medical insurance and covers unforeseen risks which may occur during the trip.

It is the duty of the travel agent to ensure that the traveller has all required valid documents before setting off on a trip abroad. If the necessary documents and immunizations are not in order, it may result in delay or cancellation of the trip.

KEY TERMS

Agent A person authorized to act on behalf of another. For example, a travel agent is authorized by the providers of services such as airlines, car rentals, tour operators, hotels, etc. to sell travel-related services on their behalf.

Air travel Travel by an airline/aircraft for the purpose of flying therein, as a passenger.

Checked-in baggage Baggage handed over by the traveller and accepted by an international carrier, in the same carrier as the traveller, for which a baggage receipt has been issued.

Consulates Office of embassies and high commissions located in major cities of a country to make visa and other services easily available.

Contingencies Something unforeseen that may occur.

Cruise Travel by a ship specially designed for leisure travel.

Customs Important security check of the government located at entry points such as airports, seaports, and border posts, to prevent illegal trafficking of goods and other items.

Duty-free shops Shops located at air, sea, and bus terminals, selling goods such as jewellery, watches, liquor, perfumes, chocolates, etc. which are exempted from local excise, hence are lower in cost than the local market.

Emigration Going out of a country.

Immigration Coming into a country.

Indemnifies Protects against penalties incurred by one's actions, compensation for injury.

Insurance policy Written contract between the client and the insurance company, which dictates the terms of the insurance. Must be signed by both the insurance company (insurer) and the person who is being covered (insured) to be valid.

Insured The individual whose name specifically appears as such in the policy.

Passport An official document required to travel outside the country which proclaims the citizenship of the holder.

Period of insurance With reference to the single-trip policy, the period from commencement of insurance cover to the end of the insurance cover or actual trip duration, whichever is less.

Physician A person who is qualified to practice medicine, a surgeon, or an anaesthetist, and has a valid licence issued by the appropriate authority for the same, provided that this person is not a member of the insured's family.

Pre-existing condition Chronic illnesses or ailments and consequences of such illnesses or ailments, existing or known to exist at the commencement of the period of insurance or for which medical advice has been sought in the last six months.

CONCEPT REVIEW QUESTIONS

1. Define the term passport. List the different types of passports.
2. Mention the documents required while applying for a new passport.
3. What is visa? Explain the different types of visas.
4. What are restricted and protected areas?
5. Explain the need for travel regulations in the tourism industry.
6. Name some insurance companies which offer travel insurance.
7. Why is it advisable to have travel insurance while going abroad?
8. What is basic travel quota scheme?

9. Why is emigration check required?
10. List the duty-free allowances for tourists.
11. What are the baggage rules for tourists?
12. Describe health regulations and explain why they need to be enforced.

CRITICAL THINKING QUESTION

A student has gone to the USA for training abroad on a four month student visa (J-1 visa). The training did not commence as scheduled but was delayed by a fortnight. The student needs to complete four months training as part of the curriculum. Explain the procedure to be followed for the extension of his/her visa.

PROJECT/ASSIGNMENT

Visit the passport office and apply for a passport for yourself or your friend and list the documents required, procedure to be followed, and time duration required for the same.

REFERENCES

Bhatia, A.K. 2001, *International Tourism Management*, Sterling Publishers Private Ltd, New Delhi.

IATA – International Travel Agents Training Programme 1997, Standard Course, *Introduction to Tourism*, IATA, Montreal.

IATA – International Travel and Tourism Training Programme 2004, *Travel Formalities*, Aviation Training and Development Institute, Montreal.

IATA/UFTAA Training Issue 2006, *Travel Information Manual IATA, Netherlands*.

IGNOU School of Social Sciences 1994, TS 1 *Foundation Course in Tourism* IGNOU, New Delhi.

Kaul, R.N. 1985, *Dynamics of Tourism: A Trilogy, Vol. I—The Phenomenon*, Sterling Publishers Private Ltd, New Delhi.

www.tourindia.com, accessed between 4 April 2008 and 15 July 2008.

www.tourismofindia.com, accessed between 4 April 2008 and 15 July 2008.

www.passport.gov.in, accessed between 4 April 2008 and 15 July 2008.

www.cbec.gov.in, accessed between 4 April 2008 and 15 July 2008.

www.usavisa.com, accessed between 4 April 2008 and 15 July 2008.

www.ukvisaservices.co.uk, accessed between 4 April 2008 and 15 July 2008.

www.mychinavisa.com, accessed between 4 April 2008 and 15 July 2008.

www.iata.org, accessed between 4 April 2008 and 15 July 2008.

www.path2usa.com, accessed on 6 February 2009.

Format for Passport Application

Government of India
Ministry of External Affairs
Passport Application Form (No.1)
(For New / Re-issue/ Replacement of Lost/Damaged Passport)
(Please tick the required category)

Signature
OR ⟹
Thumb Impression

Paste your
unsigned recent
colour
photograph.
Size: 3.5 X 3.5 cm

Please read the Passport Information Booklet carefully before filling the form, in CAPITAL LETTERS in blue/ black ball point pen only:
(CAUTION: Please furnish correct information. Furnishing of incorrect information would attract penal provisions as prescribed under the Passports Act, 1967). Please produce your original documents at the time of submission of the form.

For official use only

File Number .... Police Verification required   (Yes/No)   ECR / ECNR

....
Signature of Checking Official

Fee Amount Rs.   Cash /D.D   Bank Code   D.D No.   Date of Issue of D.D

1. Name of applicant as it should appear in the Passport (Initials not allowed)

Surname
Given Name
(with documentary proof)

2. In case of change of name/surname (after marriage or otherwise with documentary proof), please indicate the previous name/surname in full

3. Sex   ☐ Male   ☐ Female   ☐ Others

4. Date of Birth: DD ☐☐ MM ☐☐ YYYY ☐☐☐☐
(with documentary proof)
In words. _____

5. Place of Birth: Village / Town, District, State, Country (with Documentary Proof)

6. Father/Legal Guardian's Full Name (including surname, if any): (Initials not allowed)

7. Mother's Full Name (including surname, if any): (Initials not allowed)

8. If married, Full Name of wife/husband (including surname, if any). (Initials not allowed).

(1)

8 (i) If divorced/widow/widower, Please indicate the category with documentary proof.

9. Current Residential Address (where staying presently), Residing since ....
   (In case of students, please see Section III of Passport Information Booklet)

																P	I	N						

Telephone No.   Mobile No.

9 (a) If you have been resident at your current address for less than one year, please furnish other addresses
   of your residence during the last one year.
   From.................To......................   From.....................To...................
   _____   _____
   _____   _____
   _____   _____
   _____   _____

10. Permanent Address with PIN code (if the permanent address is same as the present address write "Same" only)

																	P	I	N				

11. Details of latest held/existing Ordinary / Diplomatic / Official passport(s):

(i)   Passport Office File No: ..../ Passport(s) No..................................
(ii)   Date and Place of Issue: ..../ Date of Expiry ....
(iii)   In case passport was applied for and not issued, please give File No. & Date ....
(iv)   Has your passport(s) ever been lost / damaged (if so attach FIR and give details).....................
        ....

11. (a) If you have returned to India on Emergency Certificate (EC) or were ever deported or repatriated,
        please furnish details:

        EC No., date and place of issue & attach seizure memo in original ....

        Place & Country from where deported / repatriated and reason thereof:..
        ....
        ....

12. Other Details:
    a) Educational Qualifications...
    b) Visible Distinguishing Mark, if any..
    c) Height ....cms.

(2)

13. Are you working in Central Government/ State Govt/ PSU/ Statutory Bodies (Y)es/ (N)o ☐
    If 'Yes' attach Identity Certificate (As per Annexure "B" of Passport Information booklet).

14. Are you a citizen of India by: (**B**)irth/(**D**)escent/(**R**)egistration/(**N**)aturalisation; ....
    If you have ever possessed any other citizenship, please indicate previous citizenship ....

15. "Emigration Check Not Required" status? Yes/No ....
    (Please note that all 10 and above qualified applicants are eligible for ECNR status.)
    If yes, mention the eligible category (see Section III of Passport Information Booklet) and enclose copy
    of relevant certificate/document_____

16. In case of minors (applicant below the age of 18), if **EITHER** of the parents hold a Valid Indian
    Passport or has applied for it give the following details. Please see and fill up attached Annexure-H.

	Passport/ File No.	Date & Place of Issue/ Application
Mother	_____	_____
Father	_____	_____

17. (a) Have you at any time during the period of Five years immediately preceding the date of this
        application been convicted by a court in India for any criminal offence & sentenced to imprisonment
        for two years or more? If so, give name of the court, case number and relevant sections of Law.
        (Attach copy of judgement)
        ....

    (b) Are any criminal proceedings pending against you before a court in India? If so, give name of court,
        case number and relevant sections of Law.
        ....

    (c) If answer at (b) is (Y)es, please furnish No Objection Certificate from competent court for grant of
        Passport.
        ....
        ....

    (d) Have you been ever refused/denied passport? If yes, give details:
        ....
        ....

    (e) Has your passport ever been impounded / revoked? If yes, give details:
        ....
        ....

    (f) Have you ever applied/granted political asylum by any foreign country? If yes, give details.
        ....
        ....

18. Particulars of person to be intimated in the event of death or accident:
    Name   ....
    Address   ....
              ....
    Mobile / Tel. No. / email ID ....

(3)

19. Self Declaration:

        I owe allegiance to the sovereignty, unity & integrity of India, and have not voluntarily acquired citizenship or travel documents of any other country. I have not lost, surrendered or been deprived of citizenship of India. The information given by me in this form and enclosures is true and I am solely responsible for its accuracy. I am aware that it is an offence under the Passports Act, 1967 to furnish any false information or to suppress any material information with a view to obtaining a passport or any other travel document.

        I further declare that I have no other passport/ travel document.

(Signature/Thumb Impression of Applicant)

Date ....

(Left Hand Thumb Impression if male and Right Hand Thumb Impression if female)

Place ....

20. Enclosures:

1 Proof of date of birth .... 2 Proof of Residence ....

3 Educational Qualifications .... 4 ....

5 .... 6 ....

(For Official Use Only)

Checked by Name   **Signature/date**

Granted by Name   **Signature/date**

Scanned by Name   **Signature/date**

Dispatched by Name   **Signature/date**

PERSONAL PARTICULARS FORM
(In Duplicate)

Paste your
cross signed
recent colour
photograph.
size 3.5*3.5 cm

1. Full name (Initials not allowed) ....
....

2. Sex: Male / Female / Others ....

(a) Has the applicant ever changed name?

   (b) If yes, previous name: ....

4. Date of Birth:.................................... 5. Place of Birth ....

6. Profession ....

7. a) Father ....
                        (Surname)   (Name)
   b) Mother...
                        (Surname)   (Name)
   c) Husband / wife ....
                        (Surname)   (Name)

8 a) Permanent Address & Tel. No.   8(b) Present Residential Address & Tel. No, along with
     along with Police Station   Police Station and residing since

9. If you have not been resident at the address given at COLUMN 8(b) continuously for the last one year, please furnish other address(es) with duration(s) resided (Please furnish an additional set of P P Forms for each address with Police station.
   From.................To......................   From.....................To....................

10. **References:** Names and Addresses of two responsible persons in the applicant's locality who can vouch for the applicant.
    (1) Name, Address & Tel. No.   (2) Name, Address & Tel. No.

11. Citizenship of India by: Birth ☐ Descent ☐ Registration ☐ Naturalization ☐

12. Furnish details of previous passport / travel document, if any:
    (i) Passport/Travel document No: .... (ii) Date & Place of issue ....

For Police Use Only
Recommended Passport: **YES/NO**

Signature or Thumb Impression of the applicant
(Left Hand T.I. if male and Right Hand T.I. if female)

(5)

Visa Requirements for Some Popular Destinations

Australia

Tourist visa

- Valid Passport
- Application form duly filled
- Photographs (as per requirement)
- Covering letter, from the applicant stating the purpose of tourism, and the intended duration of visit
- Foreign exchange, to be endorsed in the passport/copy of the international credit card
- Photocopies of income tax papers of last three years
- Personalized bank statement for the last three months
- Employers leave certificate (leave sanction from employer)
- In case of children, leave certificate from school must
- Sponsorship required if visiting relatives, fee as applicable

Business visa

- Valid passport for six months
- Visa form duly filled and signed, as per the signature in the passport, by the applicant
- Photographs (as per requirement)
- Covering letter on company letterhead mentioning the applicants name, designation, purpose and duration of visit
- Foreign exchange, to be endorsed in the passport/copy of the international credit card
- Invitation from the Australian party/company
- Personalized bank statement for last three months
- Photocopies of income tax papers of last three years
- Validity of the visa to be decided by the embassy

Fee

- As applicable, by draft, in favour of 'Australian High Commission', New Delhi.

    Health insurance must, if above seventy years. (All passengers above seventy years of age are required to undergo medical tests.)

    Time taken   seven to nine days

Transit visa

- Valid passport
- Four photographs
- Confirmed return ticket
- Application forms
- Covering letter
- Onward visa.

Fee Nil
Time taken Five to seven days

China

Tourist visa

- Valid passport
- Visa form duly filled and signed, as per the signature in the passport, by the applicant
- Two coloured photographs 35mm × 45mm (white background with 80 per cent of face showing clearly)
- Covering letter, from the applicant stating the purpose and intended duration of the visit
- Foreign exchange, to be endorsed in the passport/copy of the international credit card.
- Hotel booking confirmation from China itself with original round seal, address and telephone number on hotel letterhead.
- Bank statements for last six months showing minimum closing balance of Rs.1,50,000 duly stamped or original passbook.
- Last three years' income tax papers
- Fee as applicable

Business visa

- Valid passport
- Visa form duly filled and signed, as per the signature in the passport, by the applicant
- Two coloured photographs 35mm × 45mm (white background with 80 per cent of face showing clearly)
- Covering letter on company letterhead mentioning the applicants name, designation, purpose and duration of visit
- Foreign exchange, to be endorsed in the passport/copy of the international credit card
- Invitation from the Chinese party/company
- Last three years' income tax papers
- Fee as applicable payable by draft in favour of Consulate General of China, Mumbai

Time taken Four to six working days

France

Tourist visa

- Valid passport
- Visa form duly filled and signed, as per the signature in the passport, by the applicant
- Two coloured photographs 35mm × 45mm (white background with eighty per cent of face showing clearly)
- Covering letter, from the applicant stating the purpose and intended duration of the visit
- Confirmed return ticket
- Foreign exchange to be endorsed in the passport/copy of the international credit card
- Passenger's contact details
- Proof of hotel confirmation from France (with address and contact details)
- Original insurance papers
- Copy of income tax papers
- Photocopy of the passport's first page, air ticket, and insurance
  Fee As applicable

Business visa

- Valid passport
- Visa form duly filled and signed, as per the signature in the passport, by the applicant
- Two coloured photographs 35mm × 45mm (white background with 80 per cent of face showing clearly)
- Covering letter on company letterhead mentioning the applicant's name, designation, purpose and duration of visit
- Confirmed return ticket
- Invitation from French company
- Proof of hotel booking (with address and contact details)
- Foreign exchange, to be endorsed in the passport/copy of the international credit card
- Original insurance (only TATA, BAJAJ or ICICI, or any other insurance that has the 'Repatriation Column' duly filled and highlighted)
- Photocopy of the passport's first page, air ticket, and insurance

Fee As applicable, by draft
Time taken Minimum three working days

Please note all the passengers will have to come to Mumbai for finger printing at the French consulate.

Germany

Tourist visa

- Valid passport
- Visa form duly filled and signed, as per the signature in the passport, by the applicant.
- Covering letter, from the applicant stating the purpose and intended duration of the visit
- Photograph (as per requirement)
- Leave letter from employer
- Confirmed return air ticket
- Hotel confirmation
- Foreign exchange, to be endorsed in the passport/copy of the international credit card
- If employed, salary slips for last three months or Form 16A.
- Original income tax papers (for last three years)
- If any friend/relative in Germany, required original sponsorship declaration with invitee passport copies
- Medical policy with photocopy

Time taken   Three working days

Business visa

- Valid passport
- Visa form duly filled and signed, as per the signature in the passport, by the applicant
- Photograph (as per requirement)
- Covering letter on company letterhead mentioning the applicant's name, designation, purpose, and duration of visit
- Invitation letter from Germany
- Confirmed return air ticket
- Foreign exchange, to be endorsed in the passport / copy of the international credit card
- If employed, salary slips for last three months or Form 16A
- Original income tax papers (for last three years)
- Medical policy

Fee   As applicable
Time taken   Three days

A passenger travelling for the first time, needs to come in person, by taking an appointment.

Japan

Tourist visa

- Valid passport
- Visa form duly filled and signed, as per the signature in the passport, by the applicant.
- One photograph
- Covering letter, from the applicant stating the purpose and intended duration of the visit
- Proof of hotel confirmation
- Confirmed return air ticket
- Foreign exchange, to be endorsed in the passport/copy of the international credit card
- Income tax papers

Business visa

- Valid passport
- Visa form duly filled and signed, as per the signature in the passport, by the applicant
- One photograph
- Covering letter on company letterhead mentioning the applicants name, designation, purpose and intended duration of the visit
- Original invitation is must
- Confirmed return ticket
- Foreign exchange, to be endorsed in the passport/copy of the international credit card
- Income tax papers
- Salary slip

> **Fee** As applicable, by draft
> **Time taken** Three days

Malaysia

Tourist visa

- Valid passport
- Visa form duly filled and signed, as per the signature in the passport, by the applicant
- Two photographs
- Covering letter, from the applicant stating the purpose and intended duration of the visit

- Foreign exchange, to be endorsed in the passport / copy of the international credit card
- Confirmed return air ticket
- Hotel confirmation or tour itinerary

Fee   As applicable by draft favouring Consulate General of Malaysia

Business visa

- Valid passport
- Visa form duly filled and signed, as per the signature in the passport, by the applicant
- Two photographs (as per requirement)
- Covering letter on company letterhead mentioning the applicant's name, designation, purpose, and duration of visit
- Confirmed return ticket
- Foreign exchange, to be endorsed in the passport/copy of the international credit card
- Invitation to be faxed directly to the embassy by the inviting party in Malaysia and copy to travel agent with documents

Fee   As applicable, through draft favouring Consulate General of Malaysia
Time taken   Seven days

Mauritius

Indian nationals can get a visa on arrival for fifteen days.

Tourist and business visa

- Valid passport
- Visa form duly filled and signed, as per the signature in the passport, by the applicant
- Two photographs (as per requirement)
- Covering letter on company letterhead mentioning the applicant's name, designation, purpose, and duration of visit
- Covering letter, from the applicant stating the purpose and intended duration of the visit
- Confirmed return air ticket
- Exchange endorsement (minimum of USD 500 along with original exchange endorsement receipt) or
- Copy of an international credit card, along with original credit card and credit card statement for last six months
- Hotel confirmation only from the hotel in Mauritius on their letter head, including the name of the passenger and the intended check-in and check-

out dates (e-mail confirmation and travel agent's confirmations not accepted any more)
- Original income tax papers (for last three years)
- Original bank passbook/bank account statement for minimum three months

Fee   As applicable
Time Taken   Three days

New Zealand

Tourist visa

- Valid passport
- Visa form duly filled and signed, as per the signature in the passport, by the applicant
- One photograph (as per requirement)
- Covering letter, from the applicant stating the purpose and intended duration of the visit
- Foreign exchange, to be endorsed in the passport/copy of the international credit card
- Complete family details on letterhead
- Bank account statement for the last three months
- Income tax documents for the last three years

Fee   As applicable

Business visa

- Valid passport
- Visa form duly filled and signed, as per the signature in the passport, by the applicant
- Photograph (as per requirement)
- Covering letter on company letterhead mentioning the applicant's name, designation, purpose, and duration of visit
- Invitation from New Zealand
- Foreign exchange, to be endorsed in the passport/copy of the international credit card
- Original income tax papers (for last three years)
- Original bank passbook/bank statement for minimum three months

Fee   As applicable, by demand draft

South Africa

Tourist visa

- Valid passport
- Visa form duly filled and signed, as per the signature in the passport, by the applicant
- Two photographs (as per requirement)
- Covering letter, from the applicant stating the purpose and intended duration of the visit
- Proof of hotel confirmation, or sponsorship from South Africa (original affidavit B1 1355 from the sponsor in South Africa), and copy of identification documents/passport attested by foreign police, same day, when the affidavit is issued, along with the bank account statement of the sponsor
- Day–to–day itinerary
- Confirmed return air ticket
- Income tax papers
- Foreign exchange, to be endorsed in the passport/copy of the international credit card
- Leave letter
- If employed, salary slips for last three months or Form 16A
- Health requirement—also for transit passengers not leaving the airport—vaccination against yellow fever. Malaria prophylaxis is recommended.

Business visa

- Valid passport
- Visa form duly filled and signed, as per the signature in the passport, by the applicant.
- Two photographs (as per requirement)
- Covering letter in detail, mentioning the duration of visit
- Recommendation letter from the Chamber of Commerce
- Invitation from a South African party/company
- Proof of hotel confirmation
- Confirmed return air ticket
- Credit card copy or endorsement copy
- Income tax papers
- Health requirement—also for transit passengers not leaving the airport—vaccination against yellow fever. Malaria prophylaxis is recommended.

Fee   As applicable
Time taken   Ten days

Singapore

Tourist visa

- Valid passport
- Visa form duly filled and signed, as per the signature in the passport, by the applicant
- Two photographs (as per requirement)
- Covering letter, from the applicant stating the purpose and intended duration of the visit
- Confirmed return air ticket
- Foreign exchange, to be endorsed in the passport/copy of the international credit card
- Original Income tax papers (last three years)
- Original bank passbook/bank account statement for minimum three months

Fee   As applicable, by draft

Business visa

- Valid passport
- Visa form duly filled and signed, as per the signature in the passport, by the applicant
- Two photographs (as per requirement)
- Covering letter on company letterhead mentioning the applicant's name, designation, purpose, and duration of visit
- Confirmed return air ticket
- Foreign exchange, to be endorsed in the passport/copy of the international credit card
- Invitation from Singapore
- Income tax papers
- Original bank passbook/bank account statement for minimum three months

Fee   As applicable
Time taken   Three days

Switzerland

Tourist visa

- Valid passport
- Visa form duly filled and signed, as per the signature in the passport, by the applicant
- Photograph
- Foreign exchange, to be endorsed in the passport/copy of the international credit card

- Covering letter mentioning the applicant's name, designation, purpose, and duration of visit.
- Confirmed return air ticket
- Hotel confirmation
- Detailed tour itinerary
- Overseas mediclaim policy
- If employed, NOC from employer and leave letter.
- Evidence of financial status which includes letter from employer (NOC certificate), pay slips, original income tax returns for last three years, original bank passbooks/account statements for last six months.

    Fee   As applicable

Business visa

- Valid passport
- Visa form duly filled and signed, as per the signature in the passport, by the applicant
- Photograph
- Covering letter from employer on company letterhead stating –the applicant's position, length of service, whether applicant is registered for tax, reason for visit, whether expenses are being covered by company, etc.
- Invitation letter directly faxed to the consulate from Switzerland and one copy with the application
- Foreign exchange, to be endorsed in the passport/copy of the international credit card
- Confirmed return air ticket
- If employed, salary slips for last three months or Form 16A
- Overseas mediclaim policy
- Consulate may insist for personal interview in some cases

    Fee   As applicable, through a demand draft, in favour of the Consulate General of Switzerland, Mumbai

    Time taken   Forty-eight hours.

Thailand

Tourist visa

- Valid passport
- Visa form duly filled and signed, as per the signature in the passport, by the applicant
- Two photographs (as per requirement, on white background)
- Covering letter, from the applicant stating the purpose and intended duration of the visit

- Confirmed return air ticket
- Foreign exchange, to be endorsed in the passport/copy of the international credit card

Business visa

- Valid passport
- Visa form duly filled and signed, as per the signature in the passport, by the applicant
- Two photographs (as per requirement, on white background)
- Covering letter on company letterhead mentioning the applicant's name, designation, purpose, and duration of visit
- Invitation from Thailand
- Foreign exchange, to be endorsed in the passport/copy of the international credit card
- Confirmed return air ticket

Fee   As applicable, through a demand draft, from a nationalized bank favouring 'Royal Thai Consulate General', Mumbai

Time taken   Two days

UAE

Business/tourist visa

- Indian nationals intending to visit the UAE must obtain a 'No Objection Certificate' (NOC) through their sponsor in the UAE
- The sponsor must submit passport details to the Immigration Directorate for the Immigration Directorate to issue the visa.
- Processing time required for the above formalities is approximately fifteen days
- Visa is faxed to the traveller and must be carried by passenger.
- No passenger is allowed to board the flight without the NOC.
- Visa is valid for thirty days
- Visa fees is paid by the sponsor while applying for the clearance
- Incase of tourists, the invitation is valid only within blood relations i.e. husband/wife, parents/children. Invitee must send copy of the labour contract attested by Emirates Visa Section.

Time taken   Four days

UK

Tourist visa

- Valid passport

- Visa form duly filled and signed, as per the signature in the passport, by the applicant
- Two photographs (passport size, white background, without border)
- Covering letter, from the applicant stating the purpose and intended duration of the visit
- Sponsorship declaration
- Bank account statement, last three months
- Income tax documents, last three years
- Photocopy of the passport's first page
- Foreign exchange, to be endorsed in the passport/copy of the international credit card
- Leave letter from employer
- Hotel confirmation

Business visa

- Valid passport
- Visa form duly filled and signed, as per the signature in the passport, by the applicant.
- Two photographs (passport size, white background, without border)
- Covering letter on company letterhead mentioning the applicant's name, designation, purpose, and duration of visit
- Invitation letter from the UK
- Bank account statement, last three months
- Income tax documents, last three years
- Photocopy of the passport's first page
- Foreign exchange, to be endorsed in the passport/copy of the international credit card
- Original bank passbook/bank account statement for minimum three months
- If employed, salary slips for last three months or Form 16A

Fee   As applicable
Time taken   Two days
Note: As per the new rules all visa applications have to be submitted at the VFS centers only.

- All documents to be in original
- Consulate may insist for personal interview
- Should be accompanied by an authority letter for collection of passport

USA

Business visa

- One visa form, copies allowed (clear photocopy), duly filled and signed as per the signature in the passport by the applicant.

- One recent photograph (as per requirement)
- Valid passport
- Covering letter on company letterhead mentioning the applicant's name, designation, purpose, and duration of visit.
- Invitation letter from the USA
- If employed, salary slip for last three months or Form 16A required
- Tax papers and company papers are required, if self employed
- Foreign exchange, to be endorsed in the passport/copy of the international credit card
- Passenger has to go for personal interview

Tourist visa

- One visa form—copies allowed (clear photocopy) duly filled and signed, as per the signature in the passport, by the applicant.
- One recent photograph (50 mm x 50 mm) (milky white background)
- Letter from the applicant stating the purpose and duration of the visit
- Employer's certificate. Leave letter from employer if employed
- If joining any tour, require tour confirmation
- Affidavit-in-support attested by US Justice of Immigration
- If employed, salary slip for last three months or Form 16A required
- Tax papers and company papers are required, if self employed
- If invited by relatives or friends, sponsorship declaration
- Passport copies
- For partnership companies, partnership deed to be enclosed
- Foreign exchange, to be endorsed in the passport/copy of the international credit card
- Original income tax papers (for last three years)
- Original bank passbook/bank account statement for minimum three months
- Fixed deposit certificates
- Property papers
- Passenger has to go for personal interview

Fee　As applicable
Time Taken　Two days

Health Questionnaire

검역질문서 (檢疫質問書)
(HEALTH QUESTIONNAIRE)

도착연월일(到達年月日)
Arrival Date _____ / _____ / _____

선박·항공기·열차·자동차명 (船舶·航空機·列車·車輛名)
Vessel·Flight·Train·Car No. : _____

좌석번호 (座位號碼) Seat No. : _____

성 명(姓名)
Name in full : _____

주민등록번호 _____ - _____
Passport No. (护照番号) : _____

국 적(國籍)
Nationality : _____

남(男) _____ 여(女) _____   연령(年齡)
Male _____ Female _____   Age _____

한국내 주소(韓國內 地址)
Contact address in Korea.

전화(電話)
(Tel. _____)

과거 10일 동안의 체재국명을 기입하여 주십시오. (請填寫過去十天之內停留的 國家)
Please list the countries where you have stayed during the past 10 days before arrival.

과거 10일 동안에 아래 증상이 있었거나 있는 경우 해당란에 「∨」 표시를 하여 주십시오.
(過去十天之內如有以下症狀, 請左症狀前劃 「∨」)
Please check a mark 「∨」, if you have or have had any of the following symptoms
during the past 10 days before arrival.

☐ 설사(腹瀉)   ☐ 구토(嘔吐)   ☐ 복통(腹痛)   ☐ 발열(發熱·发烧)
  Diarrhea   Vomiting   Abdominal pain   Fever

☐ 기침(咳嗽)   ☐ 호흡곤란(呼吸困難)   ☐ 잦은 호흡(呼吸急促)
  Cough   Difficulty breathing   Shortness of breath

검역질문서 작성을 기피하거나 허위작성 제출하는 경우 검역법 제9조 및 제39조의 규정에 의거 1년
이하의 징역 또는 500만원 이하의 벌금 처벌을 받을 수 있습니다.
If you make a false statement concerning your health or fail to fill out the Health
Questionnaire, you may face a sentence of up to one year of imprisonment or up to 5
million won in fines, in accordance with Articles 9 and 39 of the Quarantine Act.
回避或虛假地填寫衛生檢疫單時, 依据檢疫法第九條及第三十九條的規定, 可被判以一年以
下的徒刑或500万元以下的罰款.

대한민국 국립인천공항검역소 (大韓民國 國立仁川空港檢疫所)
Incheon Airport National Quarantine Station
Republic of Korea

148mm×210mm
(황색지 70g/㎡)

Customs Declaration Form

Customs Declaration

19 CFR 122.27, 148.12, 148.13, 148.110,148.111, 1498; 31 CFR 5316

FORM APPROVED
OMB NO. 1651-0009

Each arriving traveler or responsible family member must provide the following information (only ONE written declaration per family is required):

1. Family Name
   First *(Given)* / Middle
2. Birth date   Day   Month   Year
3. Number of Family members traveling with you
4. (a) U.S. Street Address (hotel name/destination)
   (b) City   (c) State
5. Passport issued by (country)
6. Passport number
7. Country of Residence
8. Countries visited on this trip prior to U.S. arrival
9. Airline/Flight No. or Vessel Name
10. The primary purpose of this trip is business: Yes   No
11. I am (We are) bringing
    (a) fruits, vegetables, plants, seeds, food, insects: Yes   No
    (b) meats, animals, animal/wildlife products: Yes   No
    (c) disease agents, cell cultures, snails: Yes   No
    (d) soil or have been on a farm/ranch/pasture: Yes   No
12. I have (We have) been in close proximity of (such as touching or handling) livestock: Yes   No
13. I am (We are) carrying currency or monetary instruments over $10,000 U.S. or foreign equivalent: Yes   No
    (see definition of monetary instruments on reverse)
14. I have (We have) commercial merchandise: Yes   No
    (articles for sale, samples used for soliciting orders, or goods that are not considered personal effects)
15. Residents — the total value of all goods, including commercial merchandise I/we have purchased or acquired abroad, (including gifts for someone else, but not items mailed to the U.S.) and am/are bringing to the U.S. is: $
    Visitors — the total value of all articles that will remain in the U.S., including commercial merchandise is: $

Read the instructions on the back of this form. Space is provided to list all the items you must declare.

I HAVE READ THE IMPORTANT INFORMATION ON THE REVERSE SIDE OF THIS FORM AND HAVE MADE A TRUTHFUL DECLARATION.

X
_____
(Signature)   Date (day/month/year)

For Official Use Only

CBP Form 6059B (10/07)

U.S. Customs and Border Protection Welcomes You to the United States
U.S. Customs and Border Protection is responsible for protecting the United States against the illegal importation of prohibited items. CBP officers have the authority to question you and to examine you and your personal property. If you are one of the travelers selected for an examination, you will be treated in a courteous, professional, and dignified manner. CBP Supervisors and Passenger Service Representatives are available to answer your questions. Comment cards are available to compliment or provide feedback.

Important Information
U.S. Residents — Declare all articles that you have acquired abroad and are bringing into the United States.
Visitors (Non-Residents) — Declare the value of all articles that will remain in the United States.
Declare all articles on this declaration form and show the value in U.S. dollars. For gifts, please indicate the retail value.
Duty — CBP officers will determine duty. U.S. residents are normally entitled to a duty-free exemption of $800 on items accompanying them. Visitors (non-residents) are normally entitled to an exemption of $100. Duty will be assessed at the current rate on the first $1,000 above the exemption.
Agricultural and Wildlife Products — To prevent the entry of dangerous agricultural pests and prohibited wildlife, the following are restricted: Fruits, vegetables, plants, plant products, soil, meat, meat products, birds, snails, and other live animals or animal products. Failure to declare such items to a Customs and Border Protection Officer/Customs and Border Protection Agriculture Specialist/Fish and Wildlife Inspector can result in penalties and the items may be subject to seizure.
Controlled substances, obscene articles, and toxic substances are generally prohibited entry.

Thank You, and Welcome to the United States.

The transportation of currency or **monetary instruments**, regardless of the amount, is legal. However, if you bring in to or take out of the United States more than $10,000 (U.S. or foreign equivalent, or a combination of both), you are required by law to file a report on FinCEN 105 (formerly Customs Form 4790) with U.S. Customs and Border Protection. Monetary instruments include coin, currency, travelers checks and bearer instruments such as personal or cashiers checks and stocks and bonds. If you have someone else carry the currency or monetary instrument for you, you must also file a report on FinCEN 105. Failure to file the required report or failure to report the *total* amount that you are carrying may lead to the seizure of *all* the currency or monetary instruments, and may subject you to civil penalties and/or criminal prosecution. SIGN ON THE OPPOSITE SIDE OF THIS FORM AFTER YOU HAVE READ THE IMPORTANT INFORMATION AND MADE A TRUTHFUL DECLARATION.

Description of Articles (List may continue on another CBP Form 6059B)	Value	CBP Use Only
Total		

APPENDIX 8.5

Arrival and Departure Forms

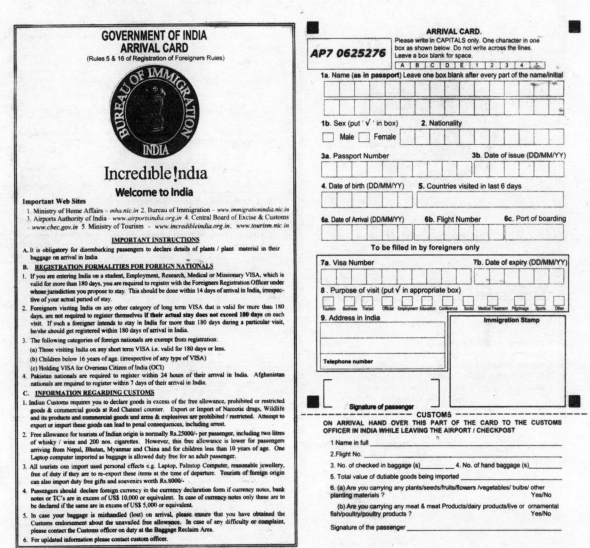

GOVERNMENT OF INDIA
ARRIVAL CARD
(Rules 5 & 16 of Registration of Foreigners Rules)

Incredible !ndia
Welcome to India

Important Web Sites
1. Ministry of Home Affairs – *mha.nic.in* 2. Bureau of Immigration – *www.immigrationindia.nic.in* 3. Airports Authority of India – *www.airportsindia.org.in* 4. Central Board of Excise & Customs – *www.cbec.gov.in* 5. Ministry of Tourism – *www.incredibleindia.org.in*, *www.tourism.nic.in*

IMPORTANT INSTRUCTIONS

A. It is obligatory for disembarking passengers to declare details of plants / plant material in their baggage on arrival in India

B. **REGISTRATION FORMALITIES FOR FOREIGN NATIONALS**
1. If you are entering India on a student, Employment, Research, Medical or Missionary VISA, which is valid for more than 180 days, you are required to register with the Foreigners Registration Officer under whose jurisdiction you propose to stay. This should be done within 14 days of arrival in India, irrespective of your actual period of stay.
2. Foreigners visiting India on any other category of long term VISA that is valid for more than 180 days, are not required to register themselves **if their actual stay does not exceed 180 days** on each visit. If such a foreigner intends to stay in India for more than 180 days during a particular visit, he/she should get registered within 180 days of arrival in India.
3. The following categories of foreign nationals are exempt from registration:
(a) Those visiting India on any short term VISA i.e. valid for 180 days or less.
(b) Children below 16 years of age. (irrespective of any type of VISA)
(c) Holding VISA for Overseas Citizen of India (OCI)
4. Pakistan nationals are required to register within 24 hours of their arrival in India. Afghanistan nationals are required to register within 7 days of their arrival in India.

C. **INFORMATION REGARDING CUSTOMS**
1. Indian Customs requires you to declare goods in excess of the free allowance, prohibited or restricted goods & commercial goods at Red Channel counter. Export or Import of Narcotic drugs, Wildlife and its products and commercial goods and arms & explosives are prohibited / restricted. Attempt to export or import these goods can lead to penal consequences, including arrest.
2. Free allowance for tourists of Indian origin is normally Rs.25000/- per passenger, including two litres of whisky / wine and 200 nos. cigarettes. However, this free allowance is lower for passengers arriving from Nepal, Bhutan, Myanmar and China and for children less than 10 years of age. One Laptop computer imported as baggage is allowed duty free for an adult passenger.
3. All tourists can import used personal effects e.g. Laptop, Palmtop Computer, reasonable jewellery, free of duty if they are to re-export these items at the time of departure. Tourists of foreign origin can also import duty free gifts and souvenirs worth Rs.8000/-
4. Passengers should declare foreign currency in the currency declaration form if currency notes, bank notes or TC's are in excess of US$ 10,000 or equivalent. In case of currency notes only these are to be declared if the same are in excess of US$ 5,000 or equivalent.
5. In case your baggage is mishandled (lost) on arrival, please ensure that you have obtained the Customs endorsement about the unavailed free allowance. In case of any difficulty or complaint, please contact the Customs officer on duty at the Baggage Reclaim Area.
6. For updated information please contact custom officer.

ARRIVAL CARD.
Please write in CAPITALS only. One character in one box as shown below. Do not write across the lines. Leave a box blank for space.

AP7 0625276

| A | B | C | D | E | 1 | 2 | 3 | 4 | |

1a. Name (as in passport) Leave one box blank after every part of the name/initial

1b. Sex (put ' √ ' in box) ☐ Male ☐ Female   **2. Nationality**

3a. Passport Number   **3b. Date of issue (DD/MM/YY)**

4. Date of birth (DD/MM/YY)   **5. Countries visited in last 6 days**

6a. Date of Arrival (DD/MM/YY)   **6b. Flight Number**   **6c. Port of boarding**

To be filled in by foreigners only

7a. Visa Number   **7b. Date of expiry (DD/MM/YY)**

8. Purpose of visit (put √ in appropriate box)
Tourism Business Transit Official Employment Education Conference Social Medical Treatment Pilgrimage Sports Other

9. Address in India

Immigration Stamp

Telephone number

Signature of passenger

- - - - - - - - - - **CUSTOMS** - - - - - - - - - -

ON ARRIVAL HAND OVER THIS PART OF THE CARD TO THE CUSTOMS OFFICER IN INDIA WHILE LEAVING THE AIRPORT / CHECKPOST

1 Name in full _____

2. Flight No. _____

3. No. of checked in baggage (s)_____ 4. No. of hand baggage (s)_____

5. Total value of dutiable goods being imported _____

6. (a) Are you carrying any plants/seeds/fruits/flowers /vegetables/ bulbs/ other planting materials ?   Yes/No

(b) Are you carrying any meat & meat Products/dairy products/live or ornamental fish/poultry/poultry products ?   Yes/No

Signature of the passenger _____

GOVERNMENT OF INDIA
DEPARTURE CARD

(Rules 5 & 16 of Registration of Foreigners Rules)

BUREAU OF IMMIGRATION INDIA

Incredible !ndia

WISH YOU A HAPPY JOURNEY

Important Web Sites

1. Ministry of Home Affairs – *mha.nic.in*
2. Bureau of Immigration – *www.immigrationindia.nic.in*
3. Airports Authority of India – *www.airportsindia.org.in*
4. Central Board of Excise & Customs – *www.cbec.gov.in*
5. Ministry of Tourism - *www.incredibleindia.org.in*
          - *www.tourism.nic.in*

DEPARTURE CARD.

Please write in CAPITALS only. One character in one box as shown below. Do not write across the lines. Leave a box blank for space.

DC6 6276286

| A | B | C | D | E | 1 | 2 | 3 | 4 | 5 |

1a. Name (**as in passport**) Leave one box blank after every part of the name/initial

1b. Sex (put ' √ ' in box)　　**2.** Nationality

☐ Male　☐ Female

3. Date of birth (DD/MM/YY)

4a. Passport Number　　**4b.** Date of issue (DD/MM/YY)

5a. Date of boarding (DD/MM/YY)　　**5b.** Flight Number

5c. Port of final destination

6. Occupation (put √ in appropriate box)

☐ Doctor　☐ Business　☐ Employed　☐ Media　☐ Lawyer　☐ Government　☐ Sports Person　☐ Other

7. Purpose of visit - for Indian nationals only (put √ in appropriate box)

☐ Tourism　☐ Business　☐ Transit　☐ Official　☐ Employment　☐ Education

☐ Conference　☐ Social　☐ Medical Treatment　☐ Pilgrimage　☐ Sports　☐ Other

8. Address in India

Telephone number

IMMIGRATION STAMP

Signature of passenger

APPENDIX 8.6

Travel Insurance Form

F. No. **OMP Proposal (New) w.e.f. 1.11.2003**

 The New India Assurance Company Limited
Regd. & Head Office : 87, Mahatama Gandhi Road, Fort, Mumbai - 400 001.
Regional Office : Sharda Centre, 2nd Floor, Behind Nal Stop, Karve Road, Pune 411 004.

PROPOSAL FORM FOR OVERSEAS MEDICLAIM POLICY
(Business & Holiday)
(To be submitted in Original with 2 copies)
(Available to persons in the age group of 6 months to 70 years)

IMPORTANT

PLEASE MAKE SURE YOU READ AND FULLY UNDERSTAND THIS DOCUMENT BEFORE YOU TRAVEL FROM THE REPUBLIC OF INDIA.

FAILURE TO FOLLOW THE INSTRUCTION GIVEN COULD RESULT IN REJECTION OF ANY CLAIM THAT MIGHT BE MADE.

THE OVERSEAS MEDICLAIM POLICY PROVIDES INDEMNITY FOR EXPENSES NECESSARILY INCURRED FOR IMMEDIATE TREATMENT OF ILLNESS, DISEASES CONTRACTED OR INJURY FIRST SUSTAINED (DURING THE PERIOD OF INSURANCE OF OVERSEAS TRAVEL SUBJECT TO POLICY TERMS AND CONDITIONS).

POLICY ALSO OFFERS PERSONAL ACCIDENT COVER

UNDER SELECTED PLANS, FOLLOWING ADD ON COVERS ARE OFFERED: -

- TOTAL LOSS OF CHECKED IN BAGGAGE
- DELAY OF CHECKED IN BAGGAGE
- LOSS OF PASSPORT
- PERSONAL LIABILITY

IN THE ABSENCE OF MEDICAL REPORTS AS SPECIFIED IN ITEM 11 (B) SUM INSURED WILL STAND REDUCED TO AN EQUIVALENT AMOUNT OF US$ 10,000 IN RESPECT OF MEDICAL EXPENSES INCURRED THROUGH ILLNESS OR DISEASE ONLY, SUBJECT TO EXCLUSION OF PRE-EXISTING DISEASE.

THE ATTENTION OF THE PROPOSER IS DRAWN TO ITEM II (MEDICAL HISTORY) OF THE PROPOSAL FORM ESPECIALLY IN RELATION TO PREVIOUS TREATMENT FOR ILLNESS OR DISEASE SUCH AS RENAL DISORDERS OR DISEASES, CEREBRAL OR VASCULAR STROKES, HEART AILMENT OF ANY KIND, MALIGNANCY, TUBERCULOSIS, ENCEPHALITIS, NEUROLOGICAL DISORDERS, GALL BLADDER DISORDER, ARTHRITIS REQUIRING SURGERY AND IF ANY TREATMENT HAS BEEN RECEIVED FOR ANY OF THE ABOVE DISORDERS AT ANY TIME IN THE PAST, SUCH TREATMENT MUST BE DISCLOSED TO THE POLICY ISSUING OFFICE.

NEITHER THE INSURERS NOR CLAIMS SETTLING AGENTS SHALL BE RESPONSIBLE FOR THE AVAILABILITY, QUALITY OR RESULTS OF ANY MEDICAL TREATMENT OR THE FAILURE OF THE INSURED TO OBTAIN MEDICAL TREATMENT.

THE PROPOSAL FORM SHOULD BE COMPLETED TO THE BEST OF YOUR KNOWLEDGE AND BELIEF, AND ALL MATERIAL FACTS SHOULD BE DISCLOSED. FAILURE TO DO SO MAY NULLIFY COVER UNDER THE POLICY ISSUED.

NOTE: Plan A - 1 & A - 2 (Worldwide travel excluding USA / Canada)
Plan B - 1 & B - 2 (Worldwide travel including USA / Canada)
Plan E - 1 & E - 2 (Corporate Frequent Travel to all destinations including USA / Canada)
Plan K (For travel to Asian countries - Japan not included)

Medical Reports are required
- A) Trip is for period over 60 days and if
  - a) insured person if over 60 yrs of age visiting USA/Canada
  - b) insured is over 70 yrs of age and visiting countries other than USA/Canada.
- B) Proposal reveals that insured had suffered from / suffering from any illness / disease.

the Proposal Form should be accompanied with 1) ECG printout with report and 2) Fasting blood Sugar and Urine Sugar, Urine Strip Test Report or any other medical report required by the company etc. along with the attached questionnaire II (B) to be completed and signed by the Doctor with minimum M. D. qualification conducting the test. In the absence of such medical tests and reports due to a shortage of time before travel, cover may still be granted subject to a satisfactory proposal form but the sum insured under policy, in respect of expenses incurred for the treatment of illness or disease shall be restricted to US $ 10,000 only, which shall not cover the cost of Medical treatment for pre-existing disease. In case of accident however the full sum insured benefit would be available.

2

I. **GENERAL INFORMATION**

1. NAME OF THE PROPOSER
   (IN BLOCK LETTERS) AS STATED IN THE PASSPORT.   :   MR. / MRS. / MISS. / MASTER

2. HOME ADDRESS & TELEPHONE NO.   :

3. PROPOSER'S ACTUAL OCCUPATION
   (Specify)   :

4. OFFICE ADDRESS   :

5. TELEPHONE NO./FAX NO./E-MAIL ADDRESS   :

6. AGE (IN COMPLETED YEARS)   :   DATE OF BIRTH

7. PASSPORT NO.   :
   DATE OF EXPIRY &   :
   NAME OF PASSPORT ISSUING AUTHORITY   :

8. PLAN OPTED FOR   :   A-1   A-2   B-1   B-2   E-1   E-2   K
   (Please tick relevant plan)

9. PURPOSE OF VISIT
   (BUSINESS / HOLIDAY TRAVEL)

10. PROPOSED DATE OF DEPARTURE FROM   :   DAY   MONTH   YEAR
    REPUBLIC OF INDIA i.e. FIRST DAY OF INSURANCE

11. INSURANCE REQUIRED FOR   :
    (Number of days)

N.B.:   1. In case of any extension of stay abroad, requiring extension of policy period, approval of issuing office has to be obtained & appropriate premium paid before expiry of policy. Request for such extension should be supported with a declaration of good health.

         2. In case of early return partial refund of premium will be permitted if the original cover is for minimum period of 60 days and unexpired period is not less than 14 days and also if no claim is lodged under the policy.

12. COUNTRIES TO BE VISITED   :
    (State approximate number of days at each place)

13. NAME, REGISTRATION NO., ADDRESS &   :
    TELEPHONE NO. OF FAMILY PHYSICIAN

11. MEDICAL HISTORY.

(A)   TO BE COMPLETED BY THE PROPOSER

PLEASE ANSWER THE FOLLOWING QUESTIONS WITH 'YES' OR 'NO' (A DASH IS NOT SUFFICIENT) AND GIVE FULL DETAILS :

1. Are you in good health and free from Physical and mental disease or infirmity.   : _____

2. Have you ever suffered from any illness or disease upto the date of making this proposal.   : _____

3. Do you have any physical defect or deformity.   : _____

4. Have you ever been admitted to any hospital/nursing
   home/clinic for treatment or observation.   : _____

5. Have you suffered from any illness / disease or had an accident
   in the 12 months preceding the first day of insurance.   : _____

6. If the answer is 'yes' to any of the foregoing questions please give full details as under :

Nature of illness/disease/ injury & treatment received	Date on which first treatment taken	First treatment completed /is continuing	Name of attending medical practitioner/ Surgeon with his address & Tel. Nos.

7. a) Have you any intention of engaging in professional sports?

   b) If so, give details. _____

   _____

8. Please give details of any knowledge of any positive existence of any ailment, sickness or injury which may require medical attention whilst on tour abroad.

I HEREBY DECLARE THAT

1. I will not be travelling against the advice of a physician
2. I am not on the waiting list of any medical treatment.
3. I will not be travelling for the purpose of obtaining medical treatment.
4. I have not received a terminal prognosis for a medical condition before this day.

Assignment:

I _____ do hereby assign the monies payable under the

_____ policy in the event of my death to my

_____ (relation to the insured

Mr / Mrs / Miss. / Master _____ I further declare that his , her receipt

shall be sufficient discharge to the company.

I further declare that and warrant that the above statements are true and complete. I consent to the insurers seeking medical information from any doctor who has at any time attended concerning anything which affects my physical or mental health, and I authorize the giving of such information to Coris International and / or their programme medical advisers. I agree that this proposal shall form the basis of the contract should the insurance be effected.

I am willing to accept the policy, subject to the terms, exceptions and conditions prescribed therein.

Signature of Proposer.   Date : _____ / _____ / _____
                                                                  Day   Month   Year

Place :

B) TO BE COMPLETED BY THE DOCTOR [To be completed by M. D. only]

1. a) History

   b) Any past history of disease, operation, accidents, investigation etc.

   c) General Examination.

   d) Systemic Examination.

2. **Electrocardiography**

   a) Does the attached Electrocardiogram in your professional opinion show any abnormalities if so, please describe :

   b) Does the abnormality represent a current illness or disease which may possibly require medical treatment during proposer's forthcoming trip?

   c) Does the Proposer now or did he/she in the past, require medication for this abnormality?

   d) Please describe any treatment taken by Proposer in the past or being taken at present

   e) Do you recommend Stress Test? If so please obtain the report on such test.

3. **Does the Blood / Urine Strip Test show any sugar ?**

4. Do you consider that Proposer is fit to travel anywhere abroad, due account being taken of the stress of air travel adversely affecting his health/medical condition?

   Signature of the Doctor   :

   Name of the Doctor   :

   Qualification   :

   Address   :

   Telephone No.   :

CHAPTER 9

Airline Geography

Learning Objectives

After reading this chapter you should be able to:
- understand the meaning and importance of airline geography
- know the various city and airport codes
- understand different time zones in the world
- appreciate the role of IATA in airline traffic facilitation
- know the various abbreviations used in the travel industry
- identify the currencies of various countries

INTRODUCTION

The advancement in technology has resulted in many developments, one of them being the development of transport. Like the other modes of transport, air transport too developed after the Industrial Revolution. Travel has become swifter and now people can travel thousands of kilometres and reach far-off destinations on the other side of the globe on the same day.

Travel for leisure or business is popular and tourists visit various places all over the world. The mode of transportation they select varies according to the availability and need, but for a long distance journey the preferred mode is always air transport.

Tourists prefer to travel by air for the following reasons:

- they have disposable income;
- it is the fastest mode of transport;
- they need to travel at short notice for business-related work; and
- air travel has become affordable with the introduction of low cost carriers.

Planning an air travel itinerary requires an understanding of world geography, the continents and oceans, world time zones, knowledge of airlines which ply on different routes, their codes and countries, cities, airports and their codes.

Airline geography covers the study of world, which is served by various airlines. It is the study of various tourist destinations around the globe which are linked by air, their routes, airports, airlines, city, and country codes. All places in the world are not tourist destinations. We have already read in Chapter 1 that a destination is a location that a traveller chooses to visit because it has various factors such as accessibility, attractions, activities, etc. which appeal to the traveller.

This chapter introduces the reader to the three IATA Traffic Conference areas of the world. It covers the various countries and cities which are linked by air, their codes, major international and domestic airports and their codes and airlines which ply on these routes. Tourism professionals need to know world geography and airline geography to enable them to plan itineraries. They need to know the location of the destination, which Traffic Conference (TC) area the city is located in, the connecting points, so that they can avoid unnecessary backtracking and choose the shortest route to save both time and money.

Airline geography is based on international standards, which need to be followed worldwide. These standards are set by IATA and have been created by International Standards Organization (ISO), based in Geneva, Switzerland. Codes for countries, cities, airlines, and airports have been created to simplify the procedures for selling and booking travel arrangements. These codes are universally accepted and are used in the travel industry.

PHYSICAL GEOGRAPHY

Before we study airline geography, let us revise some basic concepts related to geography so that we understand major airline routes, world time zones, and time differences better. Physical geography refers to the world's natural terrains or features. Land masses and water bodies are important in dictating the variety of the tourist product which can be offered at the destination. The major land masses or continents cover 29 per cent of the earth's surface. The seven continents are Europe, Asia, Africa, North America, South America, Australia, and Antarctica. The subcontinents are Central America, Australasia and the Pacific Islands, and the Middle East.

The four major oceans which cover 71 per cent of the earth's surface are the Pacific Ocean, Atlantic Ocean, Indian Ocean, and Arctic Ocean. The Pacific Ocean is the largest ocean.

Locating continents, countries, major tourist cities, and various water bodies on a map is a prerequisite to the study of travel and tourism.

A strong link exists between tourism and geography as the natural attractions and uniqueness of a destination is very often related to its geographic locations.

Geography is study of the earth and the factors that make the earth unique as well as the changes on the earth's surface brought about by the movement of people. Tourists need to travel to different destinations and geography has helped to simplify the process of measuring and indicating locations on the earth. A simple way to locate a place on the map is by using the imaginary lines of latitude and longitude.

The parallel lines which extend east to west on both sides of the equator are the latitude. The latitude tells us how far north or south of the equator, a given place is located. It is measured from the equator to the pole, the equator being zero degrees and the pole being 90 degrees.

The equator divides the world into two hemispheres.

1. The northern hemisphere or north latitude
2. The southern hemisphere or south latitude

Vertical lines called meridians, extending from the North Pole to the South Pole, intersect the parallels of latitude. They measure longitude and are not parallel to each other as they converge at the two poles. One meridian is taken as the point of reference and is called the Prime Meridian. The Prime Meridian runs through Greenwich, London.

The equator divides the world into two hemispheres—northern and southern, while the Prime Meridian divides the world into eastern and western divisions.

To understand world time zones, standard clock time, and the International Date Line, it is essential that all tourism professionals should be familiar with the basic concepts of geography as well as the major countries on the world map, before they begin reading this chapter.

They should refer to the Oxford Student Atlas for India 2004, page 5 and page 109 to clarify concepts if necessary.

WORLD TIME ZONES

The earth rotates on its axis from west to east and takes one complete day or 24 hours to complete the rotation. While half of the earth is lit by the rays of the sun and has daytime, the other half is plunged into darkness and experiences night.

Our conventional clock has 12 one hourly markings on it to which we add a.m. or p.m. to denote day or night. We tell the time using this clock. However, while preparing travel itineraries, this method is confusing and misleading because when it is daytime in one part of the globe, it may be nighttime in another area.

To remove confusion over a.m. and p.m. and to simplify the process of calculating elapsed travel times, the travel industry uses the 24-hour time clock.

In the 24-hour clock, each day begins at 00:00 hours, i.e. at midnight and progresses through each hour of the day from 01:00 hours or 01:00 am to 23:00 hours or 11:00 p.m.

The decision to create standardized time zones dividing the world into 24 time zones was taken in 1884 by the major nations of the world.

Imagine the planet earth as an orange, which has 24 equal sized segments. Each of the 24 vertical lines formed by the segments are the meridians or lines of longitude and each segment represents a time zone of one hour out of 24 hours measuring fifteen degrees. Since the earth is circular it has 360° of longitude (15° × 24 hours = 360°). When we travel from one zone to another, we have moved by one hour.

The world is now divided into 24 time zones, which begin with the Prime Meridian that we have read about earlier in this chapter, which is an imaginary line which passes through Greenwich, England and connects the North and South poles. The time at Greenwich and all other countries in this zone is called the Greenwich Mean Time (GMT) or the Universal Time Coordinated (UTC). The Greenwich Meridian or the Prime Meridian marks the starting point of every time zone in the world. The Prime Meridian is a fixed point and considered as zero (0°) degree. The time in other zones can be expressed by referring to the

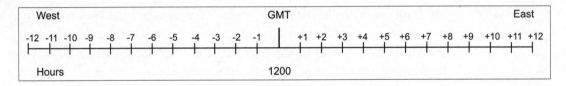

Fig. 9.1 Greenwich Mean Time

Greenwich Mean Time (GMT). The signs + (for plus) and – (for minus) are used (see Fig. 9.1) as follows:

GMT + 3 = 3 hours ahead of GMT

GMT – 3 = 3 hours behind GMT

These signs can be used for up to +12 or –12 hours.

The Scale of Hours

If we take a look at the time zones of the world and look at the map of India, we find that Mumbai is GMT +5 while Kolkata is GMT +6. This system needs to be adapted so that the local time is the same within national boundaries or groups of islands and India has adopted a uniform time zone of +5.30. The Standard Clock Time or Standard Time in India or Indian Standard Time (IST) is fixed and is the same whether you are in Gujarat or in the northeastern town of Shillong.

Daylight Saving Time

In some countries the Standard Time is modified during summer and is an hour or a fraction of an hour earlier. This is called daylight saving time (DST). For example, the standard clock time in New Zealand is +12 and DST is +13, sometime during the period October to March, which is summer time in New Zealand. The DST date may vary from year to year.

Time charts are published in all major airline guides. The complete Official Airline Guide (OAG) International Time Calculator lists the standard time in relation to GMT and DST in countries where it is applicable together with the specific period of the year.

If we know the date and time in one country, we can easily calculate what the date and time will be in another country at that moment.

Example 9.1

Using the scale of hours, one can find out what the local time in New Delhi, India is, when it is 12:00 hours GMT.

In India the standard time is GMT +5.30 all year round. This means that the local time is 5 ½ hours ahead of GMT. The local time in New Delhi is 17:30 hours when GMT is 12:00 hours.

GMT is necessary to calculate the time duration of a flight and to know the date and local time of departure of a flight and date and time of arrival. The GMT tells us the time difference between two cities.

Example 9.2

One can calculate the flying time for a British Airways flight from Mumbai to London from the particulars given below.

Date	Place	Local Time	GMT	GMT Time and Date	Flying Time
01.05.2008	Mumbai Departure	01:00	+5.30		
01.05.2008	London Arrival	07:00	+1		

Local time of different countries in different time zones, needs to be converted to a common time. The GMT time and date for both countries needs to be calculated.

In Mumbai the local time is 5.30 hours ahead of the GMT. This means that the GMT time is 5.30 hours behind the local time at Mumbai. GMT time at Mumbai would be 01:00 minus 05.30 which is equal to 19.30 hours of the previous day, i.e. 30.04.2008.

GMT time at London would be one hour before the local time, i.e. 07:00 minus 01:00 which is equal to 06:00 hours on the same date.

Flying time is the time between 19:30 on 30.04.2008 and 06:00 on 01.05.2008.

The flying time between Mumbai and London is 10 hours 30 minutes.

Date	Place	Local Time	GMT	GMT Time and Date	Flying Time
01.05.2008	Mumbai (Departure)	01:00	+5.30	19:30 hours, date 30.04.2008	
01.05.2008	London (Arrival)	07:00	+1	06:00 hours, date 01.05.08	10 hours 30 minutes

Multi-time Zone Countries

These countries have different time zones within the country, inspite of having the same national boundary. For example, USA has five time zones ranging from –5 at Indiana to –10 at Alaska, and in Australia the time zones range from +8 in Western Australia to +10.30 at Lord Howe Island.

INTERNATIONAL DATE LINE

World time is calculated in relation to the longitudinal location of a place. While the Prime Meridian passes through Greenwich, another meridian, which is located 180 degrees east of Greenwich or 180 degrees west of Greenwich, both being the same meridian is of importance. This meridian marks the change of day and is referred to as the International Date Line (see Fig. 9.2).

The International Date Line is an imaginary line running from North Pole to South Pole through the Pacific Ocean, with the date differing in the east and west, the east of the line being one day earlier. For example, if it is the 15 July in the USA, it will be 16 July in India.

Because of the International Date Line, if it is Sunday in San Francisco, California, it would be Monday in Sydney, Australia. Similarly if a tourist from India takes a flight to Texas, USA on 19 June 2008 early in the morning and the flight duration with halts is approximately 21 hours, he/she still reaches USA on 19 June around lunch time, saving nearly one day, because of the International Date Line.

Travellers may either gain a day or lose a day when they cross the International Date line. This is of particular importance to the business traveller who usually needs to arrive on a working day during normal working hours. Passengers, who travel long distance by air, often complain of jet lag because of the change in time zones. Often a full night's sleep is lost, because there is no nighttime, only daylight for over 24 hours.

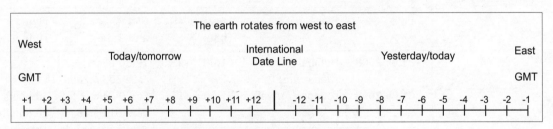

Fig. 9.2 International Date Line

After the journey, travellers may feel tired and drowsy during the day because their body clock is telling them it is midnight and time to get some rest, while the sun may be shining outside.

When travellers take long flights and cross multiple time zones in a short time span, they often experience tiredness, drowsiness, and fatigue. This feeling is called jet lag and occurs because the traveller's internal body clock is not sure whether it is day or night. Travellers may take a couple of days to return to normalcy.

While planning itineraries and specially while booking airline tickets, tourism professionals should know the following:

- The GMT should be used while calculating the time difference between two cities and that the International Date Line cannot be crossed while making calculations.
- The arrival and departure time mentioned in airline timetables is always the local time of that destination.
- Airline schedules are always published in the local time with the time variation from GMT of each city clearly specified.
- The complete OAG International Time Calculator lists all countries, its standard time in relation to GMT, DST if applicable as well as DST period.
- The elapsed travel time or the transport time is the total travelling time and covers the exact time in hours and minutes from the time of departure at the airport of origin, the transit time if any, till the time of arrival at the airport of the final destination.

Example 9.3

Air India Limited has introduced non-stop flights from Mumbai to New York. Let us study the airline timetable in terms of the International Date Line.

Air India Limited—Aircraft Boeing 777-200 LR (long range) Non-stop flight from Mumbai to New York City, John F. Kennedy Airport

Flight AI 141 BOM - NYC(JFK)				
Departure	-	Mumbai (BOM)	00:45	15 June 2008
Arrival	-	New York (JFK)	07:10	15 June 2008

The time difference between India and New York is 9:30 hours.

When it is 07:10 hours in New York it is 16:40 hours in India.

Transport time or elapsed travel time is 15:55 hours.

On the return journey, the flying time or the transport time is shorter as flying time depends on wind speed and route. Going westwards takes longer time than going eastwards.

Flight AI 140 NYC (JFK) – BOM				
Departure	-	New York (JFK)	21:30	16 June 2008
Arrival	-	Mumbai (BOM)	22:15	17 June 2008

Transport time in this case is shorter because of wind speed and is 15:15 hours. But if you look at the dates you will see that the person has been travelling for more than 24 hours and has lost a day in travelling, while in the flight to New York a day is gained.

Although each airline has its own timetables and information booklets, travel agents prefer to use a single international guide which includes the flight schedules of all airlines. The OAG World Airways Guide comes in two volumes and is simpler to refer to as compared to referring to the vast number of individual airlines timetables. It has a wide coverage and is easily available.

IATA AREAS OF THE WORLD

IATA, as we have already studied in Chapter 6, is an organization, which works for the airlines and its major role is in traffic facilitation. It helps airlines in making interline arrangements, standardizes different forms and procedures and passenger, baggage and cargo handling agreements, reservation codes, and other related matters. All procedures are computerized. This makes the exchange of traffic between various airlines easier and faster. It helps member airlines in negotiating fares.

IATA has divided the world into three areas or Traffic Conferences for the process of establishing fares and tariff related rules. Airlines which operate in and out of these areas or via these areas belong to that conference. The Traffic Conferences or Areas are as follows:

TC 1—North America, Central America, Caribbean Area, and South America
TC 2—Europe, Africa, and Middle East—including Iran
TC 3—Asia, Australia, and South Pacific islands

IATA's Traffic Conferences or Areas are not necessarily the same as continents. For the purpose of fare construction, countries located in one continent may be classified in another area. For example, Asia is included in TC 3 but Iran is included in TC 2.

Major Airline Routes

Airline routes depend on the airline, the direction of travel, and the network of airlines with their hubs. Normally airlines touch their hub (country to which the airline belongs) before proceeding to the destination. For example, Air France has its hub in Paris and British Airways has its hub in London. A British Airways flight from Mumbai to New York will fly via London.

Some airlines have more than one hub, for example, Delta Airlines has a hub in Atlanta, New York, and Salt Lake City while United Airlines have hubs in Chicago and Washington.

Air fares depend on many factors such as the route of the airline, the volume of traffic and the demand, the class of travel and the type of fare which is denoted by an alphabet. An economy or Y fare from Los Angeles to Singapore via the Pacific Ocean would be lower than the fare paid for travel if the plane flies via the Atlantic Ocean. Airlines operate on a number of different routes. For example, airlines may fly transiting the Atlantic Ocean (Trans Atlantic), transiting the Pacific Ocean (Trans Pacific), crossing both the Atlantic and Pacific Ocean or Round The World (RTW), in the Western Hemisphere (WH) or in the Eastern Hemisphere (EH). The flight route is represented by Global Indicators which are related to the traffic conference numbers. Global Indicators indicate the direction of travel on the globe. For example, Global Indicator WH refers to flight routes in area TC 1 which is in the WH, Global Indicator EH refers to flight routes in area TC 2 and TC 3 which is in the Eastern Hemisphere (EH). Other Global Indicators are SA via South Atlantic, AP via Atlantic and Pacific Oceans, TS or Trans Siberian etc. To understand airline routes and global indicators, knowing world geography is essential.

Some examples of Global Indicators

- A flight from Chicago to Buenos Aires via Panama City by United Airlines would be flying within area TC 1 or the Western Hemisphere and the Global Indicator (GI) would be WH.
- TC 1 and TC 2 or travel between area 1 and 2 via Atlantic Ocean, for example, a British Airways flight from Mumbai to Los Angeles via London would be represented by GI: AT.

- TC 3 and TC 1 or travel between area 3 and 1 via Pacific Ocean, for example, a Singapore Airlines flight from Mumbai to Los Angeles via Singapore transiting the Pacific Ocean would have a GI: PA.

CODES IN TOURISM

While preparing travel itineraries and booking tickets, tourism professionals need to be familiar with not only the TC areas of the world, the location of destinations and local time calculation, but also need information about city, airport, and currency codes. Each city having an airport is given a three letter ISO code. These codes are universal codes and are followed for airfare calculation, booking tickets, in itinerary planning, etc. For example, DEL is the city code for New Delhi and ORD is the airport code for Chicago–O'Hare Airport (see Table 9.1).

In case a city has more than one airport, each airport is referred to by a different code. These codes are also used on luggage tags and helps baggage handlers at the airport to load the luggage on to the correct flight.

Three-letter city and airport codes used in airlines industry are given in Appendix 9.1. City codes, airport names and codes of India are given in Appendix 9.2. The capital city is marked with an asterisk. The city with more than one airport has more than one code. Some examples of city and airport codes are listed in Table 9.1.

Table 9.1 Some city and airport codes

Country	City	City Code	Airport Name	Airport Code
France	Paris*	PAR	Charles de Gaulle	CDG
			Orly	ORY
Germany	Berlin*	BER	Tegel	TXL
			Tempelhof	THF
			Schoenenfeld	SXF
Italy	Rome*	ROM	Leonardo Da Vinci (Fiumicino)	FCO
	Milan	MIL	Linate	LIN
			Malpensa	MXP
	Naples	NAP		
	Venice	VCE		
United Kingdom	London*	LON	Heathrow	LHR
			Gatwick	LGW

Contd

Table 9.1   Contd

Country	City	City Code	Airport Name	Airport Code
	Edinburgh	EDI		
China	Beijing	BJS	Beijing Capital	PEK
	Shanghai	SHA		
	Hong Kong (SAR)	HKG		
	Guangzhou	CAN		
India	Delhi	DEL	Indira Gandhi International	
	Mumbai	BOM	C S M International	
Japan	Tokyo	TYO	Narita	NRT
			Haneda	HND
	Osaka	OSA		
Singapore	Singapore	SIN	Changi	
Turkey	Ankara	ANK	Esenboga	ESB
USA	New York	NYC	John F Kennedy	JFK
			La Guardia	LGA
			Newark	EWR
	Chicago	CHI	O'Hare	ORD
	Washington DC	WAS	Dulles International	IAD
			R. Reagan National	DCA

Airline Codes

Like the city codes and airport codes, every airline in the world has a unique identifying code. The IATA has assigned two-character alpha codes. These codes are also called the carrier code.

These codes are standard codes and are recognized throughout the aviation and related industries. For example, the code for Air India Ltd is AI and the code for Continental Airlines is CO. The list of airlines and their codes are given in Appendix 9.3.

Country Codes

Every country in the world has been given a two character code by IATA. These codes are standard and are recognized throughout the world. Some examples are given below (see Table 9.2). The remaining codes are given in Appendix 9.3.

Table 9.2 Some country codes

Country	Country codes
Afghanistan	AF
Canada	CA
Denmark	DK
India	IN
Malaysia	MY
Thailand	TH

Table 9.3 Currency codes of a few countries

Country	Currency	Code	Symbol
Australia	Australian Dollar	AUD	$
Austria	European Euro	EUR	•
Bahamas	Bahamian Dollar	BSD	B$
Hong Kong	Hong Kong Dollar	HKD	HK$
Hungary	Hungarian Forint	HUF	Ft
Iceland	Icelandic Króna	ISK	kr
India	Indian Rupee	INR	Rs
Indonesia	Indonesian Rupiah	IDR	Rp
Thailand	Thai Baht	THB	
Turkey	Turkish New Lira	TRY	YTL
UAE	UAE Dirham	AED	
UK	British Pound	GBP	£
USA	US Dollar	USD	US$

Currency Codes

The form of currency used in different countries of the world varies and travel professionals need to know the local currency used at different destinations as well as its exchange rate. The exchange rate varies from day to day. Each country has a currency code which is based on its country code and the first digit of its currency. For example, the country code for India is IN and the first digit of its currency the Rupee is R, so its currency code is INR (see Table 9.3). The remaining currencies and their codes are given in Appendix 9.5. The USD is the most easily exchangeable currency. All countries in the European Union with the exception of three, use the euro as their sole currency, so as to simplify business transactions not only in Europe, but also outside.

Currency codes simplify the process of identifying currencies from different countries.

Important Abbreviations

Many short forms or abbreviations are used by airlines on the ticket, in their timetables and on Miscellaneous Charges Order (MCO), etc. Travel professionals should be familiar with these abbreviations. Some of the commonly used abbreviations are listed in Table 9.4.

For smooth operations of air traffic worldwide, certain international standards need to be followed. The codes created for countries, cities, airports, airlines, currency, etc. which we have just read are universally accepted and used. Knowledge of airline geography will help tourism professionals to locate destinations, select connecting points, choose shortest routes, understand world time zones and International Date Line, and understand codes, all of which are essential while planning itineraries.

Table 9.4   Some important abbreviations

Abbreviation	Expanded form	Abbreviation	Expanded form
ACK	Acknowledge	AGT	Agent
ALTL	Alternative	BRD	Boarding
BSP	Billing and settlement plan	CHD	Child
CHTR	Charter	CRS	Computerized reservation system
DEP	Departure	DGT	Digit
EMA	Extra mileage allowance	EMS	Excess mileage surcharge
ETA	Estimated time of arrival	ETD	Estimated time of departure
EQP	Equipment (type of aircraft)	FIT	Free independent traveller
FLT	Flight	FM	From (departure city)
END	Endorsement	FRQ	Frequency (days of operation)
GIT	Group inclusive tour	GSA	General sales agent
INTL	International	ISD	Issued
MCO	Miscellaneous charges order	MPM	Maximum permitted mileage
NUC	Neutral unit of construction	OAG	Official airline guide
OW	One way	PNR	Passenger name record
PTA	Prepaid ticket advice	RES	Reservation
RFD	Refund	RER	Re-routable
REP	Representative	RR	Reconfirmed
SKED	Schedule	ST	Stops (number of stops)
TIM	Travel information manual	TKT	Ticket
TO	To (arrival city)	TRS	Travel-related services
VLD	Valid	XX	Cancel request

SUMMARY

A knowledge of world geography is essential to locate destinations around the globe and to plan travel itineraries. Airline geography is very important in tourism, especially for the purpose of traffic facilitation and fare construction. IATA has divided the world into three Traffic Conference areas.

IATA codes are an integral part of the travel industry, and essential for the identification of an airline or a logistics company, its destinations and its traffic documents. Every airline in the world has a unique two digit identifying code assigned by IATA also called carrier code. These codes are standard and recognized throughout the aviation and related industries.

Airline codes are required for passengers, baggage and cargo, for export declarations, departure reports, impending arrival reports, etc. Apart from the airline codes, country codes, city and airport codes, currency codes, other common terms and their abbreviations should also be known.

KEY TERMS

Daylight saving time A particular time of the year in some regions of the world when clocks are set forward by one–two hours to extend daylight into evening hours.

Elapsed travel time Actual time spent travelling from one destination to another. Also called transport time.

Greenwich mean time (GMT) The time at Greenwich, London which is used as a reference to calculate time anywhere in the world.

International Date Line An imaginary line or meridian that runs through the Pacific Ocean and is both 12 hours ahead of and 12 hours behind GMT and marks the change of day.

Official Airlines Guide (OAG) A guide which lists the schedule of many different carriers showing connections of up to three segments. It also contains information on carriers, baggage allowance, excess baggage charges, fares and taxes.

Prime Meridian It is the imaginary line that connects the North and South Pole and runs through Greenwich, London. The Prime Meridian is taken as the reference line for calculating time zones.

Universal Time Coordinated (UTC) Another term used in place of GMT.

Segment Segment is a portion or section of an itinerary and includes travel from one point to another. Itineraries have air segment, surface segment, outbound segment, and return segment.

Timetable Flight schedules which are specific for a carrier and which each carrier publishes on its own.

CONCEPT REVIEW QUESTIONS

1. List the continents in the world.
2. What do you understand by the terms longitude and latitude?
3. Explain the concept of 'Prime Meridian' and 'International Date Line'.
4. What is a multi-zone country? Name any three multi-zone countries?
5. What is the three-letter code for the John F. Kennedy Airport located in New York City?

   (a) ORD   (b) LGA   (c) JFK   (d) NYC

6. What is the three-letter code for the Heathrow airport in London?

   (a) LHR   (b) EDI   (c) LGW

7. What is the three-letter code of the airport Narita in Tokyo?

   (a) OSA   (b) NRT   (c) HND

8. What is the three-letter code for the following cities?

   (a) Singapore   (b) Pretoria   (c) Cairo   (d) Amsterdam
   (e) Brasilia   (f) Canberra   (g) Nice

9. Give the country codes for the following countries:

   (a) New Zealand (b) Japan   (c) Thailand   (d) the UK
   (e) South Africa

10. Give the carrier codes for the following Airlines:

    (a) Alitalia   (b) Air Canada (c) Mexicana   (d) Egyptair
    (e) Air India Limited

REFERENCES

Foster, L.D. 1994, *First Class: An Introduction to Travel And Tourism*, McGraw-Hill Book Co, Singapore.

IATA, Foundation, January 2004, *International Travel and Tourism Training Programme*, Montreal.

IATA, 2007, *International Travel and Tourism Training Programme*. Training text book. M1.12. Airfares and Ticketing 1.5.8 Edition, Montreal.

IGNOU, TS-3, 1999, *Management In Tourism, Block-6*. IGNOU School of Health Sciences, New Delhi.

Lloyd E. Hudman and Richard H. Jackson, 1999, *Geography of Travel & Tourism*, Third Edition, Delmar Publishers, USA.

Oxford Student Atlas for India, 2004, Oxford University Press, New Delhi.

http//www. asiaroom.com, accessed on 01 December 2008

http://en.wikipedia.org/wiki/Category:Airports_in_Karnataka

http://en.wikipedia.org/wiki/Bagdogra_Air_Force_Base
http://en.wikipedia.org/wiki/Rudra_Mata_Airport
http:aai.aero/allAirports/dimapur_general_info.jsp
http:aai.aero/allAirports/agartala_generalinfo.jsp
www. airlinecodes.co.uk, accessed on 01 December 2008.
www. hotelstravel.com, accessed on 01 December 2008.
www. iata_codes.htm, accessed on 01 December 2008
www. onebag.com, accessed on 01 December 2008
www. indianairlines.in, accessed on 01 December 2008
www.bharatonline.com/uttar-pradesh/travel-tips/up-airports.html
www.bharatonline.com/andhra-pradesh/travel-tips/airports.html
www.bharatonline.com/gujarat/travel-tips/airports.html
www.bharatonline.com/maharashtra/travel-tips/airports.html
www.ourairports.com/countries/IN/MM/airports.html
www.iloveindia.com/indian-airports/guwahati-airport.html
www.flights.headlinesindia.com/rajasthan.html
www.mapsofindia.com/ludhiana/airport.html

City Codes, Airport Names and Codes of Different Countries

Note: Some cities have more than one airport, hence more than one code. If no airport name is mentioned, it means that the city and airport name are the same, and they have the same code.

Country	City	Airport name	City code/ Airport code	Airport name	Airport code
		Europe			
Albania	Tirana	Rinas Mother Teresa	TIA		
Armenia	Yerevsan	Zvartnots	EVN		
Azerbaijan	Baku		BAK		
Austria	Vienna	Schwechat International	VIE		
Belarus	Minsk	Minsk International	MSQ		
Belgium	Brussels	Brussels International	BRU		
Bosnia	Sarajevo	Sarajevo	SJJ		
Bulgaria	Sofia	Sofia	SOF		
Croatia	Zagreb	Pleso	ZAG		
Cyprus	Nicosia*	Nicosia Intl.	NIC		
	Larnaca	Larnaca	LCA		
Czech Rep	Prague	Ruzyne International	PRG		
Denmark	Copenhagen	Kastrup	CPH		
Estonia	Tallinn	Ulemiste	TLL		
Finland	Helsinki		HEL		
France	Paris		PAR	Charles de Gaulle	CDG
				Orly	ORY
	Marseille	Marseille Provence	MRS		
	Bordeaux	Mérignac	BOD		
	Nice	Cote D'azur Intl.	NCE		
	Lyon	Bron	LYN		
Germany	Berlin	Berlin Metropolitan Area	BER	Tegel	TXL
				Tempelhof	THF
				Schoenenfeld	SXF
	Frankfurt	Frankfurt Intl.	FRA		
	Hamburg		HAM		
	Düsseldorf	Düsseldorf Intl.	DUS		
	Munich	Franz-Josef-Strauss	MUC		
	Cologne	Cologne/Bonn	CGN		

Contd

Appendix 9.1 Contd

Country	City	Airport name	City code/ Airport code	Airport name	Airport code
	Bonn		BNG		
	Stuttgart	Stuttgart Echterdingen	STR		
Greece	Athens	Eleftherios Venizelos	ATH		
Hungary	Budapest	Ferihegy	BUD		
Iceland	Reykjavik	Keflavik	RKV	Keflavik	KEF
Ireland	Dublin	Dublin Airport	DUB		
Italy	Rome*	ROM		Leonardo Da Vinci (Fiumicio)	FCO
	Milan		MIL	Linate	LIN
				Malpensa	MXP
	Naples		NAP		
	Venice	Marco Polo	VCE		
Latvia	Riga	Riga Intl.	RIX		
Lithuania	Vilnius	Vilnius	VNO		
Luxembourg	Luxembourg	Findel	LUX		
Moldova	Kishinev	Kishinev	KIV		
Malta	Valletta		MLA		
Netherlands	Amsterdam*	Schiphol	AMS		
	Rotterdam	Rotterdam Zestienhoven	RTM		
	Bergen		BGO		
Norway	Oslo	Oslo	OSL		
Poland	Warsaw	Frederic Chopin	WAW		
Portugal	Lisbon	Portela	LIS		
	Porto	Francisco Sá Carneiro	OPO		
	Funchal	Madeira	FNC		
Romania	Bucharest*		BUH	Otopeni	OTP
Russian	Moscow*		MOW	Sheremetyevo	SVO
Federation (West of the Urals)	St Petersburg		LED		
Spain	Madrid*		MAD		
	Barcelona	El Prat De Llobregat	BCN		
	Laspalmas		LPA		
Sweden	Stockholm		STO		
	Gottenburg	Landvetter	GOT	Arlanda	ARN
Switzerland	Berne*	Belp	BRN		
	Zurich	Zurich intl.	ZRH		
	Geneva	Geneva airport	GVA		
Turkey	Istanbul		IST		
	Ankara		ANK		

Contd

Appendix 9.1   Contd

Country	City	Airport name	City code/ Airport code	Airport name	Airport code
UK	London*	LON		Heathrow	LHR
				Gatwick	LGW
	Edinburgh	Edinburgh airport	EDI		
Ukraine	Kiev		IVE		
Yugoslavia	Belarus		BEG		

Africa

Country	City	Airport name	City code/ Airport code	Airport name	Airport code
Algeria	Algiers		ALG		
Angola	Luanda		LAD		
Botswana	Gaberone	Gaberone-Seretse Khama	GBE		
Cameroon	Yaounde		YAO		
	Douala		DLA		
Congo	Brazzaville	Brazzaville Maya-Maya	BZV		
Cote d'Ivoire	Yamoussoukro		ASK		
	Abidjan		ABJ		
Djibouti	Djibouti		JIB		
Egypt	Cairo	Cairo Intl.	CAI		
Ethiopia	Addis Ababa		ADD		
Gabon	Libreville	Leon M'Ba Intl.	LBV		
Ghana	Accra		ACC		
Kenya	Nairobi		NBO		
	Mombasa		MBA		
Liberia	Monrovia		MLW		
Libya	Tripoli		TIP		
Mauritius	Port Louis	Sir Seewoosagur Ramgoolam Intl.	MRU		
Morocco	Rabat		RBA		
	Casablanca		CAS		
Mozambique	Maputo	Maputo Intl.	MPM		
Namibia	Windhoek	Hosea Kutako Intl.	WDH		
Nigeria	Abuja		ABV		
	Lagos		LOS		
Rwanda	Kigali		KGL		
Senegal	Dakar		DKR		
Seychelles	Victoria	Seychelles Intl.	SEZ		
Sierra Leone	Freetown		FNA		
South Africa	Pretoria		PRY		
	Cape Town	Cape Town Intl.	CPT		
	Johannesburg	Johannesburg/Tambo Intl.	JNB		

Contd

Appendix 9.1 Contd

Country	City	Airport name	City code/ Airport code	Airport name	Airport code
Sudan	Khartoum		KRT		
Tanzania	Dodoma		DOD		
	Dar es Salaam		DAR		
Tunisia	Tunis		TUN		
Uganda	Entebbe		EBB		
Zambia	Lusaka	Lusaka Intl.	LUN		
Zimbabwe	Harare	Harare Intl.	HRE		
		Asia			
Afghanistan	Kabul		KBL		
Bahrain	Manama		BAH		
Bangladesh	Dhaka	Zia Intl.	DAC		
Brunei Darussalam	Bandar Seri Begawan	Brunei Darussalam	BWN		
Cambodia	Phnom Penh	Pochentong	PNH		
China	Beijing		BJS	Beijing	PEK
	Shanghai	Hongqiao	SHA	Capital	
	Hong Kong (SAR)	Hong kong	HKG		
	Guangzhou	Baiyun	CAN		
Chinese Taipei	Taipei	Taoyuan Intl.	TPE		
India	Bangalore	Bangalore	BLR		
	Delhi	Indira Gandhi Intl.	DEL		
	Mumbai	C.S. Intl. Airport	BOM		
	Chennai	Meenambakkam Airport	MAA		
	Kolkota	Netaji S.C.B. Intl.	CCU		
Indonesia	Jakarta		JKT		
Iran	Tehran		THR		
Iraq	Baghdad		BGW		
Israel	Jerusalem		JRS		
	Tel Aviv		TLV		
Japan	Tokyo		TYO	Narita	NRT
				Haneda	HND
	Osaka		OSA		
Jordan	Amman		AMM		
Korea South	Seoul		SEL		
Korea North	Pyongyang	Sunan	FNJ		
Kuwait	Kuwait		KWI		
Lebanon	Beirut		BEY		

Contd

Appendix 9.1 Contd

Country	City	Airport name	City code/ Airport code	Airport name	Airport code
Malaysia	Kuala Lumpur	Kuala Lumpur Intl.	KUL		
Mongolia	Ulaan Baatar		ULN		
Myanmar	Yangon		RGN		
Nepal	Kathmandu	Tribhuvan	KTM		
Oman	Muscat		MCT		
Pakistan	Islamabad	Islamabad Intl.	ISB		
	Karachi	Quaid-E-Azam Intl.	KHI		
	Lahore	Lahore	LHE		
Philippines	Manila	Ninoy Aquino Intl.	MNL		
Qatar	Doha		DOH		
Russian Federation (East of the Urals)	Khabarovsk		KHV		
Saudi Arabia	Riyadh		RUH		
	Jeddah		JED		
	Deharan		DHA		
Singapore	Singapore	Changi	SIN		
Sri Lanka	Colombo		CMB		
Syria	Damascus		DAM		
Thailand	Bangkok	Bangkok	BKK		
Turkey	Ankara		ANK	Esenboga	ESB
UAE	Abu Dhabi		AUH		
	Dubai		DXB		
	Sharjah		SHJ		
Vietnam	Hanoi	Noibai	HAN		
Yemen	Sanaa		SAH		
	Aden		ADE		
Australia and Pacific Islands					
Australia	Adelaide	Adelaide Intl.	ADL		
	Brisbane	Brisbane Intl.	BNE		
	Canberra	Canberra Intl.	CBR		
	Darwin	Darwin Intl.	DRW		
	Sydney	Sydney Intl.	SYD		
	Melbourne	Tullamarine Airport	MEL		
	Perth	Perth Airport	PER		
Fiji	Suva		SUV		
	Nadi		NAN		

Contd

Appendix 9.1 Contd

Country	City	Airport name	City code/ Airport code	Airport name	Airport code
French Polynesia	Papeete		PPT		
New Zealand	Wellington	Wellington	WLG		
	Auckland	Auckland Intl.	AKL		
	Christchurch	Christchurch	CHC		
Papua New Guinea	Port Moresby		POM		
Solomon island	Honiara		HIR		

North America

Country	City	Airport name	City code/ Airport code	Airport name	Airport code
Canada	Calgary	Calgary International	YYC		
	Edmonton	Edmonton Intl.	YEG		
	Ottawa	Macdonald-Cartier Intl.	YOW		
	Montreal		YMQ	Mirabel	YMX
				Dorval	YUL
	Toronto		YTO	Pearson Intl.	YYZ
	Vancouver	Vancouver International	YVR		
	Winnipeg	Winnipeg International	YWG		
Greenland	Nuuk		GOH		
USA	Atlanta	Hartsfield-Jackson Atlanta Intl.	ATL		
	Anchorage	Anchorage International	ANC		
	Boston	Logan International	BOS		
	Chicago		CHI	O'Hare	ORD
	Cincinnati	Cincinnati/Northern Kentucky International	CVG		
	Cleveland	Cleveland Hopkins International	CLE		
	Dallas	Dallas/Fort Worth International Airport	DFW		
	Detroit		DTT	Wayne County	DTW
	Houston	Houston George Bush Intercontinental	HOU		
	Los Angeles	Los Angeles International	LAX		
	Miami	Miami International	MIA		
	Minneapolis	Minneapolis/St. Paul International	MSP		
	New York		NYC	John F Kennedy	JFK
				La Guardia	LGA
				Newark	EWR

Contd

Appendix 9.1   Contd

Country	City	Airport name	City code/ Airport code	Airport name	Airport code
	Orlando		ORL		
	Philadelphia	Philadelphia International	PHL		
	St. Louis	St. Louis Lambert International	STL		
	San Francisco	San Francisco International	SFO		
	Seattle	Seattle-Tacoma Intl.	SEA		
	Washington D.C.		WAS	Dulles International	IAD
				R. Reagan National	DCA
Hawaii island	Honolulu	Honolulu International	HNL		

		Central America			
Bahamas	Nassau	Nassau Intl.	NAS		
	Freeport	Grand Bahama Intl.	FPO		
Barbados	Bridgetown		BGI		
Belize	Belmopan		BZE		
Costa Rica	San Jose		SJO		
Cuba	Havana		HAV		
Guatemala	Guatemala City		GUA		
Haiti	Port au Prince		PAP		
Honduras	Tegucigalpa		TGU		
Jamaica	Kingston		KIN		
Mexico	Mexico City	Internacional Benito Juarez	MEX		
	Acapulco	General Juan N Alvarez	ACA		
	Guadalajara	Intl.	GDL		
Netherlands Antilles	Curacao		CUR		
Nicaragua	Managua		MGA		
Panama	Panama City		PTY		
Trinidad & Tobago	Port of Spain		POS		

		South America			
Argentina	Buenos Aires		BUE		
Bolivia	La Paz		LPB		

Contd

Appendix 9.1 Contd

Country	City	Airport name	City code/ Airport code	Airport name	Airport code
Brazil	Brasilia	Presidente Juscelino Kubitschek	BSB		
	Manaus	Guararapes Intl.	MAO		
	Recife		RCE		
	Rio de Janeiro		RIO	Galeao	GIG
	Sao Paulo		SAO	Guarulhos	GRU
				Congonhas	CGH
				Viracopos	VCP
Chile	Santiago de Chile		SCL		
Colombia	Bogota		BOG		
	Barranquila		BAQ		
Ecuador	Quito		UIO		
French Guiana	Cayenne		CAY		
Paraguay	Asuncion		ASU		
Lima		Jorge Chavez Intl.	LIM		
Paramaribo			PBM		
Uruguay	Montevideo		MVD		
Venezuela	Caracas	Simon Bolivar Intl.	CCS		
	Maracaibo	La Chinita	MAR		

City Codes, Airport Names and Codes of India

City	State/ Region	Airport	Airport Code
Agartala	Tripura	Agartala Singerbhil	IXA
Agra	Uttar Pradesh	Agra Airport	AGR
Ahmedabad	Gujarat	Ahmedabad Airport	AMD
Allahabad	Uttar Pradesh	Allahabad Bamrauli	IXD
Amritsar	Punjab	Amritsar Raja Sansi Airport	ATQ
Aurangabad	Maharashtra	Chikalthan	IXU
Bagdogra	Sikkim	Bagdogra Airport	IXB
Bangalore	Karnataka	Bangalore Airport	BLR
Bhavnagar	Gujarat	Bhavnagar Civil Airport	BHU
Bhopal	Madhya Pradesh	Bhopal Airport	BHO
Bhubaneswar	Orissa	Bhubaneswar Airport	BBI
Bhuj	Gujarat	Bhuj Rudra Mata Airport	BHJ
Calcutta (Kolkata)	West Bengal	Netaji S C Bose International Airport	CCU
Chandigarh	Chandigarh	Chandigarh Airport	IXC
Chennai(Madras)	Tamil Nadu	Meenambakkam Airport	MAA
Cochin	Kerala	Cochin Airport	COK
Coimbatore	Coimbatore	Coimbatore Peelamedu Airport	CJB
Daman	Daman	Daman Airport	NMB
Dehradun	Uttarakhand	Dehradun Grant Airport	DED
Dibrugarh	Assam	Dibrugarh Airport	DIB
Dimapur	Nagaland	Dimapur Airport	DMU
Diu	Daman and Diu	Diu Airport	DIU
Guwahati	Assam	Lokpriya Gopinath Bordoloi International Airport	GAU
Goa	Goa	Dabolim Airport	GOI
Gwalior	Madhya Pradesh	Gwalior Airport	GWL
Hubli	Karnataka	Hubli Airport	HBX
Hyderabad	Andhra Pradesh	Begumpet Airport	HYD
Imphal	Manipur	Imphal Municipal Airport	IMF
Indore	Madhya Pradesh	Indore Airport	IDR
Jaipur	Rajasthan	Jaipur Airport	JAI
Jammu	Jammu & Kashmir	Jammu Airport	IXJ
Jamnagar	Gujarat	Govardhan Airport	JGA

Contd

Appendix 9.2 Contd

City	State/ Region	Airport	Airport Code
Jamshedpur	Jharkhand	Jamshedpur Sonari Airport	IXW
Jodhpur	Rajasthan	Jodhpur Airport	JDH
Jorhat	Assam	Rowriah Airport	JRH
Kanpur	Uttar Pradesh	Kanpur Airport	KNU
Khajuraho	Madhya Pradesh	Khajuraho Airport	HJR
Kozhikode (Calicut)	Kerala	Kozhikode Airport	CCJ
Leh	Jammu & Kashmir	Leh Airport	IXL
Lucknow	Utter Pradesh	Amausi Airport	LKO
Ludhiana	Punjab	Ludhiana Sahnewal	LUH
Madurai	Tamil Nadu	Madurai Airport	IXM
Mangalore	Karnataka	Mangalore Bajpe Airport	IXE
Mumbai (Bombay)	Maharashtra	C S International Airport	BOM
Nagpur	Maharashtra	Sonegaon Airport	NAG
Nanded	Maharashtra	Nanded Airport	NDC
Nashik	Maharashtra	Gandhi Nagar Airport	ISK
New Delhi	Delhi	Indira Gandhi International Airport	DEL
Patna	Bihar	Patna Airport	PAT
Pondicherry	Union Territory (UT)	Pondicherry Airport	PNY
Poona (Pune)	Maharashtra	Lohegaon Airport	PNQ
Porbandar	Gujarat	Porbandar Airport	PBD
Port Blair	Andaman and Nicobar Islands	Port Blair Airport	IXZ
Puttaparthi	Andhra Pradesh	Puttaparthi Airport	PUT
Rae Bareli	Uttar Pradesh	Rae Bareli Airport	BEK
Rajkot	Gujarat	Rajkot Airport	RAJ
Ranchi	Jharkhand	Ranchi Airport	IXR
Shillong	Meghalaya	Shillong Barapani Airport	SHL
Silchar	Assam	Kumbirgram Airport	IXS
Srinagar	Jammu & Kashmir	Srinagar Airport	SXR
Surat	Gujrat	Surat Airport	STV
Tezpur	Assam	Tezpur Airport	TEZ
Tiruchirapally	Tamil Nadu	Tiruchirapalli Airport	TRZ
Tirupati	Andhra Pradesh	Tirupati Airport	TIR
Trivandrum	Kerala	Trivandrum International Airport	TRV
Udaipur	Rajasthan	Udaipur Airport	UDR
Vadodara	Gujarat	Vadodara Airport	BDQ
Varanasi	Uttar Pradesh	Babatpur Airport	VNS
Vijayawada	Andhra Pradesh	Vijayawada Airport	VGA

APPENDIX 9.3

Airlines Codes

Airlines	Location	Airline Codes
Aeroflot—Russian Airlines	Russian federation	SU
Aerolineas Argentinas	Argentina	AR
Air Canada	Canada	AC
Air China	China	CA
Air France	France	AF
Air Holland	Netherlands	GG
Air New Zealand	New Zealand	NZ
Air India Ltd	India	AI
Alitalia	Italy	AZ
All Nippon Airways	Japan	NH
American Airlines	USA	AA
Austrian Airlines	Austria	OS
BMI British Midland	UK	BD
British Airways	UK	BA
Canadian Airlines International	Canada	CP
Cathay Pacific	Hong Kong SAR China	CX
Crossair	Switzerland	LS
Continental Airlines	USA	CO
Delta Airlines	USA	DL
Dragonair	China	KA
Egyptair	Egypt	MS
El Al	Israel	LY
Emirates	UAE	EK
Etihad Airways	UAE	EY
Finnair	Finland	AY
Garuda Indonesia	Indonesia	GA
Gulf air	Bahrain	GF
Iberia	Spain	IB
Indian Airlines	India	IC
Japan Airlines	Japan	JL
Jet Airways	India	9W
Korean Airlines	Korea	KE
KLM	Netherlands	KL
KLM UK	UK	UK
Lufthansa	Germany	LH

Contd

Appendix 9.3 Contd

Airlines	Location	Airline Codes
Malaysia Airline	Malaysia	MH
Mexicana	Mexico	MX
New England Airlines	USA	EJ
Northwest Airlines	USA	NW
Olympic Airways	Greece	OA
Pakistan International Airlines	Pakistan	PK
Qantas	Australia	QF
Royal Air Maroc	Morocco	AT
Ryanair	Ireland	FR
Sabena	Belgium	SN
Sahara Airlines	India	S2
SAS	Sweden	SK
Saudi Arabian Airlines	Saudi Arabia	SV
Singapore Airlines	Singapore	SQ
Spanair	Spain	JK
Swissair	Switzerland	SR
TACA	El Salvador	TA
TAP—Air Portugal	Portugal	TP
Thai Airways	Thailand	TG
United Airlines	USA	UA
Varig	Brazil	RG
Virgin Atlantic Airways	UK	VS

APPENDIX 9.4

Country Codes

Country Name	ISO 2-alpha code	Country Name	ISO 2-alpha code
Afghanistan	AF	Albania	AL
Algeria	DZ	Andorra	AD
Angola	AO	Antigua and Barbuda	AG
Argentina	AR	Armenia	AM
Australia	AU	Austria	AT
Azerbaijan	AZ	Bahamas	BS
Bahrain	BH	Bangladesh	BD
Belarus	BY	Belgium	BE
Belize	BZ	Benin	BJ
Bhutan	BT	Bolivia	BO
Bosnia and Herzegovina	BA	Botswana	BW
Brazil	BR	Brunei Darussalam	BN
Bulgaria	BG	Cambodia	KH
Cameroon	CM	Canada	CA
Chad	TD	Chile	CL
China	CN	Colombia	CO
Comoros	KM	Costa Rica	CR
Croatia	HR	Cuba	CU
Cyprus	CY	Czech Republic	CZ
Denmark	DK	Djibouti	DJ
Ecuador	EC	Egypt	EG
Equatorial Guinea	GQ	Estonia	EE
Fiji	FJ	Finland	FI
France	FR	Gabon	GA
Gambia, The	GM	Georgia	GE
Germany	DE	Ghana	GH
Greece	GR	Grenada	GD
Guatemala	GT	Guinea	GN
Guyana	GY	Haiti	HT
Honduras	HN	Hungary	HU
Iceland	IS	India	IN
Indonesia	ID	Iran	IR
Iraq	IQ	Ireland	IE
Israel	IL	Italy	IT
Jamaica	JM	Japan	JP
Jordan	JO	Kenya	KE
Korea north	KP	Korea	KR
Kuwait	KW	Lebanon	LB

Contd

Appendix 9.4 Contd

Country Name	ISO 2-alpha code	Country Name	ISO 2-alpha code
Liberia	LR	Libya	LY
Luxembourg	LU	Macedonia	MK
Madagascar	MG	Malawi	MW
Malaysia	MY	Maldives	MV
Mali	ML	Malta	MT
Marshall Islands	MH	Martinique	MQ
Mauritania	MR	Mauritius	MU
Mayotte	YT	Mexico	MX
Micronesia	FM	Moldova	MD
Monaco	MC	Mongolia	MN
Montenegro	ME	Montserrat	MS
Morocco	MA	Mozambique	MZ
Myanmar	MM	Namibia	NA
Nepal	NP	Netherlands	NL
New Zealand	NZ	Nicaragua	NI
Niger	NE	Nigeria	NG
Norway	NO	Oman	OM
Pakistan	PK	Panama	PA
Papua New Guinea	PG	Paraguay	PY
Peru	PE	Philippines	PH
Poland	PL	Portugal	PT
Puerto Rico	PR	Qatar	QA
Romania	RO	Russian Federation	RU
Rwanda	RW	Sao Tome and Principe	ST
Saudi Arabia	SA	Senegal	SN
Serbia	RS	Seychelles	SC
Sierra Leone	SL	Singapore	SG
Somalia	SO	South Africa	ZA
Spain	ES	Sri Lanka	LK
Sudan	SD	Suriname	SR
Swaziland	SZ	Sweden	SE
Switzerland	CH	Taiwan	TW
Tajikistan	TJ	Tanzania	TZ
Thailand	TH	Tonga	TO
Trinidad and Tobago	TT	Tunisia	TN
Turkey	TR	Turkmenistan	TM
Uganda	UG	Ukraine	UA
UAE	AE	UK	GB
USA	US	Uruguay	UY
Uzbekistan	UZ	Vatican City	VA
Venezuela	VE	Vietnam	VN
Yemen	YE	Zambia	ZM
Zimbabwe	ZW		

APPENDIX 9.5

Currency Codes

Country	Currency	Code	Symbol
Afghanistan	Afghan Afghani	AFN	
Argentina	Argentine Peso	ARS	
Armenia	Armenian Dram	AMD	
Australia	Australian Dollar	AUD	$
Austria	European Euro	EUR	•
Azerbaijan	Azerbaijani Manat	AZN	
Bahamas	Bahamian Dollar	BSD	B$
Bahrain	Bahraini Dinar	BHD	
Bangladesh	Bangladeshi Taka	BDT	
Belarus	Belarusian Ruble	BYR	Br
Belgium	European Euro	EUR	•
Belize	Belize Dollar	BZD	BZ$
Bhutan	Bhutanese Ngultrum	BTN	Nu.
Bolivia	Bolivian Boliviano	BOB	Bs.
Brazil	Brazilian Real	BRL	R$
Cambodia	Cambodian Riel	KHR	
Canada	Canadian Dollar	CAD	$
Central African Republic	Central African CFA Franc	XAF	CFA
Chile	Chilean Peso	CLP	$
China	Chinese Yuan Renminbi	CNY	¥
Colombia	Colombian Peso	COP	Col$
Congo	Central African CFA franc	XAF	CFA
Croatia	Croatian Kuna	HRK	kn
Cuba	Cuban Peso	CUC	$
Cyprus	European Euro	EUR	•
Czech Republic	Czech Koruna	CZK	Kc
Denmark	Danish Krone	DKK	Kr
Egypt	Egyptian Pound	EGP	£
Ethiopia	Ethiopian Birr	ETB	Br
Fiji	Fijian Dollar	FJD	FJ$
Finland	European Euro	EUR	•
France	European Euro	EUR	•
Germany	European Euro	EUR	•
Greece	European Euro	EUR	•
Guatemala	Guatemalan Quetzal	GTQ	Q
Honduras	Honduran Lempira	HNL	L
Hong Kong	Hong Kong Dollar	HKD	HK$

Contd

Appendix 9.5 Contd

Country	Currency	Code	Symbol
Hungary	Hungarian Forint	HUF	Ft
Iceland	Icelandic Króna	ISK	kr
India	Indian Rupee	INR	Rs
Indonesia	Indonesian Rupiah	IDR	Rp
Iran	Iranian Rial	IRR	
Iraq	Iraqi Dinar	IQD	
Israel	Israeli New Shekel	ILS	
Italy	European Euro	EUR	•
Jamaica	Jamaican Dollar	JMD	J$
Japan	Japanese Yen	JPY	¥
Jordan	Jordanian Dinar	JOD	
Kenya	Kenyan shilling	KES	KSh
Korea, North	North Korean Won	KPW	W
Korea, South	South Korean Won	KRW	W
Kuwait	Kuwaiti Dinar	KWD	
Luxembourg	European Euro	EUR	•
Malaysia	Malaysian Ringgit	MYR	RM
Maldives	Maldivian Rufiyaa	MVR	Rf
Mali	West African CFA Franc	XOF	CFA
Mauritius	Mauritian Rupee	MUR	Rs
Mexico	Mexican Peso	MXN	$
Moldova	Moldovan Leu	MDL	
Myanmar	Myanmar Kyat	MMK	K
Namibia	Namibian Dollar	NAD	N$
Nepal	Nepalese Rupee	NPR	NRs
Netherlands	European Euro	EUR	•
New Zealand	New Zealand Dollar	NZD	NZ$
Norway	Norwegian Krone	NOK	kr
Oman	Omani Rial	OMR	
Pakistan	Pakistani Rupee	PKR	Rs.
Peru	Peruvian Nuevo Sol	PEN	S/.
Philippines	Philippine Peso	PHP	
Poland	Polish Zloty	PLN	
Portugal	European Euro	EUR	•
Qatar	Qatari Riyal	QAR	QR
Russia	Russian Ruble	RUB	R
Saudi Arabia	Saudi Riyal	SAR	SR
Seychelles	Seychelles Rupee	SCR	SR
Singapore	Singapore Dollar	SGD	S$

Contd

Appendix 9.5   Contd

Country	Currency	Code	Symbol
South Africa	South African Rand	ZAR	R
Spain	European Euro	EUR	•
Sri Lanka	Sri Lankan Rupee	LKR	SL Rs
Sudan	Sudanese Pound	SDG	
Sweden	Swedish Krona	SEK	kr
Switzerland	Swiss Franc	CHF	Fr.
Syria	Syrian Pound	SYP	
Tanzania	Tanzanian Shilling	TZS	
Thailand	Thai Baht	THB	฿
Turkey	Turkish New Lira	TRY	YTL
Ukraine	Ukrainian Hryvnia	UAH	
UAE	UAE Dirham	AED	
UK	British Pound	GBP	£
USA	US Dollar	USD	US$
Uruguay	Uruguayan Peso	UYU	$U
Venezuela	Venezuelan Bolivar	VEB	Bs
Vietnam	Vietnamese Dong	VND	þ
Yemen	Yemeni Rial	YER	
Zambia	Zambian Kwacha	ZMK	ZK
Zimbabwe	Zimbabwean Dollar	ZWD	Z$

CHAPTER 10

Itinerary Planning

Learning objectives

After reading this chapter you should be able to:
- understand how an itinerary is planned and organized
- know what all the itinerary should include
- explain what all information is required while planning an itinerary
- understand how tour costs are calculated
- appreciate how the travel agents and tour operators earn their profit
- know how to work on a costing sheet, using information and different costs

INTRODUCTION

Itinerary planning, as we have read in Chapter 7, is one of the major functions and day-to-day activities of a travel agency. The travel agency may sell ready-made tour packages or design tailor-made customized tour itineraries for their clients as per their requirements. Detailed thought and careful planning is needed while preparing a tour itinerary. Itinerary planning involves a lot of work. Even though the proposed route may be familiar to the tour professional or the tour packages offered are a repeat of previous years, there are still many small things which need to be reviewed. Some tour operators may add value by including new destinations or offer some new facility or entertainment to make the tour programme more attractive, appealing, and competitive than the others. While planning the tour itinerary, the tour professional should also consider the political situation, in terms of strikes, terrorism, etc. related to the intended destination of visit.

Many tour operators have their own escorted tour programmes. These tours are prepackaged. Few alterations are made every year as per the changing likes and dislikes of the tourists. The tour planner should know the success rate of such tours and how popular they are in the market. Feedback can be taken from the past clients, colleagues, or managers regarding the tour. The tour planner while preparing the itinerary should be able to live the tour day by day, considering all important parameters of itinerary. Special events such as fairs, festivals can also be considered while planning the tour itinerary depending on the clients and their preferences. For example, the Republic day, Pune festival, Pushkar fair, Kumbh mela. These events showcase the culture of the tourist places. Tour planners can also add events on their own. These events must be suitably balanced against time, cost, the target tourists, etc. For example, senior citizens would prefer to have a relaxed tour instead of rock concerts, etc.

The tourist professional or consultant should be aware of and have sound knowledge of the destination, its geography, and the places to be visited by his/her clients. Apart from the various travel guidebooks, brochures, journals, and periodicals available, the national, regional, and state level tourism boards are also a good source of information. These tourism offices offer information on the history, culture, transport, tourist attractions, accommodation, museums, special events, fairs and festivals, etc. of a particular city or country. The various travel organizations, such as UNWTO, ASTA, IATA, etc. are also a good source of information to the professional travel agent. The Internet where one can get information within seconds at the click of the mouse, offers various search options like Google Search, etc. A tourist or anybody can get access to information on any topic or place on the Internet.

DEFINITION

The term 'itinerary' may be defined as the linking of all the journey points in a traveller's journey, i.e. from the origin point, and in between stopping points for sightseeing at the destinations and back to the point of origin, which may not always be the case.

Thus, the term itinerary is used to identify the origin, destination, and all the halts in a traveller's journey.

Each particular portion of an itinerary can be termed as a segment. For example, for the Golden Triangle sector Delhi–Agra–Jaipur–Delhi, the itinerary would consist of the following segments:

1. Delhi–Agra
2. Agra–Jaipur
3. Jaipur–Delhi

Depending on the mode of transportation between the journey points, these segments can be termed as air segment and surface segment. An air segment is one, which has air travel as its mode of transport. Similarly, a surface segment is one, which has land travel such as railway or road for its mode of transportation.

In an air segment, the departure city or airport is termed as the boarding point or departure point, whereas the city of arrival or airport is termed as off point or arrival point. Together, the boarding point and departure point are termed as city pair. For example, Mumbai–Delhi, Pune–Goa, and Jaipur–Udaipur.

For an outbound travel such as Mumbai–New York–Mumbai, Mumbai–New York will be the outbound segment and New York–Mumbai the return segment (inbound segment).

If an itinerary has a flight connection, for example, a tourist travels from Mumbai to London via Dubai but on his/her return journey he/she uses a direct flight from London to Mumbai, then his itinerary will have the following segments:

1. Mumbai–Dubai
2. Dubai–London
3. London–Mumbai

In this particular case, if the tourist has to change his flight at Dubai, then Dubai is considered as the connecting point, whereas London is the stopover point. A connecting point is thus a point where there is change of aircraft. A stopover point is one which is not a connecting point.

In an itinerary, the origin point is the first departure or boarding point whereas the destination point is the point of stopover.

A one-way itinerary is one where the passenger does not return to the point of origin, for example, Mumbai–Dubai.

A circle trip is one where the passenger returns to the point of origin. Example, Mumbai–Dubai–Mumbai.

An air segment will also have a non-stop, direct, or a connecting flight. A non-stop flight is a flight that does not have any stops between the origin point and the passenger's intended destination. In a direct flight, the passenger is not required to change any aircraft. However, the direct flights may have to make any number of stops. When two or more aircrafts are used between the origin point and the destination point, then the flights are known as connecting flights.

While planning a tailor-made customized tour itinerary, the travel agent should find out certain minute and vital details about the client's travel. Without these details an itinerary cannot be planned.

BASIC INFORMATION

The following information is required from the client by the travel agent to plan a tour itinerary.

1. Approximate dates or month of travel of the client
2. Total number of people travelling
3. Mode of travel along with the class
4. Class of hotel and type of local transport
5. The budget of the client
6. Any extra services required

Approximate Dates or Month of Travel

This information is required because during the tourist season and school vacations, most tourist places are packed to their capacity. Sometimes the hotels are also booked well in advance by the large tour operators. Getting air and train reservations are also difficult during the peak season time. For example, the months of December and January being high season in Goa, tourists may have to stay in their vehicles or at the beaches because of unavailability of rooms. For the summer season, people flock to the Himalayan states of Jammu and Kashmir, Uttarakhand, and Himachal Pradesh to escape from the hot climate in the plains.

After getting this basic information, the travel agent can accordingly recommend to his/her clients the places he/she intends to visit. Other alternatives can also be suggested to the client if there is non availability of rooms or transport services.

Total Number of People Travelling

This information is useful for booking the hotel and transport arrangements. In the case of a group of 15 or more passengers, the group can avail discount in the tariff. Hotels offer discounts to groups depending on the group sizes. The tour leader is given free accommodation and other services by the tour operator.

The other important information needed is whether any children are travelling with the passenger. The hotels charge a substantial amount depending on the age of the child. Children below five years are usually not charged anything by the hotels. Children between five to 12 years of age have to pay certain charges for an extra bed, if it is needed. However, every hotel has its own policy on the tariff of the hotel. If an extra bed has to be provided in a double room, the costing of the tour has to be done on triple occupancy basis. Thus, such minute details are necessary while planning the itinerary. Even the transport arrangements needed for sightseeing will depend on the size of the group travelling. For example, two to four people will need a car, six to eight people will need a Toyota Qualis or a van, a 14-seater mini bus will be required for a group size of 14 and a larger 35-seater bus or 55-seater bus for a larger group, depending on the group size.

Mode of Travel Along With the Class

There are various modes of travel available and the client's preference is of utmost importance. Some tourists might want to save on travel time while some might be high spending luxury tourists and prefer first or business class seats and travel by air. There are tourists who would want to enjoy the scenic beauty of the countryside and travel by rail or road while some tourists are budget conscious and will opt for a second-class train ticket or a semi-deluxe coach.

Sometimes, the tourist may prefer the privacy of a chauffeur driven car for sightseeing at tourist places or he might arrange it on his own. Such details are needed while costing of the tour.

Class of Hotel and Type of Local Transport

Tourists have a wide variety of choice of hotels to choose from depending on their budget. The luxury tourists might opt for five star hotels whereas the cost conscious tourists will prefer a standard budget hotel. Knowledge of all the different types of accommodation and local transport available is thus necessary for the tourism professional.

The Budget of the Client

This information is needed so as to find out the tour cost of the itinerary. For a high budget tourist, options of five star or four star hotel along with airline transport and a luxury car for sightseeing can be given. A middle class tourist can be given the option of a three star hotel, train journey, and an ordinary car for sightseeing. Whereas a budget conscious tourist can be suggested a two star or one star hotel, train journey, and bus for sightseeing.

Any Extra Services

Extra services such as a guide, an escort, and additional facilities such as entertainment will definitely add to the tour cost of the itinerary and so will a visit to additional tourist attractions in the vicinity.

PLANNING THE ITINERARY

After receiving confirmation from your potential client, identifying the destinations to be visited, number of people travelling, budget of the client, and booking the air and ground transport segments, the next job is to plan the tour itinerary. While planning an itinerary, the route has to be established first. The distances in kilometres between the tourist cities and the places of attractions, the approximate time taken for travelling and visiting the sightseeing places should also be considered. The name of the hotel booked for the client along with specification of meals, if any, and the day-to-day activities to be recommended have to be mentioned in the tour itinerary.

Route Map and Routing of Itinerary

The tour professional or travel agent should have a clear picture of the exact route to be followed whether it is by air, rail, or road for the client's itinerary.

An atlas, road maps, maps of individual states, cities and countries, come in handy while planning and explaining the itineraries to the clients. Railway and airline route maps and timetables are also available which can be of help to the travel agent.

Routing is very important while planning a tour itinerary. For road travel the journey should be scenic. The itinerary should be practical. Backtracking, doubling back, or routing the client in circles should be avoided, unless it is necessary.

In case of business tourists, their meeting plans should be considered, as the itinerary has to be planned according to their requirements.

Thus, the itinerary should be carefully planned and detailed out as per the client's requirements.

Pacing the Itinerary

The tour itinerary plan should be paced as per the client's requirement. The client's age and health should be considered while chalking out the itinerary. Senior citizens or old people cannot travel at a stretch for a long duration. They will prefer a relaxed tour itinerary with less walking. Similar is the case if a family is travelling with small children or for tourists with some physical disability. The assumption that younger people can travel at a faster pace is not always true and thus each and every client has to be considered on an individual basis depending upon their requirement and need to travel.

Thus, while planning the itinerary, the limitations of passengers' endurance have to be thought of. The pacing of the tour should not be too slow or too fast. To keep the itinerary moving, the pace of the itinerary should not be too fast because of which the clients are pushed continuously and become tired and irritated. This might make their trip less enjoyable. The tour should be reasonably planned with half day and full day sightseeing, and with some two or three overnight stays.

Interests of Tourists

This is one important way to add more value to the tour itinerary. The client's interests or liking can be matched with the corresponding activities and attractions of the tour itinerary. The tour professional should thus talk to their clients to know their interests. Recreational activities, educational activities, fun, games, entertainment, dance shows, cultural shows, plays, etc. can be added to the basic itinerary as per the interest of the client. Determining and matching the interests of clients requires thorough knowledge about the destination, as well as practice and expertise in planning of itineraries.

Details to be Considered

Certain minute details are important while planning the tour itinerary. Even when you plan an attractive detailed itinerary and miss out on a small point, the entire tour of the passenger may be a failure. One of the most important things to do is to check whether the sightseeing place or tourist attraction is open on that particular day when your client arrives, for example, the Taj Mahal, Agra is closed on Fridays. Also, all ground arrangements and air travel should be reconfirmed. Similarly, you should inform your clients regarding the check-in formalities at the airport, the amount of baggage to be carried and the kind of clothing, etc. suitable at the destination.

Energy Level of Tourists

The energy level of the client and the energy level needed for the tour itinerary should be matched for a successful trip. This can be done by knowing what kind of holiday or travel experience the traveller is exactly looking for. At some tourist attractions, particularly hill stations such as Shimla and Manali, large vehicles are difficult to drive. The tourists might have to walk for some kilometres to reach these attractions. Thus, the tour professional should know how much walking is required for certain tourist attractions. Older people or a family with small children may face difficulties in such situations.

Some tourists might prefer a quiet vacation near the beach or at a hill resort. Thus, the tour professional should be able to judge the energy level of the client and then match it with the itinerary.

Shopping

Many tourist cities are famous for some special things to shop for. Tourists want to carry mementos or souvenirs, purchase gifts for family and friends from the places they have visited. The travel agent should always keep some free time for shopping or leisure in the tour itinerary. For example, Rajasthan is famous for tie and dye fabrics, *morjaris*, and kundan jewellery while Aurangabad for Paithani sarees and Himroo shawls.

Many tour agents and tour operators lure tourists by highlighting shopping in their advertisements or brochures. For example, the Dubai festival, Malaysia festival, etc.

Climate

Climate plays an important role while recommending a travel destination to tourists. Not all tourists are aware of the climatic conditions of tourist places. It is the job of the travel agent to inform the tourists accordingly as to what essential clothing and accessories should be carried for the trip. Tourists should not be recommended to travel to hilly and snowy areas during the rainy season, as it may be dangerous if there are landslides, flooding, and road blockage. The flights also may sometimes get cancelled or delayed due to bad weather conditions.

Tourists always prefer to escape to places famous for good climatic conditions. In the summer season the hill stations, Himalayas, or the cooler places in the plains are the most sought after destinations.

RESOURCES FOR PLANNING ITINERARIES

Planning of tour itineraries requires expertise and knowledge of the travel destinations. As the tour professional cannot visit each and every tourist destination, the following resources (see figure 10.1) can be of help while planning itineraries.

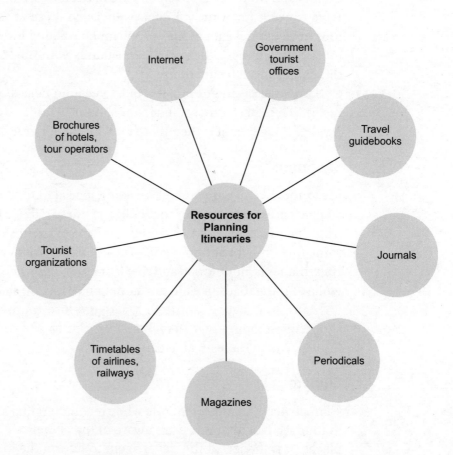

Figure 10.1 Resources required for planning itineraries

Feedback from clients

Clients feedback, whether positive or negative are a valuable source of information. Usually, a feedback form is given to the client before the tour, which has to be mailed to the travel agent after completion of the tour. The travel agent can also call up their clients and find out how their tour was.

Apart from your clients, your friends, relatives, and colleagues can also be a good source of information regarding the tourist destinations.

Government tourist offices

The national and state government tourist offices offer useful information to the tourist, and tour professionals. The information ranges from the history, geography, culture, hotels, tourist attractions, museums, fairs and festivals, special events, mode of transport available, etc. Brochures, folders, pamphlets, posters, CDs are made available at these tourist offices.

Travel guidebooks

Travel guidebooks are available at the various bookstores. These guidebooks contain important travel information for the tourist and the tour professionals. For example, *Lonely Planet.*

Magazines, Journals, and Periodicals

These are also important sources of information regarding travel. For example, *Outlook Traveller, National Geographic,* etc.

Tourist organizations

The tourist organizations are also an important source of information for the professional travel agent For example, International Air Transport Association, Cruise Line International Association, American Society of Travel Agents Association, Travel Agents Association of India, etc.

These tourist organizations publish their regular newsletter, journals, etc. for the travel industry.

Brochures of hotels and tour operators

Hotels publish their yearly tariff along with other details of various services and amenities offered in the hotel. The tariff details are of help while doing the costing of the hotel. Many tour operators also publish their brochures with the tour programmes.

Exhibit 10.1   Basic steps to be followed while planning an itinerary

When planning any itinerary, the tour professional should always try to follow the following steps:
1. Determine the places the tourist intends to visit and the number of days required at these destinations.
2. Establish the sequence of the tourist destinations the tourist intends to visit.
3. The cities should be linked so as to avoid doubling back and zigzag.
4. The political situation of the city, state or country should also be considered.
5. The geographical limitations of a particular place and the practicality of the transport options are also important for planning the itinerary.
6. Convenient and quickest mode of transportation should be planned and proper connections should be made for air/sea/rail or road.
7. When planning air itineraries, preference to lowest fares should be considered.
8. Alternative or optional itineraries or suggestions can always be given in case the clients change their mind.
9. The itinerary should be planned as per a format, which can be used always.
10. The initial information and notes taken while discussing with the client should be retained as they are of help while planning the itinerary.

Internet

The Internet is the most useful source of information which can be accessed within seconds at the click of the mouse.

Timetables

Many airlines publish their regular schedule along with the air tariff every month. The railways also publish their yearly timetable with all details. The Indian Railways publish *Trains At a Glance.*

Other examples are *Official Airline Guide* (OAG), *Passenger Air Tariff, Indian Airlines Timetable,* etc.

COSTING OF A TOUR

After planning the itinerary, the next important thing is to calculate the tour cost of the itinerary. For the costing the essential requirements are the tariff details of the hotel, meals, airline/train, ground transport cost which can be a car or coach depending on the group size of the passengers, if any guide/escort has been taken into account, or any extra services such as camel ride, elephant ride, entertainment, etc. The entire cost of the travel is then shared between the number of passengers travelling together to find out the per person tour cost on twin sharing or triple sharing basis by the travel agent.

For any kind of tour whether it is a prepackaged tour or specially designed tour, the tour planner has to keep some profit for the travel agent. The tour planner has to consider the currency rates and fluctuations for the convenience of the tourists. Because if the dollar drops against major foreign currencies, it may deter the tourists who travel for shopping and other reasons from undertaking the tour. The tour planner can always suggest to their clients how they could utilize their free time or leisure time and give information on restaurants and entertainment. The tour price quoted to passengers has to be competitive in the market, and if the cost is higher than the price of other competitors, it should be justifiable.

The standard items which are included in the costing of a tour are

- cost of accommodations
- cost of meals
- cost of transportation (air/rail/road/water)
- entrance fees, local guides, porterage (transfer of luggage by airport, railway, hotel porters), and airport taxes
- miscellaneous fees such as entertainment or any extra service to be provided to the client
- mark up

Hotel

The travel agent should be aware of the various hotels available at the tourist destinations. He/she should keep himself/herself updated on the different category of hotels, types of rooms, tariff plans, extra bed charges, taxes, meal rates, etc. There are different tariff plans as per the season i.e. regular, season, off-season, and weekend tariff. Some hotels offer special rates to corporates. Discounted rates are given to groups depending on the size of the group.

After determining the route of the itinerary the travel agent's next important task is to contact the hotels at the destinations to check the availability of rooms for the anticipated number of guests. The tour planner should know the exact number of people travelling, so as to calculate the cost of the accommodation.

For example, there are 14 people travelling to Rajasthan for eight days. The travel agent contacts the hotel for the best possible and competitive rate. The hotel offers the travel agent a net price of Rs 1800 for a double room on continental plan (i.e. room + breakfast). The travel agent may contact the chain hotels, for example, Taj, Oberoi, etc. and use only their hotels or the hotels with which he has a regular contact and good relationship. The travel agent has to also consider the location and facilities offered at the hotel for the tour.

The hotel may give the net price on an individual basis, i.e. per person rate or on room basis. When the net price is given on a room basis, the cost per person has to be calculated by dividing the room cost by the number of occupants. For example, for two people staying in one double room, Rs 900 will be the per person cost. If a third person is sharing the room, i.e. triple occupancy then the cost of extra bed is added to the cost of double room. Example, Rs 300 (extra bed) + Rs 1800 (double room) = Rs 2100. This figure is divided by 3. Thus, the cost per person will be Rs 700 on triple occupancy.

Meals

Some hotels usually, give a net rate, which is inclusive of all meals for large groups. Some have the tariff inclusive of meals, for example, only breakfast, i.e. continental plan (CP), or breakfast and any one meal i.e. modified american plan (MAP), or all meals—american plan (AP), or it can be only room and no meals european plan (EP). The hotels may also publish their meal plans along with the room tariff in their brochure. If the meal plan is not included in the tariff the guest can have meals as per the 'a la carte' menu and pay their own bills.

The travel agents usually do not include lunch in the tour cost as the guest might be out for sightseeing. Many tourists prefer a light lunch or may like to choose their own restaurants. While doing the costing, the meal cost also has to be taken into account as per the requirement of the guest.

Airlines

Knowledge of different airlines along with the airfares, air schedules, in-flight services, meals, different classes, taxes, etc. are important for the travel agent.

The tour cost may include the airfares for different sectors as required in the itinerary or it can be given separately as airfare supplement per person.

Railways

The travel agent should also be familiar with the train names, routes, schedules, and fares of major trains for well-known tourist destinations. The Indian Railways nowadays allows passengers to make reservations ninety days prior to their date of travel. The Tatkal Seva is also useful for making reservations five days prior to travelling (see Chapter 5).

If there are any train journeys in the itinerary the cost can be given as a separate supplement or it may be included in the tour cost.

Road Transport

Road transport is essential to reach the destination from the airport/railway station to have the pick-up and drop facility to the hotel, visiting the places of attractions, or for sightseeing at the destination. The tour professional should know the approximate time taken to reach the next tourist destination and for visiting places of attractions. The exact kilometres to be covered and average time taken are important while planning the itinerary. The distance has to be calculated with accuracy considering the journey and the local terrain of that area. For example, a plain area can be covered at an average speed of 40 kilometres per hour while a hilly area might be covered at a speed of 20–25 kilometres per hour depending on the vehicle used for travelling and the road condition.

If the tour planner schedules an eight hour road travel between Delhi and Shimla, he/she will have to make sure that the clients arrive in time for meals. He/she will also have to check whether it is certain that the time taken will be exact considering the stops en route for tea, lunch or en route sightseeing and shopping. The tour planner should not plan a hectic schedule for the passengers. Too much travel on a single day should be avoided. The limitations of passenger endurance should be kept in mind while planning the tour itinerary. The tour should be well paced so that travellers are not continuously pushed and tired while sightseeing.

For calculating the cost of the vehicle for the entire tour the travel agent has to contact the supplier, i.e. the transport operator. For example, if the travel agent is based in Mumbai and he/she contacts his/her transport agent at Jaipur to give him/her the best competitive rate for a 14-seater mini bus for an eight days tour, which comprises of two nights at Jaipur, two nights at Jodhpur, two nights at Jaisalmer, two nights at Jodhpur, and one night at Udaipur. The transporter gives a net rate of Rs 20,000 for the entire eight days inclusive of the driver's charges, parking, toll taxes, etc. The average kilometres covered in a day is 300 kilometres. Thus, the client has to pay for the extra kilometres or other sightseeing, which may be Rs 13 per kilometre for non-AC mini bus and Rs 16 for an AC vehicle.

Cruises

Many tour operators sell cruise packages of three to five days and more. Tourists nowadays are also opting for cruise holidays. The tour professionals should therefore be updated on the different categories of rooms, cabins, on board facilities, tariff and other details associated with cruises.

The travel agent can give the cost of the cruise as a supplement cost.

Local Guide/Escort

In India, there are English speaking and foreign language speaking licenced guides provided by the India Tourism offices. Similarly, there are local guides who are also authorized to explain the monuments or other sightseeing places. The travel agent should have a list of approved guides with their contact numbers and address available at the tourist destinations. The fee charged by the guides are for half day and full day and also night charges if any. The travel agent thus while doing the costing of the tour has to include the guide charges as applicable. Escorts are provided by the tour operator for the entire tour. For finding the per person cost, the total guide charges have to be divided by the number of people travelling. The expenses of the tour escort have also to be added to the tour cost.

Miscellaneous

If any entertainment has to be provided to the group, for example, a cultural show in the evening at the hotel or a desert safari with some touch of culture and entertainment, then the cost of this should also be included in the tour cost.

The charges for porterage may or may not be included in the tour cost. It can be given as supplement charge also depending on the preference of the tourist.

There may be other costs also, such as airport taxes, toll taxes, entrance fee for places of attractions including museums, historical forts, palaces, churches, etc. and similar other charges. These costs can be given as supplement cost.

Mark Up

Finally the mark up which is the main source of income for the travel agent has to be added to the per person cost of the tour to get the final tour cost. The mark up may vary from one travel agent to another.

Everybody in business wants to make a profit. The travel agents' main source of income is the commission which they receive from their various service providers, i.e. airlines, hotels, transport operators, etc. Hotels and transporters normally give a 10 per cent commission to the travel agents. The range of commission depends on the volume of business, which the travel agents give to these service providers. This commission is sometimes further shared by the sub travel agents also. The travel agents have to also bear the costs of office rent, salary of employees, electricity, telephone bills, Internet, etc. The amount of commission which the travel agents get is very low and inadequate for the agency to survive. Thus, in order to earn a profit the travel agents and tour operators add a mark up to the total cost of the tour before quoting it to the client. The mark up is the extra amount, which the travel agents can keep as their income. Some travel agents refer to it as service charges also. The mark up should not be too high as the business may be lost to the competitor and at the same time it should not be too low. The amount added to the tour cost as mark up is usually decided by the seniors or the management of the travel agency. The mark up is usually expressed as a percentage of the total cost price and ranges from seven to 15 per cent.

Many travel agents, tour operators, airlines, etc. while working on the cost of package tours negotiate with the suppliers such as hotels for discounted rates if they are able to give more business to the hotel. During off season many hotels offer discounted rates. In this way the travel agents' margin can be increased without increasing the price at which they sell to the clients.

While working at the travel desk and preparing itineraries and calculating the tour cost, the tour professional should be aware of the technical terms such as net rate and gross rate.

Net rate

It is the price which is charged by the supplier and has to be paid by the travel agent to the supplier. The travel agent is free to add any amount of mark up to it before quoting it to the client. This net rate is confidential between the supplier and the travel agent. The client should not have any idea of the extent of mark up. The supplier can give different net rates to different travel agents depending on the volume of business and personal relations.

Gross rate

It is quoted by the supplier to the travel agent and includes commission (expressed as a percentage of the gross rate). The commission differs from supplier to supplier on the amount of business the travel agent gives to the supplier. Normally, hotels give 10 per cent commission to the travel agent.

Profit

It is not similar to mark up. It is the amount which the travel agent gets at the end of the tour after paying the bills to the suppliers. Profit usually includes the commission earned from the suppliers with mark up added to it. Profit is also calculated on yearly basis.

Margin

It is similar to mark up in some ways. Mark up is expressed as a percentage whereas margin is the amount expressed in money.

CALCULATION OF A TOUR COST

Let us see with examples as to how an independent tour company, a travel agency, and an individual organizing a tour might determine their costs.

Example 10.1

A client Mr. Sharma approaches the executive at the travel desk for a seven nights/eight days tour to Kerala. Mr Sharma gives all the required information as stated below.

1.	Name of passenger	Mr Suresh Sharma
2.	Number of people	2
3.	Date of travel	2 May 2009
4.	Mode of travel	BOM – COK, TRV – BOM by air and a non-AC Indica car for sightseeing
5.	Hotel	Luxury hotel

The travel agent after determining the route of the itinerary will first find out the availability of seats on the airlines and then check if the hotels are also available for the same dates. Alternative airlines and hotels can be given as options if unavailable for the required dates. Similarly ground arrangements also have to be arranged for those days. The confirmation of all these bookings should always be in writing from the suppliers to be on the safer side in case of any error. The travel agent also has to decide on the inclusion of meals if any, entrance fee, porterage, miscellaneous fee, etc.

Costing sheet

Name: Mr. Sharma × 2   **Tour:** Kerala

Day	Date	Place	Hotel	Tariff			Transportation		ITNY
				SGL	DBL	FOOD	TRSF	S.S.	
1	2 May 09	Kochi	Taj Malabar		4500	CP			
2	3 May 09	Munnar	Copper Castle		2800	EP			
3	4 May 09	Munnar	Copper Castle		2800	EP			
4	5 May 09	Thekkady	Spice Village		5800	AP			
5	6 May 09	Kumarakom	Coconut Lagoon		6200	AP			
6	7 May 09	Kovalam	Le Meridian		5200	CP			
7	8 May 09	Kovalam	Le Meridian		5200	CP			
					=32,500/2				
					=16,250 PP				

Transport
AC Indica: 13,000 + 10% = 14,300/2 = 7150 PP
Non-AC 12000 + 10% = 13,200/2 = 6600 PP
AC supplement: 7150 – 6600 = 550 PP

Airfare:
BOM – COK: 5200 PP
TRV – BOM: 6000 PP
Total: 11,200 PP

Hotel	16,250
Food	
Transport	6600
Agent's comm.	
Mark up	3500
Miscellaneous	300
Total	26,650

Cost to be quoted to passenger = Rs.26,650

Abbreviations		Abbreviations	
PP	Per person	CP	Continental plan
EP	European plan	AP	American plan
SGL	Single room	DBL	Double room
TRSF	Transfers	TRPL	Triple
ITNY	Itinerary	SS	Sightseeing
AC	Air-conditioned		

As per the calculation on the given costing sheet, the tariff of the hotel is noted in the column provided for double room. The meals provided in this tariff are also mentioned. The tour professional has to check the luxury and other taxes on room and meals and add it to the room tariff. To find out the per person rate the total of all the hotels is divided by 2. In Mr Sharma's case, the total for hotel is Rs 32,500. After dividing it by 2 the cost per person comes to Rs 16,250.

The non-AC Indica car is provided by a local transporter based in Kochi. He gives a net rate of Rs 13,000 for an air-conditioned, Indica car and Rs 12,000 for a non-air conditioned car. The travel agent adds 10 per cent to this rate and divides it by 2 to find the per person cost for vehicle. The AC supplement is also calculated which comes to Rs 550.

The airfare for Mumbai–Kochi and Trivandrum–Mumbai are added. The cost of airfare comes to Rs 11,200 per person.

Mark up of Rs 3500 and for welcome drink and chocolates/flowers Rs. 300 can be put under miscellaneous.

Thus after totaling the hotel, transport, mark up, and miscellaneous rates the total tour cost comes to Rs 26,650 per person. This tour cost to be quoted to passenger can be rounded up.

Kerala tour itinerary for Mr Sharma

Date	Programme
2 May 09 (Saturday)	Departure from Mumbai by 9W 333 at 08:30 hours. On arrival at Kochi, pick up from the airport by a non-AC Indica car. Check in into hotel Taj Malabar. Visit Jewish Synagogue, old fort, Chinese fishing net, Bolghatty palace, Wellington Island. Dinner and overnight stay at Kochi.
3 May 09 (Sunday)	After breakfast departure for Munnar (140 kms–4 hours) on arrival check in into hotel Copper Castle. Evening at leisure. Overnight at Munnar.
4 May 09 (Monday)	Morning local sight seeing of Munnar. Visit Echo point, Mattupetty dam, Devikulam, Indo-Swiss dairy farm, Eravikulam National Park, Rajamalai. Overnight at Munnar.

Contd

Contd

Date	Programme
5 May 09 (Tuesday)	Morning departure for Thekkady (110 kms–4 hours). On arrival check in into Hotel Spice Village. After lunch visit spice plantation and tea factory. Evening at Leisure. Dinner and overnight at Thekkady.
6 May 09 (Wednesday)	After breakfast enjoy boat ride in Periyar lake. Visit Periyar wild life sanctuary. Proceed to Kumarakom (160 kms 4-5 hours). On arrival check in into hotel Coconut lagoon. Enjoy backwater cruise at Vembanad lake. Dinner and overnight at Kumarakom.
7 May 09	After breakfast visit bird sanctuary. Departure to Kovalam (5 hours). On arrival check in into hotel Le Meridian. Evening relax at the beach. Dinner and overnight at Kovalam.
8 May 09	After breakfast proceed for Thiruvananthapuram local sightseeing. Visit Padmanabhaswamy temple, Palace, Napier museum, Art gallery, Handicraft Institute. Overnight at Kovalam.
9 May 09	After breakfast departure for Mumbai by 9W 315 at 12:30 hours.

Tour Cost: Rs. 26,650 per person on twin sharing basis.

Tour cost includes

- accommodation on twin sharing basis
- all currently applicable taxes
- all transfers and sightseeing by non-AC Indica car
- parking at the airport
- breakfast at Kochi and Kovalam.
- all meals at Thekkady and Kumarakom

Tour cost does not include

- airfare
- entrance fee
- porterage at airport
- any personal services such as tips, laundry, etc.
- meals at Munnar and lunch and dinner at Kochi and Kovalam

Supplement cost

- AC supplement Rs 550 per person.
- airfare supplement for
  (a) Mumbai–Kochi: Rs 5200 per person
  (b) Thiruvanathapuram–Mumbai: Rs 6000 per person

Example 10.2

Costing for USD passenger

Mr and Mrs Jayant Sidhaye, an NRI couple has approached XYZ travel agency for a Golden Triangle Tour. They will be accompanied by Mr Sidhaye's foreign friends, who are two couples with one child of 12 years. So, in this particular case, they will require three double rooms with one extra bed in one of the rooms for the child. As Mr Sidhaye is an Indian, his costing will be based on INR rates, whereas for his foreign friends, USD rates have to be applied.

As per the costing sheet, the tour operator will have to make separate columns for an extra bed and double room, to calculate rates for triple occupancy and double occupancy. A separate column should be given for INR rates and food.

After filling the amount in the respective columns the total is added. To find out the triple occupancy rate, the charges of double room and extra bed are added, i.e. 145 USD + 511 USD = 656 USD. The amount is divided by 3 which comes to 218.66 which is rounded up to 219 USD per person on triple sharing basis. The per person rate on double occupancy is 511/2= 256 USD per person. For INR, it is 17,066/2 = 8533 per person. The meal coupons are given in INR. If we want the rate in USD it has to be divided by the current dollar rate. Suppose it is Rs. 42.50. Then it comes to 59 USD per person for meal coupons.

The transport rates are calculated as per the rates provided for Qualis and Tempo traveller by the transport operator for the sightseeing and transfers. The guide charges are also added for half day and full day sightseeing accordingly. A 10 per cent commission is added on the transport and guide, as these are net rates. The USD rate is calculated @Rs 42.50. The train fare is taken as Rs 600 PP and USD 15. The total entrance fees and airfare are given as supplements to the client.

Costing Sheet

Name: Mr Jayant Sidhaye and Mr Ian Garett   **Tour:** Golden Triangle

				Tariff			
Day	Date 2009	Place	Hotel	Extra bed USD	DBL USD	Food INR	INR ITNY DBL
1	17 Dec	Delhi	Oberoi Maidens	37	134	500	4288
2	18 Dec	Delhi	Oberoi Maidens	37	134	500	4288
3	19 Dec	Agra	The Trident, Agra	27	79	500	2730
4	20 Dec	Jaipur	The Trident, Jaipur	22	82	500	2880
5	21 Dec	Jaipur	The Trident, Jaipur	22	82	500	2880
				145+511 =656/3	511/2 =255.5 =256$	2500@ 42.50 =2500/	17066/2 = Rs. 8533
				=218.66	PP on DBL	42.50 =59 USD	PP
				=219 PP on TRPL			

Airfare

	USD		INR
	Adult	**Child**	
BOM–DEL	181	91	5705
JAI–BOM	161	81	4667

	USD		INR
	Dbl	**Trpl**	
Hotel	256	219	8533
Food (Meal Coupons)	59	59	2500
Tran. (Non AC Tempo)	72	72	2995
Gifts	6	6	250
Mark up	70	70	3000
Guide	11	11	428
Total	474	437	17,706

Cost to be quoted to passenger = 474 USD per person on double sharing
= 437 USD per person on triple sharing
= Rs 17,750 on double occupancy

Transport costing

		Qualis		Tempo		Guide
		Non-AC	AC	Non-AC	AC	
Delhi	Arr. trsf	3800	3800	4300	4800	495
Day 01	Parking					
	Half day s/s parking					
Day 02	Full day s/s parking					618
Day 03	Dep trsf to stn. parking					
Agra	Arr. Trsf. parking	6945	8245	7945	9245	495
	5/6 of Agra					
Day 04	Trsf to Jai via F. Sikri					
	F. Sikri parking					
Jaipur						
Day 05	Full day s/s	1355	1810			
	Elephant ride	900	900	2995	3745	618
	Parking	50	50			
Day 06	Dep trsf	640	935			
	Parking	50	50			
	Total	13740	15790	15240	17790	2721

Contd

Transport costing   Contd

	Qualis		Tempo		Guide
	Non-AC	AC	Non-AC	AC	
	+10%	+10%	+10%	+10%	+10%
	=15114/7	=17369/7	=16764/7	=19569/7	=2994/7
	=2160 P.P.	=2482 P.P.	=2395 P.P.	2796 P.P.	427.77 = 428
	@42.50	@42.50	@42.50	@42.50	@42.50
				=56.35	=65.78	=10.07
	=51$	=59$	=57$	=11$	=11$
Train fare: 600 PP @42.50 = 15 USD	+15	+15	+15	+15	
Total	=66$	=74	=72	=81	

Example 10.3

Itinerary for the Golden Triangle tour

The Golden Triangle is a luxury tour offered by XYZ travel agent for five nights/ six days to Delhi–Agra–Jaipur. It covers places of historical interest and the world famous monument of love, the Taj Mahal by moonlight.

Day	Distance or Drive	Time	Activity	Overnight	Highlight of the Day
1 Mumbai – Delhi	Air (2 hrs)	0805 hrs 1000 Hrs	Arrival Delhi by 9w 333 0805/1000. Meet and greet by travel agent representative. Transfer to the hotel by a non-AC Tempo Traveller, Welcome drink at the time of check-in. Chocolates and flowers in the room. Afternoon local sight -seeing of Old Delhi. Overnight at the hotel.	Delhi Oberoi Maidens	Welcome Drink upon arrival. Chocolates and flowers in the room. Half day local sightseeing of Old Delhi.
2 Delhi		1100 Hrs	Breakfast at the hotel. Half day sightseeing of New Delhi by a non-AC Tempo traveller.	Delhi Oberoi Maidens	Half day sight -seeing of New Delhi.

Contd

Contd

Day	Distance or Drive	Time	Activity	Overnight	Highlight of the Day
		PM	Overnight at the hotel. Breakfast at the hotel.		
3 Agra	Rail 2hrs	0630 hrs 0830 hrs	Transfer to railway station by a non-AC tempo traveller to board Shatabdi Express to Agra at 0630 hrs. Arrival Agra at 0830 hrs. Transfer to hotel by a non-AC Tempo traveller. Welcome drink at the time of check-in. Chocolates and flowers in the room. Traditional Indian Welcome.	Agra The Trident	Welcome Drink upon arrival. Chocolates and flowers in the room. City tour and visit the magnificent Taj.
		PM	Evening visit Taj by moonlight (Upto 7.30 p.m.) O/n at hotel.		
4 Agra – Jaipur	232 kms 5 hrs	0800 hrs 0930 hrs	Breakfast at the hotel Drive to Jaipur via Fathepur Sikri by a non-AC Tempo traveller, Welcome drink at the time of Check-in. Chocolates and flowers in the room. Rest of the day at leisure. Overnight at the hotel.	Jaipur The Trident	Welcome Drink upon arrival. Chocolates and flowers in the room. Enjoy the drive to Fatehpur Sikri.
5 Jaipur		0800 hrs 0930 hrs 1430 hrs	Breakfast at the hotel. A.M. visit Amber Fort with elephant ride to the fort. Afternoon, half-day city tour of Jaipur by a non-AC tempo traveller. Shopping. Overnight at the hotel.	Jaipur The Trident	Amber Fort with elephant ride to the fort, Sheesh Mahal and city tour of Jaipur including the Hawa Mahal, Jantar Mantar, the museum etc. Shop for semiprecious stones and fabric.
6 Tour ends	Air 3½ hours	0720 hrs 1050 hrs	Breakfast at the hotel. Transfer to Jaipur airport for flight to Mumbai by CD 7471 0720/1050 hrs.		Take back happy memories along with a souvenir gift and photo CD.

Tour cost

- 474 USD per person on twin sharing basis
- 437 USD per person on triple sharing basis
- Rs 17,750 per person on twin sharing basis

Tour cost includes

- accommodation on twin sharing basis.
- all currently applicable taxes.
- all transfers and sightseeing by a non-AC Tempo Traveller.
- meal coupons worth Rs 500 per person per day
- rail fare Delhi–Agra by Shatabdi Express air-conditioned chair car.
- elephant ride at the Amber Fort, Jaipur
- parking at airport and railway station
- english speaking guide.

Exclusive highlights of the tour

- traditional Indian welcome
- welcome drink upon arrival
- chocolates and flowers in the room
- elephant ride at the Amber Fort
- souvenir gift on departure
- a photo CD upon return in receipt of one tour photograph and feedback letter from client

Tour cost does not include

- airfare
- entrances
- porterage at airport or railway station
- any personal services such as tips, laundry, etc

Supplement cost

- AC Supplement cost USD 9 per person and for INR Rs 401 per person on twin sharing basis
- entrance Supplement USD 99 per person and for Rs 373 on twin sharing basis.
- airfare Supplement for
  - (a) Bombay–Delhi 9W 333 0805/1000
        Adult USD 181 per person and for INR: Rs 5705 per person.
        Child USD 91 per child

(b)   Jaipur–Bombay CD 7471 0720/1050
adult USD 161 per person and for INR: Rs 4667 per person.
child USD 81 per child

Note: **Entrances at the sightseeing places**

Delhi Red Fort, Qutub Minar, Humayun's Tomb, and Jantar Mantar: USD 35 per person and INR Rs 53

Agra Taj Mahal, Sikandra, Agra Fort, Itmad-ud-daulah and Fatehpur Sikri: USD 58 per person and for INR: Rs 85

Jaipur City Palace, Observatory, Museum and Amber Fort: USD 6 and for INR: Rs 235

Note:

- The tempo traveller is available as per the sightseeing places mentioned at Agra and Jaipur and for Delhi it is for one half day and one full day (minimum kilometres 200 avg. per day).
- Agra can be visited for half day sightseeing for four hours in the evening.
- The hotels at all the places are centrally air-conditioned.
- Information on Son et Lumiere show: It is held at Red Fort. There are 2 shows, i.e. 0700 p.m. to 0800 p.m. in Hindi and 0830 to 0930 p.m. in English.

Example 10.4

Itinerary for one-day Pune Darshan city tour (01 day)

This itinerary is of a day trip to the places of interest in Pune by bus and is available everyday.

Day 1: Departure from Deccan Bus Stand, Railway Station, Pune at 0900 a.m. by M.T.D.C. semi luxury bus for Pune Darshan city tour. Visit Chaturshrungi Devi temple, Pune University, Pataleshwar temple, tribal museum, Raja Kelkar museum, Shaniwarwada, Parvati, Aga Khan Palace, Shinde's Chhatri, Katraj Snake Park, and Saras Baug. Tour ends in the evening.

Example 10.5

Itinerary for Romantic Escapade in Goa three nights/four days (for honeymoon couple)

This is a special luxury package offered by XYZ Travels for newly married couples to spend their honeymoon in Goa which is one of the most romantic places.

Day	Activity/Programme	Overnight
1 Mumbai	Arrival Goa by air. Meet and greet by XYZ representative. Transfer to the hotel by a non-AC Indica car. Check-in at hotel. Champagne and cute heart shaped chocolates in the room. Rest of the day at leisure. A candle light dinner in the room and overnight at the hotel.	Goa The Marriott
2 Goa	Breakfast at the hotel at Palmaeri restaurant. Half day sightseeing. Visit Bom Jesus church, beaches of North or South Goa. A relaxing body massage. Dinner and overnight at the hotel.	Goa The Marriott
3 Goa	Breakfast at the hotel in Palmaeri restaurant. Day at leisure. Dinner at Wan Hao/Simply Fish and overnight at the hotel.	Goa The Marriott
4	Breakfast at the hotel. Transfer to the airport for onward journey.	

Tour Cost: Rs 15,200 per person.

Tour cost includes

- airfare BOM – GOI – BOM
- accommodation on twin sharing basis
- all currently applicable taxes
- breakfast and dinner on all days
- a non air-conditioned car for transfers and sightseeing in Goa

Exclusive highlights of the tour

- a candle light dinner in the room.
- cupid's Bay view room
- champagne and cute heart shaped chocolates in the room
- midnight steam and Jacuzzi
- souvenir gift on departure courtesy XYZ Travels

Tour cost excludes

- any personal services such as tips, laundry, etc.
- lunches
- entrance fees
- guide
- porterage at airport

Example 10.6

Tour Itinerary for Fairy Queen

The Fairy Queen is a sixty seater luxury train built in 1855. The Indian Railways offers a unique two-days all inclusive package tour on the heritage chair car from New Delhi to Alwar, Rajasthan.

Day 1 Saturday	
0830 hrs	Reporting at the Delhi Cantonment railway station
0900 hrs	Fairy Queen departs
1300 hrs	Lunch on Board
1500 hrs	Arrival Alwar Railway Station
1520 hrs	Arrival Sariska by air-conditioned coach
1630 hrs	Arrival Hotel Tiger Den (RTDC)
1930 hrs	Theme dinner/Night Stay at Hotel
Day 2 Sunday	
0630 hrs	Jeep safari for Sariska National Park
0930 hrs	Return from Sanctuary and breakfast at Hotel
1200 hrs	Departure Sariska by air-conditioned coach to Alwar Railway Station
1245 hrs	Arrival Alwar Railway Station
1300 hrs	Fairy Queen leaves Alwar
1320 hrs	Lunch on Board
1600 hrs	Light Refreshment on Board
1845 hrs	Fairy Queen arrives at Delhi Cantonment Station

Special attractions

- Cultural programme and theme dinner, night stay at the Hotel Tiger Den.
- Jeep safari for the Sariska National Park.

Tour cost includes

- all meals
- pickup, drop and sightseeing by air-conditioned coaches
- jungle Safari in open jeeps (05 tourists in each jeep)

Tour does not include

- personal expenses
- entrance fees during sightseeing
- any other item not specified

Example 10.7

Tour Itinerary for Deccan Odyssey

The Deccan Odyssey is the newest and one of the finest luxury trains of India with all the modern facilities available on board. This super deluxe train has been launched by MTDC in association with the Indian Railways.

The itinerary of Deccan Odyssey includes seven nights/eight days of memorable visits to many beautiful cities, historical monuments, exotic beaches, caves, temples, etc. The train leaves Mumbai on Wednesday from Chhatrapati Shivaji Terminus.

Day 1 Wednesday

Departure in the evening from Chhatrapati Shivaji Terminus (CST) Mumbai

Day 2 Thursday

Morning arrival at Ratnagiri Railway Station. Departure by AC bus for Ratnagiri town excursion. Visit Thibaw Palace, Bhatye viewpoint, local markets and Lokmanya Tilak's memorial. Proceed to Ganapatipule Beach.

Lunch and free time at Ganapatipule beach resort. Noon (Optional): Tuk-Tuk ride in and around Malgund. Late in the afternoon proceed to Jaigad Jetty for backwater cruise. Board the bus for Ratnagiri railway station. Board the train. Dinner on-board.

Day 3 Friday

Morning arrival at the Sindhudurg Nagari Railway station. Departure by AC Bus to Malvan Jetty. Visit Sindhudurg fort. From jetty proceed to Tarkarli beach resort. Lunch and free time at Tarkarli beach resort. Enjoy backwater cruise. Visit Laxmi Narayana temple, lacquer handicrafts, paintings and furniture at the "Shilpagrama" the art and craft centre at Sawantwadi town. Watch cultural programme performed by local artist. Late in the evening board the train at Sawantwadi railway station. Dinner on-board.

Day 4 Saturday

Morning arrival at Karmali, Goa. Board the bus to reach Old Goa. Visit St. Augustine Church, Basilica of Bom Jesus, Church of St. Francis. Departure to Hotel. Lunch and Free time on the beach. Evening board the train from Madgaon railway station. Dinner on-board.

Day 5 Sunday

Morning arrival at Kolhapur City. Board the bus to visit New Palace, Bhawani Mandap, Mahalaxmi temple, Shalini Palace. Watch cultural programme and visit handicraft stalls. At noon board the train at Kolhapur station to depart for Pune. Lunch on-board. On arrival at Pune board the bus to visit Raja Dinkar Kelkar Museum. Board the train from Pune railway station. Dinner on-board.

Day 6 Monday

Morning arrival at Daulatabad station. Proceed by road to visit Daulatabad, Ellora caves, a World Heritage site. After lunch visit Bibi-ka-Maqbara. **Optional: Back to train.** Free time to shop Paithani, Himroo, Bidriwork from showrooms. Evening board the train from Aurangabad railway station. Dinner on-board.

Day 7 Tuesday

Morning arrival at Jalgaon railway station. Board the bus to visit Ajanta caves—World Heritage site. At noon board train at Jalgaon railway station. Proceed to Nashik. Lunch on-board. On arrival at Nashik Road railway station board the bus to visit Panchawati Ghat, Kala Ram Temple. Evening board the train at Nashik railway station. Farewell dinner on-board.

Day 8 Wednesday

Morning—Arrival at CST, Mumbai
Journey ends

Example 10.8

Tour Itinerary for Palace on Wheels

A royal holiday in historic coaches representing the princely states of colourful Rajasthan. One can board the Palace on Wheels for a week-long luxury cruise through fascinating Rajasthan. The train leaves New Delhi on Wednesday from Safdarjung Railway station.

Day 1 Wednesday

New Delhi Tour begins at 09.30 hrs.

After a day tour of New Delhi's India Gate, Lotus Temple, Qutab Minar, and more sights and lunch at a restaurant the group moves to the station. Reporting Time 16.00 hrs. Dep. 18.30 hrs.

Departure from Delhi Safdarjung Railway station.

Day 2 Thursday

Jaipur Arrival 03.00 hrs. Departure 19.30 hrs.

Visit Hawa Mahal or the Palace of Winds, Amber Fort with elephant ride. Lunch at a five star hotel followed by visit to City Palace, Museum and Observatory.

Day 3 Friday

Jaisalmer Arrival 09.00 hrs. Departure 23.45 hrs.

Visit the yellow sandstone fort, Nathmalji-ki-haveli, Patwon-ki-haveli and Salim Singh-ki-haveli. Shop for fine pattu shawls, mirror work and embroidered articles, wooden boxes, trinkets, silver jewellery and curios. After lunch on board enjoy camel ride on the sand dunes of Sam. Dinner and cultural porgramme at a Five Star hotel.

Day 4 Saturday

Jodhpur Arrival 07.00 hrs. Departure 15.30 hrs.

Visit Mehrangarh Fort, the grand palaces within—Moti Mahal, Sheesh Mahal, Phool Mahal, Sileh Khana, and Daulat Khana. Near the fort complex lies Jaswant Thada, and a group of royal cenotaphs made of white marble. After lunch at a Palace hotel, return to the Palace on Wheels. Shop for exquisite handicraft articles including the famous breeches, embroidered shoes, metal curios, silverware, paintings and tie and dye fabrics while at Jodhpur.

Day 5 Sunday

Sawai Madhopur Arrival 04.00 hrs. Departure 10.30 hrs.

After breakfast visit Ranthambhor National Park, covering an area of 392 sq. kms. and home to more than 300 species of birds, the tiger, hyena, ratel, jackal and fox, etc. Upon return to the Palace on Wheels, departure for Chittaurgarh.

Day 5 Sunday

Chittaurgarh Arrival 16.00 hrs. Departure 05.30 hrs (next day). After lunch on board visit Chittaurgarh Fort. Proceed to Udaipur.

Day 6 Monday

Udaipur Arrival 07:30 hrs. Departure 17.30 hrs.

On arrival at Udaipur, the Lake City, visit marble palaces—the Jag Niwas (Lake Palace) and the Jag Mandir, near Lake Pichhola. After lunch at a Five Star Hotel, a visit to the City Palace.

Day 7 Tuesday

Bharatpur Arrival 06.30 hrs. Departure 11.45 hrs.

After breakfast visit the world famous bird sanctuary, Keoladeo Ghana National Park, the nesting place for thousands of Egrets, Siberian Cranes, migratory Water Fowl, and other species of birds.

Day 7 Tuesday

Agra Arrival 14.30 hrs. Departure 22.00 hrs.
Visit to Fatehpur Sikri and the world famous Taj Mahal.

After dinner on board and a good night's sleep arrive at Safdarjung Railway Station at 06.00 hrs. on Wednesday.

Planning itineraries, as we have just read is not a simple task and requires detailed knowledge about the product as well as details about the client especially for customized tour itineraries. The tourism professional should ideally visit the destination and posses first hand updated information about the tour. The costing of the tour should be done carefully to cover all heads of expenditure and ensure that the tour rates are competitive yet profitable to the travel agency.

SUMMARY

Itinerary planning requires detailed and thoughtful planning, as it is one of the major operations for a travel agent and tour operator handling all kinds of tours. Besides seeing the customer's likes and dislikes the travel agent and tour operator also has to consider certain other external factors of a destination such as the political stability, the climate, etc. while planning any itinerary. The travel agent and the tour operator should be well versed with all the basic requirements for making an itinerary. The tour professional should have a sound knowledge of the geography of the place, the climatic condition, the best season to visit a particular destination, the duration of stay required at the destination, the distances in kilometres, different mode of transport available, hotels, shopping, and any fairs and festivals, etc. All the information required for planning an itinerary can be gathered from the state tourism offices, guidebooks, periodicals, journals, national and international tourist organizations, brochures of tour operators, colleagues, feedback from clients, Internet, etc.

After planning the itinerary, making reservations for hotels and transport, the next job is costing of the tour. The tour professional has to negotiate with the suppliers to get the best possible rates. While doing the costing the profit of the firm should be taken into account. All the basic costs of accommodation, meals, transport which may be airfare, train fare or car/coach travel depending on the size of the group, entrance fees, guide fees, miscellaneous charges, mark up, etc has to be included for costing a tour. The tour cost is given on an individual basis, i.e. per person cost, which can be on double occupancy or triple occupancy as per the requirement.

KEY TERMS

A la carte A separate price for each item on the menu.

American plan (AP) Hotel accommodation, which includes three meals in the room rate.

Bermuda plan (BP) Hotel accommodation with a full American style breakfast included in the room rate.

Check-in A process at the airport, which includes checking documents, issuing a boarding pass and accepting baggage and permitting the passenger to go to the departure lounge. In the hospitality industry it means greeting and registering a guest, verifying the method of payment and handing over room keys.

Check-in time Time at which a passenger should report and register at an airport terminal. In a hotel it is the time at which the room is ready for occupancy.

Circle trip A travel plan with stop over which returns to the point of origin by a different route and does not retrace the route.

Continental breakfast A light breakfast which normally includes beverages such as tea, coffee, cocoa and milk; bread rolls, butter and preserves such as jam/ marmalade.

Continental plan (CP) Hotel accommodation which includes a continental breakfast in the room tariff.

Double occupancy A room rate for two adults occupying the same room.

Double room A room with a double bed, suitable for two adults.

English breakfast A heavy breakfast which includes fruit juices, breakfast cereals, variety of egg preparations, meats, toast, and beverages

European plan (EP) Hotel accommodation in which no meals are included in the room tariff.

Group inclusive tour (GIT) When a particular number of passengers travel together they pay a subsidized GIT fare.

Incentive travel A specially designed trip arranged for agents or employees of a firm along with their spouses as a reward for outstanding performance

Miscellaneous charges order (MCO) Proof of prepayment. A voucher authorizing specified services to be provided to the person's named on the voucher or form.

Modified american plan (MAP) Hotel accommodation in which breakfast and either lunch or dinner are included in the room tariff.

Off-season rate Highly discounted room rates offered during lean season or a period of low occupancy.

Package A combination of travel related services such as air transportation, accommodation, car rental, etc.

Persons approximately (PAX) It means number of people which can fit into a particular space.

Plan A room rate, which is inclusive of meals.

Rack rate The normal published tariff of the hotel room, which is offered to the general public, without any discounts.

Room rate The price of a particular room in the hotel based on its location, size, bedding, amenities, and occupancy.

Single A room rate for one adult staying in the room.

CONCEPT REVIEW QUESTIONS

1. Define itinerary planning.
2. What kind of basic information is required from the clients for planning an itinerary?
3. What are the benefits of a group tour? How does it work out cheaper than the regular tours?
4. Give the importance of the information required of the number of people travelling.
5. Different people have different energy levels. Comment.
6. Give the importance of climate while planning an itinerary.
7. What are the basic steps to be followed while planning any tour itinerary?
8. List the basic items included in the costing of a tour.
9. Explain mark up, net rate, gross rate.
10. Discuss the importance of product knowledge in itinerary planning.
11. What all things should be considered while costing a tour?

PROJECTS/ASSIGNMENTS

1. A school approaches your travel agency for a study tour of 7–8 days for their students of age group of 13–14 years. How will you go about it?
2. A couple approaches you for a weekend tour. What suggestions will you give them? Plan an itinerary for the same.
3. Plan an itinerary for a honeymoon couple to a nearby destination for 3–5 days.

REFERENCES

Foster, D.L. 1994. *First Class: An Introduction to Travel and Tourism,* Second Edition, McGraw-Hill Book Co, Singapore.

IGNOU, TS-3 – *Managerial Practices in Tourism* – 1 Block.

Reilly, R.T. 1991. *Handbook of Professional Tour Management,* Second Edition, Delmar Publishers Inc, Canada.

CHAPTER 11

Tourism Product

Learning Objectives

After reading this chapter you should be able to:
- understand the concept of tourism product
- understand the nature of tourism product
- know the special characteristics of a product in tourism
- differentiate among the terms—tourism product, attraction, and destination
- classify the types of tourism product
- differentiate between tangible and intangible products

INTRODUCTION

When tourists decide to travel to a particular destination, they look forward to a pleasurable experience in terms of a safe and comfortable journey, good accommodation and meals, interesting attractions and leisure activities. These are the expectations or products, which the tourist is willing to spend money for. All these are components of the tourism product. Before we define 'tourism product' let us understand the meaning of the term 'product'.

A product in general can be a thing, a place, a person, an event, etc. which satisfies the needs of the person purchasing the product. The product which is offered to the consumer must have some need satisfying qualities. This product can be exchanged for some value. The value is of importance for mutual satisfaction for both supplier (producer) as well as the receiver (consumer) of the products.

The product is always characterized by 'pull factors' and it motivates the consumer to purchase it as it has the ability to satisfy a need of the consumer. Thus, a product is anything that can be offered to the market for attention, acquisition, or consumption and is capable of satisfying a need or want.

The tourism industry is a service industry and provides products which are nothing but services. The service product refers to an activity or a set of activities that a marketer offers to perform, resulting in satisfaction of a need of the customer or the target market.

Products which fulfill or satisfy the customers' leisure, pleasure, or business needs at places other than their own place of residence are known as tourism products.

A tourism product can be either a tangible item, for example, a comfortable seat in an aircraft or the food served in a restaurant or an intangible item, for example, the quality of services provided by a cruise liner or scenic beauty at a hill resort. In general, in almost all the cases, the tourism product is a combination of both tangible and intangible items. This combination of different components results in giving the tourist the total travel experience and satisfaction.

Philip Kotler (Kotler and Keller 2006) defines the concept 'service' as a product from marketing viewpoint. 'A service is any act or performance that one party can offer to another that is essentially intangible and does not result in the ownership of anything. Its production may or may not be tied to a physical product.'

The product from the tourism industry perspective can be viewed at two levels. They are as follows:

1. The total product which has a combination of all the service elements consumed by tourists throughout the entire tour. This product can be an idea or an expectation.
2. The explicit components of tourism products, such as attractions, accommodation, transport, and other facilities which are elements of the total tourist product.

DEFINITION

The product in tourism industry is the complete experience of the tourist from the time the tourist leaves home till the time he/she returns back.

The product may be defined as the 'sum total of physical and psychological satisfaction it provides to the buyers'.

In the tourism industry, the basic raw material used in the formulation of a tourism product is the country's natural beauty, its climate, history, culture, and the people. The other essential elements are the existing facilities or the infrastructure, which are necessary for the stay to be comfortable and it includes water supply, electricity, roads, transport, communication, services and other ancillary services (refer to Chapter 4).

Thus, we can understand that the tourist/tourism product is the sum total of a country's tourist attractions, transport systems, hospitality, entertainment, and infrastructure which is offered to the tourist, and if well designed and developed, will result in consumer satisfaction.

Tourism products are nothing but various services offered to the tourists, and falls under the category of service product (see Fig. 11.1).

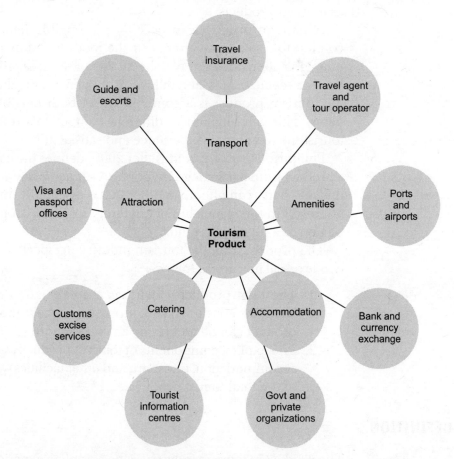

Fig. 11.1 The tourism product is an amalgamation of a variety of goods and services
Source: Adapted from Jha (1995)

CHARACTERISTICS OF TOURISM PRODUCTS

Tourism products are mainly service products or services which have several characteristics like intangibility, inseparability, perishability, variability, etc. (see Fig. 11.2).

For example, in business tourism, conference planning and management is a service offered by large hotels and convention centres. Fairs and festivals are events which are offered for enjoyment only at a particular time of the year and these are perishable and variable. In India, cultural attractions in the form of dances and music can be seen and enjoyed. Other products which tourists consume like wildlife, and flora and fauna are natural products.

Intangibility

Commodities are tangible products which have physical dimensions and attributes which can be seen, touched or, tasted while service products

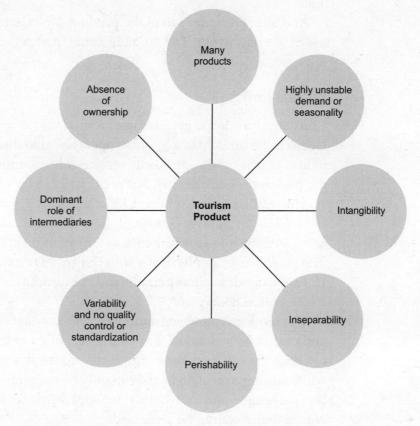

Fig 11.2   Distinct characteristics of tourism product

are intangible and cannot be seen, touched, or measured, but can only be experienced. The tourism product can be anything like a package tour, an airline ticket, or a stay in a hotel. The purchase of a package tour to the Far East is nothing but purchasing an experience or buying a dream as we cannot show the product we have purchased to our friends.

The timely performance, efficiency of service, getting the baggage quickly are the intangible items of tourism product. These aspects are very important for the business travellers who travel frequently. Similarly, noisy air-conditioners, other guests talking loudly in the restaurant, etc. are all part of the meal experience which is real but intangible and even though the tangible aspect, i.e. the meal served is good, the overall experience is poor. The product has both tangible and intangible elements.

Intangibility means the product cannot be directly seen, tasted, felt, or heard prior to the purchase and consumption. The only tangible item we get before purchase are the tickets or receipts for payment we have done.

And after consumption of the product we have memories of the tour which are intangible. The tangible items from a tour are in the form of souvenirs.

Inseparability

Consumer products, for example, a motorcycle manufactured at New Delhi can be brought to a Mumbai outlet and sold there. In case of tourism industry the products are mostly services which cannot be separated from the person or the company that provides it.

This can best be explained by a guide or escort who provides the services to the tourist. The guide has particular skills which are used along with the infrastructure such as any monument or place of attraction. The guide has to go physically with the group to explain the monument. Here the service is inseparable and the product exists only when the consumption takes place.

The production and consumption of the product occurs simultaneously and cannot be separated. The tourist has to go to the site of production to utilize the product. For example, the courtesy shown by an airhostess while serving a meal on board can only be experienced in the aircraft by the passenger and not before or afterwards as the production and consumption cannot be separated.

Perishability

Any tangible good or product can be manufactured and stored for a certain period of time and sold or used at a later date. For example, pens can be manufactured, stored in the warehouse for few months, and can be sold when there is a demand.

However, the service product cannot be stored in a warehouse and sold at a later date. For example, the airline cannot store 100 unsold seats of a flight scheduled to depart on 12 March 2008 to sell it on 13 March 2008. The unsold seats have no value at all. The service industry faces such problems due to fluctuating demands, as demand for air travel is more in mornings and evenings, or in some sectors which are heavily booked, while in other sectors, seats may remain unsold.

To avoid the loss of unsold products and overcome the losses incurred due to the perishable nature of the product, the airlines offer last minute sales or standby rates at drastically reduced rates. These rates indicate that although they are not getting profit they are minimizing losses and at least earning some revenue.

It is due to perishability that the hotel industry also offers heavy discounts along with transport operators especially during off season.

Variability/Heterogeneity

In tourism industry, services are rendered by humans to humans. These services have a high level of variability, when producer and consumer interact. The human element makes standardization of the product a difficult task. The services rendered vary from person to person and from time to time.

The guide's or escort's behaviour may not be consistent every single day. Family problems, ill health, or stress may affect his/her interest in the job, concentration in his/her work and ultimately his/her performance. Good tidings, minimum personal problems, and an interested audience help in boosting one's performance. The waiter in a restaurant will not be uniformly efficient on all days of the week for similar reasons.

To avoid variation in services and to maintain the standards in delivery of the products, the hotel industry, tour operators, and airlines have introduced computerized reservation systems (CRS). Such systems minimize human contact and errors. The tourism service providers also provide training to their staff who need to directly interact with the tourist.

Major travel companies who have their branches all over the world, have developed standard operating procedures (SOPs) to maintain uniformity in rendering services.

Dominant Role of Intermediaries

In all the industries, manufacturers play a major role in product components, design, distribution, promotion, and pricing. This is not the same in the tourism industry. Sale intermediaries such as tour operators, travel agents, reservation agents, hotel brokers, etc. play a dominant role. They enjoy a superior position in travel trade. They are the ones who decide to a large extent which services will be sold and to whom. They also decide at what time and which types of services are to be offered as well as pricing policies and promotion strategies.

Absence of Ownership

If you buy a computer, the ownership of the computer is transferred to you but when you hire a car, you buy the right to be transported to a predetermined destination at a predetermined price. The tourist or consumer cannot own the car or the driver of the car. The same is the case with the hotel industry. The hotel rooms can be used by a tourist during the hotel stay and the tourist acquires the right to certain benefits that the seller or hotel offers, but the ownership of the rooms remains with the hotel.

This can be further explained by a tourist purchasing a ticket of Deccan Odyssey, the exotic journey showcasing the rich cultural heritage of Maharashtra, or an aircraft which brings the tourist to the destination. The ticket allows them to use the services on board which they offer, but the customers do not own the product.

The tangible product can be bought and ownership can be transferred to the buyer whereas the tourism product being a service product, services can be bought for only consumption. The ownership remains with the person or organization which is providing the service. Kathakali, the famous dance from Kerala can be enjoyed by viewing it, but the dancer cannot be owned.

Manufactured by Many Producers

In case of tangible products, one manufacturer produces a total product. In tourism industry, the tourist product cannot be provided by a single enterprise. Each of the components of the tourist product is highly specialized and when combined together makes the final product.

The hotel industry produces guest nights or hotel rooms, and airlines fly passengers as their products. The travel agent's products are the bookings done on that day and in case of a museum or an archeological site, the product is measured on the basis of the number of visitors who visited the site on that day.

But from the tourist's point of view, the product he/she purchased was a single product—a Kerala package tour which covers the complete experience of his/her visit to a destination. The Kerala package tour is a total product for the tourist.

In other words, to a tourist, tourist product is not an airline seat or a hotel room or ticket to museum or guide services but it is a combination of all the above stated services manufactured by different producers which makes a complete product.

This is peculiar to tourism product and hence requires greater co-ordination in marketing the product.

Highly Unstable Demand/Seasonal Product

The demand for tourist products depends on many factors such as season, economy of the destination, political factors, social factors, etc. Except for the seasonal factor all other factors can be made favourable. Season is a factor which affects the tourism industry greatly.

Seasonality means the time period when the tourist destination is frequently visited by tourists which is for a limited period of the year. Almost all tourist areas have a short season which is called peak season which often may be as short as three months.

This seasonal usage of the product creates unemployment and also has an impact on transportation and hospitality services as well as most other services.

Along with unemployment, investment is greatly affected by seasonality.

Political unrest and economic instability caused by currency fluctuation and inflation have an impact on tourism demand but this may be temporary.

To tackle the problem of seasonality and unstable demand, the suppliers of tourism services have different pricing strategies. For example, the hotel tariff will be higher in peak season, in mid-season it will be moderate and in lean or off-season the rates of the product will be very low, i.e. off-season discounts are offered to combat the problem of seasonality. Sometimes the product is also offered in combination with other products like a package tour.

NATURE OF TOURISM PRODUCT

The nature of tourism product comprises two different types of travel to the destination. These are non-discretionary and discretionary travel.

In non-discretionary travel, undertaking travel is a must and the traveller has to travel to a particular destination and does not have much choice. These are business travellers travelling to attend a conference or a family travelling to their hometown for a wedding or a funeral, or a student flying back to college, etc.

Discretionary travel is concerned with choice; the traveller can select the destination/attraction and time of travelling, for example, to stay at home and relax, drive to a nearby beach resort, or fly to Malaysia for a vacation.

Both these travel segments have different needs and wants. For example, advertisement will affect the discretionary traveller because of choice.

In both the discretionary and non-discretionary travel, the nature of tourism product is the purchase of intangible services.

TYPES OF TOURISM PRODUCT

The tourism product which is a combination of tangible and intangible products can be a thing, an event, or a place which motivates the tourists towards it.

There are three ways in which tourist products can be classified (see Fig. 11.3).

Natural, Human-made, and Symbiotic Tourism Products

Natural tourism products are the natural attractions found all over the world like beaches, deserts, hills, mountains, climate, flora and fauna, islands, etc. These are nature's gifts to human beings.

Human-made products include fairs, festivals, cuisine, architecture, monuments, shopping, etc. Entertainment centres in the form of a theme park such as Disneyland, USA or the shopping festival at Dubai, etc. are also created products which offer a wide range of services for pleasure, leisure, or business.

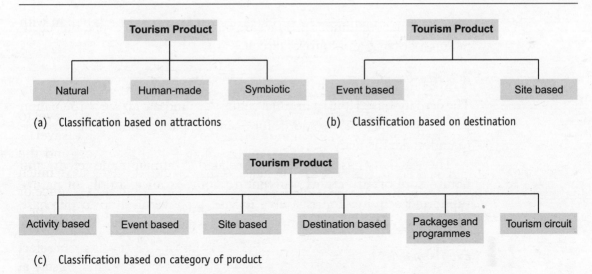

(a) Classification based on attractions

(b) Classification based on destination

(c) Classification based on category of product

Fig. 11.3 The tourist products can be classified in many ways

Symbiotic tourism product does not come under natural or human-made category. Marine park, flower festival, wildlife sanctuary, water sports are few examples of tourism products which are combination of products created by blending natural attractions and built attractions. The resources are provided by nature which are converted into the product by humans. But nature remains the core attraction and these are best examples of a symbiotic association of nature and humans.

Event-based and Site-based Tourism Product

In an event-based product, the event is the core element in the tourism product, for example, the Goa carnival in Goa, the Khajuraho dance festival at the Khajurao temples or the World Cup cricket matches are all event-based tourist products where tourists visit the destinations to attend the event. These events are seasonal.

In a site-based tourism product, it is the site which motivates the tourist to visit the place such as the Taj Mahal at Agra, Corbett National Park at Nainital, river rafting in Karnataka, etc.

Site-based products are open to tourists practically throughout the year.

Based on Category of Product

Here the products are visualized as a continuous whole or as a series ranging from a simple activity which may constitute the product to an entire circuit. Continuous product are based on activity, event, site, destination, package, and tourism circuit.

Activity-based

The activity-based tourist product centres around the active participation of tourists. In adventure sports, for example, paragliding, the tourist has to undertake the activity.

These activity based products are related to human-made activity and nature supported activity. Adventure sport is an example of nature supported activity. Tourists have to visit a souvenir shop to purchase handicrafts which is an example of human-made activity.

Event-based

There are many events which attract tourists. For some events the places are fixed such as Elephanta festival, Mumbai and for some the places vary such as the venue for the Olympic games. Tourists visit such places as spectators or as participants.

Site-based

Sites also offer attractions. These sites are specific. Museums at New York, Temples of Hampi, or beaches of Hawaii are all destination specific sites.

Destination-based

Many cities in the world are themselves a tourist attraction. The city itself may attract tourists specially if they are country capitals or state capitals, for example, Washington DC, New Delhi, Mumbai, etc. These cities also offer plenty of other attractions to the tourist.

Packages and programmes

Under this category come the offers which are complimentary and are offered by service providers. For example, free casino tickets to participants of a conference. These add-ons increase the attraction of the tourist product. Programmes are add-ons or optional products offered to customers. They are always provided with core attractions which make the product more effective and attractive. For example, post conference excursion tours. These tours are beneficial to service providers as delegates get to see new places and in turn spend more money at the attraction.

Delhi–Jaipur = 261 km
Jaipur–Agra = 228 km
Agra–Delhi = 200 km

Fig. 11.4   The Golden Triangle circuit
Courtesy: Rohit Sanas

Tourism circuit

They are a combination or multiple chain of destinations marketed as one product. Circuits are always beneficial to tourists as they offer a variety of attractions which are otherwise not possible to experience. For example, pilgrimage circuits like the Buddhist circuit and Char Dham yatra. Char Dham includes Gangotri, Yamunotri, Kedarnath, and Badrinath as one product. Figure 11.4 shows us the Golden Triangle circuit in India.

As we see, many types of tourism products are available while many more are being developed to attract tourists to the destination. It is the overall quality of the tourism product which determines the tourist experience and tourism planners should design products keeping tourist satisfaction in mind. This is a challenging task because of the unique nature of the tourism product.

SUMMARY

The product in tourism is a service product and refers to an activity or set of activities that a marketer offers to the customer and results in satisfaction of a need or want.

It fulfils the customer's pleasure, leisure, or business needs at places other than their own place of residence. The tourism product differs from the manufactured product or goods. Goods or commodities are tangible products which can be seen or touched while the tourist product is a service product and has both tangible and intangible elements. The characteristics of tourism products are perishability, heterogeneity, lack of ownership, dominant role of intermediaries, intangibility, inseparability, and seasonality. A tourism product is an amalgamation of a variety of products and services offered by many producers. The tourism product which is a combination of tangible and intangible products can be a thing, an event, or a place which motivates the tourist towards it and can be largely classified as natural and human-made products.

KEY TERMS

Inseparable Cannot be separated from the person responsible for providing the service.

Intangible Something which cannot be seen, felt, smelt, or tasted but can only be perceived.

Perishable product A product which has a particular life span after which it does not have any value. Cannot be stored.

Supplier of services The tourism suppliers which provide services to the intermediaries like airlines, hotel industry, etc. to sell.

Tangible product The product which can be seen and touched by human beings.

Target market The selected market used to attract potential tourists.

CONCEPT REVIEW QUESTIONS

1. Define tourism product. How is the tourism product different from the commodity product?
2. What are the distinct characteristics of a tourism product?
3. Explain the role of intermediaries in manufacturing the tourism product.
4. Explain the effect of seasonality on tourism product.
5. How can you classify tourism products?
6. State whether the following sentences are 'true' or 'false'.
   (a) Tourists can see the tourism product before the purchase.
   (b) The ownership of tourism product is not transferred to the tourist.
   (c) The tourist season cannot be extended.
   (d) Political situation and economy of the destination do not have any impact on tourism product.

CRITICAL THINKING QUESTION

Identify and briefly describe the tangible and intangible aspects of the services provided by the following:

(a) An airline
(b) A fine dining restaurant
(c) A theme park
(d) A museum

PROJECTS/ASSIGNMENTS

1. Identity the tourism products available in your city and classify them based on the category of the product.
2. Prepare a collage of tourism products available in your state.

REFERENCES

Bhatia, A.K. 2001. *International Tourism Management,* Sterling Publishers Pvt. Ltd, New Delhi.

Gupta, I.F. and S. Kasbekar 1995, *Tourism Product of India*, G.A. Publications, Indore.

IGNOU Booklets for Tourism Studies and MTM programmes.

Jha, S.M. 1995, *Tourism Marketing,* Himalaya Publishing House, Mumbai.

Keyser, H. 2002, *Tourism development*, Oxford University Press Southern Africa, Cape Town.

Kotler, P. 1996, *Marketing for Hospitality and Tourism*, Third Edition, Pearson Education, Delhi.

Kotler, P and K. Keller, 2006, *Marketing Management*, Tenth Edition, Dorling Kindersley Publishers, New Delhi.

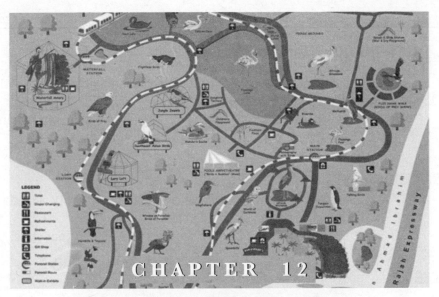

CHAPTER 12

Tourism Marketing

Learning objectives

After reading this chapter you should be able to:
- define and explain the terms market, marketing, and selling
- explain the concept of marketing and need for market segmentation
- understand the need for market research and for forecasting the demand for tourism products
- identify the components of the tourism marketing mix
- appreciate the characteristics of the tourism product and its effect on marketing
- appreciate the role of FAM tours in tourism promotion
- understand the reasons and problems of seasonality in tourism
- know how a tour brochure is designed

INTRODUCTION

Marketing has been recognized as the most important management activity in the tourism industry today. Being the fastest growing industry in the world, the world tourism arrivals and receipts have shown a steady growth. The number of people directly employed in this industry as well as the foreign exchange receipts is on the rise.

The principal suppliers of tourism products and services, such as airlines, hotels, car rentals, travel agencies, etc. are growing in number and there is strong competition amongst them. Their survival and growth in the tourism industry will depend to a large extent on their marketing approach.

Countries are competing with each other to market their destinations; travel agents, and tour operators compete to market package tours; hotels compete with one another to sell their rooms; and airlines compete with each other to market their seats (see Fig. 12.1). Competition is seen in all service sectors like restaurants, transporters, event managers, guides, escorts, and in all secondary constituents of the service industry. It is especially important because of the perishable and intangible nature of the tourism product, and requires a professional approach. Before we study about the need for tourism marketing, let us understand the meaning of the term 'marketing' and see how it differs from 'selling'. The terms marketing and selling are often misunderstood; marketing means much more than simply selling or promoting a product.

The term market was originally used to describe a physical place where buyers and sellers gathered to exchange goods and services. To a marketer, a market is the set of all the actual and potential buyers of a product.

Suppliers of tourism products have realized that their products cannot attract the buyers in the market or not all the buyers in the same way. Buyers are too many, widely scattered across the globe, and differ in their needs.

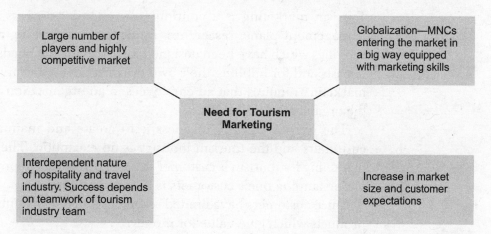

Fig. 12.1 Some of the reasons why marketing of tourism products is necessary

Sellers have recognized the need to identify their market segment and target that market. In this case the seller develops products and marketing mixes to meet the demands of the selected market segment. For example, Meadowlea developed salt and cholesterol-free spread to meet the demands of people suffering from lifestyle-related diseases. Target marketing helps sellers to focus their marketing efforts and promotional campaigns on existing and potential buyers instead of diluting the effort through mass marketing. Organizations can develop the right product for each target market.

Suppliers of tourism products and services have realized that to remain in business they should know what the customer's needs, wants, and expectations are. Their business should focus on creating and maintaining satisfied profitable customers. Customers are attracted and retained if their needs are met. If their expectations are exceeded, they are overjoyed and they talk favourably about their experience. This is what tourism marketing is all about—'customer satisfaction' and 'customer delight'. Satisfied customers return to the same travel agent, restaurant, hotel, cruise line, or car rental firm and keep these suppliers in profitable business. The aim of marketing, therefore, is to know and understand your customer so well, that the product or service you are selling fits their requirement perfectly and they buy it without your having to make much effort to sell the product.

DEFINITION

Tourism marketing is a continuous sequential process in which the management plans, researches, implements, monitors, and evaluates activities which have been designed for satisfying the needs and wants of tourists and for fulfilling their own organizational objectives. Successful marketing requires that all employees in an organization work towards the organizational objectives.

The purpose of any business is to create and maintain profitable customers and the tourism industry is no exception. The main goal of marketing for tourism is customer satisfaction leading to profit. Therefore understanding one's customers is the bottom line.

Since customers have limited resources and many wants, they choose products which give value for money.

Marketing activity is carried out based on some concepts. These are discussed as follows:

Production concept

It believes that consumers will prefer products which are easily available and highly affordable and that the management should focus on production and distribution channels. Customer satisfaction tends to get overlooked.

Product concept

It believes that consumers prefer existing products and these need to be developed further. They look at the present product with blinkers and overlook the possibility of developing entirely different products.

Selling concept

It believes that unless the organization concentrates on large scale selling and promotional activities, the consumers will not buy the product. It focuses on getting the maximum possible sales through increased advertising and discounts and not on creating a product to satisfy customers.

Marketing concept

Marketing concept is a recent business philosophy which believes that organizational goals can be achieved once we determine the needs and wants of the target market and deliver the service in a more effective and efficient manner as compared to our competitors. The target market is the clearly defined group or groups of potential customers chosen for specific marketing attention.

The marketing concept starts with the needs and wants of the target customers and coordinates all activities which affect customer satisfaction, while the selling concept focuses on the seller's need. It assumes that customers will not buy enough of the product unless the manufacturer uses promotional techniques such as advertising and personal selling. It points out that goods are not bought, they have to be sold.

The marketing concept focuses on the buyer's need. It assumes that when a product meets and exceeds customer's wants, selling is not necessary, and a product should sell itself without any extra promotional effort.

Selling aims at profit through sales volume, i.e. more sales more profit, whereas marketing aims at profit through serving customers' needs or demands. Such companies make profit by creating and maintaining customer satisfaction.

Societal marketing concept

The latest marketing concept is the societal marketing concept which keeps the consumer and the society needs, wants, and interests in mind. It is based on determining the needs, wants, and desires of target markets and delivering the service product more effectively and efficiently than its competitors. Apart from meeting or exceeding expectations, the consumer's and the society's well-being in the long run is focused upon. For example, airlines and hotels are promoting smoke-free international flights and no smoking floors to reduce the harmful effects of passive smoking. The Orchid Hotel, Mumbai, an ecotel, has eco-friendly practices as its unique selling proposition (USP) and also supports eco-friendly causes. The customers of such hotels are a part of save your planet programmes and are also willing to pay a premium for their suites.

MARKET SEGMENTATION

In the marketing context, both the existing and prospective customers for the product are together referred to as the market. For example, hotels are used by tourists for board and lodging, when they are on a tour. Although the need may not be there today, it is likely to be there in future and hence they are prospective customers and part of the marketing effort is aimed at such prospective customers. However all persons who need lodging facilities are not prospective customers for five star hotels. Many tourists travel on a tight budget and the market for five star hotels is only a part of the total market of hotel users. Such parts are called segments of the market.

Apart from lodging, hotels offer many facilities to people such as fine dining restaurants, health clubs, discotheques, swimming pools, beauty parlours, etc. Different groups with different needs and expectations constitute different segments. For example, some schools have contracts with star category hotels for teaching swimming to children. The segment using the pool for training are very different from the regular hotel guests in terms of age, behaviour, hours spent in pool, use of restaurant facility, etc.

A segment is discreet, identifiable, and distinguished by characteristics such as purpose, needs, motivation, behaviour, and benefits.

The tourist market may be segmented on the basis of the following characteristics:

- geography or place of origin of tourists
- demographic characteristics
- purpose of travel
- psychographic characteristics
- behavioural characteristics
- income, etc.

We have seen that there are various ways to segment a market and the next step lies in selecting an effective way so that the best segmentation base or combination of bases is selected. The segmentation base should be such that all people within a segment are as similar or homogenous as possible and the segments are as different from each other. The size of the target market should be large enough and have long term potential. They should be easy to reach and accurately selected.

There are two distinct sequential steps called market segment analysis in market segmentation. They are as follows:

1. Dividing the whole market into groups or market segments with common characteristics by using specific segment bases.
2. Selecting those market segments or target markets that the organization is best able to serve.

Markets consist of buyers, and buyers differ from one another in more than one way. They may differ in their wants, resources, buying attitudes, and practices. Each buyer is unique, but as it is not possible to create customized products for each buyer, it is necessary to categorize them into broad classes or segments with similar characteristics.

Need for Market Segmentation

The basic reason for market segmentation is that if we try to appeal to all potential customers and have an untargeted approach, our efforts are wasted. This is because there are groups of customers who are just not interested in buying our services. Table 12.1 shows the basis for segmentation.

Good marketing means selecting the segments that are most interested in specific services and aiming the marketing plan at them. The main reason for segmentation is to direct or focus our efforts and finances in the most productive way. This can be done by asking the questions who, what, how, where, and when.

Table 12.1 Basis for segmentation

Bases	Variables	Examples
Geographic	Region	Continents, countries, states, cities
	Population density	Less than 5000, 5000–20,000, 20,000–50,000, etc.
	Development	Rural, urban, suburban, slum
	Postal code	
Demographic	Age	Under 6, 6–11, 12–19, 20–34, 35–49, 50–64, 65+
	Gender	Male, Female
	Family size	1-2, 3-4, 5+
	Occupation	Business/service/retired/student/housewife/unemployed
	Education	Primary or less, middle school, X Std, XII Std, graduate, P.G. and above
	Nationality	Indian/American/British/French
Purpose of travel	Leisure	Vacation, VFR
	Business	Sales and marketing, MICE
	Other purpose	Health, agro, special interest
Psychographic	Social status	Lower class, middle class, upper middle class, upper class
	Life style and personality traits	Activities, interests, and opinions of self and the world
Behavioural	Use frequency and usage status, brand loyalty	Frequent travellers, non-users, previous users, regular and potential hard core loyals, split loyals, shifting loyals, switchers
Annual income	Income	Below 2 lakhs, 2 to 4 lakhs, 4 to 6 lakhs, 6 to 8 lakhs, 8 to 10 lakhs, and above 10 lakhs per annum

- Who   : Who is our target market?
- What   : What are they looking for?
- How   : How should we develop our marketing programme to fit their needs and wants?
- Where : Where do we launch our promotional campaign?
- When   : When should we promote our services?

After selecting the target market, we are better focused for identifying the needs and wants of the group.

There is no single way to segment a market and different segmentation variables have to be tried out.

Selecting Market Segments

Each market segment has different needs and expectations. Different organizations cater to the needs of different segments and decide which segments they would like to cater to. A segment is identified on the basis of the objectives and capabilities of the organization and the organization will plan and execute all activities keeping the needs, wants, and desires of this target market in mind. For example, if the hotel is targeting business tourists, then it should advertise in business magazines, have conference facilities such as a conference hall and a business centre with latest audiovisual aids, teleconferencing facilities, secretarial facilities, wi-fi connectivity, Internet access in all rooms, have multi-cuisine restaurants, a bar, and a special floor in the hotel reserved for lady executives.

The business tourist looks for a reputed hotel in a good location, a large table with bright lighting in the business classroom, data ports for a modem connection, easy to reach electrical points, multiple phones, and a comfortable chair.

Once an organization has chosen its target market segments, it must decide on its market positioning.

A product's position is the place the product occupies in the consumer's mind when it is compared with competing products. Today, the consumer has access to a lot of information and he/she makes a mental note of a product and a company's position. The role of the marketer is to plan the position to give his/her products the greatest advantage in the selected target markets and then design marketing mixes to create the planned positions.

Products are positioned based on specific product attributes. For example, Kerala advertises its backwaters and ayurvedic massages. Products are also positioned on the wants they fulfill or the benefits they offer. For example, Sentosa Island Resort advertises itself as a fun place, while Dubai promotes its image as a shoppers' paradise. Products can also be positioned for certain class of users, for example, Singapore Science Centre has exhibits ideal for students. A product can be positioned against the competitor's product highlighting the location as an advantage.

The marketer must select which of the qualities need to be highlighted to give it the right competitive advantage. Each product should develop its own USP and promote it. The USP should be visible, of distinct importance to the buyers, superior, difficult for the competitors to copy, affordable, and profitable.

PRODUCT LIFE CYCLE

The product in tourism is a bundle of benefits and satisfaction for the tourist. What consumers want today may not be the same as what they expect tomorrow. Consumers' needs, wants, and expectations are constantly changing as more competitors are entering the market and offering added benefits to their products.

Every product has a life cycle through which it progresses and the length of the life cycle varies from one product to another. The product life cycle displays five distinct phases in relation to the sales history of the product.

The product's life begins with the introduction or launching of the product in the market and ends when the sales decline or the product dies at a later stage or at the end of the life cycle.

Figure 12.2 shows the five phases a new product passes through from inception to decline stage in the product life cycle.

Introduction or launch

When a new product is launched in the market, the consumer needs to know about the product. This is achieved through promotional campaigns and advertising. Expenditure on promotions is high as customers are

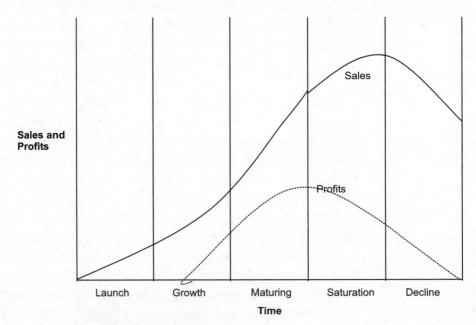

Fig. 12.2 Product life cycle

being motivated to try the new product, sales are low as the product is new in the market, and there are low or no profits.

Growth

In this phase, the product or service starts getting accepted by consumers. Market acceptance means that both sales and profits show a steep increase. Promotional expenditures remain high and product image is built. There may be an increase in the number of distribution channels.

Maturity

This is the stage when the product has been accepted by most of the target market and is well established in the market place. Many outlets are selling the product and offering it at a competitive price. At this stage, product manufacturers look for ways to hold on to their market share.

Saturation

This is the stage when sales and profits have reached their peak or saturation points and are now stagnant. The product has penetrated the market place to the maximum degree possible. Technological advancements and mass production have made it possible to lower the price and make it available to a larger market. This stage may last for a couple of years.

Decline

In the last stage, the demand falls and obsolescence sets in. New products need to be introduced and old products need rejuvenation. Sales are low, profits decline, advertising expenses are low. This is a critical stage requiring management decisions on rejuvenating the product or dropping the product as demand is low.

The lifecycle for tourism products and services is becoming shorter because of the changing needs and wants and changing life styles of the consumer as well as the rapid advances in the field of technology. Product manufacturers as well as marketers need to keep this in mind while planning the marketing strategy. The stage at which the product is in its life cycle can help identify opportunities and threats for undertaking marketing decisions.

Marketers and manufacturers should understand the concept of the product life cycle as it can be a major factor in successful and profitable product management and helps marketing managers to plan their promotional campaigns more effectively. Promotional costs in the first stage are high as the new product has to be made visible to the market. Familiarization tours or FAM tours for travel writers, media persons, and travel agents are organized at this stage. Profits are highest during maturity stage and saturation stage and gradually decline. If profit levels are to be maintained, advertising expenses should be reduced for sometime, letting the product sell on its own reputation and later on rejuvenating the product. The product life cycle serves as a guideline for formulating a marketing strategy and alerts an organization to take remedial action. The market for the product during the launch stage would be the segment with high disposable incomes sensitive to value and status of trying out a new product. At the maturity stage, a wide market is reached and marketers have the task of highlighting the merits of the product vis-à-vis the competitor's products. A decline in sales sends off a danger signal that the product should be either revitalized or allowed to die its own death and later replaced. In terms of tourist products, it means adding move activities or attractions to sites at destinations, or in a restaurant offering different cuisines and checking out what the competitors have to offer and their price structure.

THE MARKETING MIX

The marketing mix is one of the fundamental tools in marketing. Generally the marketing mix comprises the four 'P's namely:

1. Product
2. Price
3. Place
4. Promotion

These are the four factors which need to be mixed to enable a business to achieve its marketing objectives. A product has to be developed and designed, its price has to be determined, it has to be promoted, and made available in the target market. Each of these four factors needs thought and planning by the marketer to match the customer's expectations.

The tourism industry being a service industry needs a fifth 'P' which is an integral part of service. The fifth 'P' in tourism stands for people, processes, and physical evidence. Let us see how each 'P' is of relevance in designing the 'marketing mix'.

Product

The product/service is one of the four basic elements in the marketing mix and as we have read earlier in Chapter 11, it can be anything that can be offered to a market for use or consumption that might satisfy a need or want. From the tourism point of view, the product covers the complete tour experience from the origin of the journey till the tourist returns home. Refer to Chapter 11 for more details about the product in tourism.

Price

Once the tourism business has identified the product, it must decide on the price at which it is going to be offered to its customers. The term price in tourism is what a customer has to pay to obtain the product. The price in tourism may be hotel tariff, air fare, car rental, guide rate, and entry fee. For some products such as museums, shopping malls, science attractions there may be no price at all. Pricing plays a critical role in the marketing mix and therefore should be set very carefully. Customers relate price to quality and the nature of the product. Pricing is an art and a product's price should be sufficiently low to be perceived as good value for money to customers, yet high enough to make profit for the business.

Overpricing and under pricing

If the price is too low, the product may be perceived as inferior in quality and customers may not buy it. If the price is too high, customers have certain expectations which if not met, lead to dissatisfaction. Marketing should be aimed at not only customer satisfaction, but also customer delight, i.e. offering the customer more than what he/she expects.

The success of a tourism business is based on setting the right price. Competitor's prices and prices customers are willing to pay should be determined in advance through market surveys.

Various pricing policies which may be used are as follows:

Market penetration price

This is usually used when a new product is to be introduced in the market. The price is kept low to attract customers or to undercut competition.

Discount pricing

This pricing policy is widely used in the tourism industry. A discounted price is offered for certain products, such as airlines offering two for the price of one or 'take your spouse free', 15 per cent off, or hotels not charging for children, etc.

Discretionary pricing

Tourism businesses can use their discretion and alter prices by market segment, time, or place of purchase. For example, lower prices may be charged during lean season, lower entrance fees at museums for students or early bird prices for the first 100 bookings.

Competitive pricing

This pricing is based on the prices charged by competitors or the going rate for the product. For example, car rentals will frequently charge very similar prices as higher charges would result in losing business to competitors.

Market-skimming pricing

Exclusive tourism products often adopt high price policies to retain their brand image, exclusive status and superior quality. Target customers are willing to pay exorbitant prices for the quality product and service offered as this is a status symbol. For example, the Palace on Wheels and Deccan Odyssey are luxury trains-cum-attractions with high charges but are always booked to capacity and booked one year in advance.

Space tourism scheduled for 2009 is already fully booked.

Large tourism businesses have very complex pricing structures. An airline company may have many different prices and although all passengers in the economy section of a given flight are travelling from the same place of origin to the same destination, they all may have paid a different price for the similar category seat because of a vast combination of pricing policies which are in force (refer to Chapter 5).

Place

The place or the distribution channel is another important component of the marketing mix (see Table 12.2). Because of the perishable nature of the tourism product, selecting the right distribution channel is critical for the success of any tourism business. Tourism managers must choose the right place or distribution channel to ensure that it reaches the target markets.

Tourism businesses may sell their product directly to customers via the Internet or indirectly through intermediaries such as travel agents

Table 12.2 Distribution channels in travel and tourism marketing

Distribution channels	Marketing directly to customers	Principal suppliers such as hotels, airlines, car rentals, etc.
	Marketing through intermediaries	Travel agents, general sales agents, tour wholesaler, speciality intermediaries, tour operators
	Marketing through technology	Telephone, Internet

and tour operators. Intermediaries increase the selling capacity of the organization by providing sales outlets at places near to the customers. The choice of intermediaries is important as they are in direct contact with customers and can influence levels of quality and satisfaction. Large organizations often use more than one distribution channel for marketing the product. Read Chapter 7 and Global Distribution Systems (GDS) in Chapter 16.

Promotion

Promotion is one of the main marketing functions for a tourism business. Once the product has been designed, developed, attractively priced, and made available to the target customers through distribution systems, it needs to be promoted to highlight its USP and let the agents and customers know how your product is better than your competitor's product.

All promotional work should be based on the AIDA principle.

A—Attention
I—Interest
D—Desire
A—Action

The attention of the potential customer is sought and interest is created through colourful pictures and bold letters. Desire is created by offering a discount with the advertisement and action is triggered off by giving details of place to contact such as address, timings, directions to reach, contact numbers, e-mail address, and the website address.

To create awareness about the service product, and to persuade the customer to purchase the product, what is important is what you communicate to the target market about the product.

Promotion is vital because of the high level of competition in the tourism industry and customers need to be motivated or stimulated to try out a new product. There are a number of different tools which are used to promote tourism products. These include advertising; public relations; publicity; sponsorship; brochures; sales promotions; personal selling; and direct marketing such as telemarketing, networking, exhibitions, and tradeshows. These tools are referred to as the promotional mix elements.

The promotional mix elements include the following:

Advertising

It is a form of communication that appears in the media to inform and persuade the consumer to buy the product. Advertising is carried out by a number of media such as newspapers, magazines, journals, brochures, display boards, radio, television, motion pictures, etc. It appears as space in a print media or time slot on the radio or television. It requires a substantial budget if it is to be successful.

The advertiser should know whom the advertisement is meant for, what thoughts need to be put into the tourist's mind so that a liking is developed for the product, i.e. what message needs to be communicated and which media is to be used as well as when and how often must the advertisement appear. A full coloured advertisement in glossy print of high quality gives a tangible dimension to the product.

Public relations

It is defined as the sum total of activities designed to build and maintain good relations between a tourism company and its public (i.e. customers, suppliers, government organizations, stakeholders, employees, the press, and the community). Public relations (PR) or publicity does not need any budget and is yet the most powerful and valuable promotional tool. Publicity is generally used for generating awareness, building recognition, and creating a favourable image. Tourism is a popular topic for the media to cover and if there is some newsworthy item, it can get good publicity through the media. When any tourism product is launched, leading personalities are invited for the inaugural function along with reporters and journalists. Press releases with major highlights are kept ready and brochures are distributed. The product gets publicity through write-ups by the press quoting what others feel about the product, thus giving it more credibility than advertising.

The Government of India has been promoting the country as a tourist destination around the world through *Incredible India* road shows. These shows project the great concept of Indianness which celebrates the diversity of India. Road shows have been staged in Europe, Singapore, and in Shanghai, China. They include folklore, theatre, traditional dance, and music depicting the vast potential India has to offer. *Incredible India* festivals have been held in London, New York, Singapore, Berlin, and Beijing.

Negative publicity is also tackled by the India Tourism offices around the world. The offices are briefed about the current situation so that people can log-in and clear their doubts. Three such recent incidents were the Chikungunya epidemic scare, the negative stories published by London newspapers about a British teenager's murder in Goa, and the 26/11 terrorist attacks on Mumbai which resulted in the cancellation of bookings.

Personal Selling

This tool is used by travel agents or tour operators while making a presentation to a customer or a group on various packages, destinations, hotels, etc. for the purpose of making a sale. Personal selling becomes effective when the sales person has complete knowledge about the customer, the product being sold, and the competitors, and has a good presentation as well as excellent presentation skills.

Sales promotion

These are short term incentives offered to customers to motivate them to purchase the product or to sales people for achieving certain targets. For example, the frequent flyers programme offered by airlines to customers or incentive tours to Singapore/Malaysia to travel agents for achieving a given target are some examples of sales promotion.

Networking

It is the art of meeting and maintaining contact with tourism suppliers and potential customers at social gatherings like events, launches, meetings, get-togethers, conferences, etc. Networking is an excellent way of keeping pace with the latest developments in the industry and promoting tourism products.

Attending travel tradeshows

Trade shows are held annually for suppliers from the travel trade as well as consumers. These are mega events, for example, the International Travel Exchange (ITB) in Berlin and the World Travel Market (WTM) in

London. These are platforms for sharing developments in the travel trade and can give wide exposure to the delegates as well as the products.

Membership

Membership of tourism organizations helps tourism businesses to network and also offers discounts for advertising of their products in their association's publications.

Many products are available on the Internet and tourism businesses have felt the need to have their own websites along with distributing the product through travel agents. Refer to Global Distribution Systems Chapter 16.

MARKETING OF SERVICES

Services marketing has extended the traditional marketing mix of four 'P's to seven 'P's and has added people, processes, and physical evidence to the tourism marketing mix. The components of the extended marketing mix are interrelated and can be controlled by the tourism professional. In any service industry, it is the people who deliver the product; the service or process is quite complex with many minute details which need to be looked into and the services/product offered can only be evaluated by consumers at the place of consumption, i.e. physical evidence. People, processes, and physical evidence are therefore essential components in managing the quality of the service and creating customer satisfaction.

For example, tourism is a high contact service with different people being part of the tourism product and being multifaceted there are many complex service processes involved. Because of the unique characteristics of the tourism product, physical evidence gives tangibility to the intangible product.

People

A tourist undertaking a holiday abroad first encounters people from the point of origin of the journey connected with the trip.

The airline ground staff at the check-in counter, the flight attendants in the aircraft, their attitude and behaviour, whether they are helpful and courteous or indifferent and curt will reflect on the image of the airline. Tourists judge the quality of an airline on the basis of the people they employ. The time taken for the process of checking in, the wait in long queues, filling up of forms, and completing formalities, the assistance from airline staff in filling up forms, etc. will all reflect on the overall quality of service.

Process

Process includes all procedures, steps, schedules, and activities, etc. which are followed to carry out any activity. Some processes are compulsory like filling up an embarkation and disembarkation form, while others are practised to facilitate easy control over various activities. Some processes are complex and time consuming and need to be simplified or else they would have a negative influence on the customers. Many flight attendants assist passengers on board in filling their disembarkation forms or fill the same for them.

Physical Evidence

Physical evidence is closely related to the tourism product and since services are intangible in nature, it is difficult to estimate the level of satisfaction the tourist would derive from the product. Physical evidence helps the tourist to judge and select the product from a variety of options. Since the tourist cannot see, evaluate, or compare products prior to making a decision whether to purchase the product or not, it is necessary that the source of information projects an image of what the tourist could expect by purchasing the product. For example, India Tourism offices abroad are projecting a grand image of *Incredible India* to attract tourists and convince them that India has a lot to offer.

Physical evidence tries to give tangibility to the intangible service product, be it the office building, its cleanliness, comfort, and ambience; uniforms of staff; quality of visiting cards, letterheads, brochures, tickets, other publications of the tourism industry; prior experiences of tourists in the form of appreciation letters, etc.

FAMILIARIZATION TOURS

Familiarization (FAM) tours are educational tours and are an excellent marketing tool for reaching out to travel professionals, journalists, and trade delegates.

The focus of FAM tours is to apprise, enlighten, and provide first hand information and real life experience of the tourism product to the intermediaries who form part of the distribution system, as well as the opinion makers in tourism. The opinion makers are journalists, travel writers, television crew, radio persons, incentive tour operators, outbound tour operators of other countries, and dignitaries who are capable of influencing the public.

FAM tours are necessary because of the intangible nature of the tourism product which cannot be seen, felt, or experienced by the prospective customer before the purchase. These products are generally purchased through intermediaries who need to have first hand information to market the product and FAM tours play a major role in this.

The entire effort of the FAM tour is geared to bring the opinion makers and suppliers to actually experience what the destination has to offer to its tourists. They can decide about the merits and demerits of the product and accordingly inform or influence the prospective buyers through press releases, write ups in travel magazines, presentations, etc.

The purpose of a FAM tour may vary according to the following two reasons:

1. The aims of the organization/destination, for example, what market segment it wants to target.
2. The stage of the product life cycle a product/destination is in, for example, launch stage, rejuvenated stage, etc.

Need for FAM Tours

There are several reasons why FAM tours are needed. They are discussed as follows:

Destination promotion and image building Today, every country or destination wants to increase its tourism earnings and therefore FAM tours are regularly organized by various service providers to attract potential tourist generating regions to the destination.

Introducing new products All new tourism products, however strong they may be, need to be introduced to the right intermediaries, at the right time, at the right place, at the right price. For example, the Deccan Odyssey needs to be experienced. No amount of photographs, brochures, etc. can bring alive the grandeur and pleasure of travelling on board this luxury train; but if a travel writer, personally experiences it and writes his views for many readers to read it, then the effect would be dramatic and the response would be positive.

Damage control FAM tours are an effective tool in dealing with any negative image situation related to health, safety, and security of tourists.

In such cases, the opinion makers are the specialists from different fields who visit the destination to study the situation and give their own account of the facts.

Publicizing events   Most destinations are promoting special events to attract tourists. For example, India Tourism organizes FAM tours covering events like fairs and festivals to promote these events abroad.

Therefore, one can see the importance of FAM tours in the tourist products' promotion, launching, reducing negative impacts, and for publicizing any special event. FAM trips are made more effective by including innovative ideas like including an activity programme, welcome greetings, sending a follow-up mail, etc. All sectors of the industry benefit from using FAM tours as a promotional strategy. Practically all sectors are involved in planning and organizing a FAM tour depending on the tourism product to be marketed. National tourism board offices, airlines, hotels, archaeological survey department, forest department, restaurants, etc. both belonging to government or privately owned, are involved in preparing the itinerary for the tour.

MARKETING RESEARCH

Tourism managers need information about the market or consumers, the competition, the trade, and the distribution system before undertaking the marketing plan. Research is the first step in plan preparation, and is defined as a systematic collection and analysis of data relating to the marketing of goods and services.

Tourism professionals need to understand which markets they wish to serve, which products to sell, what prices to charge, which place or distribution channel to select, and which communication tool to use to promote the product. Because of the multi-faceted activities in the tourism industry, tourism professionals need an in depth knowledge of the service's marketing mix to enable them to make a viable plan. The marketing research process is closely linked to the development of an effective marketing mix.

Market research means to investigate the market, gather information objectively, understand, analyse and use the details for problem solving and decision making, i.e. for the betterment of the tourism product. There is a difference between the terms 'marketing research' and 'market research'. The term marketing research covers a wider variety of aspects including research into new products, price, and distribution channels, publicity, and consumers, whereas market research is concerned with the consumers and their behaviour patterns. The main purpose of market and marketing research is to reduce as much guess work or assumptions as possible. Research has two main aims—firstly, it minimizes risks when plans are being made and secondly, it can monitor performance after implementation of the plan.

Thus, market research is an ongoing continuous process and involves re-assessment of chosen strategies. Especially in the tourism industry, research helps to identify opportunities for product development; make investment decisions for new ventures; and choose locations, themes, and levels of service required; and arrange for any diversification of product.

A variety of data is gathered and used by the tourism industry. The data may include statistical data of tourist profiles like age, gender, occupation, etc. statistical data on tourist behaviour such as choice of destination, frequency of holidaying, budget, time spent on vacations; tourist satisfaction; competition analysis, etc. Market research is thus an important tool for effective marketing, planning and management of tourism businesses.

Advantages

Some of the advantages of marketing research are

- understanding the customers and the market;
- identifying opportunities for product development;
- developing an effective marketing mix;
- helping in problem solving;
- minimizing risks as guesswork is reduced;
- monitoring performance after plan is implemented; and
- helping in future marketing decisions.

Disadvantages

Some of the disadvantages of marketing research are

- one may not get reliable data;
- errors are likely to occur if responses are wrongly interpreted;
- the sample size may be too small and may not represent the population; and
- the choice of sample itself may be incorrect.

The various research methodologies are based on the fact that research can be quantitative or qualitative. Data may be gathered from primary or secondary sources.

Quantitative Research Methodology

This method involves statistical analysis and answers the questions—How much? and How many? These involve numerical and statistical data to test a hypothesis or generalization. Some of the main attributes of quantitative approaches are as follows:

- Identical questions and methods of recording are used which make data compilation easy.
- The sample size is quite large and is in consideration of the issue.
- Statistical analysis is used for drawing inferences.
- Closed questions are asked to facilitate use on computers and give statistical outputs. 'Yes', 'no', 'don't know', etc. are used and thus elaborate judgment is not present.
- It uses scoring/rating scales such as excellent/v. good/good/fair/ satisfactory/poor, etc. A scale of one to 10 is used for rating opinions.

Advantages

Some of the advantages of quantitative research methodology are as follows:

- Since the sample sizes are large they represent the population and hence some judgments can be made easily and confidently.
- Data can be easily summarized and analysed using computers.

Disadvantages

Some of the disadvantages of quantitative research methodology are as follows:

- This method is impersonal and does not give subjective information.
- It involves a lot of time and effort as large samples are required to be gathered.
- Poorly framed questions may cause bias and misinterpretation.
- The problems of those individuals who have not/will not take part in the survey are not highlighted.

Qualitative Research Methodology

It is used to probe ideas, feelings, and attitudes. It answers questions such as 'What did you like about the destination'.

Qualitative research is undertaken to provide the basis for designing quantitative research. Some of the attributes of qualitative research are as follows:

- It aims at gathering more in depth information by using open ended questions.
- Usually the interviewer tries to initiate people to share their thoughts on a topic such as—why does a tourist prefer to visit Spain rather than India.

Advantages

Some of the advantages of qualitative research methodology are as follows:

- It provides invaluable information about people, their experiences, motivations, attitudes, etc.
- It is more personal in nature.
- The purpose of the research is more for understanding and not just for statistical analysis.

Disadvantages

Some of the disadvantages of qualitative research methodology are as follows:

- As a small number of people are involved, generalizations cannot be made.
- Analysis of qualitative research involves judgments made by the researchers, thus objectivity may be hampered.

There are other research methodologies such as primary data collection and secondary data collection.

Primary Data Collection

Primary research or field research is original data generated by new research carried out in tourist generating market. It involves first hand information collection. Research techniques include sample surveys, interviews, and observations. Primary research covers both quantitative and qualitative data. The population from which information is required is defined and a statistically valid sample of the population is drawn. Field research includes sample surveys and motivational research (see Fig. 12.3). Choosing the samples and developing the questionnaires are important parts of the research design. Motivational research concentrates on forecasting the motives behind travel. It gives us an insight into the attitude of the tourist and what their expectations are. Data can be collected personally, through mail surveys or telephonic interviews.

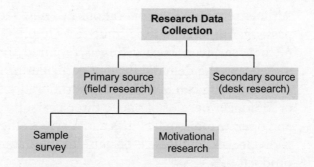

Fig. 12.3   Classification of data collection methods

Secondary Data Collection

Secondary or desk research is information collected for purposes other than solving a present problem, i.e. the researcher becomes the secondary user of the data. Secondary data can be obtained from international tourism organizations such as UNWTO, IATA, etc. which regularly publish statistical information, from national organizations, state tourism boards, trade associations, airlines, hotels, etc. All published sources of data constitute secondary research. Before undertaking any research, it is advisable to find out if the information required already exists.

TOURISM FORECASTING

Tourism planners need to predict the demand for the product they are developing and marketing. Since most markets do not have a stable demand, accurate forecasting becomes a crucial factor for the success of any organization.

Forecasting is the art of estimating future demand by anticipating what buyers are likely to do under a given set of conditions (Kotler 1996). Tourism managers need to base their decisions on certain assumptions such as behaviour pattern of customers; competitors' strategies; past sales; seasonal variations; erratic events such as heavy monsoons, recession, etc.

Forecasting helps managers to maximize their profits. Poor forecasting may lead to overstaffing, understaffing, excess inventories, inefficient operations, and customer dissatisfaction. Accurate forecasting keeps suppliers prepared for the anticipated demand for their product. For example, the Indian Railways runs special trains during the holiday season to take care of the large number of passengers travelling during vacations.

Airlines planning their operations in a new sector will want to know the passenger demand on the route so as to plan the frequency and quality of their services. Forecasting is required to design the product and understand the demand for that particular product.

Forecasting can be done for short durations like seasonal forecasting or for longer periods of one to three years. It is needed to plan, develop, and operate tourism facilities and services efficiently and profitably, and is of special significance because of the nature of the services and the product.

SEASONALITY IN TOURISM

All types and forms of tourism have seasonality as a component. There are peak seasons, lean seasons, or off seasons for a destination or a tourist generating market. If one were to analyse tourist arrivals at any destination, one would observe monthly fluctuations. In case of individual services, the seasonality concept can be further applied to demonstrate weekly or hourly fluctuations. There is more rush on weekends and public holidays in a museum or at a resort. There may be more rush in morning or evening flights in comparison to afternoon flights. Such analysis is extremely important from the marketing point of view as it helps in deciding the marketing mix.

Seasonality refers to variations in the demand for tourism products which makes it difficult for providers of tourism products and services to sustain business all year round. Demand for tourism products such as accommodation, transportation, etc. is seasonal. Tourist resorts experience a fairly high degree of seasonality, with demand peaking during vacation periods and in summer months.

Products can be designed, rejuvenated, or dropped as per the seasonal requirements. Separate prices may be charged for lean seasons along with a different promotion policy. Manpower requirements would be higher in peak season and lower in lean season. This may affect recruitment patterns adopted by the employers. Sometimes even capacity utilization is affected. Goa is a typical example of seasonality. Seasonality in tourism does not only mean climate of the seasons of the year. Seasonality is of different types and the tourists' seasons emerge because of different reasons. These are as follows:

Climatic seasonality This is related to the natural climatic seasons in a year. Tourists move from hot climatic regions towards cooler destinations in summer months like the hill stations which experience peak season.

Non-climatic attractions Non-climatic attractions or institutionalized seasonality in tourism emerges out of religious, cultural, ethnic, and social aspects of human life. Festivals, pilgrimages and fairs, public holidays, industrial holidays, and school vacations dictate seasons which are decided by humans.

Social pressure Social pressure or fashion is another aspect which brings about or affects tourism seasonality. This has been termed as social seasonality. The rich and famous class of society sets certain trends wherein it becomes socially necessary to participate, for example, travelling abroad for honeymoon.

Sporting season This is another aspect which has resulted in tourist activity. Winter sports such as skiing and water sports such as surfing are examples of this type. There is a lot of tourist movement during major sporting events such as the Olympics, cricket World Cup, Commonwealth Youth Games, etc.

Tradition This also plays a role in seasonality. Many people take holidays at peak seasons because they have always done so and old habits are difficult to change, for example, a family plans a holiday when schools are closed for long durations. Even when children are grown up, the family still takes a holiday during those months because they are habituated to taking a break during that time.

Seasonality is an important issue because seasonal fluctuations create certain problems for both the destination as well as the producers of tourism services. During the peak season, carrying and serving capacity is exceeded and there is a shortage of trained labour. The lean or off-season brings in a different set of problems such as:

(a) a decline in profits;
(b) high maintenance costs and underutilization of infrastructural facilities;
(c) unemployment; and
(d) shutting down business.

In fact, both off seasons and lean seasons in tourism are always seen as a problem because of a reduction in the volume of the business and subsequent reduction in profits. Investors hesitate to invest in business as the returns on investment are low.

Seasonal Marketing

Both over utilization and under utilization of resources are undesirable and ideally seasonality should be evenly distributed. This helps in preserving the destination at the sametime providing year round employment in this industry.

Marketing professionals should focus on the following:

- Extending the peak season by planning additional attractions and events before or after peak season.
- Organizing events which are not affected by climatic conditions, for example, indoor events like meetings, conferences, etc. The MICE industry can help solve the problem of seasonality and benefit both the providers of services as well as the workers who are unemployed during off-season by organizing business meetings, conferences, and conventions. Customers can benefit from off season discounts while tourism suppliers can keep their business going.
- Offering promotional packages during lean season.
- Establishing additional seasons after a detailed study of the climate, culture, and natural attractions. For example, destinations are being promoted to enjoy the snowfall, get wet in the rain, watch natural waterfalls, etc.
- During off season, for international tourists, domestic tourism should be promoted. Off-season promotional and pricing campaigns such as special packages, special fares, price reduction, seasonal discounts, and extra services should be introduced. Discounted pricing will attract tourists who otherwise cannot afford the holiday and do not mind going during off season. However, off-season marketing should be planned well in advance and the incentives and discounts should be attractive enough to bring tourists to the destination during lean season. This will help service providers to continue working throughout the year and overcome the problems caused by seasonality. In Goa the monsoon season is gaining popularity and Goa is being marketed as 'Goa: Monsoon Magic'. Every hotel and resort is offering heavy discounts. Although the sea is rough and beaches are deserted, boat cruises down the river Mandovi still operate. Five star hotels and resorts become suddenly affordable, charging only half the seasons' rate. Traditional festivals such as the Sao Joao festival of fertility are promoted to attract tourists.

DESIGNING A TOUR BROCHURE

All tourism service providers need some form of printed literature which gives detailed information about the organization and acts as a booking mechanism. Printed material may be in the form of a flier, a leaflet, a post card, a rack brochure, a fact sheet, a multi-page colour brochure, a map, videos, or DVDs. All this is called collateral material and being the first point of contact, it is important that they portray the correct image of your company and product.

Before designing a brochure it is important to know the following.

- The objective of the brochure—Why it is being designed?
- The target market—Who is going to read it?
- The place of distribution—Where would they be when they read it?

A brochure is a printed material used for promotion of goods as well as services. It contains important information and features about a certain product/service.

From hotels to tour operators, everybody needs to use a brochure. A good brochure, though expensive to design and create, is a must for selling the product and also to make the customer aware of the unique features being offered.

For example, brochures for visitor attractions are designed to enhance a visitor's experience by providing complete basic information in a convenient format. Figure 12.4 depicts a user-friendly map in a visitor attraction brochure. A brochure describes the attraction, its opening and

Fig. 12.4 A well-designed map is informative and useful and is often preserved after the trip as a memento
Source: www.birdpark.com/sg/visitorinfo/parkmap.html

closing time, a detailed user friendly map, directions to reach by road, rail and the location of various facilities on a map, etc. at the attraction.

Purposes

A brochure in tourism serves several purposes. These are discussed below.

Image building   The brochure is the first contact point of the consumer with the service provider and hence the paper quality, colours, layout, and photos create an image in the mind of the consumer. Hence while designing a brochure all these features must be paid attention to.

Tangibility to the intangible   A brochure acts as a medium to display how the actual product would look and its properties, as well as all facilities and amenities offered by the establishment.

Source of information   It provides information that is relevant to a consumer. Technical specifications, added advantages, etc. can be highlighted to draw the customer's attention to the USP.

Positive decision making   A brochure motivates a consumer to buy a certain product or service just by looking at the brochure.

Features which are desirable in a well-designed brochure are as follows:

- effective message;
- proper font size and legible layout;
- quality paper and printing;
- clear and appropriately sized photographs;
- relevant information and features; and
- any added advantages such as discounts, etc.

The tourism marketer should always remember that—'A brochure is an important promotional tool as it acts like a silent sales person for the company'.

We have read that marketing is much more than a business function and all tourism professionals should study and interpret the needs and wants of the target customer. This should be used to design a product-service combination which will satisfy the customer. It should provide good value, fulfil the needs, and motivate customers to purchase the product, at the same time ensuring a profit for the organization. Marketing is considered the most important management activity in the tourism industry as its survival and growth depends to a larger extent on the marketing approach as the number of competitors is vast and because of the nature of the tourism product.

SUMMARY

Marketing has been recognized as the most important management activity in the tourism industry which is growing at a rapid rate. It is especially important because of the perishable and intangible nature of the tourism product. Suppliers have realized that to remain in business, they should know what their customers expect from them. The aim of marketing is to know the customer so well that the product or service meets their requirement perfectly so they buy it without the supplier having to make much effort to sell.

Since customers vary in their requirements, marketers need to identify their market, study their needs, develop a product, and create a marketing mix to meet the demands of the selected market segment or target market.

The product needs to be advertised and promoted so that the target market is aware of the newly launched product or revitalized old product. Various communicational and promotional campaigns can be used. Tourism professionals rely on brochures to promote their offerings. Before they promote the product they prefer experiencing the product, so that they have first hand information. FAM tours are jointly organized by suppliers for travel professionals and the media to promote and give publicity to the product. Suppliers would benefit from the publicity as they would get more business.

While marketing of tourism products, the seasonality aspect should be kept in mind, with an aim to extend the tourist season. This would help conserve the destination and at the same time solve the problem of unemployment and other related problems faced during off-season.

KEY TERMS

Advertising A paid form of non-personal tourism product or service by an identified sponsor.

Allocentric traveller An adventurous traveller who seeks new destinations and is inquisitive.

Behavioural segmentation Dividing a market into groups on the basis of consumer's attitude, knowledge, and use or response to a product.

Compost Microbial decomposition of organic matter over a period of time under moist, warm, aerobic conditions with the formation of manure.

Customers' needs The gap between what the customers have and what they would like to have.

Eco-tels These are environment sensitive hotels that use eco-friendly practices in running the business so as to conserve natural resources, reduce waste, minimize pollution, and maximize sustainability. Also called 'green hotels'.

Geographic segmentation Dividing a market into separate geographic units such as neighborhoods, cities, states, regions, nations, continents.

Income segmentation Dividing a market into different income groups.

Lifestyle Way of living characterized by the way people spend their time, things they consider important, and what they feel about themselves and the people around them, i.e. their activities, interests, and opinions.

Market The set of all actual and potential buyers of a product.

Market segmentation The process of dividing the total market into more or less homogenous groups or segments each of which has certain characteristics and product preferences. Segmentation may be done on the basis of age, gender, income, status, behaviour patterns, etc. The purpose of segmentation is to identify the target group and direct the marketing efforts on that particular group thereby reducing promotional costs.

Marketing mix The four elements such as product, price, promotion, and place of distribution along with people, process, and physical evidence for a service product.

Marketing research A process of systematically gathering and analyzing information and data about customers and markets.

Mid-centric traveller Is in between allo-centric and psycho-centric and exhibits some characteristics of both and forms the bulk of the tourist market.

Opinion makers Leaders and people within a reference group who exert influence on others because they possess a special personality, knowledge, skills, or other characteristics.

Physical evidence Tangible clues in the form of promotional material, the environment of a firm, and its employer who portray the image of the quality of offering.

Press release A written document used to communicate newsworthy information to the media.

Primary data Information which is collected for the first time for a specific purpose.

Psycho-centric traveller Seeks familiar, tried and tested destinations which are secure and is an unadventurous traveller.

Psychographics Psychological profiles of customers.

Sales promotion Increasing sales volume by giving short term incentives to motivate a person to purchase a product or service.

Secondary data Information that has already been collected and compiled or used previously.

Tourism markets Tourist generating areas or countries.

CONCEPT REVIEW QUESTIONS

1. Describe the difference between the marketing concept and selling concept. Which concept do you feel is ideal for the tourism industry?
2. Why do tourism planners need to undertake market research?
3. Explain the significance of the following:
   (a) Tourism forecasting
   (b) FAM tours
   (c) Tour brochures
   (d) AIDA
4. How can the MICE industry help to overcome the problem of seasonality?
5. What is meant by market segmentation and why is it necessary?
6. Describe the various stages in a product life cycle?
7. Explain the promotional mix elements that can be used to promote tourism offerings.

CRITICAL THINKING QUESTION

1. Why do tourism managers need to understand the tourism consumer's behaviour patterns?

REFERENCES

George, R. 2007, *Managing Tourism in South Africa*, Oxford University Press Southern Africa, Cape Town.

India Today, Tourism Special, May 2008, The Great Indian Holiday, Incredible India, Living Media India Ltd, Thomson Press India Ltd, Faridabad.

Jha, S.M. 1995, *Tourism Marketing*, Himalaya Publishing House, Mumbai.

Kotler, P., J. Bowen, and J. Makens 2002, *Marketing for Hospitality and Tourism*, Second Edition, Pearson Education (Singapore) Pvt Ltd, Indian Branch, Delhi.

Medlik, S. 1996, *Dictionary of Travel, Tourism and Hospitality*, Second Edition, Butterworth Heinemann, Oxford.

Morrison, A.M. 2002, *Hospitality and Travel Marketing*, Third Edition, India Edition, Delmar, Thomson Hearing Inc, Haryana.

Tourism Marketing, TS-6, 1993, IGNOU, New Delhi.

CHAPTER 13

Customer Service Skills

Learning objectives

After reading this chapter, you should be able to:
- understand the importance of the customer to tourism business
- know the desirable qualities a tourism professional should possess
- differentiate between the terms customer satisfaction and customer delight
- demonstrate skills in answering the telephone
- appreciate the importance of both verbal and non-verbal communication
- know the techniques to be used for selling a product
- understand how one should handle difficult customers and situations
- appreciate the need for using the phonetic alphabet

INTRODUCTION

Customer service is the backbone of the tourism industry. It involves much more than just giving travel-related information, issuing tickets, and making reservations or providing personal attention to a customer before, during, or after a travel-related purchase. Good customer service today does not end with customer satisfaction. With the increased competition, service providers aim at customer delight. In this context, customer service could be defined as follows:

'Customer service is concerned with generating customer emotions or feelings of happiness and surprise by the way we meet and exceed their expectations.'

Exceeding customer expectations and surprising them by going out of one's way to give that extra service which gets a 'Wow!' response from the customer, is achieving 'customer delight'.

To be able to achieve this, tourism professionals require the skills to understand and get along with people, be alert, use refined selling techniques, know their product and the competition, and have good public relations.

We have read in Chapter 11 that the tourism product which the customer purchases is a service product which the customer cannot own but can only experience. This experience is created when the product is delivered or consumed and the experience may be a pleasant experience if the person delivering the product has combined both customer service skills and technical skills. Customers feel happy and content when their needs and wants are met and service is beyond their expectations. Let us differentiate between these three terms, namely—needs, wants, and expectations.

Needs   Human beings have certain basic requirements that are necessary for life such as food, clothing, shelter, belonging, recognition, etc. which need to be satisfied. These basic requirements are called needs.

Wants   Wants are the forms in which people communicate their needs. They are influenced by the individual's personality, society, and his/her culture.

Expectations   Expectations, or what one looks forward to, differ from person to person depending on the socioeconomic status and past experiences.

Everybody needs food as a basic requirement for survival, but what they want as food differs depending upon their food habits. An European would want fish and chips for dinner while an Indian would want chappatis, dal, and bhaji. Customers would expect the meal to be served hot with the requisite accompaniments. If they are served a complimentary beverage and dessert which they did not expect, they would be delighted.

Customers have different needs and requirements and successful tourism professionals need to understand their customers well. They need to know who their customers are and what is it that they want. Just like they need to know the product they are selling, they also need to know who is going to buy the product. Customers differ from one another in many respects. Some are very budget conscious while others may not mind spending money on themselves while on vacation. The idea of a vacation and activities to be undertaken vary vastly from one person to another and so do food habits and choice of entertainment.

There are basically two types of customers in any business:

1. Internal customers
2. External customers

Internal customers

These customers are those who provide services to the external customers or guests and include the employees of a tourism organization as well as the suppliers of goods. If excellent customer service is to be achieved, it is necessary that each employee in the organization is customer conscious, irrespective of whether he/she is in direct contact with the guest or not. Good customer service depends on the team effort of the employees and timely delivery of supplies. Guest service and satisfaction are an employee's primary responsibility. In the service industry it is very important to satisfy the needs of the internal customer according to his/her level in the organizational hierarchy, if the needs of the external customer have to be met.

External customers

The main external customers in the tourism industry are the tourists or guests who pay for the tourism products or services. While the customer is the actual purchaser of the tourism product, he/she may not be the consumer. A tourist buying a package tour is both customer and consumer, while a corporate travel department which makes travel arrangements for its employees is the customer of airlines and hotels, and its employees are the actual consumers.

Customers may be individuals, or groups from social, professional, or voluntary organizations and associations, travelling for business or leisure. All these customers approach the travel agent to fulfil certain needs and wants in terms of transport, accommodation, food and beverage, tickets or passes for attending special events, etc. These requirements may differ from customer to customer depending on the purpose of travel as well as many other factors such as budget, etc. Hence, understanding one's customers and their specific needs, wants, and expectations will help one to serve them better.

IMPORTANCE OF CUSTOMER SATISFACTION

Good customer service is important as it leads to satisfied customers as well as employees. It is the sign of a professional organization. Happy customers speak highly about the organization and remain loyal to the organization. Employees get job satisfaction, appreciation, and rewards for a job well done in the form of praise from the customers and employees, service tips, etc. All tourism professionals should realize the fact that satisfied customers are the best source of advertising for the travel house. They recommend the travel house to their friends and relatives, and speak highly about their travel experience. The number of customers increases as new customers are motivated to try out the product. Since travel business is entirely dependent upon customers, satisfied customers keep travel agents in business and contribute in a big way to their prosperity and reputation.

Customers have certain expectations which are as follows:

- recognition (for old customers), remembering names
- up-to-date information
- immediate action
- warm sincere welcome
- highly knowledgeable staff
- assistance at all stages
- full and undivided attention
- excellent interpersonal skills
- keeping up commitments and promises
- meeting and exceeding their expectations

Satisfied customers feel they are valued and are important to the organization (see Exhibit 13.1). Their expectations have already been

Exhibit 13.1   The customer is important

The customer is important
• The customer is the most important person in the tourism industry.
• Without customers we do not have a business.
• Customers choose their travel consultant and they have many options to choose from.
• They select a place which they feel will provide efficient service.
• They judge our service depending on how they have been treated.
• If they are satisfied they are our best source of advertisement.
• If we understand our customers and their needs and requirements, we can serve them better.
• If our customers are delighted, they come back as repeat customers.

met or have been exceeded. Customers expect prompt efficient service. The atmosphere in the travel house should be professional and pleasant with no noisy arguments or complaints. This is good for the image of the organization.

CREATING GOOD CUSTOMER RELATIONS

Good customer relations evolve out of employees working together in coordination and cooperation with each other. Each employee should be customer conscious even if he/she is not in direct contact with the customer. Every employee contributes to the total guest service experience either by directly interacting with the customer or indirectly by working behind the scene. A successful professional uses both technical skills and interpersonal skills such as empathy, etiquette, speaking skills, listening skills, body language, etc. while providing service. Good customer relations begin with simple things which tourism professionals should be aware of. The first step in customer interaction begins with creating a good first impression on the customer.

A good first impression is created by a good personality. You have to present yourself before you present your product. You are the ambassador for your travel house. If you are not presentable, it is very likely that you will not be heard. Always remember that the first impression is the best and lasting impression and one does not get a second chance to make a first impression. A good personality means much more than a well groomed person.

Grooming Standards and Personal Hygiene

Personality is defined as the sum total of the habitual qualities and behaviour of a person as expressed by physical and mental activities and attitude. Good grooming is an essential part of one's personality. Refer to Table 13.1 for some of the basic grooming standards.

Some of the personal hygiene standards are as follows:

- One should make it a point to follow good habits. Bad habits, such as biting one's nails or digging one's nose in front of others should be avoided.
- One should use a good deodorant after bathing and carry a clean ironed handkerchief.
- Personal hygiene should be observed every day; especially washing one's hands well before and after meals and after visiting the toilet is mandatory.

Table 13.1 Basic grooming standards

Gentlemen		Ladies	
Hair	Healthy, clean and shampooed, well trimmed and combed	Hair	Clean, shampooed, and conditioned.
		Long hair	Tied into a neat bun
		Short hair	Well brushed, away from forehead and ears.
Beard and moustache	If present—well trimmed if not, clean shaven	Make-up	Should be light and natural and should highlight your features. Refresh make-up during the day.
Shirt	Clean, well ironed, no missing buttons, white or light shade matching tie and trousers	Jewellery	A thin chain, small ear studs, and a simple bracelet or thin bangles look elegant. Avoid flashy make-up and chunky jewellery.
Trousers	Well fitted, well pressed	Perfume	A fresh, flowery fragrance which is subtle could be used. Avoid strong overpowering perfumes.
Shoes	Simple design, clean, and polished.	Clothes	Outfit whether Indian or Western should be clean, comfortable to wear the whole day
Socks	Match with shoes, change daily		in pleasing colours and designs which give an elegant look. Clothing should be modest and not provocative and ensure that saris and dupatta's are pinned in place and tops are not sleeveless.
Deo	Use a deodorant after bathing	Deo	Use a deodorant after bathing.
		Footwear	Comfortable well fitted with a moderate heel which match your outfit. For example, shoes and natural coloured stockings match western outfits, while sandals or slippers are worn with Indian outfits such as salwar-kameez or sari. A common uniform designed for all employees with a name tag gives a professional outlook.
Nails	Short, clean, and trimmed	Nails	Should be well trimmed and filed. Hands should be manicured and nail polish, if used, should not be gaudy or chipped.

- A balanced diet, adequate sleep, recreation, and exercise are needed to keep one physically fit and mentally alert. Exercise firms up the muscles and increases one's stamina, at the same time helping one to maintain a good figure and physique.

All the factors enumerated in Table 13.1 contribute not only to our health and personality, but also to our work efficiency.

First Impressions

First impressions are formed in the first 30 seconds when you meet a customer. Since you are representing your company, the impression you create is that of your company so make sure it is positive and is not the reason to lose a prospective customer.

The customer judges the travel professional by the images which they portray about themselves when they first meet their customer. These images are of three types namely:

1. Visual
2. Vocal
3. Verbal

Visual

What the customer sees in terms of your appearance, clothes, posture, make-up, shoes, etc. speaks volumes about you. Body language, your reactions, eye contact, gestures, and even a simple handshake sends out subtle messages. Visual impressions are very strong and sometimes you may be saying something, but your body language may be revealing an opposite message. In such cases the customer may feel uncomfortable. So make sure you greet the customer with a sincere smile and maintain eye contact but do not stare. A smile can put the customer at ease and can convey many messages such as—I am happy to see you, you can ask me questions; I know my job and can help you. Everyone likes to be greeted with a sincere smile and friendly eye contact.

Vocal

The way you speak and modulate your voice can give an impression of your interest and professionalism. The tone of your voice can tell whether you sound interested in hearing what your customer has to say or do you sound bored or sarcastic. The speed and volume of your speech also needs to be regulated. Do you speak loudly or is your voice so loud that the receiver has to be held away from the ear or is your voice too soft and unclear that they have to strain their ears to hear?

Vocal images are very important, especially when you cannot see the caller and have to make your impression on the basis of what is heard.

Verbal

The words you use in your conversation are very important. Is your language grammatically correct? Do you use correct words and pronunciations? Is your language simple and easy to follow or are you using slang language and difficult terms? Does the customer comprehend what you are trying to convey?

Other desirable qualities

To be successful in the service industry, you should also develop the following qualities:

- have a positive attitude
- be friendly and courteous
- be creative
- be well mannered and polite
- maintain a cheerful disposition
- build a good personality
- be patient and respectful
- have good communication skills
- be empathetic
- always be attentive and alert
- work in a quick and efficient manner
- show enthusiasm and be eager to serve
- be optimistic
- be knowledgeable and well read
- display honesty and fairness
- have a problem-solving nature
- have a good memory
- use common sense

TELEPHONE SKILLS

The telephone is the most widely used instrument to communicate and is the first point of contact for most customers. If it is used skillfully, it can be a very powerful marketing tool as a large percentage of business in the travel industry is transacted over the telephone.

The tone of your voice and how you speak is very important as the customer cannot see you. Vocal and verbal images are very important for any transaction over the telephone. Your voice has to convey all the messages which your smile or eyes would convey if you were facing each other. A sincere smile can get reflected in one's voice and one can also project one's personality and attitude through the way one converses over the telephone.

The travel professional should also remember that while communicating via the telephone there is a possibility that certain problems may be encountered, such as:

- The telephone connection may not always be clear. There may be disturbances or the battery may be low.
- The customer's facial expressions cannot be read.
- Customers may get distracted while speaking and attention span may be low.

Hence, utmost care should be taken while communicating with customers over the telephone and control your voice so that the message you send is the one you really want to convey.

While answering telephone calls, the following should be kept in mind.

1. Answer the phone within three rings. If the phone keeps ringing unanswered, it suggests that the agency is unprofessional and may tempt the customer to call another travel agency.
2. Greet the customer as per the time of the day and identify the agency and yourself by saying 'Good morning, Girikand Travels, this is Neha speaking, how may I assist you?'
   An informal way of greeting would be 'Hi! Melanie speaking, how may I help you?'
3. Listen carefully to what the customer asks and repeat what is said to check that you have understood correctly. Ask the name of the caller, so that you can use it to give a personal touch to further conversation.
4. Smile while talking and modulate your voice so that you sound warm, friendly, and professional. Speak clearly and somewhat slowly and make sure you pronounce words correctly.
5. While answering the customer's queries, be brief and to the point. Remember, it is the customer who has made the call. Long answers may confuse the customer and may be irrelevant. If the customer keeps on talking off the point, then it is better to take control of the conversation and ask necessary questions to get straight answers.
6. If you cannot provide the information needed, inform the customer that you would be connecting to another department and would keep the call on hold. Ask the customer whether you should put the call on hold or whether you should call back. If the line is busy or the concerned person is unavailable, do not

keep the customer on hold indefinitely. Ask the customer whether he/she would like to remain on hold or whether you could call back shortly with the required information. Note down the contact details of the customer and remember to call back as committed.

7. Make a note of customer's instructions and repeat what you have noted. Do not leave instructions to memory as one may miss out important information. Formats for customer's enquiries may be available at some organizations, and note taking is a good habit and prevents unnecessary complications for future communication.

8. Be courteous and patient with the customer, listen politely, and do not rush the customer to disconnect.

9. Thank the customer for calling and showing interest in your agency and if required give a date when you would call back. Note the same in your dairy.

10. Make sure that you call back on the given date.

PHONETIC ALPHABET

As we have read earlier, in any travel organization, people are likely to spend a lot of time on the telephone. Often the telephone lines are unclear and some people's accent makes understanding what is being said difficult. Getting a message across is difficult and in such cases you may often have to dictate or to hear names in the phonetic alphabet. To increase clarity and reduce confusion, people use the phonetic alphabet (see Table 13.2), wherein each letter of the English alphabet has been given a name.

Table 13.2 Phonetic alphabet

Letter	Code Word	Letter	Code Word
A	Alpha	N	November
B	Bravo	O	Oscar
C	Charlie	P	Papa
D	Delta	Q	Quebec
E	Echo	R	Romeo
F	Foxtrot	S	Sierra
G	Gold	T	Tango
H	Hotel	U	Uniform
I	India	V	Victor
J	Juliet	W	Whisky
K	Kilo	X	X-ray
L	Lima	Y	Yankee
M	Mike	Z	Zulu

The names given to each letter have been specially chosen because they do not sound like anything else and there is little scope for error. Thus, phonetic alphabet is a means of giving correct information such as client's details with a minimum possibility of error.

Example 13.1

The following customer's name and address has to be transmitted correctly:

Neha   Roday

Aundh Camp

Pune

Using the phonetic alphabet, the following message will be given over the telephone.

NEHA—November, Echo, Hotel, Alpha

RODAY—Romeo, Oscar, Delta, Alpha, Yankee

AUNDH—Alpha, Uniform, November, Delta, Hotel

CAMP—Charlie, Alpha, Mike, Papa

PUNE—Papa, Uniform, November, Echo

PRODUCT KNOWLEDGE

Every travel professional should be well versed with the product which is being sold by his/her organization. Product knowledge goes hand in hand with good sales and customer service skills. The secret of success as a travel agent or tour operator depends on how well you know your product and how much confidence your customers have in your knowledge, judgment, and ability. In tourism this means that you should know both the product and service you are providing and the method by which the service will be provided. All staff working in the travel agency should have sound knowledge about the product (see table 13.3). For example, if the product you are selling is a resort in a hill station, you should have thorough knowledge about the facilities available at the resort such as number and type of rooms, banquet facilities, recreational activities, amenities, the altitude of the hill station, climate, wind chill factor, flora and fauna, etc. Customers have all kinds of queries, hence product knowledge includes much more than what is printed in the brochures. It includes general knowledge about the area, its culture, history, geography, political party in power, local holidays, and days the market is closed.

Table 13.3   Product knowledge

Destination	Packages
Main attractions	Different package options
Travel documents required	Special interest tours
Accommodation	Local city tours
Year round climate	Excursions
Culture and cuisine	
Currency and exchange rate	
Safety and security	
Communication facilities	
Health and other hazards	
Political situation	
Transport	**Principal Suppliers**
Type of transport	Reputation or brand image
Reservation system	Financial standing
Route	Services offered
Timetables and fares	Quality of service
Services offered en route	Commission percentage
Connections	Reliability
Distance of terminal from city	
Baggage restrictions	
Transfers	

To increase product knowledge, the tourism professional can have easy access to many different sources of information. He/she should only ensure that the information gathered is current information or has been updated as the industry is constantly witnessing many changes.

Product knowledge includes detailed information about the following:

1. Destinations
2. Types of transport to reach destination
3. Various tours and packages
4. Principal suppliers

Sources of Information

The most reliable source of information is a tourism professional's personal experience. A tourism professional should make it a point to personally visit certain destinations on their own accord or with FAM tours. Customers who have returned from a tour and other professionals from the field can give first hand knowledge of the product. The tourism professional gathers information through various sources and systematically stores and upgrades the information for future use. A good quality atlas helps in locating remote places and preparing itineraries and is a bible for the tourism professional.

Other sources of information are as follows:

- brochures, guides, news bulletins, and promotional literature published by principal suppliers, government tourist offices, tourism organizations; directories for hotels, restaurants, and shopping;
- internet—websites on travel and tourism;
- documentary films, and presentations made by tourism professionals;
- newspapers—reports, articles, and write-ups by travel writers;
- television and radio programmes;
- posters and advertisements;
- statistics from the tourism ministry; and
- journals and magazines—travel trade magazines, hospitality magazines, current affairs magazines.

THE SALES PROCESS

Every principal supplier or intermediary is faced with a challenging task of selling travel related services to the customer, if they are to remain in business. The number of service providers and the competition is growing at a rapid pace, giving the customers a number of options to choose from. Selling the travel product is their basic goal. This makes it necessary to know their product; understand who their customers are, and what is it they want. Every customer who calls on a travel agent or tour operator has different needs and requirements.

Selling means understanding the customer's specific requirements, giving them all the information they need, suggesting travel plans, assisting them in taking a decision, and influencing them to purchase the travel product.

In a travel agency or tour operating organization the following interaction takes place stepwise across the counter.

The steps in the selling process are discussed as follows:

1. Initial contact
2. Building rapport
3. Getting the initial information
4. Finding out what the customer really wants or qualifying the prospect

5. Analysing the information or analysis
6. Recommendations
7. Overcoming objections
8. Getting the commitment or closing the sale
9. Follow-up

Initial Contact

The initial contact is generally made by the buyer who walks into the travel agency or makes a phone call and begins the conversation by expressing a need or a desire.

The opening statement may be highly specific and to the point as:

I need a flight ticket from Pune to New Delhi on 1 July in the morning.

Or it may be ambiguous as

I need a holiday and would like to leave town for a few days.

Building Rapport

Greet the customer and if in person, give a smile, establish eye contact, and extend a handshake. If you are on the phone, smile before you speak to add warmth to your voice. Express your pleasure in meeting them and if you know them personally, ask about their job, hobbies, etc. Your greeting should be sincere, to give the customer confidence that he/she is in the right hands.

When a prospective client walks in, stop any private conversation or reading and give him individual attention. Listen without interrupting and concentrate on what is being said. If the telephone rings, ask a colleague to answer the call or tell the caller that you will call back as soon as possible.

Apart from establishing rapport, try to gauge their needs and their level of commitment to travelling.

Getting the Initial Information

After the initial greeting, ask the client to be seated and introduce yourself. The client will normally tell you his/her name which you must remember and use in your conversation. Write down the name so that you do not forget it or call him/her by another name, as this is a sensitive issue. There are many things you need to know before you can give any advice. The basic information which is needed includes

- Where is he/she planning to travel?
- When and how would he/she like to travel?
- For how many days does he/she plan to stay?
- How many people would be travelling?
- Is it holiday or business travel?
- If purpose is holiday, what are his/her interests?
- What are the full names of the travellers?
- What is his/her budget?
- Does he/she require accommodation?

It is important to note down the client's name, address, telephone number, and e-mail id.

Since 90 per cent of the sales transactions in a typical travel agency involve air travel, the class of travel—first class, business, or economy ticket should be ascertained. The information gathered may be entered directly into a computer reservation system (CRS) as the client answers or if answers are complex, it may be written down with a promise to respond with your recommendations within a stipulated time frame.

Finding Out What the Customer Really Wants

After gathering the initial information, it is necessary to probe deeper to know the real needs of clients. It is important to check if the destination the traveller has asked for, really meets his/her needs and is his/her budget realistic. Getting the initial information and finding out what the customer really wants are a part of the qualification process also called 'qualifying the prospect'.

Qualifying is the process of determining a client's needs to see whether you have a product or service to satisfy those needs. Prospects are the people who call on your organization and express interest in your products/services. Prospects may or may not become customers. It is necessary to qualify a prospect as one has to decide whether the person inquiring about the travel is really serious and whether the prospect has any potential to use your service. The travel professional then decides on how much time and effort can be spent on such a prospect, and also which products and services should be recommended.

Analysing the Information or Analysis

After qualifying the prospect and assessing the needs, the travel agent analyses the information to prepare a recommendation.

While analysing the information, focus on cost and convenience and offer the lowest available price to earn the sale and remain competitive, unless the client has requested for a particular fare.

Focus on the benefits and features of the product to fulfil the underlying needs of the client. Focus on facilities like the centrally heated swimming pool at the resort for youth who are fond of swimming. Benefits or features include climate, budget, special interests, sightseeing, etc. Physical constraints if any need to be considered such as travelling with young children, a physical disability, etc. Analysis provides a useful foundation for presenting the recommendation.

Recommendations

The agent presents his/her recommendations which he/she feels will provide the maximum satisfaction within the client's allotted budget. Convince the client that you have understood his/her needs and wants and the product you recommend is best suited to him/her. Do not confuse the customer with too many options or with irrelevant details. Let the client participate and keep him/her actively involved and be a part of the decision process.

Overcoming Objections

Sometimes the customer may not accept your recommendations. Listen carefully to what your customer is saying so that you can clearly understand the customer's problem with your recommendation.

Sometimes the problem may be due to misunderstood communication on either side, in which case you can keep asking questions till you understand the customer's requirements and the customer understands the proposal which you have recommended. If you still feel your recommendation will meet the customer's needs, you may once again explain its benefits to the customer, discuss the issues raised and tell him/her that he/she has a point, but highlight the advantages of your suggestion. If he/she still seems reluctant, make a new recommendation or modify the original recommendation till your customer seems satisfied. Tourism professionals should anticipate objections and should be prepared for them as they are a normal part of the sales process. Objections are generally requests for more information and indicate that the customer has not been totally qualified.

Getting the Commitment or Closing the Sale

After having spent valuable time with the customer and the customer gives some indication of interest in your recommendations, it is in your interest to get a commitment and close the sale at the earliest. Closing the sale means getting the business. Help the customer in making up his/her mind. Do not just hand over brochures and leave the final decision to the customer or ask him/her to call back whenever he/she decides. Give him/her a reason to make a decision like this is peak season and the best accommodation may not be available later.

The sale may be closed by saying the following:

- The deposit for the tour is Rs 5000.
- Would you like to pay by cash, cheque, or by card?
- Shall I book executive class or economy?
- I am sure your family will enjoy the tour.
- Do you wish to board from Chennai or Mumbai?

If you cannot get a commitment for closing the sale, get a commitment to talk again or give a commitment saying you will call back on Thursday to check what the customer has decided. In this way, the sales process remains open and there is no ambiguity. However if there still seems to be no commitment, it is best to terminate the sales conversation graciously.

Always remember that if you do not help your customer decide, he/she will go to your competitor and you will lose the sale.

Follow-up

Follow-up refers to the sales efforts that take place after closing the sale. It includes the following:

- request for payment;
- accept payment and handover airline tickets, hotel vouchers, etc.
- give necessary instructions for time to check-in at the airport, baggage size, and allowance (checked-in as well as cabin or hand baggage), reconfirmation procedure for return flight if any, etc.
- congratulate your customer on the decision and emphasize any special offer or discount available;
- reassure your customer that you are always there to serve them if they experience any problem and ask them to call when they return; and
- if you do not hear from them, make sure you call and enquire about their trip; make note of any feedback which needs immediate attention and incorporate the same in the next tour.

Let your customers know that you care about them and hope to see them again as repeat customers.

HANDLING CUSTOMER COMPLAINTS

When people use the services of a travel organizer for undertaking travel for leisure or business, they have high expectations of the tour. They find it difficult to accept things going wrong and often confront the first staff member they find if they have any problem. The complaint may not be related to you or your job but they still expect you to look into the matter and resolve the problem, hence it is important that all staff members know the organization, its products and develop customer service skills. You cannot tell the customer that you are not aware of this and you should not pass the buck on to someone else.

Customers may complain for a variety of reasons. The most common causes for complaints are related to the staff, the equipment, facilities, or treatment given to the customer. The reasons for some of the complaints are as follows:

* customer does not get a special request which was promised by the sales executive;
* staff misunderstands what the customer says or wants;
* front desk staff forgets to pass on a message;
* equipment in the room is not working or is damaged;
* room service is missing;
* linen has not been changed or is soiled;
* customer has been kept waiting;
* customer feels he/she is not getting what he/she has been charged for or promised;
* food served is not hot, water is not chilled; and
* crockery smells of stale food served earlier.

If you want to achieve customer loyalty, you must listen to the complaint, treat it as a genuine complaint, be sympathetic, and handle it as per company policy. Every service personnel should understand that a complaint is a very important source of information about the quality of their services or products. It is better to know about the complaint and regard it as an opportunity for improvement rather than having a dissatisfied customer who does not complain but silently vows never to come back to your organization.

Different reactions are observed from customers who are unhappy about your product or service. Some are aggressive and speak loudly in public, while others are timid and keep their grievance to themselves. Some others remain calm and composed and insist on what they feel are their rights. Any complaint should be dealt with as per the guidelines given below.

- Listen to the customer's complaint. Listen patiently and attentively to what the customer has to say even if he/she is shouting. Do not interrupt or show any sign of anger, fear, or resentment.
- Identify the problem and make a mental note of important facts. Seek additional information if required but do not appear to doubt what is said.
- Empathize with the customer, say you are sorry and understand how the customer feels. Do not be too apologetic and do not argue as your customer is already annoyed and upset and this will just make matters worse.
- Thank the customer for bringing the problem to your notice and appreciate the trouble he/she has taken in informing you.
- Tell him/her that you will look into the matter immediately and inform the company. Let the customer understand what you and the company can and will do about the complaint.
- Do whatever can be done immediately. Inform the concerned staff and department about the lapses so that they can ensure there are no repeat complaints. Keep a record of the complaints and check that they do not recur.

Customers' comments are an invaluable source of information and need to be documented. This information whether in the form of a complaint or a compliment needs to be filtered back to the appropriate person or department. Compliments are strong motivators; they boost ones morale and help in raising service standards and growth of the organization. Be gracious while accepting compliments and make a mention of the positive feed back received in weekly staff meetings. Display such positive letters or comment cards on the notice board.

When dealing with problems, always try and put yourself in the customer's shoes. Think how you would like to be treated if you were in his/her situation. Showing empathy will help you in finding the right solution.

The tourism professional should always remember that any problematic situation needs to be tackled right away. If you are unsure about what to do, ask your superiors and act immediately.

Do not ignore the guest or the complaint hoping it will go away. It will not. It will cause loss of goodwill and is bound to reappear. You cannot make excuses or try to justify what has happened as customers are not interested in excuses, they want results. They want to know that you are concerned and are looking into the matter.

Tourism professionals should hone their customer service skills if they wish to remain in competition and do profitable business. The very nature of the tourism product is such that both technical skills and customer service skills are necessary for a successful sale. Tourism organizations should emphasize the importance of customer satisfaction and focus on grooming and training their staff to develop desirable qualities, knowledge and personality traits. Excellent interpersonal skills will go a long way in creating and retaining satisfied and delighted customers.

SUMMARY

The customer is the backbone of the tourism industry because without a customer to purchase the tourism products, there can be no business at all. Customer service today aims at much more than just satisfying the consumer of the tourism product or service, but is concerned with generating feelings of happiness and delight, which meet and exceed their expectations.

Tourism professionals require people skills. Customers have different needs and requirements. They come from varied backgrounds. A successful professional will use both technical and interpersonal skills and begin by creating a good first impression. The importance of a good personality, immaculate grooming, physical fitness, and communication skills cannot be underestimated. Good qualities are an added advantage in the service industry and should be developed. The importance of these qualities should be highlighted.

Since a large percentage of business is transacted over the telephone, all calls should be answered professionally. To sell any product, having adequate product knowledge and knowing from where to gather the latest up-to-date information is equally vital to the success of any programme. The product will be purchased by the customer once he/she is satisfied and it is the job of the travel professional to recommend a suitable product and close the sale. Qualifying the prospect to ensure that the customer is interested and has the potential to travel needs to be ascertained, likewise, overcoming objections and getting a firm commitment or closing the sale are two important steps.

Customers are likely to have some complaints at sometime during their travel, which need to be handled with utmost care ensuring that the customer loyalty is retained.

KEY TERMS

Body language The personality trait of using facial expressions, gestures, sign language, and grooming which convey certain messages in a social and cultural context.

First impression The first and lasting impression that one forms within 30 seconds to five minutes of meeting a person.

Grooming The personality trait of dressing or the external persona which meets and surpasses the perception, in the social and cultural context of society.

Interpersonal skills Skills involving relations between people, which are required by all professionals to understand, empathize, and relate to different customers in order to gain an insight into sub-conscious and conscious mind of individuals.

Personality The inner and outer contextual meaning of the whole being of an individual, referring to the perception of the external characteristics, internal persona, traits, habits, gestures, body language in the social, and cultural context.

Product knowledge Detailed information about the travel product in terms of the facilities at the destination, mode of transport available, various packages, and principal suppliers of various services.

Selling Influencing the customer to buy your product after having given all the information required for the proposed trip and suggesting a travel plan most suitable for the customer.

CONCEPT REVIEW QUESTIONS

1. Discuss the physical aspects which one should focus on to portray a pleasing personality.
2. Explain the importance of product knowledge for all tourism professionals.
3. Explain each of the following phrases in a paragraph.
   (a) A complaint is really an opportunity.
   (b) The first impression is the last impression.
   (c) It is necessary for the sales persons to qualify the prospect.
4. From where can a tourism professional gather latest information about a destination?
5. Briefly explain the steps involved in the sales process in a travel agency.
6. Why are telephone handling skills of special importance in a travel agency?
7. What are the main causes of customer complaints? List any five and suggest preventive measures.

CRITICAL THINKING QUESTIONS

1. List the qualities which are desirable in a tourism professional and evaluate how many of the listed qualities you possess.
2. As an escort for an international tour, explain the procedure you would follow and steps you would take if a customer complains about the amenities in the hotel room.

PROJECTS/ASSIGNMENTS

1. Visit any two travel agents who handle outbound packages and ask for information regarding package tours to Europe. Observe the staff and the office and write down which of the two agencies you feel is more customer oriented. Which of the two would you select as your travel consultant. As a future customer give reasons for your choice.
2. Identify any five star hotel in your area. Call the central reservation number and request for information on room availability after a fortnight. Ask for the different types of rooms available and the room rates but do not make a booking. Keeping telephone handling skills in mind, write down your observations.

REFERENCES

Andrews, S. 2007, *Introduction to Tourism and Hospitality Industry*. Tata McGraw-Hill, New Delhi.

Baker, S. and J. Huypen 2006, *Principles of Hotel Front Office Operations*. Thomson, Australia.

Clark, M. 1996, *Interpersonal Skills for Hospitality Management*. Thomson, London.

Davidoff, P.G. and D.S. Davidoff 1996, *Sales and Marketing for Travel and Tourism*, Prentice Hall, New Jersey.

IGNOU Schools of Social Sciences TS-1 Foundation Course in Tourism. 1994, *Tourism Marketing and Communications*, Berry Art Press, New Delhi.

International Travel and Tourism Training Programme 2004, *IATA Training Manual—Foundation*. IATA Aviation Training and Development Institute, Montreal, Canada.

Kotler, P., J. Bowen, and J. Makens 2005, *Marketing for Hospitality and Tourism*, Third Edition, Pearson Education, Delhi

SATS 1997, South Asia Integrated Tourism Human Resource Development Programme. *Training Manual Entry Level Front Office, Colombo, Sri Lanka*, India Offset Press, New Delhi.

Weaver, D. and M. Opperman 2004, *Tourism Management*, John Wiley and Sons Inc.

CHAPTER 14

Impacts of Tourism

Learning Objectives

After reading this chapter you should be able to:

* understand the significance of tourism in the economic development of a nation
* explain what is meant by the multiplier effect
* understand the problems unregulated tourism can have on the host society
* appreciate how tourism can help in preserving culture and environment
* realize the need for environmental conservation
* understand the role of stakeholders in developing responsible tourism
* explain the terms carrying capacity and sustainable tourism development
* appreciate the necessity for framing tourism legislations

INTRODUCTION

In the preceding chapters we have already read about the importance of environment as a foundation for tourism development. We have also discussed the role tourism plays in economic development of a nation. However, while promoting tourism development at a destination, tourism planners should ensure that the fragile environment and attractive landscapes which are the very basis for tourism are not destroyed through over-utilization.

Two possible situations arise between tourism and the environment. They are as follows:

1. To live in harmony with nature so that tourism is sustained.
2. To exploit the environment and natural landscape by encouraging excessive number of visitors and building so many facilities that there is no natural wealth or scenic views left.

The very purpose of visiting the attraction is lost through over-utilization of the destination for profit maximization. The continued development of hotels and resorts in strips running parallel to lakes, waterfalls, and coastlines, is a cause of concern. Ribbon development results from the desire of every property owner to get a view of the lake, the waterfall, or the sea. Such properties fetch premium prices and high profits to the developers at the cost of the environment. Tourism activities leave their impact on the destination, and if the capacity of the destination is over-exploited, the attractiveness of the destination or the very reason for tourists to visit the destination is lost. Pristine beaches, sand dunes, wetlands, mangroves, coral reefs, and rare species of flora and fauna which are the very basis for tourism may be destroyed due to the over-use of a destination. Tourism development, if well planned and managed can yield steady profit for a long duration provided the environment is conserved.

A symbiotic relationship between tourism and the environment will help sustain tourism for the host population as well as the guests or tourists. It will have the least negative impacts on both the hosts as well as the environment and will preserve the destination for the future generations. The responsibility of conserving the destination lies with the tourism planners.

ECONOMIC IMPACTS

Tourism contributes significantly to the economic development of a nation and for this reason governments are prepared to invest public funds for the development of tourism in a country. Public funds are invested in developing infrastructure such as construction of roads, airports, etc. and private investors are encouraged to construct hotels, resorts, and transportation because of the perceived economic benefits of tourism. India's GDP has been growing at over eight per cent on an average since 2004 and is expected to touch the nine per cent mark in the coming years.

Travel and tourism industry contributes about 5.8 per cent to the Indian GDP. The government is encouraging the private sector to invest in accommodation, entertainment, food and beverage sector, etc. by providing incentives to the developers of facilities such as tax holidays and is encouraging public–private partnership (PPP) projects. Tourism promotion can be a very good tool in boosting economic development through creating new jobs, and income generation opportunities, earning a substantial amount of foreign exchange, and development of backward regions. Certain economic costs have to be incurred if tourism has to develop as an economic activity. These costs need to be planned and managed well if the business has to run profitably.

Economic benefits of tourism include

- employment generator
- increased tax revenue
- foreign exchange earner
- rural development promoter
- improved infrastructure
- increased gross domestic product

Employment

The tourism industry has tremendous capacity to generate both direct, indirect, and induced employment. Since it is a highly labour intensive industry and many jobs involve low-skilled work, it is beneficial to the vulnerable and unemployed sectors of the local community as formal education and prior work experience are not mandatory. Jobs created through tourism are spread across many sectors of the economy such as hospitality sector, transport sector, retail sector, manufacturing sector, travel and tour operations, etc.

Hotels, restaurants, airlines, other transport operators, tourist offices, travel agents, guides, tour operators, etc. provide direct employment to people at different levels in the organizational structure. Indirect employment through tourism includes all ancillary service providers such as florists, taxi drivers, electricians, plumbers, furnishers, etc. Shops and emporia selling local handicrafts and handloom products provide a marketing outlet to thousands of craftsmen, weavers, and artisans. A general increase in tourism at a destination will stimulate growth of employment in other areas as well. This type of employment is called induced employment, such as more retail outlets, schools, housing facilities for employees, etc.

Many jobs created by tourism are in remote areas where job opportunities do not exist or are scarce, for example, in hill stations many families depend on tourism for their livelihood. Local hotels, attractions, restaurants, transport, etc. provide direct employment to the residents. Tourism provides a broad spectrum of jobs ranging from highly trained managers in five star hotels and resorts to waiters, guides transport workers, artisans, etc.

Tax Revenue

Tourism activities are also an important source of taxation revenue. Many taxes are hidden, i.e. they are a part of a package or included in the cost of the airline ticket so that tourists are unaware of such taxes. Tourists also generate taxation revenue through the purchase of tourism offerings which are subject to sales tax, service char ge, value added tax (VAT), etc. Some taxes are ad valorem taxes, i.e. set as a percentage of the price, while others like airport departure tax and visas are specific amounts.

Tourism generates both direct and indirect revenue for the government. When people are employed on tourism projects, the government receives revenue through income tax and VAT on goods purchased. The operation of tourism establishments contribute to the government's revenue pool in many ways such as gambling taxes for running a casino, food licence for preparing and servicing food, import duties on imported articles, entry fee at attractions, etc.

Apart from curbing leakages, the economic benefits through tourism can be further enhanced by the following measures:

1. Increase the amount of money spent by tourists at the destination by
    (a) Providing a greater variety of attractions and activities which will increase the duration of stay and encourage repeat visits.
    (b) Attracting alternative forms of tourism.
    (c) Organizing shopping festivals.

2. Local ownership and management of tourism facilities at destinations through
    (a) Bed and breakfast establishments at destinations where there is a shortage of hotels.
    (b) Encouraging agritourism, ecotourism, cultural tourism, rural tourism and farm stay with local entertainment.
    (c) Involving local community in a wide variety of services such as handicrafts, laundry, gardening, and ayurvedic medications.

Tourism contributes to government revenue through

- airport taxes, fees, and levies
- entrance fee at attractions
- hotel and restaurants registration fees and licences; for example, liquor licence
- travel agents and other tourism businesses registration/licence fee
- corporate income tax on profits
- import duty on items directly imported for tourism sector, for example, alcoholic beverages
- local taxes like property tax
- personal income tax
- parking charges
- VAT on goods purchased

Foreign Exchange

Tourism has emerged as one of the largest foreign exchange earning economic activity in India. Foreign exchange earnings from tourism are computed by the Reserve Bank of India (RBI) as part of its exercise to collect balance of payment statistics. Tourism is the only export trade that earns large amounts of foreign exchange without reducing national resources and without actually exporting any material skill. Inbound tourism is the largest source of foreign exchange earnings and tourism has been rightly called an invisible export.

Rural Development

Tourism creates jobs in the underdeveloped regions and in rural areas. For example, rural tourism and ecotourism are popular forms of tourism which generate employment opportunities and prevent the migration of villagers to the densely populated urban slums. Because of tourism activity in the region, basic amenities develop and raise the standard of living of the rural poor.

Improved Infrastructure

Infrastructure is one of the basic requirements for successful tourism at the destination. Tourism stimulates infrastructural development like good airports, network of roads, sanitary systems, and water purification plants etc. which not only benefit the tourists but the hosts as well and improves their quality of life.

Gross Domestic Product

International and domestic tourism combined generate up to ten per cent of the world's gross domestic product (GDP). This figure varies from one country to another. In a growing economy, there is an increase in GDP every year. The GDP reflects economic growth. This, however, does not mean that the entire population is benefiting from economic growth, as the distribution of income in developing countries is uneven. Tourism should aim at economic development, i.e. an improvement in the socioeconomic status of all people in a given population and not only a privileged few. To measure economic development we need to use other indicators which measure longevity, educational attainment and an acceptable standard of living.

Governments encourage the development of tourism because of the income it can generate specially in terms of foreign exchange earned. The income generated by tourism has a positive impact on a country's GDP, balance of payments, and government revenue. However some of these figures may be misleading unless they are corrected for leakages.

Leakages

It refers to the process through which tourism receipts are withdrawn or leave the destination's economy. This happens when money is spent on buying goods and services from another economy or when money is put into savings. The smaller the economy, the greater the likelihood that tourism needs have to be imported. If many goods/services used by the tourism industry need to be imported, tourism is said to have import leakages. See Table 14.1 for sources of leakages in tourism.

Table 14.1 Leakages in tourism

Cost of imported goods and services for tourists	Food items, alcoholic beverages such as whisky, liquors, wine, flowers, etc.
Cost of capital investments	Investment in quality construction material, equipment, machinery for constructing tourist facilities
Foreign financial commitments	International franchises management fees or royalty
Payments to foreign tourism suppliers	Foreign airline carriers, tour operators abroad
Tourism development costs	Cost of financial incentives provided by the government for investment in tourism
Training and promotional expenditure	Overseas training of officials, promotional costs overseas, travel expenses for attending trade fairs
Payment incurred for importing goods	Currency conversion charges, banking fees, and commissions
Demonstration effect	Increase in demand for imported goods by locals

Leakage is siphoning of income from the income flow of a destination. Foreign exchange leakages occur when a country uses a large number of goods and services such as building materials, food and beverages, machinery and equipment, furnishings and furniture, foreign consultants, management fees, etc. Other forms of leakages include increased consumption of imported goods because of demonstration effect, costs incurred by government in providing financial incentives, export of profits to foreign owners, MNCs, etc. The real earnings from tourism can be determined only after all leakages, i.e. payments made of parties outside the country have been adjusted.

Leakages can be curbed by the following measures:

Use of local resources   Local raw material, for example, building material will add to the local flavour of the destination.

Local ownership   Local ownership and control of hotels and restaurants should be encouraged and governments should provide maximum financial incentives.

Promotion of local foods and beverages   Local foods and beverages prepared under high standards of hygiene and sanitation may be modified to increase their acceptability.

Conducting local training programmes   Inviting trainers from within the country would help the income to remain within the economy.

Ensuring quality and safety   Tourism providers should be more quality and safety conscious so that tourists are agreeable to trying out local products and do not demand goods from their home countries.

The Multiplier Effect

Money earned from tourism activity is a major contributor to the national income of a country. Without considering receipts from domestic tourism, international tourism receipts alone contribute vast amounts.

New money entering the economy in any form, be it investments, government grants, remittance from workers abroad or tourist expenditures—stimulates the economy not once but several times as it is respent. The flow of money generated from tourist spending or any source multiplies as it passes through various sections of the economy because of the multiplier effect.

Let us consider the following example. An international tourist pays a hotel for his/her accommodation and meals. The hotel uses part of the money to purchase provisions such as groceries, meat, bread, linen, and flowers from the supermarket, bakery, furnishings store, and florist respectively. Some of the money is used for salaries and wages to staff and casual labour, some is kept aside for savings, and some used for payment of property tax. The payment made by the tourist to the hotel is a direct expenditure, while expenditure by the hotel on daily supplies is an indirect effect of the original expenditure which the tourist made. The waiter working in the hotel spends part of his salary on purchasing provisions, part on house rent; and the additional payment received as tips for good service on toys for his child and on a special outing for the family. This shows that as income levels rise due to tourism, some additional personal money is spent at the destination. These are induced benefits of tourism.

The bakery will use the money received from the hotel to buy flour, margarine, and eggs from the wholesale suppliers, on the workers' wages, on paying electricity bill, and on taxes. The expenditure made by the baker is induced expenditure.

If we study each round of expenditure, we see that a proportion of money goes to the local suppliers, the residents as salaries and wages and to the government in the form of taxes. Money which is saved or spent on imported goods will cease to circulate in the economy, loses its stimulative value and is called a leakage. Leakages are far lower in economies where businesses supply and support each other and amount spent on imports is low. The concept of the multiplier is based on the interdependence of the different industrial sectors of the economy. The strength of linkages between these different sectors, determines the size of the impact multiplier. For example, if the linen needed by the hotel is not available in the furnishings store or is of poor quality, there is no inter-industrial linkage to increase the positive impact of tourism on the industry. In such cases, linen will need to be imported and the local economy will not get the benefit.

If the hotel receives more guests and associated income, the amount spent by the hotel in the local economy will be more, and will result in a chain reaction of increased production, income, and expenditure which will be reflected throughout the economy. Because of the interdependency of various sectors, any change in tourist's expenditure will bring about a change in the economy's level of production and income.

The size of the tourism multiplier will be determined by the number and strength of the linkages within the economy as well as the various sources of leakages. While intersectional linkages maximize the positive economic impact, because of the multiplier effect, leakages, lower the multiplier effect as money is withdrawn from the economy through imports.

The economic impact can thus be increased by supporting and creating strong linkages within the tourism industry and minimizing the leakages.

Tourism can also create risks and negative economic impacts at the local destination such as increased cost of living due to increase in the prices of essential commodities like food, house rent, etc. Opportunity costs of tourism in rural areas which is the cost of investing in tourism instead of traditional farming, also gets affected.

Excessive dependence on tourism may have some risks in case of emergency situations. Like natural calamities or terrorist attacks in which case tourists may abandon a destination indefinitely.

ENVIRONMENTAL IMPACT

The environment is a powerful resource for tourism as it plays a major role in attracting tourists to the destination. Tourism causes both positive and negative impacts and impacts are greater if the environment is underdeveloped or fragile. It was only in the mid-1960s after the growth of mass tourism that people realized that nature is an exhaustible resource and that tourism and related activities leave their mark on the environment. Before we study the impact of tourism, let us understand the meaning of the term 'environment'. When we refer to the environment we generally mean the natural or physical features of a landscape. This includes the four divisions that our planet earth has been divided into namely, atmosphere, biosphere, hydrosphere, and lithosphere. Each of these spheres have their own distinctive characteristics, support various life forms, and are a distinct part of most tourist attractions. All these spheres have an interdependent relationship and together create conditions that are conducive for life to survive and grow on our planet. The environment thus functions as a live system and any major disturbance in any one sphere will have a profound effect on and disturb the delicate balance of the ecosystem.

The term environment has been defined by many individuals. The simplest definition is 'the environment is a given set of conditions in which one lives and is influenced, and in turn influences these set of conditions'. The environment is composed of different components namely physical, biological (also called natural components), and social (human-made components). The physical components or a biotic component of the environment include the non-living elements in the environment such as latitude, altitude, location, temperature, rainfall, soil, etc. Each of these factors has an influence on the natural environment. The biological components include life forms which are classified as producers, consumers, and detrivores or scavengers. All these form part of the food chain. In the environment all elements are inter-related and interdependent on the various food chains such as terrestrial (land) food chain, marine food chain, etc.

A combination of different food chains forms a food web.

Food chains generally have three to four levels of energy transfer, also called a tropic level. The tropic levels represent the basic framework for all ecosystems.

The social environment is the third component of the environment. Early humans had a limited interaction with their natural environments and lived in harmony with nature. Technological advances and political factors have had a great impact on the level of development and the level of interaction with the natural environment under the banner of tourism development. Natural resources have been exploited, artificial resources have been created, and wastes are piling up. All this has resulted in attraction, modification, and degradation of the natural environment (see Exhibit 14.1). The extent of the changes and damage is so severe that if tourism developers do not change their approach, it will not only endanger tourism activities but also the very basis for survival of humankind.

Exhibit 14.1 Tourism Environment

From the tourism perspective, the tourism environment comprises of the following:

1. **Natural environment**
   - (a) Beaches
   - (b) Caves
   - (c) Water bodies—lakes, rivers, and oceans
   - (d) Forests
   - (e) Hill stations
   - (f) Wildlife

2. **Built environment**
   - (a) Accommodation and built facilities
   - (b) Transport infrastructure
   - (c) Theme parks
   - (d) Dams and reservoirs

3. **Natural resources**
   - (a) Air
   - (b) Water
   - (c) Climate—temperature, rainfall, snow, glaciers

The major negative impacts of tourism on the environment include

- environmental pollution
- depletion of natural resources
- land erosion
- loss of natural habitats
- traffic congestion
- garbage trails

Environmental Pollution

The largest negative impact of tourism is pollution of air, water bodies, land surface, and noise pollution in areas of tourism activity. This pollution is mainly caused by various modes of transportation and construction of tourist accommodation.

Transport pollution is caused by an increase in road and air traffic. This also results in noise pollution, especially if airports are located in the heart of the city. Aircrafts produce toxic nitrogen oxide during take-off and landing. Noise and air pollution in Hong Kong has reduced ever since the airport was shifted from the city to Lantau Island. Water-based sports and water transportation are major causes of oil spills.

Architectural pollution of the natural landscape because of haphazard construction of hotels, resorts, and conference centres and other high rise unsightly concrete structures also gives rise to visual pollution. For example, at the Niagara Falls, Canada, every other hotel is called Falls View and new high rise buildings were being constructed, each higher than the other to give a view of the breathtaking Horseshoe Falls from the hotel room.

Depletion of Natural Resources

Natural forest resources are lost through deforestation, when forest land is used for development of buildings for tourism or when trees are felled for fuel and camp fires. Careless behaviour by tourists like throwing lighted cigarette stubs or not extinguishing campfires can cause forest fires. Many locals earn their livelihood through medicinal plants and herbs collected from forests. Deforestation deprives them of this activity. Graffiti on trees, caves, and monuments mars the beauty of the environment. Scarce natural resources, such as water are often affected in areas where swimming pools and golf courses need to be maintained.

Land Erosion

Mass tourism and reckless behaviour on the part of the tourists often result in this problem which is seen mainly on nature trails, hill stations, and coastal areas. Deforestation for construction of new facilities or to clear vast stretches of land on hill slopes for winter sports and construction of ski-lodges is one of the major causes of erosion of the rich soil cover. Construction of hotels and other tourist facilities on the beach can erode sand dunes and affect marine life. The marine ecosystem is particularly fragile and is damaged by irresponsible tourism such as driving vehicles on long stretches of beaches disturbs birds which breed in coastal areas. Removal of forest cover is a common cause for landslides in hilly areas.

Loss of Natural Habitats

Indigenous plants and animals may lose their natural habitat by damage resulting from tourism activities (see Exhibit 14.2). Animals in jungles are not used to the noise of vehicles or passengers and may get stressed out by the disturbance caused by insensitive tourists on safari tours. Presence of a large number of visitors may affect the food habits and

Exhibit 14.2   Impact of tourism on natural resources

Natural resources such as water, wildlife, forests, mountains, islands and beaches bear the impact of tourism. Hotels, swimming pools, water sports, and golf courses, can put critical pressure on water resources, especially in areas of water scarcity. Oil spills, trash, and plastic waste dumped into the sea by callous water transporters and cruise ships have led to the death of millions of birds and marine mammals who mistake plastic bags for jelly fish and swallow them.

Fragile coral reefs are damaged by inexperienced scuba divers accidentally stepping on them or by propellers of boats.

Trampling and damage of vegetation by feet and vehicles and destruction of vegetation by erosion or by gathering wood and plants and lighting campfires is another impact of tourism. Beaches, sand dunes, wetlands, mangroves, and threatened and endangered flora and fauna are destroyed by unplanned tourism. Killing animals to supply goods for the souvenir trade is a major outcome of tourism. Poaching and illegal trade in wild animals and their products which are sold to tourists at phenomenal prices is still rampant in forests. For example, poaching and hunting have led to the extinction of the Indian cheetah. Demand for ivory ornaments and animal hides have led to a considerable reduction in the elephant or rhinoceros (for ivory horn) and tigers, zebras, and other wild animals (for hides). Wild animals' fur, skin with head and tail, tusks, or feathers are still traded illegally at phenomenal prices. The number of wild animals like the crocodile, hippopotamus, lion, tiger, leopard, one-horned rhinoceros, gorilla, and elephant are steadily depleting.

breeding of animals. Marine creatures and coral reefs get damaged by propellers of boats.

Fires used to clear forests for land use have triggered an ecological disaster with poisonous smog blanketing most of South-East Asia. The heavy air pollution has resulted in respiratory tract and skin problems in people residing in Singapore, Malaysia, and Indonesia.

Traffic Congestion

This is a common problem encountered at many destinations due to a large number of tourist vehicles ranging from cars to tourist coaches and caravans. Vehicles parked in a haphazard manner on narrow roads and no parking zones can mar the beauty of scenic drives and popular destinations creating traffic jams, inconvenience to both locals and tourists, damage to roads and pavements/footpaths and an increase in road accidents as well as air pollution.

Garbage Trails

Garbage is a common cause of land and water pollution and the presence of improperly disposed waste at any destination is not only aesthetically unappealing but also damages the plants and animals in that area. Non-biodegradable waste builds up in the environment and is an eye sore. Biodegradable wastes can alter the soil and attract animals into tourist areas. The use of the oceans to dispose untreated sewage from tourist accommodation on the beach or from cruise liners is a major problem which environmentalists are aware of and laws to enforce clean oceans are being practised in some areas. The use of polythene bags and plastic bottles while travelling from one island to another by water transport is being monitored in Andaman and Nicobar islands. Tourists are given bags made of natural material to carry their belongings and are charged a refundable deposit for the same.

Like tourism, the environment too has its impact on monuments. Exhibit 14.3 is about the world famous Ajanta Caves.

Positive Impacts on the Environment

The tourism industry generally pollutes the environment to a lesser extent as compared to most manufacturing industries especially if eco-friendly tourism is propagated.

Tourist destinations, such as national parks, wildlife and bird sanctuaries, gardens, and hill stations help in maintaining the ecological balance.

Exhibit 14.3   Environmental impact on Ajanta Caves

The Ajanta and Ellora rock cut caves in Aurangabad, Maharashtra contain world famous Buddhist, Hindu, and Jain art in the form of sculptures and paintings and have been accorded 'World Herit1age Site' status by UNESCO. The paintings depict the life of the people during the eighth century.

The paintings have been damaged by microorganisms, soil seepage of rain water, chemicals used to protect the paint, fumigants, and vehicular pollutants. An afforestation drive on 500 hectares land near the caves was implemented in 1992. Trees restrict soil particles from entering the caves, reduce the scorching effect of the suns rays, and reduce wind velocity.

The carrying capacity in the caves should be fixed as warmth and moisture through breathing can help micro-organisms to multiply, which damage the paintings. Certain plants stop the growth of these microbes and they should be planted. Paintings have been damaged by graffiti; hence protection of the caves is necessary. Rain water seepage from cracks in the rocks has been controlled by laying pipelines, thereby controlling moisture.

The caves should be kept cool and dry and tourist behaviour should be kept in check. Regular fumigation should be done to control microorganisms and bats in the caves. Visitors' vehicles are not allowed near the foot of the caves but parked in special parking zones and only special buses are operated to ply from 'T point' up to the foot of the caves.

Some important positive impacts are

- the environment in these areas is kept free from industrial pollutants like smoke, noise, and industrial liquid wastes;
- such activities help in maintaining ecological balance;
- historical sites are preserved and restored;
- endangered species are protected in national parks and wildlife sanctuaries;
- coral reefs and other forms of marine wealth are protected;
- forest areas are protected;
- revenue generated from visitors' charges or donations invited from visitors can help conserve wildlife and endangered species, for example, Jurong Bird Park, Singapore and Night Safari, Singapore, request visitors to contribute towards maintaining the creatures in these built natural attractions;
- natural attractions help create awareness about the environment and educate the public through wild life education and interpretation; and
- provides for captive breeding programmes for endangered species of wildlife in zoos.

SOCIOCULTURAL IMPACTS OF TOURISM

Although the tourist is a temporary visitor at a destination, he/she leaves behind lasting impacts on the host community. The economic impact of tourism, i.e. the dollar or other foreign currency is consumed or invested by the host but what the host has seen or learnt in the brief encounter with the tourist is often retained and imitated. The demonstration effect in terms of language, clothing, and behaviour pattern, often leave their lasting marks in underdeveloped and developing countries.

Aspects of Tourist–host Relationships

The aspects of tourist–host relationships are as follows:

- Since tourists are temporary visitors, the relationships are superficial and short-lived, with limited expectations and trust.
- The hosts have to work to provide a satisfactory tourism experience to the tourists. This work begins from the minute the tourists reach the destination. If they do not get adequate financial benefits or are required to undergo hardships, it will be reflected in their behaviour.
- Tourism being a commercial activity, the hospitality shown by the service providers and their courteous behaviour may be a put on act and not genuine feelings towards tourists.
- Because of linguistic and cultural barriers, the interactions may create misunderstandings especially in certain sensitive issues.
- In the context of the guest and host, tourism is an unequal and unbalanced experience. Most tourists are strangers in unfamiliar surroundings. They stand out from the host population terms of physical appearance, i.e. colour of skin, hair and eyes; the language they speak or understand; their dress and mannerisms. They have disposable money, have mostly lived in cities and look forward to a pleasant and memorable experience. The hosts view tourists as superior beings, having unlimited spending money, coming from affluent, developed nations and hence try to imitate them.
- Tourism is a service industry, and since the tourists have the spending power, they assume the superior position and may look down upon the hosts.
- The host is knowledgeable about the destination, sightseeing places, routes, prices, etc. while the tourist is ignorant and is at a disadvantage in this respect.

Tourist–host Interactions

Tourism involves social interaction between the tourist and the residents or hosts. This interaction may bring about a change in the norms and values of a society, the prevailing dress code and trends in general. Social impacts are visible sooner than cultural impacts.

Along with social interaction, tourism brings people from different cultural backgrounds together and results in a cultural exchange. Cultural impacts refer to long term changes in arts and crafts, religion and rituals, community structure, etc.

Sociocultural impacts of tourism are inter related and result from the interaction between two distinct groups of individuals—the tourists and the residents. However, most interactions between the tourists and the residents are at a superficial level and take place in the following situations.

Social interactions

While sharing common resources and facilities at the destination, for example, travelling in local buses and trains, bathing on the beach, or having meals in restaurants. They are basically social meetings with little interaction.

Economic interactions

While using facilities specially created for tourists like guide and escort facilities, different types of accommodation or shopping for handicrafts and souvenirs. They involve buying, selling, and bargaining.

Cultural interactions

While studying their culture by stepping out of the 'tourist bubble' and experiencing their lifestyle through visits and home stays. Interactions with locals, community leaders, and visiting places of cultural significance or seeing staged performances which depict indigenous cultures. The intensity of the interaction is maximum in this case.

Impacts on Society

The impact tourism will have on society varies from destination to destination and depends on the nature of tourism, attitude of the hosts, background of the tourist, and the strengths and weaknesses of the destination. Figure 14.1 depicts some of the negative impacts of tourism on society.

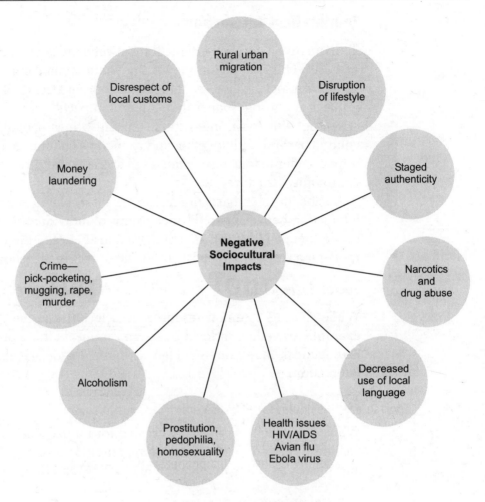

Fig. 14.1   Some of the negative impacts on society

Although tourism cannot be blamed for all social evils, it is a known fact that the presence of strangers, temporary visitors, floating populations, or even the armed forces may accentuate such social problems. To the host population, tourism is a mixed blessing. The positive impacts are:

- develops entrepreneurship
- provides jobs, increased income, and quality of life
- creates an economic multiplier
- preserves heritage
- revives arts and crafts
- helps national and international integration by breaking down linguistic barriers

- develops facilities and infrastructure
- revives vernacular languages

Since tourism leaves its mark and never leaves a host society or culture unchanged, the negative impacts are minimized by the positive impacts and sufficient remedial measures are being taken up by tourism organizations and the government to resolve the social evils in society. Many tourism organizations like UNWTO, IATA, UFTAA have raised their voice and passed resolutions against this menace. Governments, NGOs, and local bodies are taking measures and sensitizing their citizens travelling abroad against drug abuse and the consequences if caught with drugs.

THE DEMONSTRATION EFFECT

It is an outcome of the guest-host relationship where residents who perceive the tourists as superior beings, try to copy their behaviour. The demonstration effect is most visible in the younger generations who may be discontented with their own lifestyle and try to emulate the tourists. This is seen in dressing up like the tourist—casual attire, flowery shirts, couple of cameras hanging around the neck, sun glasses, comfortable footwear, floppy hats, etc. and discarding the traditional outfits. Locals may migrate from villages or small towns to cities in search of better incomes, women folk joining the work force, all of which bring about changes in the social structure.

Attitude

It refers to the behaviour pattern of both the tourist and the host. As tourism grows, local infrastructure which was adequate for the host community, needs to cope with the tourism related stress. The degree of acceptability of or irritation of the host community is expressed by the attitude of the host towards tourism related activities which affect their quality of life. How the hosts perceive tourists is well presented by Doxey (1975) (see Table 14.2).

The *Irridex* (derived from 'Irritation Index') represents the increasing irritation of residents as the impact of visitor numbers increases (see Table 14.2).

This model is a simplification of the complex relationships and sets of attitudes that develop between tourists and host communities. The specific ability of host communities to accommodate or tolerate tourism, and the attitudes which are formed as a consequence, are known to differ from

Table 14.2   Irridex model of community attitudes

Stage	Host community attitude	Characteristics
Stage 1	Euphoria	• Small number of visitors • Visitors seek to merge with the local community • Host community welcomes tourism • Limited commercial activity in tourism
Stage 2	Apathy	• Visitor numbers increase • Visitors are taken for granted • The relationship between tourists and the host community is more formalized
Stage 3	Irritation	• The number of tourists grows significantly • Increased involvement of external commercial concerns • Increased competition for resources between tourists and residents • Locals concerned about tourism
Stage 4	Antagonism	• Open hostility from locals • Attempts to limit damage and tourism flows

Source: Doxey 1975

community to community, and are determined by a number of factors, including the number of visitors, types of visitors, length of visit, and cultural distance between hosts and guests. The type of contact, characteristics of the destination, and specific community groups also act as determinants (Keyser 2002).

The guest-host impacts range from minimum to maximum and are influenced by the number of tourists, duration of stay, their behaviour and attitude towards each other and how stressful the interactions are.

CULTURAL IMPACTS

Culture is one of the major attractions or motives to travel for tourists. Tourists travel to study and experience the culture of different societies.

They are attracted by cultural events, handicrafts, traditional dress, religion, dance, music, folktales, customs, ceremonies, and food. Culture includes one's behaviour, beliefs, language, and the way of life of a group of people during a particular period of time. Apart from creating awareness about one another's culture, tourism has a marked influence on various aspects of a society's culture. When tourists visit an unknown destination, and are unaware about local customs and practices, a conflict situation may arise. Culture shock and cultural arrogance are often the reasons for causing conflict between the tourists and the host. Culture shock results from witnessing a totally different lifestyle or behaviour and may be experienced by either the guest or the host. Lack of communication and understanding can cause such situations. Cultural arrogance arises when there is a continual intentional disregard of local customs and insensitivity to the feelings of the host. For example, tourists who do not take off their shoes while visiting a temple or take photographs when they are requested not to do so are displaying cultural arrogance.

Tourists need to recognize and respect local cultures and need to be briefed on how to behave before they interact with the locals. Knowing and understanding the local culture can help minimize the negative impacts.

Culture and Authenticity

Mass tourism has resulted in a shift from authentic natural culture to contrived culture and tourism planners are fulfilling the quest for knowing and enjoying culture.

While tourism helps in preservation of culture and rejuvenation of traditional art forms, sometimes locals cannot meet the demands or sell handicrafts at low prices. The demand for large quantities of artifacts at cheaper prices has led to commercialization of material culture which is either mass produced in a factory or imported from abroad. In both cases, there is loss of authenticity.

This may lead to disappointments and misunderstandings for both tourists and residents. Handicrafts are time consuming and authentic crafts involve a lot of effort while the number of articles produced per day is low. Mass produced or factory produced crafts are cheaper and often the tourist is disappointed to note that the artifact purchased in one country has the manufacturing label of another country.

Museums may display authentic exhibits such as original sculpture and paintings which have been preserved, while in contemporary museums many of the exhibits are reproductions. Museums at forts and monuments often display models of original artefacts used by great leaders of that era, while some other museums have life-size figures sculptured from wax or plastic. Folk dances and music during religious rituals in villages and urban public spaces retain their authenticity. But when performed on stage or as part of a cultural festival, they become part of the contrived form of culture. This form is popular both in India and abroad and cultural festivals are being staged and used to promote India abroad.

There is a visible shift from authentic to touristic low-cost package tours. Mass tourism focuses on staged culture creating a tourist bubble which separates the tourist from the local life at the destination. For example, the cruise down the river Mandovi showcases Goan culture through songs and folk dances aboard the ferry, which are staged to attract mass tourists.

Cultural tourism has expanded to cover heritage tourism and includes sites such as residences of royalty, historical buildings, artifacts, and traditions which have been passed on from one generation to another.

Minimizing Negative Impacts on Culture

To minimize the negative impact, it is necessary to ensure that tourism develops gradually so that the local residents have sufficient time to adapt to the change and understand and participate in tourism development in their region. The local residents should be informed about the benefits that tourism brings to the destination and how everyone has a role to play in tourism promotion and hospitality towards the guests.

Negative impacts on culture can be minimized by doing the following:

- Management of the tourists is important as sometimes they are the cause of the problem. Tourists need to be sensitized about the social norms and customs which are in practice at the destination.
- Providing appealing and informative interpretation can be another way of minimizing negative impacts on culture. Interpretation is the process by which the significance of the site is explained to the visitors. It can be done by a guide, by signage, brochures, books, tourist guides, i.e. both verbal and written methods may be used.
- Tourism professionals should prepare a code of conduct for tourists and provide travellers tips to ensure that sensitive issues are not overlooked.

A form and scale of tourism development that is appropriate for the local society and takes into consideration the social carrying capacity should be included. Exceeding the social carrying capacity or the tolerance levels of the locals will create two negative impacts. They are

1. Residents will be irritated or resentful of the visitor's presence.
2. Tourists/visitors will be dissatisfied with their destination experience because residents will not be friendly or hospitable.

POLITICAL IMPACTS

The growth and development of tourism depends on the political forces that govern the country. The impact is more marked in developing countries. Both internal political structure as well as international politics have a marked impact on the tourism policies and tourism growth in a country. If there are political upheavals and unrest in one part of the world, the impact is felt in other parts of the world, affecting tourist flows into the country. For example, air travel to and over Libya was banned by the international community after the bombing of an aircraft over the Scottish town of Lockerbie. This was a political decision to pressurize Libya to hand over the bombers for trial. By imposing this ban, travelling to Libya became extremely complicated. Visitors were forced to fly to neighbouring countries and travel by land to reach Libya because of the ban on air travel. Political decisions are very powerful decisions and policies formulated by the government affect each and every aspect of tourism such as currency exchange, airline operations, operations of MNCs, cross border movements of people and goods, currency, documents required for international travel, health regulations, etc.

Tourism is affected by the international relationships between different nations and the impacts that follow from the national tourism policy. Some policy decisions of the government act as a stumbling block to travellers like imposing a ban to travel to certain countries, visa policies, etc. The earlier policy limiting the amount of foreign exchange outbound tourists from India could carry has been abolished.

Levels of taxes imposed on tourism activities by the government have an impact as they can promote or discourage the flow of international tourists. The high taxation and more complicated travel requirements will make people think twice before undertaking a journey. Exit taxes, visa and passport requirements and charges, foreign exchange restrictions, entry and exit restrictions, special permits, etc. all act as deterrents to travel.

Changes in the political scenario also have a marked impact on tourism. For example, after the downfall of the Apartheid regime, many tourists chose South Africa as a destination instead of the usual popular destinations.

Terrorism, incidences of violence, political unrest, and natural disasters have serious consequences and have a direct impact on tourism and tourists avoid not only the destination but the country as well. After the 9/11 terrorist attack on the World Trade Centre in New York in 2001, there was a decline in travel by Americans and to the USA. There was a general slump in global tourism, many people lost their jobs and tourism industry was in serious financial crisis especially travel agents and tour operators who had invested heavily in accommodation and airline bookings.

The recent 26/11 terror attacks on Mumbai, India led to heavy cancellations of bookings for events, cruises, hotel stays, luxury trains, festivals, etc. Travellers planning to head to Goa, Kerala, Lakshadweep, etc. to celebrate New Year's Eve, changed their minds, resulting in massive financial losses for the tourism industry.

India Tourism is organizing hospitality tours inviting outbound tour operators from Europe to visit India so as to reassure them about tourists' safety and security.

Tourists look for destinations which have political stability, peace. and security as these are key words for promoting tourism.

MEASURES TO REGULATE TOURISM IMPACTS

The impact of tourism on the environment is a serious issue which needs to be addressed immediately, if tourism is to survive. Environmental impacts can be minimized by using management tools such as carrying capacity, visitor and traffic management, LAC, environmental impact assessments, and sustainable tourism development.

Carrying Capacity

The number of visitors and the type of developmental activities to be made available at a destination are based on the carrying capacity. The concept of carrying capacity is not new and has been followed by several disciplines such as agriculture, engineering, etc. Simply defined it means determining the maximum capacity which a building, an infrastructure or a facility could sustain with regards to its number of users. Farmers use this technique to calculate the number of cattle which can graze on a farm of a certain size for a specified period of time without causing negative impacts on the soil such as soil erosion, compaction, and delayed regeneration of pastures. Builders use this technique while constructing structures. Exceeding the carrying capacity will result in negative impacts.

In tourism carrying capacity means that level of tourism activity at a destination that could be maintained without having any adverse environmental, economic, social, or cultural impacts on the destination and the host population.

Carrying capacity is the maximum number of people who can use a site without an unacceptable alteration in the physical environment and an unacceptable decline in the quality of the experience gained by visitors (Wall and Mathieson 2006).

The initial concept of carrying capacity used half a century ago, referred mainly to the physical carrying capacity of buildings or the biological carrying capacity used by farmers. The term tourism carrying capacity has wider dimensions which include the overall quality of the visitors experience at the destination. The dimensions of carrying capacity are interrelated and influence one another.

They include

- environmental carrying capacity
- physical carrying capacity
- economic carrying capacity
- socio-cultural carrying capacity
- perceptual carrying capacity

If a destination is to remain popular and continue to attract new and repeat tourists, all the above mentioned dimensions need to be considered.

Environmental carrying capacity

This refers to the maximum number of visitors who can use an area without causing any permanent damage or change in the ecological systems. If the environmental carrying capacity is exceeded, it will result in destruction of the fragile environment, its flora and fauna, irreversible damage to the ecosystems, soil erosion along footpaths and loss of habitat for endangered species. Environmental carrying capacity can be determined by the conservation importance of local flora and fauna, water quality of lakes and rivers, shells and coral on beaches, marine life, soil erosion sensitivity, etc.

Physical carrying capacity

This dimension refers to physical space and the number of people or vehicles that can be accommodated by the available services, infra-structure, and facilities. This includes the availability and adequacy of transportation, accommodation, food service establishments, attractions, and tourist facilities at the destination. It also includes the infrastructure in terms of utility facilities like water supply, waste disposal systems, electric power, and telecommunications as well as facilities related to health and safety. All these have upper limits in terms of the number of people who can be safely accommodated or supported. Every hotel, vehicle, or restaurant has its maximum carrying capacity which should not be exceeded. For example, in Singapore the number of private cars on the city roads is restricted by charging heavy taxes.

Economic carrying capacity

This dimension refers to that extent of tourism development in a region that provides optimum overall economic benefits to the host population without distorting the economy. Uncontrolled or unplanned tourism is likely to result in inflation and shortages of essential commodities. Tourism projects which can provide gainful employment to the local community should be developed.

Sociocultural carrying capacity

This refers to the local community's perception towards all tourism related activities, the number of tourists and their involvement in tourism activities without having a detrimental influence on their lifestyles and activities. It is that level of tourism that helps maintain and preserve historical monuments, local arts and crafts, customs and traditions as well as values and beliefs. Exceeding this capacity could lead to a hostile attitude towards tourists and deterioration or transformation of historical, cultural, and built resources.

Perceptual carrying capacity

This refers to the number of tourists who can be accommodated at an attraction or at a destination without affecting the overall quality, the enjoyment, and the comfort level at the destination. Too many people, congestion, and overcrowding in small spaces has a psychological impact leading to an unfavourable tourism experience. An optimum number of people are acceptable, beyond which the tourist experiences discomfort. What level is optimum depends on what the tourists perceive as overcrowding and how comfortable they are in a crowd. The perceptual carrying capacity is how tourists perceive the destination, their attitude, and levels of acceptance and tolerance. It is the point at which the tourist begins to find a visit unacceptable.

Tourism carrying capacity refers to the type and extent of tourism development and visitor use that does not result in environmental problems or destruction of ecological systems, generate social problems or loss of cultural identity, exceed infrastructural capabilities, depreciate visitor satisfaction levels or go beyond the capabilities of resource managers to manage change (Keyser 2002).

Factors affecting carrying capacity

As we have read, carrying capacity has many dimensions and a large number of factors affect the carrying capacity of a destination. These factors range from the type of tourism to technological advances in the region. However, the overall carrying capacity of a destination is often determined by a single factor. It is this most limiting factor which determines the true carrying capacity of a destination, and this may not necessarily be related to environmental issues. For example, a destination may receive lesser tourists than the environment can support, but more than its host population may accept. The sociocultural dimension should also be considered while deciding on carrying capacity.

A destination may have adequate rooms to accommodate 5000 tourists per night, but may have a sewage plant which can handle only 2000 tourists staying overnight, in which case the carrying capacity will be 2000 tourists and not 5000 tourists as untreated sewage will make the physical environment unacceptable.

Carrying capacity concept in tourism is very complex and many factors need to be considered while determining the level of tourism which can be accommodated, without hampering the quality of the destination experience in the years to come. The factors affecting carrying capacity are shown in Table 14.3. While the carrying capacity approach attempts to prevent over utilization of the destination by identifying an upper limit to the number of visitors to an area, experience has shown that it is not necessarily the number of visitors which create a negative impact, but the visitor's behaviour which is more important. Sometimes, even a few visitors can cause irreparable damage to the environment in certain cases. For example, graffiti on walls of monuments, rocks or tree trunks; littering at picnic spots; throwing polythene bags and bottles in water bodies; collecting coral and shells from beaches; throwing lit cigarette stubs in sanctuaries and parks; damaging flora and fauna, trampling on rare plants, scaring away wildlife, poaching, etc. Exceeding the carrying capacity especially at religious places has led to the loss of innocent lives in stampedes during the Hajj pilgrimage and Mandharadevi stampede

Table 14.3 Factors affecting carrying capacity

1. Tourist Volume of tourists, type of tourist, duration of stay, educational level, age, purpose of visit	Mass tourism has a greater impact, while independent tourists, SIT have lesser impacts. Tourists who are aware of the environmental issues may tend to protect and prevent destruction and damage.
2. Destination Geographical concentration of visitors, seasonality, types and forms of tourism, physical environment	Attractions closely located in dense clusters will have a greater impact, especially during tourist season. A fragile environment like an island rain forest can be easily destroyed if carrying capacity is exceeded as compared to a built attraction.
3. Local factors Economy-developed/ underdeveloped, government, tourism policy, availability of local resources, technological development	A developing country is more susceptible to the negative impacts of tourism as compared to a well developed country with ample local resources, technological advancement in all areas and minimum leakages due to imports. The greater the local resources and government support, the greater the economic benefits to the locals with minimum negative social impacts. The wider the economic and cultural gap, the bigger the impact.
4. Other factors Guest-host relationship, degree of interaction	The more the interaction, the greater the demonstration effect.

at Wai in Maharashtra. In all these cases, the tourists' behaviour is the main cause of these tragedies.

Visitor and Traffic Management

We have read in carrying capacity that the number of visitors and their behaviour are the two main factors which need to be controlled to minimize negative environmental impacts of tourism. Visitor management techniques are widely used at popular tourism spots. According to Page and Dowling (2002) there are two types of visitor management techniques. They are

1. Hard measures and
2. Soft measures

Hard measures

They aim to restrict entry and usage by regulating the number of tourists. This is achieved by adjusting the opening time, charging higher entry fees during peak hours, using walkalators to regulate time spent at popular spots, warning signage such as not to litter or feed the animals, etc.

Soft measures

They aim at influencing visitor's behaviour and attitude and are designed to inform or educate the visitor. Boards displaying codes of conduct to be followed, measures to prevent degradation of fragile flora and fauna, etc. help conserve the environment and add to the knowledge of tourists.

Private vehicles add to environmental pollution and traffic jams leading to loss of precious time, missing transport connections or reaching attraction at closure time. The traffic at the destination can be controlled by discouraging the use of private vehicles by charging heavy taxes and toll. Singapore is an excellent example of traffic control. Tourists have easy access to quality public transportation both by road or rail at an affordable price with good frequency and electronic information display boards. Roads have speed control and are in good condition with proper signage. Traffic management at the site includes designated drop-off points and parking for tourist's coaches, park and ride services, moving walkways, etc.

Limits of Acceptable Change

Managers at tourism sites are now following the limits of acceptable change (LAC) approach to resource management which was developed in the 1970s by the US Forest Service. In this approach, all stakeholders, namely the host population, the tourists, the principal suppliers, the local government, and the NGOs are equally involved in the decision making process. Every agency and individual concerned decides on and accepts an approach to manage a particular site and the solutions to be introduced to manage visitor pressure.

The LAC processes plans, selects indicators, establishes standards for each indicator, sets the limits of acceptable change and agree on the action to be taken once the indicators are reached. The team monitors and reviews the LAC indicators for example the duration of queuing time outside an attraction. If there are long queues and crowding for a particular attraction, the possible solutions to this problem could be

- increasing the timing of the attraction by an hour each in the morning and evening;
- reducing the length of tour so that more batches could be covered;
- using walkalators so that there is no crowding at specific spots and time of tour can be controlled; and
- opening additional sites or routes.

Some indicators need to be monitored several times during the day.

The carrying capacity and LAC approach are useful tools for managing tourism at a destination and can help in preventing accidents, enhance visitor experience and have beneficial impacts on the host, their economy, culture, and environment.

Estimation of carrying capacity is one of the most challenging tasks faced by tourism managers today. There are many diverse opinions on as to which method is best for establishing and measuring the carrying capacity of an attraction or a destination and how many tourists are too many.

While modern tourism continues to grow beyond its carrying capacity in many destinations, many sites have proposed upgradation of existing facilities without deteriorating the tourist's experiences. Some of the technological advancements are water recycling plants in areas of water scarcity; cable cars, helicopters in hilly areas; waste management plants; desalination plants in coastal areas etc.

Environmental Impact Assessment

New tourism development and land use projects now require an environmental impact assessment (EIA) before they begin any development work. EIAs evaluate the overall effect the development will have on the environment and identity measures to reduce the negative impacts. EIA is carried out by consultants and is a legal requirement in some countries.

EIAs take into consideration the following:

- total cost of development;
- all beneficiaries and all possible benefits which may arise;
- those who are likely to be adversely affected by the project;
- other developmental options which have lesser negative impacts;
- steps which are being taken to reduce negative impacts.

Sustainable Tourism Development

A sustainable tourism destination is the product of careful planning, management, and monitoring of tourism development.

Mass tourism has expanded rapidly since the post world war era. Many countries have reaped the benefits of tourism without paying much attention to the negative impacts. Along with economic development, tourism has also been responsible for a wide range of detrimental impacts on the natural and physical environment like devastation of flora and fauna, disruption of natural habitat, traffic congestion; air, water, and land pollution, destruction of natural landscapes and obstructing scenic views by unplanned and haphazard constructions, etc. While tourism can help in sustaining arts and crafts and tradition and festivals, it may also be responsible for cultural change and disrupting the morals, values and beliefs of the host population because of the demonstration effect.

The concept of sustainability has become a fundamental issue in tourism development and growth. During the 1960s people became increasingly aware of environmental problems like destruction of rare habitats, pollution, acid rain, etc. and related it to the unplanned growth of industries. From the birth of the environmental era in the mid-1960s, arose the concept of sustainability. People began to realize that the earth's natural resources were limited and if not conserved, would ultimately get exhausted. After the debate at the Earth Summit in 1992 at Rio de Janeiro and the World Summit on Sustainable Development at Johannesburg, world leaders, politicians and the society, seriously took up the issue of sustainable development to ensure that present and future generations should be able to benefit from tourism resources.

Sustainable tourism means achieving a particular combination of numbers and types of visitors, the cumulative effect of whose activities at a given destination, together with the actions of the servicing businesses, can continue into the foreseeable future without damaging the quality of the environment on which the activities are based (Middleton 1998).

The sustainable development approach ensures that future generations everywhere will have adequate resources to sustain themselves and maintain a reasonable quality of life. Achieving sustainability is now the underlying principle for tourism development. Destination planners and managers are now faced with a new challenge. They need to meet the increasing demands of experienced and seasoned tourists while balancing the fragile and diminishing resources at the destinations, preserving indigenous cultures and traditions, and accepting social responsibility for the negative impacts on the host community.

Governments and societies have realized the need to plan and manage economic growth objectives within the limits of the environment and to keep the growth of the tourism sector under check.

Tourists and tourism planners and suppliers have realized that the environment is the most fundamental ingredient of the tourism product. Any tourism activity changes or modifies the environment, i.e. it creates an impact. Proper planning and management can help minimize negative impacts and help create positive impacts. Sustainable development is intended to reduce the tension and friction created by the interaction between the various sectors of the tourism industry, the tourists, the host population, and the environment, i.e. all the stakeholders of the tourism industry. See Fig. 14.2 for some of the advantages of sustainable development.

Sustainable tourism development includes the following:

- conserving and enhancing resources for tourism which can be used by both residents and tourists in the present and future;

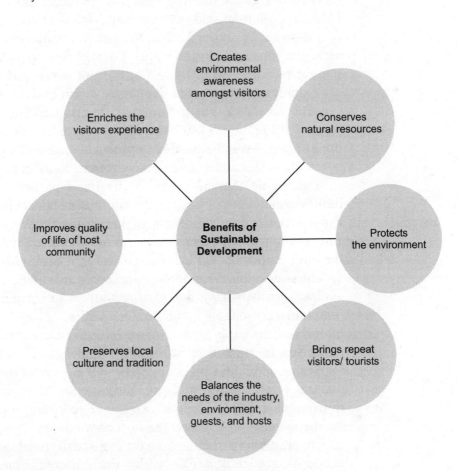

Fig. 14.2 Some of the benefits of sustainable development

- development projects which are compatible with the society and culture of the tourism destination;
- marked improvement in the standard of living of the host population;
- meeting the expectations of tourists and attracting repeat visitors;
- respect for the host community and measures to protect the environment;
- meeting the needs of visitor facilities and maintaining them well;
- maintaining tourism resources by applying conservation techniques and promoting campaigns to create funds for maintaining wildlife; and
- developing suitable visitor facilities and services at the site for the convenience of tourists and cleanliness of destination.

All tourism-related activities should be well planned, located, designed, and managed in an environmentally friendly and culturally sensitive manner so that the environment is not congested, polluted, or degraded and there are no social tensions.

Local communities are involved in tourism planning in the area from the inception of the project and they participate and benefit from tourism. Sustainable tourism development embraces a community involvement and participation.

Responsible Tourism

The concept of 'responsible tourism', is based on the concept of sustainable tourism development and was the theme for the FHRAI annual convention for this year. It is a positive approach by all the partners in the industry to plan, manage, market, and compete with other partners in a responsible way.

Responsible tourism means

- the tourism industry is responsible to the environment and promotion of environment friendly practices;
- the government is responsible to develop linkages with the local community;
- the responsibility of local communities is towards tourists safety and comforts; etc.
- the responsibility of both employers and employees in tourism, to each other, and to the customers;
- responsibility to respect, invest, and develop local cultures and prevent their exploitation; and
- responsible tourists who observe local norms and practices.

TOURISM LEGISLATION

Although tourism is said to be the world's largest industry, very little attention has been paid to framing national and international laws.

Tourism consists of industries and activities that stretch across both public and private sectors. Tourism businesses are affected by the actions of different levels of government and operate in a diverse legal environment, with a variety of laws and regulations. Some of the various legislations which directly or indirectly affect tourism are

- laws pertaining to trans-border movements such as visa regulations, customs, foreign exchange, immigration rules, etc.;
- laws related to transportation such as airline regulation, fares and tariffs, laws related to road transport—permits, licences, etc.;
- laws related to food and beverage production storage and service like PFA Act 1954, municipal health laws, licences, liquor permits, grading of restaurants, etc.;
- laws related to accommodation like classification of hotels as five star deluxe to one star;
- consumer protection laws related to health, hygiene, quality, etc. consumer protection act;
- labour laws related to employers working conditions, minimum wage act, etc.;
- laws related to conservation of monuments, historical sites, and environmental protection such as the Wildlife Protection Act, Forest Conservation Act, and the Ancient Monuments Act; and
- laws regarding the functioning of tourism organizations at various levels.

The legal environment of tourism activities becomes even more complicated once international borders are crossed. Tourists have no right in international law to enter the territory of a state of which they are not nationals. This means that each state is entitled to decide which tourist may enter its territory and under which conditions.

When international tourists have made arrangements with say Indian tourism businesses before they enter the country, in the likelihood of any problem, which country's legal system governs these contractual relationships is the question which may arise. While the Indian tourism business will want Indian law to apply, the foreigner would like to follow the legal system in his own country. The tour package may have been purchased at a trade fair in one country, for a tour to another country by a tourist from a third country.

This issue could be addressed by inserting a clause in the contract stating which courts will have jurisdiction in the case of a dispute. Legal issues in tourism are often complex and need expert legal advice, hence framing of tourism laws is necessary.

Travel is a legal right of all individuals. Tourism laws are needed in order to regulate, permit, promote, enforce, empower, or ban both commercial and leisure activities of both the service provider as well as the tourist. Figure 14.3 which shows us why these laws are necessary. Tourists should have a redressal mechanism or get rightful compensation for transgression of rights and regulations. The Government of Jammu and Kashmir has enacted a special legislation—Jammu and Kashmir Registration of Tourist Trade Act to protect the interests of tourists. Under this legislation, various officers of the State Tourism Department have been vested with magisterial powers, including the powers of compounding, in cases of harassment, cheating, over charging or pestering tourists.

To revive tourism which was the main source of income of more than thirty per cent of its population, the state government has taken many

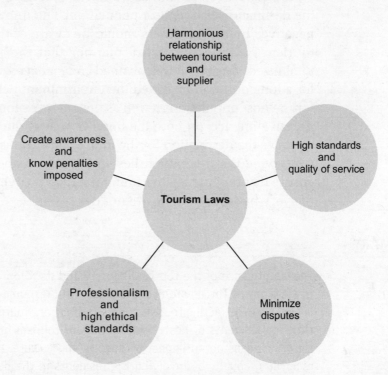

Fig. 14.3 Tourism laws are needed for these reasons

steps like formulating a special package for reviving and developing tourism in the state.

The Ministry of Tourism is the nodal agency for formulation of national policies and programmes and for coordinating various activities of tourism in India. Apart from various planning, monitoring, and coordinating activities the ministry is responsible for formulating tourism legislation.

Two of the functions of the attached office, i.e. Directorate General of Tourism are

1. Regulation, that is
   (a) Approval and classification of hotels and restaurants
   (b) Approval of travel agents, tour operators, and tourist transport operators, etc.
2. Inspection and quality control
   (a) Guide service
   (b) Complaints and redressal

The National Policy of Tourism 2006 has covered the issue pertaining to Tourism legislations in India.

Tourism development, as we have read, always leaves its impact on the destination and its host population. The impact may be positive or negative. Tourism planners should be aware of these impacts and plan tourism activities in such a manner that the negative impacts are minimized. Tourism, if well planned and managed, can yield steady profits for a long duration provided the environment will help sustain tourism for the host population as well as the guests or tourists. It will have least negative impacts on both the hosts as well as the environment and will preserve the destination for the future generations. The responsibility of conserving the destination lies with the tourism planners who should ensure that the fragile environment and attractive landscapes which are the very basis for tourism are not destroyed.

SUMMARY

The significance of the tourism industry and its role in economic development is well known. The environment is a powerful resource for tourism as it plays a major role in attracting tourists to the destination. Tourism results in interactions with the residents or host, the suppliers of tourism products and services and the NGOs, causing an impact on society and culture. Negative impacts can be removed gradually by involving the residents in the development process. The tourism activity to be developed should be acceptable to the residents and at the same time should be a source of income to them. The positive and negative impacts on the environment should be kept in mind while undertaking any developmental activity. All stakeholders should know that the environment is an exhaustible resource which needs to be preserved for the future generations. The extent of damage by unplanned and unregulated tourism can be so severe that it can destroy the very basis of tourism. The carrying capacity should be kept in mind to give the visitors a satisfying destination experience and the extent of development should be such that tourism is sustained for the future generations to enjoy.

Since tourism is growing at a rapid rate, the framing of tourism legislations to protect the interests of both the tourists as well as the service providers needs to be done. This is a difficult task considering the different nature of the sub-sectors which comprise this industry. However, the state governments are forming tourism laws which will help in smooth functioning of tourism related activities.

KEY TERMS

Atmosphere Is the body of air that surrounds our planet and is most dense close to the earth's surface. It is composed mainly of nitrogen (78%), oxygen (21%), carbon dioxide (0.03%), and other gases (less than 1%).

Biosphere Is the life bearing layer and is composed of all living organisms like plants, animals, microbes, etc. which exist from up to three metres below the ground to thirty metres above it and in the top 200 metres of the oceans and seas.

Demonstration effect Tendency for local residents to be influenced by behaviour of tourists and to imitate their mode of dress, food habits, etc. and assimilate it as their own.

Environment Means the total of the things or circumstances which surround us and may refer to the natural or built environment or some other set of conditions or influences like economic, sociocultural or political environment.

Environmental Impact Assessment (EIA) A set of procedures to assess in advance, the likely effects of a tourism development project on the environment. It is a legal requirement in many countries such as the USA and countries of the European Union.

Gross domestic product (GDP) Is the total market value of all final goods and services produced in a country in a year.

Hydrosphere Is composed of all the water forms on or near the earth like oceans, rivers, lakes and even the moisture in the air, ice and snow.

Interpretation Is the process of explaining the significance of the place the tourists have come to visit.

Leakages Withdrawal of demand from an economy when money is spent on buying goods and services from another economy, for example, money spent on imports or when money is put into savings.

Lithosphere Is the solid rocky inorganic crust covering the entire surface of the earth from the tallest mountain to the deepest trench.

Sustainable tourism Term used to describe all forms of long term tourism which are in harmony with their physical, social, and cultural environment and meet the present needs as well as the future generation needs.

CONCEPT REVIEW QUESTIONS

1. Explain the term 'Multiplier Effect' in tourism.
2. What do you understand by the term 'leakages'? How can you minimize leakages in the tourism industry?
3. What type of impact does tourism have on the coastal region?
4. What measures would you suggest to minimize the adverse impact of tourism on hill stations?
5. Discuss the economic impact of tourism on a developing country.
6. What are the positive impacts of tourism on the environment?
7. Explain the following

   (a) Need for sustainable development
   (b) Physical carrying capacity
   (c) Guest-host interrelationships

CRITICAL THINKING QUESTIONS

1. Do you feel that there is a need for having tourism laws? What would be your recommendations for healthy functioning of the tourism system?
2. Discuss the sociocultural impact of tourism which is likely to be observed on tourism activities in rural India.

PROJECT/ASSIGNMENT

Visit any monument or garden and observe the impact of tourism on the same. What measures would you suggest to minimize the impacts?

REFERENCES

Bhatia, A.K. 2001, *International Tourism Management*, Sterling Publishers Private Limited, New Delhi.

George, R. 2007, *Managing tourism in South Africa*, Oxford University Press Southern Africa, Cape Town.

IGNOU 2001, *Tourism Impacts*, MTMIO, New Delhi.

Keyser, H. 2002, *Tourism Development*, Oxford University Press Southern Africa, Cape Town.

Middleton, V. 1998, *Sustainable Tourism: A Marketing Perspective*, Butterworth-Heinemann, Oxford.

Page, S.J. and R. Dowling 2002, *Ecotourism*, Prentice Hall. Harlow.

Pednekar, H., S. Pendse and P. Dongre 2006, *Environment Education,* Sheth Publishers Pvt Ltd, Mumbai.

Wall, G. and A. Mathieson 2006, *Tourism: Change, Impacts and Opportunities*. Pearson Prentice Hall, Harlow.

www.ibef.org, accessed on 1 September 2008.

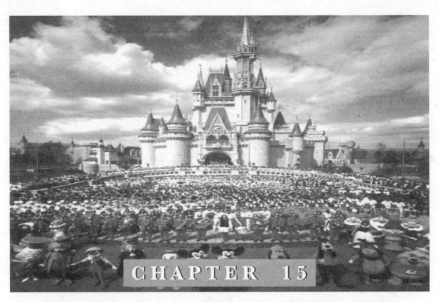

CHAPTER 15

Attraction Planning and Development

Learning Objectives

After reading this chapter you should be able to:
- understand the need for planned tourism development
- understand why travel motivators should be kept in mind while planning for tourism
- examine the basic principles underlying attraction development
- know the role of the public and private sectors in tourism planning and development
- review factors which must be considered while selecting a location
- appreciate the need for conducting a feasibility analysis and cost–benefit analysis

INTRODUCTION

Tourism is one of the fastest growing service sectors and the need for planned development is of utmost importance. All tourist attractions require a planned development approach if they are to remain as attractions in the years to come. Many natural attractions which have developed spontaneously need planned rejuvenation so that they continue to attract tourists and repeat visitors. Unplanned and unregulated tourism has an adverse impact on society, culture, ecology, and the economy in the long run.

Tourism planning is very necessary because tourism is a diffused and complex activity, made up of a variety of elements such as attractions, infrastructure, etc. These elements are developed by developers and then consumed by tourists who exhibit a diversity of demands. However, there is always a gap between demand and supply. This gap is bridged by using multiple resources which are specific to tourism.

Tourism development influences not only tourists and developers but also other sectors of society. It is directly related to economy in general and may have an impact on the environment at large.

If different tourism sectors do not develop harmoniously, costs may increase and problems may arise. If different developers have contradictory objectives or when they do not see eye to eye, growth would be uncontrolled in some sectors. Thus, what is important is 'integrated tourism planning', i.e. proper planning of all aspects such as physical, legal, promotional, financial, economic, marketing management, social, and environmental aspects. Good planning will ensure desired results and systematic working to achieve success.

Today's tourism developer knows that just having the five 'A's of destination development, i.e. accessibility, accommodation, attractions and activities, amenities, and affordability does not lead to automatic progress but to mass tourism which has destroyed many destinations completely. Mass tourism can result in permanent damage or irreversible changes in the environment. It not only changes the appearance of the environment but also damages ecosystems and habitats permanently. According to the United Nations Environment Programme (UNEP), nearly 75 per cent of the sand dunes on the Mediterranean coast between Gibraltar and Sicily have disappeared either due to resorts built on them or through erosion caused by clearing land for development. Tourists used to flock to Mahabaleshwar, a once popular hill station in Maharashtra, India, to enjoy the natural beauty and spend time peacefully in the midst of nature. Today, the tourists visiting Mahabaleshwar face traffic jams, garbage trails, water scarcity, harassment by touts, and high charges from hawkers. Food and entertainment stalls are spilling onto the already congested roads, and taxes are collected at every point. The natural beauty is lost by the congestion of people, vehicles, poor waste management, and haphazard development. It is no wonder that tourists avoid Mahabaleshwar and ask travel agents to recommend other weekend getaways.

The maximum benefits from tourism and optimal utilization of the tourism resources can occur only if it is backed by proper planning and management.

NEED FOR PLANNED DEVELOPMENT

Planning is the backbone for any industry and the tourism industry is no exception.

Planning is necessary because of the following reasons:

- A tourism plan works as a guideline for new entrants in tourism.
- Since tourism is a multisectoral and fragmented activity involving other sectors, a plan helps in integrated tourism development.
- It helps in matching tourism markets and tourism products correctly without compromising on environmental and sociocultural objectives.
- Since tourism can bring various direct and indirect economic benefits, planning helps in maximizing economic benefits.
- Tourism planning helps to achieve cultural conservation objectives, i.e. by optimizing the benefits and preventing the problems.
- Careful planning helps in determining the optimum type and level of tourism that will not degrade the environment but help in achieving environmental conservation objectives.
- The right type of planning can ensure that the natural and cultural resources for tourism are indefinitely maintained and not destroyed in the process of development, i.e. lead to sustainable tourism development.
- Planning can help to upgrade and revitalize existing outdated areas and plan for modern and latest tourism development, i.e. new tourism areas with flexibility for future growth.
- Planning helps in providing adequate human resource with the requisite skills and capabilities by organizing education and training programmes for the existing labour force.
- Planning provides a rational basis for public and private sector in investment planning, by preparing a detailed year-wise action plan depicting the stages in the development of the project and time frame for completing interconnected events and activities.

Planned tourism development needs formulation of special organizational structures, marketing strategies, and promotional programmes, laws and regulations which should be in tune with the 'National Tourism Policy'.

PLANNING PROCESS

Attractions play the most important role of drawing people to a destination. Most people tend to think of a destination in terms of the most well known or primary attractions and they travel to see and experience those attractions. When most foreigners think of India, an image of the Taj Mahal (Fig. 15.1) comes to their mind. Similarly, any thoughts about Paris, France bring the image of the Eiffel Tower (Fig. 15.2) to our minds. The attractions at a destination entice, lure, or attract tourists to the destination and they are the most powerful elements of the supply side of tourism. Attractions are used by marketers to create a destination image. The various attractions are owned by the government, non-profit organizations, or the private sector. Because they contribute significantly towards revenue generation and the visitors' experience, they need to be planned and managed well. Planning is an orderly process which is concerned with anticipating and regulating change and preparing a set of decisions for achieving goals set by the organization for an organized future.

Tourism planning is a complex process which considers the various aspects as well as the segments of the tourism industry. Tourism is an economic activity with everyone from the government to the private

Fig. 15.1   The Taj Mahal, Agra, India

Fig. 15.2 Eiffel Tower, Paris, France

sector, locals or hosts, and the tourists having a stake in it. To reap such harvests it is essential that tourism is planned in a logical sequence.

Basic Steps

Basic steps in planning for tourism include the following:

Defining the system It is necessary to define the scale, size, character, and purpose of the plan.

Formulating objectives to give direction Objectives must be comprehensive and specific with a time frame for completion.

Data gathering Basic data needs to be collected through research or fact finding. Data can be gathered, quantified, and qualified by

- preparing a fact sheet;
- conducting a market survey;
- undertaking site and infrastructure surveys; and
- analysing existing facilities and competition.

Analysing and interpreting The many pieces of information must be interpreted so that facts gathered will have meaning. Once this is done, a set of conclusions and recommendations is drawn out that leads to the making or conceptualization of a preliminary plan.

Preliminary planning Based on the earlier steps, alternatives are considered and solutions are drawn and tested. Scale models for land use, sketches to depict the development image, financial plans, site surveys, and layout plans to show investment need phase wise, etc. are prepared.

Approving the plan Plans, drawings, scale models, estimates of cost, estimates of profits, chances of success, or failure can be seen.

Making the final plan All aspects covered need to be defined, for example, in case of a destination—a definition of land use, plans for infrastructure facilities such as roads, airports, bike paths, horse trails, sewage, water, etc.

Implementing This means putting the tourism plan into operation. It also follows up, monitors, and evaluates. Good planning provides mechanisms that give continuing feedback on the tourism project and the levels of consumer satisfaction reached.

Reasons for Planning

Attractions need to be planned and managed for the following reasons:

- environmental conservation
- preservation and restoration of monuments
- sustainable development
- enhanced visitor satisfaction
- to increase the destination life cycle
- for promoting the attraction
- revenue generation

It is necessary to strike a balance between optimum enjoyment and appreciation of the attraction by the visitors without degradation of the attraction and its environment by tourism activities.

VARIOUS LEVELS AT WHICH PLANS ARE PREPARED

Tourism plans are prepared at different levels. They are discussed as follows:

International Level

At the international level, planning, marketing, and cooperative activities are undertaken by international organizations such as UNWTO, ICAO, and IATA (refer to Chapter 6).

National Level

The national level planning takes place within a country by its government. It focuses on overall tourism development within the country such as defining tourism objectives, formulating a tourism policy, identifying major tourist attractions, designing tourism development regions, marketing, research, and legislation, etc.

Regional Level

At the regional level, planning is done for a state, a province, or a tourist circuit like the Buddhist circuit in India, etc. Regional policies are formed within the framework of the national tourism policy or plan and are more specific and include transportation networks and regional access, tourism development areas, attractions, accommodations, and other facilities and their marketing and promotional strategies, etc.

Destination Level

Destination level or local level planning is more specific than regional planning. A destination zone is an area which has a large and diverse amount of attractions and services to satisfy several travel market segments, for example, MICE tourists, leisure tourists, medical tourists, etc. Local bodies play an important role in destination development and their suggestions should be taken into consideration while preparing the tourism development plan.

Site Level

This is the most popular and sought after level of tourism planning. Individual land and property owners employ the services of professional planners to plan and design their property. For example, farm owners plan rural tourism and agritourism projects. The demand for new forms and types of tourism have made this a profitable venture. Tourism entrepreneurs have recognized the business opportunity and tax benefits given by the government and are investing in tourism in a big way.

PRINCIPLES OF ATTRACTION DEVELOPMENT

The principles of attraction development are discussed in the following section.

Listing

The first principle of attraction development is to take an inventory of existing and potential attractions in the area. To collect this information, the destination needs to be surveyed and a survey format should be prepared to know the attractions already present in the locality.

- archaeological sites
- birthplaces or residence of well-known people
- caves
- exhibition grounds
- hills
- monuments
- museums
- sound and light shows
- theatres
- temples
- antique and handicraft shops
- cemeteries
- churches
- gardens
- historic buildings
- mountains
- prisons
- snow
- theme parks
- waterfalls, beaches, lakes

While collecting this information, it is necessary to keep the special features of the area in mind, for example, water bodies, hills, snow covered peaks, etc. which could form a part of the attractions in future.

Apart from the various attractions, both existing and potential, it is also necessary to survey and evaluate the institutional elements.

These include

- present development policies and plans of the government for the next five years;
- government structure and tourism organizations in the region;
- policies for investment in tourism development projects, availability of capital, and other incentives to encourage private sector investments in tourism projects;
- tourism legislation and regulations already in force in terms of standards of hygiene, building construction norms, etc.; and
- tourism and hospitality training institutes and training facilities available.

This information is necessary while preparing the development plan. For example, if a large number of trained manpower is required, special training programmes can be conducted at tourism training institutes if they are available.

All types of existing attractions should be listed and categorized into three categories, namely, natural attractions, cultural attractions, and human made or built attractions (refer to chapter 4).

Evaluation

Many attractions may be present in a given area, but not all may be worth visiting. Attractions should be evaluated in terms of their

- quality
- authenticity
- uniqueness
- activity potential
- popularity or number of visitors to the attraction
- category of attraction, i.e. primary attraction or secondary attraction

Quality

Is the attraction worth visiting? Does it provide value for money? These are some of the questions which come to the minds of tourists when they plan a tour.

Authenticity

It is important to note if the attraction is genuine and original or it is an imitation. Tourists look for authenticity in alternative forms of tourism such as agritourism, cultural tourism, etc. Built attractions or non-authentic attractions need to constantly upgrade or improve product quality if they want to remain in business, as they can be easily substituted.

Uniqueness

Tourists seek something different and exciting at the destination. They are not interested in seeing something they have already experienced at some other place. Both authentic and non-authentic destinations can have their USP, for example, the Horseshoe Falls are unique to Niagara Falls, Canada and are authentic, whereas the number of casinos at Las Vegas are unique to the area but non-authentic.

Activity potential

Tourists need something to do once they reach the attraction. If they have sufficient activities, they stay at the attraction for a longer time.

Activities should be compatible with the attraction and should maintain the sociocultural and environmental integrity of the destination.

Popularity

Popularity or the number of tourists, who visit the attraction, the mode of transportation available, and the distance visitors travel, tell us a lot about the attraction.

Category of attraction

An attraction may be either a primary or secondary motivator for travel. Very often, secondary attractions are most visited even if they are not the main reason of travel. For example, for business tourists, the main motivation for travel is business related, however, after work is over, they visit local attractions in the area.

Development Strategy

After attractions have been listed and evaluated, the next step would be the development of an attraction mix strategy to promote the attraction. This strategy includes the following:

Organic bunching

This is the grouping together of like attractions or supporting attractions to create a synergistic effect. Some attractions are insignificant by themselves and benefit by being a part of the attraction mix. Organic bunching results in greater tourist traffic to the cluster than the sum of what each small attraction could attract by itself. Some attractions are unique and can be a primary attraction by itself and do not need the support of others. Smaller attractions located on the periphery of unique or major attractions, benefit from the flow of traffic to major attractions as tourists take a halt at these places en route.

Thematic appeal

The theme approach is gaining popularity for events and attractions after the roaring success of Disney theme parks. Almost any attraction can have a theme which may be based on fantasy, escape, any period of history, rural lifestyle, urbanization, etc. Generally, themes help in psychologically transforming the individual to a different place and time including places of make-believe and fantasy.

Themes are created to make the attraction unique as the tourist is looking for something different or unusual from the routine.

For example, a spice products manufacturer, with the production unit located in a rural area, developed the processing plant and surrounding land into a tourism attraction. The attraction includes a guided tour of the manufacturing unit/processing unit which uses environment sensitive practices such as solar energy, vermiculture, bio-gas plants, water recycling plants, and composting. Other attractions include an exhibition of spices, a visit to the spice garden to see how spices are grown, lunch prepared using the spices, a sales counter for spice products, and brochures highlighting the medicinal properties of spices.

Except for the factory, the rest of the attraction was developed by using indigenous products for construction and the theme was a typical rural set-up.

FEASIBILITY ANALYSIS

Any attraction needs some amount of investment and investors are interested in knowing whether the attraction will provide a return on investment. And if yes, how much. Irrespective of whether the attraction is owned by the government or belongs to the private sector, justifying the continuance of an existing attraction or estimating potential economic contributions of a proposed attraction in terms of costs and benefits is necessary.

The feasibility analysis studies the potential demand for the attraction and its economic feasibility tells us whether the attraction we plan to develop will make money.

Development may be in terms of rejuvenating an existing attraction or developing a potential attraction.

Certain questions need to be asked such as:

- What tourist product will be developed?
- Whom is the product being developed for?
- Where is the market?
- Are there any competitors in the vicinity?
- What is the size of the market?

LOCATION

The location of the site in the destination area needs to be considered and this depends on the nature of the attraction and whether it is a primary or a secondary attraction. A stand-alone primary attraction like a self-contained resort would consider the existing transportation network and infrastructural facilities available. A secondary attraction needs to select a location near other supporting attractions.

A primary attraction is the main attraction at a destination. An example of a self-contained primary attraction is Sentosa Island Resort at Singapore and Disney World at Orlando, Florida. They are the main reasons for selecting the destination. Examples of secondary attractions in Singapore are the Singapore River Cruise, the Singapore Zoo, shopping at Little India and China Town, etc. They are not the main travel motivators, but depend on the primary attractions for their survival.

Many other factors need to be considered such as a study of the

- supply/demand analysis
- transportation modes serving the area and cost of available transport
- land ownership and price
- trained human resource
- government policies in force
- tax concessions to private investors
- existing infrastructure
- safety and security
- services available in the vicinity
- source of finance
- competitors

IDENTIFYING THE MARKET

The market area for an attraction needs to be identified and because of the intangible nature of the tourism product, this is not an easy task. As the attraction becomes more complex, the market area increases and may be as large as the world or as small as a city. The market depends on the attractions and activities available at the site (refer to Chapter 12).

The site should be selected keeping the target market in mind.

COST–BENEFIT ANALYSIS

Cost–benefit analysis is a ratio measure of the relative benefits accruing to the attraction developer versus the costs incurred in development and operations.

In any new venture, it is practically impossible to accurately predict the volume of sales because of a large number of variables. However, it is essential to estimate the expected revenues. The location decision can be finalized only after revenues are estimated.

When the government or the public sector organizations plan to develop attractions, their main motive is social welfare and not profit making. The benefits are hard to quantify in this case. Most public sector undertakings do not make a profit and in such cases the focus should be on cost-effectiveness rather than revenue maximization.

Although the tourism industry is dominated by the private sector, it is developed and managed to a large extent by the government. In India, a large number of visitor attractions such as monuments, national parks, skiing slopes, trekking trails, etc. are on publicly owned and managed lands. Most of the infrastructure such as electricity, water supply, police force, fire brigade, etc. is owned and managed by the government. Formulating tourism policies and legislations and promoting and marketing India as a destination is also done by the government.

The private sector is involved in investing in tourist facilities and services where the profit margin is high. The accommodation sector, transport sector, tour operators and travel agents, commercial food and beverage establishments, entertainment, and activities are mainly the responsibility of the private sector. In the private sector, operations are profit motivated and benefits are defined as revenue accruing to the owners of the operations. In this case, revenues may be substituted for benefits and a revenue/cost analysis should be calculated.

Revenues are defined as the sum of all sales accruing to the attraction operation.

In any tourist attraction, revenues may flow from many different sources such as accommodation which is the largest single revenue generator, food and beverage, entrance fees, sale of souvenirs, etc. All sources of revenue need to be estimated on an annual basis for the expected life of the operation. This is not an easy task and involves forecasting of sales. Each revenue generating operation needs to be considered to arrive at the annual total revenue estimates.

Cost Estimation

Costs incurred in operations are basically of two types, fixed and variable. Fixed costs are costs which are incurred regardless of whether tourists visit the attraction or not. For example, land taxes, interest on loans, salaries, etc. are fixed costs. They do not change with the level of use. Variable costs are costs incurred on food and beverage, laundry service, etc. and depend on the volume of guests. These are estimated on the basis of expected visitors. Projected revenues and costs should be estimated on an annual basis because of the seasonality factor so that both lean season and peak season use is covered. The life expectancy of the attraction is another consideration which is far more complex as it is difficult to predict whether the attraction will remain popular in the future years. While analysing revenues/costs, the life expectancy is assumed to be 10 years. The figures for revenues and costs in future are then discounted to achieve present value rates as the value of the rupee at present will be worth much more than it will be in the future.

Based on these findings, a detailed implementation plan is prepared which specifies the sequence of activities, time schedules, and responsibilities. The plan is carefully studied and redrafted after receiving recommendations, feed back and approval from various experts. It needs the approval by the final authority, i.e. the government or for the private sector by the board of directors before it is actually implemented.

Implementation means putting the final plan into operation. It also includes regular monitoring and evaluation to ensure that development is progressing according to the plan.

MANAGING A HISTORIC SITE

Historical monuments have always been major tourist attractions. These are heritage sites which need to be preserved and maintained. These monuments are outstanding examples of traditional architecture and were specially designed for civil and religious use or as residences for the rulers of that era. These structures were well planned and constructed with permanent materials and have survived through centuries to tell their tale. Historical sites include monuments such as ancient palaces, forts, historical houses, memorials mausoleums, prisons, statues, battle fields, etc. If they are not preserved they will crumble into a heap of rubble. The planning process should take the following into account:

- conservation
- restoration
- interpretation
- visitor facilities (toilets, shops, parking, refreshment, etc.)
- promotion and
- revenue generation

Monuments can be used to develop heritage tourism, for example, palaces, forts, and havelis are being converted into heritage hotels. Monuments help us understand the living environment and lifestyle of ordinary people of the past and present and interpret these in an interesting manner to tourists.

Part of the monument complex can be converted into a museum depicting settlements and lifestyles in the form of pictures, models, actual articles, etc. With the help of a survey and analysis of the archaeological and historical features, the conservation needs will be determined.

Steps to be followed for managing a large monument complex are

1. Objectives for development and conservation should be determined. These would be based on the regional and national policy. The main objectives of managing a historic site are

    (a) To provide enhanced visitor satisfaction, at the same time to promote and preserve the historic monument for the future generations and bring the monument back to life through simulated shows and interpretation.

    (b) To ensure that the visitor takes back both tangible memories in the form of souvenirs, picture postcards, brochures, CDs, books, etc. as well as intangible memories of the visit.

2. Special surveys and analysis of archaeological features and historical features need to be studied. Archaeological Survey of India (ASI) monitors the preservation and maintenance of monuments to prevent deterioration and decay from setting in. It has a challenging task of restoring the monuments and maintaining the original images for which special materials need to be used.

3. Visitor carrying capacity should be restricted to a certain number as there is danger of site deterioration through excessive congestion.

4. Direct access to very fragile features should be prohibited and these areas should be cordoned off. Visitors should have a good view of the exhibits which may be placed at a height or in glass showcases.

5. The site should be explained to visitors through the following:

    (a) Proper display of directional signs and notices in English and in regional language.

    (b) Historical description of the site through plaques on the wall at the exhibit.

(c) Brochures, audio-video material related to the site, and souvenirs.

6. The guides appointed should have a pleasing personality, be well groomed with effective communication skills and sound knowledge of history and architecture. Additional knowledge of a foreign language is desirable. Interpreters could be called for foreign groups.

7. Tourist sensitization measures need to be taken to maintain the sanctity of the place. Proper rules and behavioural expectations from tourists should be put up in clear print at the entrance.

8. The presentation should be effective and interesting. Life animators or technical means such as dioramas with mannequins, historical artifacts, etc. should be used to recreate major historical events.

9. The originality should be retained and the events, exhibits, and shows should be kept as authentic as possible. To recreate the culture, organize performances of dance and music using the monument as the backdrop. A light and sound show could be organized in the evening (two shows per day, one in English and one in Hindi). These shows will help narrate and illuminate the site's features and relate important events that took place in the past.

10. Visitors facilities and services in the form of restrooms, restaurants and refreshment stalls, drinking water fountains, umbrellas to protect from the rain and sunshine during the day as the site is large, prams for infants and pushchairs for toddlers, caps, and walking sticks and wheelchairs for the old and infirm should be made available for a nominal refundable deposit at the gate.

11. Landscaped gardens should be created around the monument.

12. The approach road should be well developed with signage and street lights.

13. Souvenir shops should be available to suit all ages and purses. These would be located near the exit of the monuments.

14. Visitor use plan indicating logical access and exit points along with visitor flow should be put up at the site.

15. Continuous monitoring should be done to check visitor satisfaction levels. Feedback forms should be discussed weekly.

16. Sociocultural and environmental impacts because of visitor use should be assessed.

17. For site maintenance and preservation, government agencies like the Archaeological Survey of India should be contacted.
18. Any expansion plan should be in tune with architecture of monuments.
19. There should be continuous management of resources.
20. An entry ticket would be charged which should be nominal for locals and five times the amount for foreigners.
21. Resources would be generated through entry fee, sale of souvenirs, and refreshments which would go towards maintenance of the monument, over head expenses, and cleanliness of visitor facilities.
22. Original, authentic arts and crafts should be priced at higher rates to generate revenue which could be used for promotional campaigns.

If historic moments are to be preserved for our future generations, prompt action is necessary. Overcrowding and overuse of monuments deteriorates the attraction and needs controlling as visitors tend to spoil the monuments and surrounding trees with graffiti leading to loss of precious heritage.

THEME PARKS AS ATTRACTIONS

A theme park is a special type of tourism attraction which is not necessarily related to the natural or cultural resources of a destination. Theme parks are oriented to particular themes such as fantasy, futurism, history, adventure, flora, fauna, unusual geographic places, or a combination of these. They are generally profit making business and have goals that are purely profit driven and provide an income to the owners or shareholders. They not only attract tourists, but also a large number of day visitors including local people.

Theme parks (Fig. 15.3) offer simulated experiences, live shows, thrilling rides, shopping facilities, and a variety of food and beverage outlets for the visitors to choose from. They are a relatively modern concept of developing tourist attractions and are the most popular leisure attractions for families today. All facilities revolve around the central theme of the park.

For example, Walt Disney World's Magic Kingdom in Florida, USA has Mickey Mouse and other Walt Disney characters in costume moving around in all facilities and activities around the massive park. Also available are Mickey Mouse shaped ice creams and snacks, Mickey Mouse

Fig. 15.3 A theme park

fluoroscent stamp for re-entry, Mickey on all souvenirs and articles, etc. all in keeping with the theme.

The Jurong Bird Park and the Night Safari in Singapore are two popular leisure attractions based on birds and wild animals respectively. At the Jurong Bird Park more than 600 species of birds are conserved and displayed in their natural setting. The park offers several theme areas related to the central theme like various bird shows, world's tallest man-made waterfall, a walk-in aviary, an air-conditioned monorail to take visitors around the park, a simulated mid-day thunderstorm followed by a cool light drizzle, the ambience of a rainforest vale of tropical Northern Australia, walk-in exhibits, gift shops, restaurants, information centres, etc. Visitors have the option of becoming members of wildlife unlimited. They are encouraged to take photographs with the birds, the net proceeds of which go to the Birds Research and Conservation Programme (see Fig. 15.4).

Some theme parks are not-for-profit organizations, their main aim being unique visitor experiences which provide entertainment as well as education. A part of the proceeds from such parks go towards conservation of nature.

Hence, a theme park is an extensive, usually commercial, leisure park that may extend over many many hectares of land. It normally includes several theme areas of indoor and outdoor presentations or displays,

Fig. 15.4 A tourist takes home memories of colourful feathered friends

activities and amusements with animation. Added to these attractions are well-developed catering, retail, and other visitor services.

Themes may be historical, geographical, environmental, social, technological, or futuristic and of many other types. They are decided upon to stimulate, educate, and entertain the visitors. Infrastructure costs are high and often accommodation and other tourist facilities are also provided in such parks.

The national or regional tourism plan identifies whether a theme park is appropriate for an area and if so what type and size is suitable. If no plan exists, a special feasibility study for a proposed park has to be conducted. This study examines the market potential; determines type, size, and location of park; analyses its costs, revenues, and financial feasibility. The site for the special attraction itself should be large and often adjacent undeveloped land is an asset to develop related tourist facilities such as accommodation, employee housing, etc.

The infrastructure in terms of road, rail, air, water supply, electric power, sewage and solid waste disposal, telecommunications, safety, security, etc. needs to be studied while planning a theme park. High standards of physical maintenance of the facilities are essential features to be incorporated in the plan.

The location of the theme park is an important criteria which needs careful consideration. Theme park planning cannot be done in isolation but needs to be coordinated with planning of the region. The land in the vicinity of the park can be developed in an integrated manner. Large theme parks can generate considerable development and employment in their regions. Unplanned projects can result in serious environmental problems and discomfort to locals because of shortages of essential commodities and price rise, traffic jams, water scarcity, water accumulation, etc. Walt Disney World's Magic Kingdom in Florida, USA, Ocean Park in Hong Kong are international examples of successful theme park planning. Anand Sagar is a spiritual theme park at Shegaon, Maharashtra; Essel World, Water World Appu Ghar, etc. are other examples of theme parks on a small scale.

The need for planned development of attractions is of utmost importance if they are to remain as attractions in the years to come. Many natural attractions which have developed spontaneously need planned rejuvenation so that they continue to attract tourists and repeat visitors. Unplanned and unregulated tourism has an adverse impact on society, culture, ecology, and the economy in the long run.

Integrated tourism planning which includes proper planning of all aspects such as physical, legal, promotional, financial, economic, marketing management, social, and environmental aspects is the need of the hour. Tourism planning is a complex process which considers the various aspects as well as the segments of the tourism industry. Tourism is an economic activity with everyone from the government to the private sector, locals or host, and the tourists having a stake in it. To reap the benefits of tourism, it is essential that it is planned and managed logically.

SUMMARY

Tourism is growing at a very fast pace and needs planned development if the attractions and destinations have to remain. Natural attractions and cultural attractions need planned conservation. If tourism development is not planned, there will be no tourist attractions for 5 'A's of tourism will attract mass tourists, which has a ravaging effect of the destination if it is not backed by proper planning and management.

Tourism planning and policy formulation is necessary for many reasons and planning should be done at all levels, namely, site, destination, regional, national, and international. The main purposes of planning and managing destinations are environmental conservation, preservation and restoration of heritage sites, sustainable development, enhanced visitor satisfaction, increasing the destination life cycle, promotion and revenue generation. Principles of attraction, planning should be followed such as taking an inventory of all types of attractions both existing and potential, evaluating the quality and quantity of existing attractions, and grouping similar attractions or symbiotic attractions together for capturing a larger market. A feasibility analysis and a cost benefit analysis needs to be done before preparing the final plans. The life expectancy of the attraction should be kept in mind while analysing revenues and costs. On the basis of findings a final plan which will be implemented is prepared. The plan should have a mechanism for monitoring and control and should be approved by the authority.

Theme parks are gaining popularity and are being designed and built at destinations all over the world. They normally have attractions and activities for all age groups. They are planned and developed keeping a particular theme in mind. All attractions need planned development and good management if visitor satisfaction is to be enhanced and repeat visits encouraged.

KEY TERMS

Authenticity That which is genuine or original and not an imitation, made by using local skills and indigenous materials and not produced in a factory on a large scale.

Expenses Costs incurred in connection with the earning of revenue.

Feasibility analysis A detailed study of a project proposal to see whether the project is capable of being carried out and is practicable.

Fixed costs Costs which remain constant, irrespective of the quantum of output within and upto the capacity that has been built, for example, rent.

Heritage properties Properties which provide tangible links between the past, present, and future and is based on the culture and history of the natural and built environment.

Monuments Historical sites such as ancient forts and palaces, memorials, mausoleums, battlefields, and residences of famous personalities, each of which has a story to tell.

Revenue Is the total amount realized from the sale of goods or provision of services, plus any earnings from interest, dividends, or other items of income.

Theme park A special built tourist attraction based on a dominant theme and generally a commercial leisure park spread across a large expanse of land.

Variable costs Costs which vary in direct proportion to the output, i.e. they increase or decrease if output increases or decreases, for example, direct material cost, labour cost, etc.

CONCEPT REVIEW QUESTIONS

1. Why is planned development needed in the tourism industry?
2. List and briefly explain the basic steps to be followed while planning for tourism.
3. Why do attractions need to be planned and managed?
4. At what levels are tourism plans prepared?
5. State the principles of attraction development. On what basis are attractions evaluated?
6. Explain the following terms:

   (a) Feasibility analysis (b) Authenticity
   (c) Cost–benefit analysis (d) Types of costs

CRITICAL THINKING QUESTION

You are given the job of managing an old museum in your locality. How would you go about this task?

PROJECT/ASSIGNMENT

Visit any theme park and make a list of all the attractions and activities available. Find out the most popular attractions in the theme park and the age group they cater to.

REFERENCES

Andrew, S. 2007, *Introduction to Tourism and Hospitality Industry*, Tata McGraw-Hill, New Delhi.

Bhatia A.K. 2001, *International Tourism Management*, Sterling Publishers Pvt Ltd, New Delhi.

Gartner, W.C. 1996, *Tourism Development,Principles, Processes and Policies*, Van Nostrand Reinhold, USA.

George, R. 2007, *Managing Tourism in South Africa*, Oxford University Press Southern Africa, Cape Town.

Ghosh, B. 2000, *Tourism and Travel Management*, Vikas Publishing House Pvt Ltd, New Delhi.

Kaul, R.N. 1985, *Dynamics of Tourism: A Trilogy Vol. III Transportation and Marketing*, Sterling Publishers Pvt Ltd, New Delhi.

Keyser, H. 2002, *Tourism Development*, Oxford University Press Southern Africa, Cape Town.

Seth, P.N. and S.S. Bhat 1993, *An Introduction to Travel and Tourism*, Sterling Publishers Pvt Ltd, New Delhi.

CHAPTER 16

Emerging Trends in Tourism

Learning Objectives

After reading this chapter you should be able to:
- understand the need to keep abreast of the emerging trends in the industry
- know the current changes in all sectors of the industry worldwide
- describe the effects of rapid growth on the aviation sector
- understand the need for formulating a tourism policy
- appreciate the benefits of information and communication technology to the service providers, the customers, and the intermediaries
- discuss the niche tourism forms which are emerging

INTRODUCTION

Tourism is characterized by constant change and development, and trends indicate what will happen in the future. The UNWTO had identified, in the year 1998, trends that will influence global tourism until 2020. It has forecast that international tourism will continue to grow at the average annual rate of 4.3 per cent a year until 2020, while receipts from international tourism will increase by 6.7 per cent a year. The growth of the tourism industry will be rapid in the twenty first century, with one billion international arrivals by 2010 and 1.6 billion international arrivals annually by 2020. Some important points of the forecast are as follows:

- There will be an increase in multiple, relatively short duration trips by travellers from industrialized countries.
- Foreign holidays will become popular amongst people from developing countries.
- Long-haul travel will grow slightly faster than intra-regional travel and will increase from 18 per cent in 1995 to 24 per cent.
- Tourists will be more discerning in their search for quality and value for money, which will influence their choice of destination.
- Environmental consciousness will increase and destination selection will be based on environmental quality.

The UNWTO Tourism 2020 Vision predicts that by 2020, one out of every three trips will be a long haul journey and long haul travel which was 24 per cent of all international tourism in 1995, will increase to 32 per cent by 2020. Europe has been forecast to remain the lead tourism region, followed by East Asia Pacific in second position by 2010. China will be the world's top destination by 2020 and will become the fourth most important tourist generating market.

CHANGING SCENARIO OF THE TOURISM INDUSTRY

Customers are always looking at services that give them a unique experience along with comfort and value for money. With the increasing competition, hotels are redefining the concept of hospitality and are going all out to make the customers stay an exciting, extra special and memorable event. They are pampering travellers with the latest and the best in services and products. Some important trends in tourism are as follows:

- The experienced traveller looks for rare, authentic vacations in remote and less well know places, as against luxurious five star vacations. The trend is towards ethnic and rural tourism.
- The emphasis is on rest, relaxation, health and wellness, especially for tourists with high income and less leisure time.
- Frequency of trips is increasing while travel distance and duration of stay is decreasing and neighbouring country tourism is gaining popularity.

- Tourists have realized the need for something different and nature specific featuring premium holidays and select destinations.
- The high-end luxury traveller looks for spa facilities, luxury cruises, wild life safaris, premium holiday packages, wellness holidays, spiritual getaways etc.
- Travel agents and tour operators are focusing on FIT and students as the GIT market is quite saturated and on MICE and SMERFs.
- Incentive travel schemes to employees, distributors, and associates to recognize and award performance are on the rise. Incentive travel now includes exotic and unusual locales such as bush-dinners in Africa, a private Jet tour over the cliffs of Grand Canyon, a helicopter ride over the Twelve Apostles in Melbourne, a music extravaganza at the Paradis Latin in Paris, etc.
- Tourist products include special interest products and niche products such as tours to the North Pole and Antarctica and musical cruises, exclusive spas and luxury yachts in Greek waters, cultural tourism in Leh and Ladakh.

More entertainment options are being offered to tourists at the destination. Some are discussed as follows:

Casinos Casinos are the mainstay of the economies of Las Vegas, Macau, and Monte Carlo. Gambling Tourism is being promoted by simplifying entry procedures at such destinations. For example, no visa is required for Indian visitors at Macau.

Sound and light shows Superior quality light and sound shows are being organized at historical sites to help the tourist to re-live the events of the past. For example, the mesmerizing 50 minute Son-et-Lumiere spectacle at the Khajurao temples' western complex, evokes the life and times of the great Chandela kings and traces the story of the unique temples from the tenth century to the present day.

Human-made attractions Human-made attractions and clusters of attractions are popular and cater to the expectations of a diverse age group and social background, for example, Sentosa Island Resort in Singapore.

Tourism clusters between 100 and 500 acres located up to 150 kilometres from cities, which are primarily designed for domestic tourists for weekend breaks with family, will also serve to attract international tourists. The facilities and attractions may have hotels, restaurants, skating rinks, lakes with boating and sailing facilities, golf courses, tennis courts, and indoor games.

SMERFs

The dominant segment of MICE travellers is facing competition from a fast emerging segment to and around Asia, who travel for social, military, education, religious, and fraternity reasons (SMERFs). The SMERFs are the resilient groups, who are budget conscious and do not mind gathering during non-peak times if expenses can be saved. The SMERFs collectively form a huge market and have vast untapped potential for the developing or recovering Asian travel markets. SMERFs travel for a purpose and not just to see places. They are willing to travel abroad despite the economic cycle, travel off-season and off the beaten track to save on transport and accommodation. Social travel includes people participating in sports teams, talent and dance organizations, or as volunteer workers for events, etc. Asia's military needs civilian transport for its estimated 32 million soldiers on the move and thier proceeding on leave itself is a highly significant market. The education travel market specially studying or visiting Singapore as part of a study tour has tremendous potential. The Singapore Tourism Board is targeting 1,50,000 international students particularly from Asia by 2015. Indian students are discovering India's cultural heritage and school groups are emerging as a valuable market because of repeat tours. Asia is recognized as the birthplace of Hinduism and Buddhism and religious tourism is on the rise. The government's policy to develop joint tourist attractions such as the Buddhist circuit in Taiwan, China, Sri Lanka, and India has increased. Pilgrimages are being organized for inbound tourists usually for more than one destination. India has well-established tour operators to cater to both domestic and foreign tourists. Fraternal travel, though not as significant as educational or religious travel, is considering Asia as a possible destination for international gatherings. Fraternal groups include Rotary International, Lions Club International, etc. which are large groups. As SMERFs are not high spenders, SMERF planners can look for second and third-tier cities.

TOURISTS WITH SPECIAL NEEDS AND THE DIFFERENTLY-ABLED TOURIST

Senior citizens are a growing segment of the travelling public and often need wheel chairs, walkers, canes, or crutches. Many international destinations are friendly towards these travellers. In India, some hotels and tourist spots have facilities for the disabled, mostly out of compulsion and not because of genuine concern. Awareness for the need of accessibility for all including the disabled and making the destination disabled-friendly can be done by providing

- ramps for wheel chairs instead of steps;
- escalators in shopping areas;
- braille on elevator panels, restrooms, and directional signs;
- telephones with flashing lights for hearing impaired;
- wash areas and toilets which can accommodate wheel chairs and have extra railings;
- ambulifts at airports;
- disabled-friendly transport such as buses and trains for a person on wheel chair;
- seperate counters for disabled travellers;
- designated parking facilities;
- attitudinal change in service providers and the public;
- soft skills training on how to transfer guests with mobility problems, how to speak to the disabled depending on the nature of the disability, for example, one should not shout while talking to guests with hearing impairment; and
- assistance services at destination.

Differently-abled or disabled tourists with special needs should have accessibility to most destinations. For example, Vivekananda Rock Memorial in Kanyakumari has been redesigned to suit the needs of the disabled during its recent renovation. Basilica of Bom Jesus at Goa has wheel chair facility available at the church.

Anand Sagar of Shri Gajanan Maharaj Sansthan, at Shegaon in Maharashtra has been designed keeping the needy, old, infirm, and disabled in mind.

EMERGING TYPES OF TOURISM

Many new forms and types of tourism are being developed to meet the needs of the growing tourist market. All forms of innovation in tourism are being promoted keeping specific needs of different tourism in mind such as culinary tourism, tea tourism, film tourism, highway tourism, etc. Some of the emerging forms are discussed in this chapter at length while the reader is just introduced to the other forms.

Cruise Tourism

Cruising to exotic locales in different parts of the world is no longer a niche activity limited to the upper echelons of society. Refer to Chapter 5 for details on cruise liners. The cruising culture has spread from Europe and the Americas to India. Cruise holidays on luxury floating resorts are gaining popularity as cruise operators are offering affordable packages for all budgets ranging from one day to a number of days for all age groups. The cruise tourism industry in the country is set to witness an over three-fold rise by 2010 as number of domestic and international passengers at Indian ports is expected to increase to 600,000 a year by 2010 from the current 180,000. Besides, number of domestic and international cruise liners entering Indian ports is also growing as the country is emerging as a major destination for cruise tourism, according to the study, 'Developing Ports as Cruise Tourism Hubs in India', by FICCI—Evalueserve.

In 2007–08, about 54 cruise companies including international players sought permission to enter the circuit in India, the study said. If the government focuses on developing physical infrastructure, streamlining immigration and custom checks processes and takes recourse to viability gap funding in building infrastructure, the country's tourism industry could see a three-fold increase in the domestic and international cruise passengers.

A cruise policy formulated by the Ministry of Tourism, India is soon to be implemented and is expected to boost international cruise business in the country. The only international cruise company that is presently functional on the Indian coast is Ocean Cruises India.

The entire cruise development plan which includes building infrastructure such as new passenger and cruise terminals is scheduled to be activated through public–private partnership mode. It is proposed that cruise operators get some concessions in income tax, excise duty, customs duty, corporate tax and service tax, and other benefits to increase passenger landings.

Floating Luxury Hotel

QE2, the famous 70,000 tonne luxury ocean cruise liner which was launched in 1967 by the Queen of England, will soon become a luxury floating hotel.

The ship has been purchased by Dubai World Company, which also owns the P & O Shipping Company. The ship will be berthed at a specially constructed pier at luxury Palm Jumeriah, the world's largest human-made island.

Heritage Walks

This is a new trend which is eco-friendly and is gathering momentum in India. A two-hour guided heritage walk to study the history which is reflected in the architecture, local way of living, craft, and culture of old parts of city untouched by urbanization is being popularized by the State of Gujarat at Ahmedabad and by other states too. Dwelling owners are being given financial assistance to preserve their properties.

Spiritual Tourism

Spiritual tourism is one of the most popular forms of tourism today. It is also called pilgrimage or religious tourism and involves travel to religious places for spiritual benefit. Many people today follow the path of their gurus, and find solace in their preaching and discourses. Tour operators are developing special packages for the spiritual tourists.

Floating spiritual villages in the tranquil backwaters of Kerala, offer corporate executives an unforgettable experience and choice of spiritual and health therapies and discourses from spiritual gurus, all inside houseboats and floating cottages.

Space Tourism

One of the most advanced technological developments to be witnessed by humankind and one of the costliest types of tourism, is a trip to space which at present costs approximately USD 20 million. Space tourism as defined by the Space Tourism Society covers

- travel to the earth's orbit and sub-orbit;
- travel to planets beyond the earth's orbit, for example, to Mars;
- earth-based simulated experiences at NASA centre and entertainment based experiences; and
- cyber space tourism experiences.

Some of the companies promoting space tourism are Virgin Galactic, Space Adventures, Starchaser, Blue Origin, Bigelow Aerospace, etc.

Space tourism will give the space tourist the unique and thrilling experience of viewing the earth from outer space. More affordable sub-orbital flights are currently priced at USD 2 million, flying at an altitude of 100 to 160 kilometres in space and letting the tourists experience weightlessness for a few minutes, be amongst the stars, and view the curved earth below.

Space Adventures Ltd is working on circumlunar missions to the moon at a passenger price of USD 100,000,000. Space stations are being set up and old space stations are being converted to space hotels. Bigelow Aerospace has launched the first inflatable model called Genesis I in July 2006 and Genesis II in June 2007.

The first commercial space station is scheduled be set up by year 2010. Orbital and sub-orbital space tourism is intended for the rich and famous and although the cost of a flight may reduce, it seems it will be ill afforded by the common man.

Underwater Tourism

The deep seas have always been an attraction for tourists whether it is fun and frolic on the beach, viewing the coral reefs on the seabed or marine creatures in ocean parks. The latest addition to deep sea attractions are restaurants and hotels submerged in the sea. The Hydropolis in Quingdao, China is a hotel under the Yellow Sea, which is scheduled to open sometime in 2009, and will offer rates comparable to five star hotels.

Another hydropolis under construction is the 220 suite, luxurious underwater hotel in Dubai situated 60 feet beneath the Persian Gulf. In keeping with the theme, the hotel will be shaped like a jelly fish with bubble-shaped suites and will be connected to land via a submerged transparent train tunnel.

The Jules Undersea Lodge at Key Largo, Florida which was once an authentic underwater research station, now offers overnight packages to tourists from 13:00 hours to 10:00 hours at USD 475 which include diving gear, a gourmet dinner, and breakfast. The access to the hotel is via scuba diving 21 feet below the surface of the sea.

Underwater tourism also includes visiting wreckages of famous ocean liners which lie deep down on the ocean bed and travelling in submarines to study the marvels of the water kingdom.

Perpetual Tourism

This is a term used to describe people who are perpetually on the move and stay in one country for a set period of time only so that they can avoid the legal obligations which arise out of permanent residency, for example, paying of income tax which is mandatory if a person stays for 122 days in one country. They adopt this lifestyle to be free from the laws that govern citizens of a country.

Perpetual travellers (PTs) are people who live in such a way that they are not considered legal residents of any of the countries in which they spend time. By lacking a legal permanent residence status, they seek to avoid the legal obligations which may accompany residency, such as income and asset taxes, jury duty, and military service. For example, while PTs may hold citizenship in one or more countries that impose taxes based solely on residency, their legal residence will most likely be in a tax haven. PTs may spend the majority of their time in other countries, never staying long enough to be considered as residents.

Virtual Tourism

This allows a tourist to visit a destination sitting comfortably in an arm chair, confined to the home. Virtual reality helps them to explore different regions of the world, visit sites without having to book tickets, apply for visas or spend money, i.e. without having to physically travel.

It is a boon to those who do not get an opportunity to travel or do not have the time and money to travel.

It also helps tourists wishing to travel, to decide on a destination for a holiday and shows them what they can expect to see. Technology is used to take tourists on a panoramic tour to give an all-round unbroken view of the destination, which makes them virtually feel they are at the place. People are made to sit in the centre of a dome-shaped room which has screens all around. The Internet, multimedia packages, and the television along with travel literature are used for the virtual experience.

Dark Tourism

Dark tourism or black tourism is a pilgrimage to places where people gave up their life for the nation or where famous personalities breathed their last. The Cellular Jail at Port Blair, the death site of St. Peter in Rome, the crash site where Princess Diana lost her life, the Nazi holocaust, World War II sites, etc. are places people visit to pay homage to the departed souls or are curious to see.

Disaster Tourism

Tourism professionals are cashing in on destruction caused by various disasters to satisfy the curiosity of people to witness the extent of damage caused by various natural and human-made disasters by organizing guided bus tours to such sites. Prominent among such sites are Ground Zero in New York, where the twin towers of World Trade Center were razed to the ground following the 9/11 terrorist attack, the sites of destruction which bore the brunt of the 2004 tsunami and Hurricane Katrina, etc.

Extreme Tourism

This involves travelling to risky places or participating in dangerous events. This is a niche tourism product for the physically fit, daredevil tourist who is aware of the risk, yet is inclined to experience what majority tourists would not dare to imagine and includes ice diving in the White Sea, trekking through dense jungles, etc. Some types of niche tourism are shown in Exhibit 16.1.

Exhibit 16.1 Some niche tourism types

Type/form	Description
Accessible tourism	The ongoing effort to make all tourist locations accessible to people from all walks of life, regardless of their state of health, age, or disability.
Arctic and Antarctic tourism	Trips to the South Pole and North Pole are being promoted by tour operators. It includes visits to pristine landscapes to watch birds, marine mammals, and polar bears. Helps increase awareness about the sensitive environment, leading to its preservation.
Ancestry tourism	Also known as 'genealogy tourism', it is travel undertaken with the aim of tracing one's ancestry, visiting the birthplace of one's ancestors and going back to one's roots.
Cycle tourism	Includes trips to places of tourist interest either overnight or excursions in which leisure cycling is a fundamental and major part of the visit. It is gaining popularity because of increased awareness about the need to preserve one's health and the environment.
Dark tourism	Also called 'black tourism' or 'grief tourism', it includes visits to sites associated with death, suffering, and disaster such as visits to battlefields, prisons and the notorious Nazi extermination camp at Auschwitz in Poland.
Ecotourism	Ecological tourism is a form of minimum impact tourism that appeals to ecologically and socially conscious individuals and includes travel to natural areas where flora, fauna, and cultural heritage are the primary attractions.

Contd

Exhibit 16.1 Contd

Type/form	Description
Film tourism	Includes visits to locations where films are made or where television serials are in production. People travel to gain information on filmmaking, to attend film festivals and fan events around the world.
Food tourism	Food and beverage are vital components of the tourism experience. It is travel to various destinations to gain a unique insight into food and beverages served, experience different food customs, visit food festivals, culinary schools, or spice gardens.
Gay tourism	Also known as 'pink tourism' or 'LGBT tourism', it is a form of niche tourism marketed to gay, lesbian, bisexual, and transgender people to travel to LGBT-friendly destinations or people wanting to travel with other LGBT people. Gay tourism is at its peak during special gay events such as annual gay pride parades, gay neighbourhood festivals, or gay games.
Hedonistic tourism	Travel by the self-indulgent in pursuit of physical pleasure and social life.
Jazz tourism	It is a form of tourism for Jazz music lovers and include musical concerts delivering the very best in Jazz.
Life-seeing tourism	This form of tourism involves indulging in purposeful activities that match the tourist's interests and actually seeing the area for life's enrichment and not only experiencing the high points of a given location. Generally travel is undertaken during off season.
Moral tourism	Travellers who strive to do no harm and respect traditions and taboos of the host are morally driven, are environmentalists and human rights activists, and are called moral tourists. They do not take souvenirs from the environment but pick up litter and believe in taking photographs and leave only footprints behind.
Off-beat tourism	Travel to off-beat destinations to enjoy fascinating sights not mentioned in tourist books or visits to relatively newer fields such as ayurvedic villages, travel for yoga therapy, etc.
Research tourism	This is travel undertaken for discovering, interpreting, and developing methods and systems for the advancement of human knowledge on a wide variety of disciplines.
Shock tourism	Also called 'extreme tourism', it includes travel to dangerous places or participation in dangerous events like travelling across the Chernobyl zone or ice diving in the White Sea. This form of tourism is popular in Russia, Peru, Chile, Argentina, and North Pakistan.
Tribal tourism	Travel to explore the striking features of tribal life around the world is gaining popularity. India, Africa, and Latin America are major destinations. India has 577 tribes mainly in Chattisgarh, Jharkhand, northeastern states, and Andaman and Nicobar Islands. People travel to witness tribal festivals, rituals and weddings, and also to study the flora and fauna of the states.

Contd

Exhibit 16.1 Contd

Type/form	Description
Volunteer tourism	This form of tourism gives people an opportunity to have a holiday as well as work on social and conservation projects. These tourists get the satisfaction of contributing to a worthwhile project, experience new activities and enhance their skills. Volunteer tourists are hardworking, dedicated, and committed.
Wedding tourism	This form of tourism is on the rise in India and tour operators are packaging special wedding tours. India lures young couples to celebrate their wedding in grandeur and magnificence in true Indian style. The opulent wedding celebrations which last for several days are a treasure trove of our culture and traditions.
Wine tourism	Travel undertaken for tasting, consumption, or purchase of wine often at or near the source. It includes travel to wine regions around the world, visits to wineries, wine stomping, wine festivals, wine tours, visits to vineyards and to restaurants who offer unique vintage wines.

PRESENT ACCOMMODATION SCENARIO

There is a shortfall in tourism accommodation in our country. The number of rooms in hotels in star category approved by the Ministry of Tourism, India was 1,00,000 at the end of 2006–07 of which 30 per cent were five star/five star deluxe category. A shortfall is one of the reasons for an unprecedented increase in room tariff making it unaffordable for the upper middle class leisure traveller and the MICE segment as well. By the year 2010 India is anticipating 10 million international tourists. The estimated shortfall in tourist accommodation in the country will be 150,000 rooms of which 100,000 will be in the budget category or the no-frills hotels. Land prices and shortage of land for budget hotels has been identified as one of the main reasons for this deficit, especially in metros where the land cost may amount to 30 to 50 per cent of the project cost against the international norm of 10 to 15 per cent.

Measures taken by the Central/State Government

To overcome the shortfall in tourist accommodation, the Government has recommended the following seven measures:

1. Land use conversions within city limits, for example, from agricultural, institutional, or residential use to hotel use.
2. Allowing a higher floor area ratio (FAR) in areas of no congestion with compulsory underground parking.

3. Giving land on long term lease or revenue-sharing basis. For example, at Uttarakhand under the public–private partnership (PPP) the Uttarakhand Tourism has entered into a collaboration with hospitality major Emaar MGF to develop an international standard 200-room five star hotel and state-of-the-art convention centre for 1200 people in Dehradun, the state capital.

    The project under the build-operate-transfer model will be set up at a cost of Rs 200 crores on a ten acre plot owned by the State Government. The land has been handed over to Emaar MGF on a 30 year lease and the group will hand over the hotel to the State Government after the expiry of the lease term. The State Government hopes to earn Rs 7 crore a year from the hotel project through two per cent revenue-sharing and lease rent.

4. Additional land near many of the 48 non-metro airports and two metro airports will be made available for hotel construction of PPP.

5. Hotels and hotel-like properties of state government corporations which are being run at suboptimum levels or at a loss could be given to professional private sector hoteliers on the basis of international competitive bidding.

6. Adoption of single window clearance of hotel projects.

7. Encouragement of the bed and breakfast schemes whereby owners of suitable residential accommodation are registered for offering accommodation to tourists and are treated as non-commercial activity. They are given tax concessions such as relief from luxury tax and VAT and are charged residential rates for electricity and water supply.

TOURISM DISTRIBUTION SYSTEMS

There has been a marked change in the distribution of tourism offerings in the past few years as new technology has enabled consumers to directly access the tourism product. The tourism distribution systems are discussed in the following section.

Information and Communication Technology

Every minute of the day, there are changes and developments in inform-ation technology. Information and communication technology (ICT) has changed the business of selling travel and travel agents will need to change with the times if they wish to remain in business.

Travel distribution has been most affected by information and communication technology. Prior to the advent of ICT, making reservation was a tedious process. Travel agents had to phone different airlines, hotels, etc. to check the availability of seats and rooms and the fares and tariffs. This information had to be conveyed to the customer, who would then decide and inform the agent and the agent in turn would then phone and make the booking. If the hotel was located abroad, communication was via telex or fax as making international calls was very costly. Today, Internet-based booking systems, with their facilities to search, compare, and buy tourism offerings, have revolutionized the tourism industry. It has now become simple for consumers to purchase full package holidays via the Internet without approaching the travel agent. Nowadays, both the principal supplier as well as the customer has a wide choice of distribution methods to choose from, ranging from travel agencies, virtual or online travel agencies, Internet, call centres, tourist information offices, electronic point of sales (EPOS) systems, supermarkets, sales representatives, destination management companies, and travel clubs.

Traditional travel agents need to compete by developing specialized knowledge to maintain their competitive edge. ICT has provided both benefits and threats to travel agencies.

Benefits

It has helped travel agents by simplifying reservation procedures by providing fast and efficient service, choice of fares and seats and almost instant confirmations, increased access to information, computerized data bases of customers, efficient billing and ticketing systems, compiling reports, preparing complicated travel itineraries, etc. as well as letting them have an online presence of their own.

With ICT, travel agents can give their customers a virtual tour of the destination, before finalizing the tour. Tourism destination websites can be accessed to get customized information on the destination chosen like pictures of hotels, tourist attractions, weather conditions, passports, visas and health requirements, etc.

Threats

Traditional travel agents are threatened by the competition which has arisen because Internet access has given the customer direct contact with the tourism suppliers such as airlines, hotels, tour operators, etc. Travel agents and tour operators now have to compete with new forms of business-to-consumer technology such as e-tickets and ticketless travel where passengers are not issued a coupon or ticket but only a reference number. These technologies are bypassing both the travel agent and the airline global distribution system (GDS) and selling directly to consumers. Airlines are opting for these technologies as they help reduce costs and speed up the check-in processes.

Developments in ICT has helped in getting the product out to the consumers in the most effective and economical manner.

Global Distribution Systems

The global distribution system (GDS) is a computer reservation and information system that is often operated by multiple airlines, used by travel agents and other travel professionals. It contains information on all types of travel products like hotels, airlines, insurance, etc. The GDS connects the principal suppliers and the travel agents. It checks the availability of services, makes bookings and is capable of printing tickets through a printer in the office.

GDSs link all parts of the distribution system, i.e. airlines, travel agencies, car rental companies, and hotel chains. They offer easy access and enable users to book their complete package of requirements from airline tickets, accommodation, car hire, etc. using one computer terminal and Windows operating system. A Windows-based program on a personal computer helps the user to move from Word into the GDS and back without changing computers. The user can move from one window to another without having to sign off from one program to access another.

The GDS network

The personal computer in the travel agency is linked to other personal computers in the office by cables, phone lines, or fiber optics to form a computer network. Computers in a network can exchange and share information as well as a printer. The personal computer receives and sends information to and from the GDS.

The GDS is a central computer that comprises of a huge database along with system and application software. This central computer is connected to various public and private networks. Every computer/ terminal that is on these networks can communicate with the GDS via several different interfaces. Figure 16.1 shows us how systems are accessed.

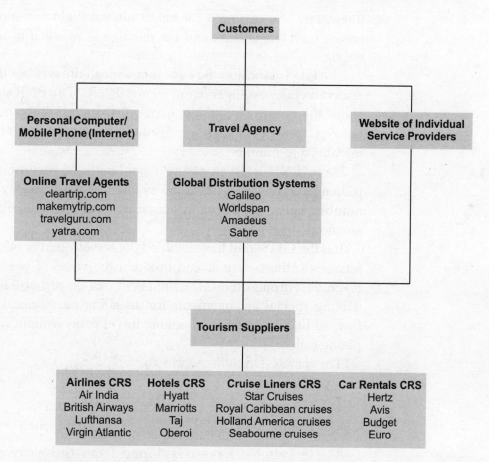

Fig.16.1 GDS networks
Courtesy: Rohit Sanas

These interfaces establish user-friendly dialogue with the GDS through graphical representation of data. For example, a customer may request information of all flights between Mumbai and Delhi on a particular day that departs from Mumbai between 08:00 hours and 10:00 hours. The interface he/she chooses may be a travel website which he/she accesses through a web browser, for example, Internet Explorer, Mozilla, Firefox, Opera, etc. He/she submits his/her query by entering the above information on a simple data entry form. The GDS replies to his/her query by providing information which will be displayed by the interface in the form of a report showing all available flights. The interface may allow the user to sort the list of available flights by fare of ticket, time of travel, etc. The customer can select his/her flight and if required hotel, cruise, travel insurance, and car rental, and proceed to book the same online.

The GDS associates the customer with all the services that he/she has reserved via a passenger name record (PNR). The PNR stores all details about the customer like last name, first name, title, address, services booked, credit card number, details of travel agent, and frequent flier membership number.

Every PNR is given a single booking reference number after the passenger's reservation details have been closed and saved. This PNR number helps the agent in accessing passenger details and making amendments if necessary.

It is the GDSs that have enabled the travel agent to offer a bouquet of services to the customer and broaden the vistas of business as well as revenue. Through the GDS the agent can do just about anything like making special arrangements for an ailing passenger, creating a full-fledged FIT itinerary, or changing travel dates without making a single phone call.

The main GDS in the world are

- Galileo
- Abacus
- Apollo
- Sabre
- Amadeus
- Worldspan

These systems have developed from the early computerized reservation systems (CRS) which were developed by airlines to solve their problem of handling reservations manually. The first CRS was introduced in 1976 by United Airlines and Apollo was installed in travel agencies. By 1987, CRS was installed by practically all the travel agencies in the USA.

Since 1987, large CRS have extended their products and services and changed into world wide or GDS.

Today, principal suppliers have their own CRS and are linked to one or more of the GDSs. After a number of alliances and mergers with several cross-ownerships there are six main GDSs as mentioned above.

ONLINE TRAVEL AGENTS

They are the new breed of virtual travel agents who are taking over a major share of reservations online and offline from the traditional travel

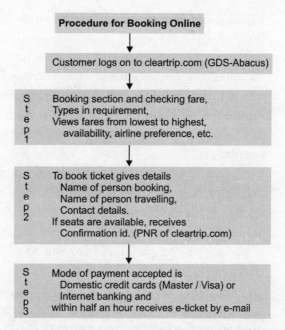

Procedure for Booking Online

↓

Customer logs on to cleartrip.com (GDS-Abacus)

↓

Step 1
Booking section and checking fare,
Types in requirement,
Views fares from lowest to highest,
   availability, airline preference, etc.

↓

Step 2
To book ticket gives details
   Name of person booking,
   Name of person travelling,
   Contact details.
If seats are available, receives
   Confirmation id. (PNR of cleartrip.com)

↓

Step 3
Mode of payment accepted is
   Domestic credit cards (Master / Visa) or
   Internet banking and
within half an hour receives e-ticket by e-mail

Fig. 16.2 Three basic steps in booking tickets online

agents. They account for approximately 30 per cent bookings on GDS, mainly of domestic air tickets.

Domestic ticketing is predicted to be mainly online because of e-ticketing. Some popular online travel agents (OTAs) are cleartrip.com, makemytrip.com, yatra.com, arzoo.com, akbartravelsonline.com, travelguru.com, etc. Figure 16.2 shows the basic steps in booking tickets online.

If there is any change in fare between booking the ticket and making the payment, the OTA contacts the customer regarding the increase in fare by e-mail to check if increased fare is acceptable.

THE ZERO PER CENT COMMISSION ERA

Airline companies were initially paying travel agents a commission on airline tickets which was nine per cent then reduced to seven per cent and five per cent in 2005 and proposed zero percent commission from 1 October 2008. The national carrier issued a written statement to all agents associations announcing its decision to move to nil commission effective 1 October 2008. Jet Airways and Kingfisher Airlines have also taken the same decision. While the proposal for zero per cent commission has been submitted, a few international airlines are still paying a five percent commission to travel agencies, but how long this situation will continue is debatable.

In a move to control costs, airlines have decided to decommission the travel agent. The agents are the primary distributors of the airlines and this decision has led to a strained relationship between the two parties. Travel agents depend on the airlines' commission for their existence and this decision will have a drastic effect, especially for the small ticketing agents.

Travel agents play a vital role in promoting and selling airline products and approximately 80 per cent of airline tickets are distributed through agents. With the nil commission decision, travel agents have united and associations are discussing strategies and considering boycotting booking of air tickets completely. However, in the talks between the airline and the travel agent, the GDS which connects the two also needs to strategize and convince the travel agents to continue booking tickets on their platform, otherwise their revenue earnings would decrease as the airlines are paying the GDSs a minimum of USD 4 as distribution fees per flight segment. The GDSs have the advantage of providing a single point of sale, where agents can contact different airlines without the need to search across various airline portals. This not only saves valuable time and costs but also increases efficiency.

The GDS does not depend only on airlines as it has non-air segments like hotels, trains, and car rentals. In the hospitality sector the GDS Galileo has 220 hotel chain codes with over 77,000 hotel properties, of which over 30,000 properties have best available rates. The commission offered to the agent for buying non-air inventory over the GDS for hotel rooms are ten per cent and hotel bookings may be for a couple of days, which amounts to a substantial figure.

Even if airlines do not pay the travel agent for booking airline tickets, they would still be required for the other services such as booking cruises, hotel accommodation, car rentals, etc. and giving that personal touch to travel.

India has witnessed a rapid growth of tourism in the new millenium with tourist arrivals and foreign exchange earnings going up steadily. The World Travel and Tourism Council had rated India as one of the five fastest growing tourism economies of the world. A survey conducted by 'Conde Nast Traveller' reveals that India is preferred to many other tourist destinations like France, Singapore, and Switzerland.

National Trends

Due to the global economic meltdown and terror attacks, the tourism industry has faced rough weather, but people are still travelling to India.

According to initial figures prepared by the Union Ministry of Tourism (MoT), there has been a six to eight per cent jump in foreign tourist arrivals in 2008 over the corresponding year 2007. In 2008 the tourist arrivals to the country were 5.3 million as compared to 5.08 million in 2007. Foreign exchange earnings from this sector also showed a growth of eight per cent at USD 11.5 billion in 2008 as against USD 10.70 billion registered in 2007. There has been an increase in traffic to the tune of 75 per cent with employment generation up by more than 43 per cent between 2002 and 2007. It is estimated that more than USD 6.5 billion of investment has already come for the construction of new star hotels.

While the shortage of rooms in major metros is adversely affecting the flow of tourists to the cities, construction of approximately 14,656 rooms for the Commonwealth Games 2010 in Delhi is in process.

Several countries have transformed their economies by developing their tourism potential. The Indian economy is undergoing a major transformation and with an annual growth of eight per cent, India has become the second most favoured destination for foreign direct investment (FDI). The government has recognized the enormous potential of tourism for contributing to economic growth and the manifold benefits which accrue from planned tourism development (see Chapter 14).

In the Eleventh Five Year Plan, the working group on tourism has recommended a target of 10 million international arrivals by 2011. However, in its vision document, the Ministry of Tourism forecasts the achievement of this target by 2010, the present figures of international arrivals being five million international arrivals. To achieve the target of ten million arrivals, the principal source markets will be diversified, infrastructural facilities such as airports, roads, civic amenities at tourist destinations will be improved, air seat capacity and connectivity will be increased and their will be huge publicity campaigns.

The principal source markets would include Israel, Spain, China, Japan, South Korea, Australia, Brazil, Argentina, etc. which offer high growth potential. The plain also stresses on the need to concentrate on countries with a large Indian population such as South Africa, Mauritius, Kenya, Malaysia, Fiji, etc. for higher tourist arrivals from these countries.

The baby boomers group in North America and Europe would be targeted and encouraged to visit India by fostering in them the desire to enjoy diverse cultures and discover one of world's oldest civilizations.

State tourism development corporations are framing their tourism policy and strategies to promote tourism in their respective states.

For example, the state of Jharkhand is planning an aggressive strategy to overhaul its entire setup, to promote itself as a strong destination for tourism. The state is planning to launch a portal for its department of tourism, which will possess detailed information about districts, cuisine, special tourist destinations, art, and culture. This unique site will provide communication points, road, and rail routes with maps for tourists. Adventure tourism like aero-sports, toy trains, and other activities has also been planned. The state is also planning to install a strong International Tourism Management System (ITMIS) which will aim at offering a platform for an internal messaging system. All tourism-related information will be stored and be easily accessible like acts and policies, land acquisitions, tourist analysis data, etc.

TRAVEL INDUSTRY TRENDS

The business environment in the travel industry is constantly changing. Some of the trends which are likely to change the structure of the tourism industry and the way in which tourism businesses interact are as follows:

Disintermediation

This trend affects the travel distribution system and means elimination of the intermediaries, i.e. the traditional travel agent from the distribution chain. With the advances in ICT, giving customers direct access to travel information to make their own travel arrangements, OTAs, and e-ticketing are a threat to the travel agent. Adapting to new technologies and using them correctly is a challenge which agencies have to take up.

Decommissioning of the travel agent by the airlines and travel agents having to charge a service fee to the customers as they will not be receiving any commission from airlines, may lead to the following two trends:

1. Customers may book tickets directly from the airline's website to save on paying service fee to the travel agent.
2. Corporate executives who need a seat at short notice and change travel plans more frequently than leisure travellers will still book tickets through the travel agent as they are not worried about costs and do not have sufficient time to spend booking their own travel.

The personal interaction with the travel agent cannot be replaced by the impersonal bookings via the Internet.

Integration

Because of increasing competition amongst principal suppliers in the tourism industry, tourism businesses form links with other companies in order to survive and take over the competitors. Integration is an economic concept that describes the formal linking arrangements between organizations.

Linking may take place vertically or horizontally between organizations in the distribution system (Fig. 16.3).

Horizontal integration

It takes place when two similar organizations such as two airlines merge and or are amalgamated or where one is taken over and absorbed by the other. Such integration helps the airline to gain a wider market share of the airline sector and helps reduce operating costs by sharing of administration offices.

Vertical integration

Vertical integration takes place when an organization at one level of the distribution chain links with an organization at another level (see Fig.16.3). For example, if a tour operator buys its own hotel or an airline acquires

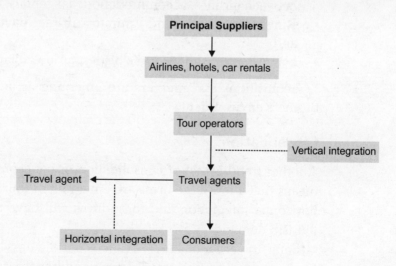

Fig. 16.3 The distribution channel in tourism

its own tour operations company. This type of integration helps in expanding tourism business by offering a wider range of products and services. It also helps in gaining control over more elements of the tourism supply chain like if a tour operator owns and operates its own hotel, it can ensure availability of rooms, reasonable room tariff, quality of supplies, and quality of service in a better way.

Vertical integration is called forward when a business links with another business one level down or closer to the customer, for example, the airline acquiring its own tour operator. It is called backward integration when links are formed one level up like in the case of the tour operator buying its own hotel.

Integration includes links such as mergers, acquisitions, takeovers, alliances and generally results in change of ownership. Strategic alliances give the organization added opportunities for rapid growth and global presence which an individual organization may find difficult to achieve.

Integration does not necessarily involve ownership. For example, in a merger, a company may take over and combine the operations of another business with its own operations. The two companies combine to form one corporate structure that retains its original identity like Air India and Indian Airlines merging to form NACIL.

Integration can also mean that businesses agree to work together and form alliances. For example,

- the frequent flyer programme involves cooperation agreements between airlines, accommodation, car rentals, florists, etc.;
- Kingfisher Airlines and Emirates Airlines have formed an alliance; and
- Star Alliance is the world's biggest airline alliance.

Acquisitions and mergers are emerging as an integral part of the business environment.

Consolidation

Another trend is that of consolidation or concentration. Concentration means that a few large firms are emerging in tourism globally, through horizontal integration and these firms will have the majority share of tourism demand.

Some travel companies are called consolidators because they combine bookings from several travel agents and benefit from group fares.

TRENDS IN THE AVIATION INDUSTRY

Trends in the aviation industry include the following:

Bilateral Agreements

This is an older trend. It is an agreement concerning relationships between two countries in which they agree on reciprocal privileges not extended to others. For example, India has entered into bilateral agreements with Indonesia's national carrier, Garuda Indonesia. However, the need of the hour is liberalization of traffic to prevent fragmentation in the industry.

Code Sharing Agreements

This involves use of the same airline identification code for two or more sectors which may be operated by different airlines, designed to promote the use of airlines for connecting flights.

Interline Agreements

These are agreements between two or more airlines/carriers which enable one carrier to include the services of another carrier in its tickets and to share the revenue. Air Astana, the national carrier of the Republic of Kazakhstan has entered into an interline agreement with Indian domestic carrier Kingfisher Airlines on a pro-rata fare basis. Both airlines will help promote each other's country as a tourism destination.

Joint Ventures

A joint venture is a contractual agreement in which two or more separate parties are involved in the joint ownership of business units, joint participation in financial outcome, and also management and operation of the venture.

Public–private Partnership

We have already read about public–private partnerships (PPP) earlier in this chapter. It is essential to attract investment in the tourism sector in order to upgrade infrastructure facilities as well as to market tourism destinations. Many tourist destinations all over the world have been privatized and are running successfully. The model of PPP should be suitably applied to tourist destinations in all states and union territories in India.

The privatization policy will help tourism in the following respects:

- It will develop the destination as a tourist centre and provide necessary amenities.
- It will help to preserve our heritage and culture which require considerable resources.
- The private investor will work to promote the destination in order to recover his investment. This will boost marketing of the destinations in India.

For example, the Uttarakhand government encourages private sector participation in the development of infrastructure projects including special economic zones, food parks, theme parks, tourism destinations, roads, airports, civic infrastructure, etc. (see Exhibit 16.2).

DEVELOPMENTS IN AVIATION

India's civil aviation sector has witnessed a meteoric boom over the last few years. With the sudden and breakneck growth in aviation, many

Exhibit 16.2 Tourism industry in Uttarakhand

The state of Uttarakhand has accorded tourism the status of 'thrust industry' and offers many opportunities for development of tourism and related activities and services. It is the first state in India to have created a tourism development board by legislation as the highest body to function as promoter, adviser, regulator, and licencing authority for tourism in the state.

The Ministry of Commerce and Industry, Government of India has announced a concessional industrial package for the state of Uttarakhand. The list of thrust industries which can avail of incentives for their new projects include the following:

- ecotourism
- hotels, resorts, and spas
- entertainment/amusement parks
- rope ways

The objectives of the new projects include the following:

- There will be 100 per cent exemption on entertainment tax for all new multiplex projects for five years and thereafter 30 per cent for next five years.
- New projects would be entitled for capital investment in plant and machinery up to Rs 30 lakhs.
- Rebate/deferment facility in the payment of luxury tax for new tourism units for five years from commencement date 100 per cent.
- Exemption on entertainment tax for five years for new amusement parks and new ropeways.

positive and negative developments have occurred from designing the 'first airline suite in the sky' and redefining luxury and comfort, and woo customers to travel by business class and first class, to making air travel affordable to the common man, and running into losses and causing congestion in the skies. Let us take a look at the emerging aviation industry.

Cost Cutting Measures

With the prices of Aviation Turbine Fuel (ATF) spiralling, there has been a rise in air fares that has led to a slump in out bound tourism. FIT, leisure and MICE-related travel has slowed down. Large corporate houses have been cutting short their travel plans.

In the present scenario, the cruise market is picking up and children are permitted to travel free with parents. Travel agents are promoting road and rail holidays to various destinations. Quick monsoon weekend getaways are becoming quite lucrative. The tourist is looking forward to relaxing in spas and resorts to de-stress from the tensions and hectic work schedules which are a permanent feature of urban lifestyle.

Airlines are looking for ways to reduce unnecessary expenses and may curtail unprofitable operations.

Our national carrier Air India is working on a plan to reduce losses by Rs 1000 crore annually, by cutting capacity through rationalization of routes and removal of loss-making routes. It is checking the possibility of taking the polar route for its non-stop flights to New York from Mumbai and New Delhi to reduce flight time by one and a half hours on the two routes and save on fuel consumption.

The present problem faced by airlines is overcapacity and seats going at low prices. Aircrafts can be given on lease to international carriers to generate revenue.

Air Cargo Management

Airlines are trying to make maximum use of its available resources to counterbalance high costs. India has potential to develop into a global air cargo hub, because of its geographical location and trade relations with other countries, and is being viewed as an alternate source of revenue to overcome rising fuel costs and the big investments which have been made in purchasing larger aircrafts.

New generation aircrafts offer 15–20 tonnes of cargo space while others are in the process of converting passenger airlines to freighters.

Air India Holidays

It is promoting packages to the north-eastern states. Customized international packages have been prepared as LTC has now been extended even to international leave for employees.

Low-cost Carriers

Low-cost carriers (LCC) or the no-frills airlines follow a strategy to offer passengers discounts on actual fares for seats booked in advance.

Jet Lite, the 100 per cent subsidiary of Jet Airways has introduced Apex-21 special advance purchase fares which must be purchased at least 21 days prior to departure date of the first segment. They are for passengers travelling economy class on several domestic routes. In case of cancellations, only the applicable tax component is refundable. Sama Airlines, the Saudi Arabian LCC has introduced flights to India.

Air Tanzanian will provide the non-existing direct link to India. Direct flights will ease access and create more demand, giving tourists more time at the destination, as a lot of time and effort is lost in catching connecting flights. International destinations have recognized the potential of the Indian market for inbound travellers.

Bar Coded Boarding Passes

After using technology successfully for e-ticketing, it is now being used for the convenience of boarding the aircraft. A single boarding pass for all routes is to be introduced shortly. The bar coded boarding passes (BCBP) is convenient to customers as it can be printed at home and will be read by bar code readers placed at airports. In future this facility will be available on mobile. The benefits of BCBP as per IATA statistics are 80 per cent reduction in paper costs, 40 per cent reduction in equipment replacement costs, and reduction in airport staff.

Helicopter Travel

The Government of India has realized that helicopter operations are most suited to the country because of its diverse land forms. The national helicopter company Pawan Hans Helicopters Limited (PHHL) has thirty five helicopters and is planning to induct 20 more shortly and increasing it further to 100 in the current Five Year Plan (2007 to 2012). The increase in fleet is for inter- and intra-city circuits enabling faster travel. Helicopters are being hired for marriages, flower droppings, and even for religious tourism and the demand is rapidly increasing. Medical tourism will need heliports to enable them to operate easily in extreme and remote locations. Portable, cheap heliports like roof top heliports, portable helipads, landing dollies etc. can be used in any terrain. The helicopter's ability to take off and land vertically without runways and its restricted seating capacity are two of its biggest advantages. Helicopters can fulfill the need for faster and uninterrupted travel because of the usually vast distance between airports and business centres, along with high density, slow paced traffic, and traffic jams. This results in the traveller spending the same time taken for say a Delhi–Mumbai flight (two hours) to reach the city from Mumbai airport.

To meet the need for trained pilots, PHHL has signed an MoU with the Indian Air Force (IAF) allowing IAF pilots opting for premature retirement to join PHHL. The Union Budget 2008–09 has removed customs duty on helicopter simulators for training pilots.

Air Charters

Air charters are the fastest mode of transport available on short notice with quickest accessibility to remote areas. The non-scheduled or charter operations are growing at a phenomenal rate. The need for quick and safe transport has instigated corporates to acquire their own aircraft and helicopters or contact private air charter operators for their domestic and international travel. Corporate giants can cover three to four cities in India during a day and report to headquarters the next morning, saving precious executive time. A new air charter service with 10 very light jets (VLJs)—the Eclipse 500 is to be launched in India shortly and will enhance business travel in India.

Airports

New age airports developed through PPP have brought about airport modernization in India's key metros. Green field airports have space to generate non-aeronautical sources of revenue like retail. Private airports developed on city outskirts are more spacious, offer shopping and dining facilities, and help enhance passenger experience. Multi-nodal airports are being planned for the convenience of passengers.

Redesigning Aircraft Cabins

Airlines are introducing incessant innovations to provide the ultimate in luxury in their in-flight services. Some examples are as follows:

1. Delta Airlines and master sommelier Andrea Robinson have introduced a sophisticated wine programme and a new in-flight programme revealing little-known travel tips called 'local flavours' which will help customers find the very best in travel, food, and wine destinations. The new wine programme is one of the many enhancements planned for its international business elite service.

2. Singapore Airlines, Delhi–Mumbai routes offer the following comforts:

   (a) Fully flat bed-cum-seats in first and business class.
   (b) Travellers can access their seats without disturbing fellow passengers, as a 1-2-1 seat configuration is used.
   (c) Large comfortable seats, with furnishings and amenities designed by French fashion house Givenchy.
   (d) Economy class seats have been upgraded to provide personal space and more legroom.
   (e) In-flight entertainment with more than 1000 on demand options and movies to suit the passengers' tastes, have been introduced.
   (f) USB port is provided for business travellers.
   (g) Crew members have undergone special training in customer service.

3. Jet Airways has re-defined privacy and luxury with its new First Class product—the first airline 'suite' in the sky, offering its First Class customers additional privacy and luxury in the new Boeing 777–300 ER aircraft. Some of the features include dual sliding doors, the world's longest first class bed at 83 inch length, dining for two, an eight point massage system, state-of-the-art entertainment, extensive menu choices served on hand painted Bernardaud porcelain, French Champagnes, and many more celebrated brands.

Some interesting developments in aviation in the future include the following:

- India will require approximately 1001 planes between 2008–27.
- India's first 787 dream liner will be inducted in Air India's fleet in Q42009.
- Congested skies in metros such as Mumbai and Delhi will clear up by identifying newer domestic markets for international operations and adding new city pairs domestically.

- Smaller cities are likely to have more international airports.
- India has adapted point to point operations.

The aviation industry has tremendous future potential and with additional and state-of-the-art aircraft, and innovative in-flight services, there will be a need for trained staff and aviation training institutes, to meet the growing demand for trained personnel in this sector.

E-passports

E-passports will be available to the general public from 2009 in India. The new e-passport would include a chip inside the passport which would have all information about the person travelling along with the person's finger prints. These passports are expected to simplify the process of passing through checks and in reducing frauds.

TRENDS IN CATERING

Globalization has resulted in the mingling of cultures and food habits. With the movement of chefs across the world and food shows on TV, the traditional food service customer has a deluge of food options and is ready to savor new gourmet opportunities. Fusion cooking has resulted in recipes modified to suit the local palate and the adventurous customer is constantly reaching out for new gastronomic experiences.

Better hygiene and sanitation is being followed in kitchens and Hazard Analysis and Critical Control Points (HACCP) is becoming an important norm for food safety standards. Food presentation and buffet table decorations is being given more importance. Chefs are flamboyant and extravagant, and at times loud. They do not hesitate experimenting with new ideas. Display kitchens and more interactive and live cooking are in vogue. More signature dishes are being prepared in honour of a guest which may or may not be repeated. New cuisine themes are in vogue and New World wines are gaining importance. Lounge bars, hookah bars, and takeaway bars have become huge revenue earners.

Tourists look for different experiences and restaurant owners are working on different, sometimes bizarre, themes to attract visitors. For example, Belgium offers 'Dinner in the Sky' in a restaurant 18,000 feet above the ground. The first ever undersea restaurant in the world was opened at The Hilton Maldives Resort and Spa in 2005, offering diners a 270 degrees panoramic underwater view of coral reefs five metres below the waves of the Indian Ocean.

NEED FOR TRAINED STAFF

Recognizing the need for skilled professionals in the field of hospitality and tourism, many new institutes offering degree, diploma, and short term certificate programmes in travel, tourism, and hotel management are being set up. The Indian Association of Tour Operators (IATO) is set to open its own travel and hospitality institute in Bhopal. The institute will be a joint venture between IATO and the Madhya Pradesh Tourism Department.

To bridge the gap between the existing course syllabus and the industry requirement, extensive research is being carried out to design a programme which will meet the present requirements.

One of India's largest travel houses, Akbar Travels of India has launched Akbar Academy which offers career courses in travel and tourism.

Tourism will continue to develop at a rapid rate in future too, as long as the human race exists, because any kind of movement is not possible without the providers of tourism products and services.

ENVIRONMENTAL CONCERNS—GOING GREEN

We have read about the impact tourism has on the environment in Chapter 14. This chapter covers what is being proposed in the future. Some countries such as Sri Lanka are working towards a carbon clean environment and are planning to track carbon emissions left by tourists.

Ecotels and ecotourism is being promoted in a large way and tourists are selecting destinations and preferring hotels which follow environmentally friendly practices.

Global Warming

Aviation contributes two per cent to world emission levels. Airlines are reviewing and updating technology to reduce their carbon footprint. Airlines can reduce their emissions by adopting the following measures:

Efficient aircraft

By investing in more efficient aircrafts and engines and in optimizing operations. Some aircrafts can be retrofitted with technical devices at the tip of the wings (winglets), new engines, and new surface treatments that reduce drag or air resistance. Optimizing operations would mean minimizing the number of empty seats flown by changing flight frequencies, routes, and timetables. ICAO has published a catalogue on 'operational opportunities to minimize fuel use and reduce emissions'.

EU emissions trading scheme

Under this scheme which started in January 2005, about 11,500 industrial installations which are responsible for nearly half of all EU's CO_2 emissions are covered. Operators of these installations receive emission allowances, giving them the right to emit a certain level of CO_2 per year. If their emissions are expected to exceed their allowance, they can take measures to reduce their emissions or they can buy additional emission allowances, whichever is cheaper.

However, if their emissions are lower than their allowances, they can sell their surplus allowances or save them to cover future emissions. This scheme puts a cap on overall emissions from these installations and creates awareness about this problem.

Use of solar energy

The IATA has become an institutional partner of Solar Impulse, the solar airplane that is scheduled to fly around the world without fuel and zero carbon emissions. The first test flights are scheduled for early 2009 and in 2011 the CEO of IATA and President of Solar Impulse are planning to fly around the world with five stopovers in a single-seater plane. The plane will fly by day and night, and will be propelled by solar energy only. IATA will assist in air traffic control clearance for this project.

IATA aims to achieve zero carbon emission technology within the next 50 years. At present two per cent of global carbon emissions are from the aviation industry. Research into alternative fuels and aircraft design can also help in minimizing carbon emission.

IATA's four pillar strategy to address global warming are as follows:

1. Invest in new technology
2. Fly planes effectively
3. Build and operate efficient infrastructure
4. Encourage improved fuel efficiency and a reduction in CO_2 emissions by giving positive economic incentives

IATA has set a target to improve fuel efficiency by 25 per cent by 2020. ICAO has endorsed the strategy and the target set, at their assembly in September 2007.

GOVERNMENT INITIATIVES FOR TOURISM

To promote domestic tourism, the Union Government has relaxed its LTC rules for central government employees to travel to the north eastern states of the country. Central government employees are permitted the use of private airlines, many of which offer low fares, while availing LTC, with the provision that the reimbursement would be restricted to the entitled class by train. Group A and B categories would be entitled to travel by air from their place of posting to a city in North Eastern Region (NER) while other categories could avail this facility from Guwahati or Kolkata. This move by the Centre will certainly help to promote tourism in the NER as the central government officials form a large section of the market. The NER is expecting an increase in tourists during Diwali and winter vacations.

Indian Railways Catering and Tourism Corporation (IRCTC) has launched the Mahaparinirvan Express, a nine-coach, air-conditioned train from Chennai on a 15-day Buddhist circuit of key sites associated with Gautama Buddha. The passengers will travel by night and go sightseeing by day in special buses. The train will halt at Guntur, Aurangabad, Bhopal, Agra, Delhi, Gonda, Gorakhpur, Varanasi, Gaya and Bhubaneswar.

The tourism industry is changing constantly to include new markets, innovative products, and untouched destinations where the sky is no longer the limit. Newer and developing technologies are enabling travellers to venture into outer space or traverse the ocean floor for a leisure trip. The market today, unlike the market of the past includes all humans giving them the right and freedom to travel and express themselves while tourism professionals develop special packages for events and activities of their interest. The government's involvement too in tourism related activities is increasing as the benefits to the economy can be tremendous, and newer forms of tourism will be seen.

SUMMARY

The tourism scenario is changing at an unimaginable pace with more number of people taking to holiday breaks or moving away from there usual place of work to take up new assignments. The UNWTO has forecast a Tourism 2020 Vision which shows a growth in international tourism and environment consciousness in the tourist.

While the number of tourists is on the increase there is also stiff competition amongst the principal service providers, with each one trying to out do the other in terms on innovative offerings. In India, the growth of tourism has been rapid during 2001–06 and a target of 10 million arrivals by 2011 is expected to be achieved. State governments are drawing up tourism policies for increasing tourist activity in their state. The government is offering tax incentives to promote private investors to develop tourism and invest in hotels, amusement parks, convention centres, etc. through PPP projects.

While new types of tourism are emerging, the industry is opening its eyes to the need for the disabled and elderly traveller. Tours to outer space and accommodation underwater, visits to dark, dismal, and disaster struck sites to view the aftermath, to offer assistance or pay homage to the departed souls are newer future forms of tourism.

The trends in the industry reveal strategies to outlive competition, gain power, and cut unnecessary expenses. Mergers, acquisitions, alliances, consolidation, public–private partnership, joint ventures, and disintermediation are some of the trends. There has been a marked change in the distribution of tourism offerings. With the advent of information and communication technology, the customer has direct access to the service providers, reducing the role of the travel agent. The present travel agents feel threatened because of talks about decommissioning and the presence of OTAs who are taking over a major share of reservations. They have become popular because booking tickets for airlines, hotel reservations, and renting cars has become a simple three step process carried out by the click of a button.

The GDS is a computer reservation and information system that is often operated by multiple airlines and used by travel agents for booking airline tickets, insurance, hotel reservations etc. It connects the principal suppliers and the travel agents, i.e. it links all parts of the distribution chain.

The aviation industry is growing at a rapid pace, offering affordable flights via low cost carriers to the middle class and upgrading facilities in the business and first class to offer a unique innovative tourist product. While the tourist as well as the industry are becoming environment conscious, airlines are seeking measures to reduce carbon emissions and accommodations are using ecofriendly measures to reduce global warming.

The future trends are going to be as imaginative as the mind wanders and as bizarre as is acceptable to society.

KEY TERMS

Baby boomers People born in the USA during the 'baby boom' years of 1946–64. As people in this age group show greater inclination to travel, they are expected to provide a boost to demand for travel and hospitality-related services.

Computer reservation system (CRS) A CRS for an individual airline containing information on that airline only and used by employees of that airline.

Global distribution system (GDS) A GDS is global distribution system for travel products such as tickets of different airlines, various hotel rooms, car rentals etc. It is used for checking the availability of services, processing reservations, making changes if necessary, and ticketing. It contains information on all types of travel products.

Green field airport An airport built on undeveloped land usually outside a city, built from scratch on a new site. For example, the Hyderabad Airport.

Interface An interface is a pictorial representation of files, date and programmes stored in the computer on the computer screen.

Internet The Internet is a world wide network of computer networks which are linked to each other through telecommunication links.

Long haul journey Journey where travel time exceeds six hours.

Multi-nodal airports Help ease congestion and improve passenger experience (with train connectivity) as seen in international airports like Changi Airport, Singapore.

Pro rata According to the calculated share or proportionate share.

Search engine Search engines are applications, such as Google, Yahoo, etc. that facilitate searching for information on the world wide web. To search for information, a key word needs to be typed.

World Wide Web World Wide Web is part of the Internet and has been developed so that information can be easily accessed from the Internet.

CONCEPT REVIEW QUESTIONS

1. Define the following:
   (a) Disintermediation
   (b) Decommissioning
   (c) Computer reservations system
2. What measures are airlines proposing to cut costs in view to the spiralling aviation turbine fuel prices?
3. What are the new innovations in in-flight services in the business and first class?
4. Discuss some of the schemes offered by the government to promote domestic tourism in India.
5. Discuss the trends in the food and beverage industry.
6. Explain the significance of the following:
   (a) Public–private partnership
   (b) Horizontal integration
   (c) Global distribution systems

CRITICAL THINKING QUESTIONS

1. Discuss the major technological developments that have influenced the distribution system in tourism.
2. Do you think there is a need to have a tourism policy? Who all in your opinion should be part of the policy formulation team?

REFERENCES

Andrews, Sudhir 2007, Introduction to Tourism & Hospitality Industry, McGraw-Hill Co.

Express Aviation World January 2008. *Supplement to Express Travel World*.

Express Travel World, *Indian Express Newspapers (Mumbai) Ltd* November 2006 (Vol. 1/No. 12) January 2008, February 2008, March 2008 (Vol. 3/No. 4) June 2008, July 2008 (Vol. 3/No. 829), August 2008.

George, R. 2007, *Managing tourism in South Africa*, Oxford University Press Southern Africa, Cape Town.

Hospitality, Pub, The Institute of Hospitality, 82 Surrey Issue 7, September/October.

International Travel and Tourism Training Programme 2007, *Foundation Course Text book*, 5.8 Edition, Montreal, Geneva.

Keyser, H. 2002, *Tourism Development*, Oxford University Press Southern Africa, Cape town.

Medilik, S. 1996, *Dictionary of Travel, Tourism and Hospitality*, Butterworth-Heinemann, Oxford.

Pune Mirror 8 September 2008 page 4, *The Times of India*, Publication.

Tourism Policy of Maharashtra 2006.

www.spacetourismsociety.org, accessed on 12 September 2008.

www.wikipedia.org, accessed on 12 September 2008.

www.jul.com, accessed on 12 September 2008.

www.info.hktdc.com, accessed on 12 September 2008.

www.wikipedia.org/wiki/winetourism, accessed on 5 January 2009.

www.wikipedia.org.dark_tourism, accessed on 5 January 2009.

www.wikipedia.org.shock_tourism, accessed on 5 January 2009.

www.indianholidays.com, accessed on 5 January 2009.

www.tourismthailand.org, accessed on 5 January 2009.

www.sustrans.org.uk, accessed on 5 January 2009.

www.books.google.co.in, accessed on 5 January 2009.

www.eturbonews.com, accessed on 5 January 2009.

www.filmtourism.blogspot.com, accessed on 5 January 2009.

www.wikipedia.org/wiki/LGBT_tourism, accessed on 5 January 2009.

www.bravenewtraveler.com, accessed on 5 January 2009.

www.ecotourism.org, accessed on 5 January 2009.

Let us have a look at the Tourism Policy of Maharashtra 2006.

TOURISM POLICY OF MAHARASHTRA 2006

The Maharashtra Tourism Development Corporation (MTDC) has realized the vast tourism potential of the state and the need to attract foreign visitors who land in Mumbai and do not visit other places in Maharashtra. Under the slogan 'Maharashtra Unlimited' the state has prepared an action plan for five years (2007 to 2012) which includes the following:

- Development of infrastructure at tourist destinations with the help of the private sector and giving them tax incentives.
- Proper approach roads to increase accessibility to tourism destinations with rail and air linkages for important destinations and wayside amenities.
- Development control regulation at destinations.
- Strengthening of bed and breakfast schemes in remote areas where hotel accommodation is not available. This scheme has a twofold purpose—it creates facilities for tourists specially those interested in rural tourism and is a source of revenue for the locals.
- Recreational facilities at destinations with a view to encourage day visitors to stay overnight.
- Developmental projects under public–private partnership at selected destinations.
- Identification of new World Heritage Sites and conservation and development of Ajanta, Ellora and Elephanta caves, and Chhatrapati Shivaji Terminus.
- Maharashtra's rich culture and tradition in the form of folk art, folk dances and folk songs, festivals and local cuisine would be identified and the artist and their troupe would be registered on the tourism portal, to promote cultural tourism.
- The handicraft industry would be promoted by identifying and training the artisan, and promoting their crafts through bazaars and haats.
- To develop pilgrimage circuits in the state.
- Rural tourism, agricultural tourism, and wine tourism will be promoted in appropriate areas.
- Fort/fort circuits of historical significance and architectural excellence will be developed and conserved.
- Application of information technology for tourism.
- Information kiosks to be set up at entrance terminals of important airports, railway stations, interstate bus terminals, and prominent places with online booking systems.

- Creating awareness about tourism as an activity, preserving our environment and safety measures.
- Providing tourism police and other safety and security measures specially for beach tourism.
- Training and capacity building of service providers will be carried out in coordination with the 'Athiti Devo Bhava' programme of the Central Government.
- Formation of a committee for coordination and monitoring of development and creation of a special task force.
- Thorough organizational review of the various departments of MTDC keeping the developmental needs in mind.
- Nodal office in New Delhi to help in liaisoning, marketing, and promotion of Maharashtra's tourism product like Deccan Odyssey, etc.
- Single window clearance system for new projects.
- Developing a mechanism to collect tourist statistics.
- Evaluation and outcome budgeting for each department and avoiding bad investments by undertaking feasibility studies.

The following units are eligible for incentives under the Tourism Policy 2006 with effect from 1 November 2006.

- Hotels, heritage hotels, resorts and health farms, health and wellness spa, and units registered under the bed and breakfast scheme of MTDC
- Motels and wayside amenities
- Apartment hotels/service apartments
- Water sports and amusement parks
- Arts and crafts villages
- Golf courses
- Camping, caravanning, and tent facilities
- Arial ropeways
- Convention centres
- Development of hill stations
- Adventure tourism projects
- Houseboats
- Ecotourism projects
- Museums and aquariums
- Projects approved by classification committee of the Tourism Department of the state government or Government of India

Tax Incentives Offered

The following tax incentives are under the tourism policy for Maharashtra:

Tax exemption will be available to new units and expansion of existing units (as per the conditions set out earlier) in respect of the following taxes, up to

100 per cent of capital investment or completion of the eligible period of five, seven, or 10 years, whichever is earlier. The tax exemption will be available to eligible units falling within the eligible areas for a period of five, seven, and 10 years respectively for A, B, and C areas. Refer to Fig. 16.4 for financial incentives for the promotion of tourism in India.

The certificate of entitlement and the eligibility certificate shall automatically stand cancelled on completion of the above period or the limit prescribed for eligible investment.

List of taxes

1. Total exemption from luxury tax (as applicable to hotels) for a period of seven and 10 years depending on the location of the tourism project in the B and C zones respectively and 50 per cent exemption for a period of five years in A zone. Refer to Table 16.1 for the different zones.
2. Total exemption from entertainment tax/amusement tax for a period of five, seven, and 10 years depending on the location of the tourism project in the A, B, and C zones respectively.
3. Total exemption from stamp duty for the projects located in B and C zones and 50 per cent exemption from stamp duty for projects located in A zone.

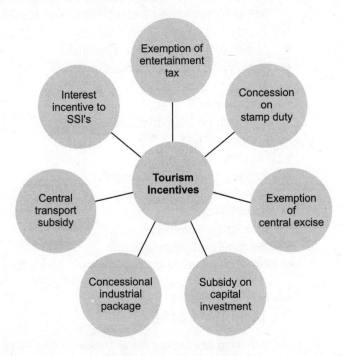

Fig. 16.4 Financial incentives for tourism and entertainment offered by the government with a view to promote tourism in India.

Table 16.1 Designated tourism areas for availing tax incentives

Area (as proposed in Tourism Policy 2006)	Investment (Rupees in crores)	Employment generation
Zone A Mumbai and its suburbs, Navi Mumbai, Thane, Pune, and Pimpri Chinchwad municipal corporations	100	500
Zone B All municipal corporations except areas in Zone A and A class municipalities	50	300
Zone C All districts of Maharashtra except areas in Zone A and Zone B	25	100

Electricity concessions

Electricity duty will be levied at industrial rates for the respective period.

Other concessions

1. Seventy five per cent exemption from registration charges and 50 per cent concession from payment of permit charges for sightseeing buses registered as such as approved by the transport authority, having minimum seating capacity of 25 seats and operating in Municipal Corporation areas and hill stations.
2. Total exemption from property tax and non-agricultural tax to all tourism projects run/owned by MTDC.
3. The water rate/tariff shall be levied at maximum industrial rate.
4. Property tax shall be charged at residential rate.

No development zones

Many tourism areas can attract a number of foreign as well as domestic tourists provided suitable areas/plots can be offered to such projects. As government has allowed IT activities in no development zones (NDZ), tourism activities such as entertainment centres which include small golfing facilities, tourism villages, handicraft displays with no extra FSI should also be considered in the NDZ.

Renewal of licences

Tourism projects require various licences and clearances like lodging house licence, eating house licence, Police permissions, licence under the Shop and Establishment Act, licence under the Food and Drug Administration Act, etc. These licences have to be renewed every year. By this Policy 2006, these licences/

permissions will require renewal every five years instead of the present annual renewal.

Mega Project

Tourism was given the status of industry in 1999. The Cabinet has recently approved a policy for mega projects in the industries sector. Since tourism is also regarded as an industry, and has the greatest employment generating potential, a policy similar to the policy for industrial mega projects, is proposed for the tourism sector.

The tourism sector is an employment intensive sector. A single room in a three to five star hotel creates nine direct employments and 18 indirect employments. Moreover, apart from the skilled, even the unskilled, and semi-skilled can be absorbed in the tourism sector.

Considering the above, it is proposed that the benefits/incentives of 'mega project' as envisaged by Industry Department, should be made available to tourism projects also.

Apart from the incentives mentioned above, the Government of Maharashtra has declared additional incentives to promote tourism in the rural and backward areas of the state. See Fig.16.4 for various incentives offered.

One of the problems in tourism development is the non-availability of encumbrance-free land for the purpose of tourism. A potential investor in the industrial sector gets industrial land as per his choice in the various industrial areas developed by the Maharashtra Industrial Development Corporation (MIDC). The MTDC does not have a similar pool of land available with it. Similarly the MTDC does not have powers of land acquisition like the MIDC. Therefore the tourism potential at many places remains unexploited or exploited haphazardly. It is, therefore, proposed to bring an investor-friendly land policy for tourism on the lines of the industrial policy.

MTDC's Mahabhraman Programme

MTDC is actively working on promoting the untapped destinations around the state and is working along with travel agents and service providers like hoteliers, resort owners, adventure tour operators from the untapped regions under the title of 'Mahabhraman'. The project also aims at attracting and retaining the large number of business travellers who use Mumbai as a stopover destination.

This programme is a public–private initiative to promote tourism in the state. For example, the Tapola River Camp is one of the five properties owned by Nature Trails Resorts and is part of the MTDC's Mahabhraman. Mahabhraman also helps new travel companies to get the required permissions and licences.

Other state tourism boards also are set to overhaul existing properties and are laying emphasis on responsible tourism.

Index